Early Modern East Asia

This book presents a great deal of new primary research on a wide range of aspects of early modern East Asia. Focusing primarily on maritime connections, the book explores the importance of international trade networks, the implications of technological dissemination, and the often unforeseen consequences of missionary efforts. It demonstrates the benefits of a global history approach, outlining the complex interactions between Western traders and Asian states and entrepreneurs. Overall, the book presents much interesting new material on this complicated and understudied period.

Kenneth M. Swope is a Professor in the Department of History at The University of Southern Mississippi, Hattiesburg, USA.

Tonio Andrade is a Professor in the Department of History at Emory University, Atlanta, USA.

Asian States and Empires
Edited by Peter Lorge, Vanderbilt University

The importance of Asia will continue to grow in the twenty-first century, but remarkably little is available in English on the history of the polities that constitute this critical area. Most current work on Asia is hindered by the extremely limited state of knowledge of the Asian past in general, and the history of Asian states and empires in particular. *Asian States and Empires* is a book series that will provide detailed accounts of the history of states and empires across Asia from earliest times until the present. It aims to explain and describe the formation, maintenance and collapse of Asian states and empires, and the means by which this was accomplished, making available the history of more than half the world's population at a level of detail comparable to the history of Western polities. In so doing, it will demonstrate that Asian peoples and civilizations had their own histories, apart from the West, and provide the basis for understanding contemporary Asia in terms of its actual histories, rather than broad generalizations informed by Western categories of knowledge.

Early Modern East Asia

War, Commerce, and Cultural Exchange

Essays in Honor of John E. Wills, Jr.

Edited by Kenneth M. Swope and Tonio Andrade

Routledge
Taylor & Francis Group

LONDON AND NEW YORK

First published 2018 by Routledge

2 Park Square, Milton Park, Abingdon, Oxfordshire OX14 4RN
52 Vanderbilt Avenue, New York, NY 10017

Routledge is an imprint of the Taylor & Francis Group, an informa business

First issued in paperback 2019

Copyright © 2018 selection and editorial matter, Kenneth M. Swope and Tonio Andrade; individual chapters, the contributors

The right of Kenneth M. Swope and Tonio Andrade to be identified as the authors of the editorial material, and of the authors for their individual chapters, has been asserted in accordance with sections 77 and 78 of the Copyright, Designs and Patents Act 1988.

All rights reserved. No part of this book may be reprinted or reproduced or utilised in any form or by any electronic, mechanical, or other means, now known or hereafter invented, including photocopying and recording, or in any information storage or retrieval system, without permission in writing from the publishers.

Notice:
Product or corporate names may be trademarks or registered trademarks, and are used only for identification and explanation without intent to infringe.

British Library Cataloguing-in-Publication Data
A catalogue record for this book is available from the British Library

Library of Congress Cataloging-in-Publication Data
A catalog record for this book has been requested

ISBN: 978-1-138-23522-9 (hbk)
ISBN: 978-0-367-87822-1 (pbk)

Typeset in Times New Roman
by Out of House Publishing

Dedicated to the memory of John E. Wills Jr.

Contents

Illustrations

Contributors

Editors

Tonio Andrade is a Professor of History at Emory University. From the beginning of his career as a historian, he has benefited from the advice and inspiration of Jack Wills. Andrade's books include *The Gunpowder Age: China, Military Innovation, and the Rise of the West in World History* (2016), *Lost Colony: The Untold Story of China's First Great Victory over the West* (2011), and *How Taiwan became Chinese: Dutch, Spanish, and Han Colonization in the Seventeenth Century* (2008). His articles have appeared in *The Journal of Asian Studies, The Journal of World History, Late Imperial China, Itinerario, The Journal of Chinese Military History, The Journal of Medieval Military History, The Journal of Early Modern History*, and other journals.

Kenneth M. Swope received his B.A. at the College of Wooster and his M.A. and Ph.D. from the University of Michigan. He previously taught at Marist College and Ball State University. He was the General Buford Blount Professor of Military History (2015–17) and currently serves as Director of Graduate Studies in History at the University of Southern Mississippi. He is also a Senior Fellow of the Dale Center for the Study of War & Society and Book Review Editor of *The Journal of Chinese Military History*. He is the author of *A Dragon's Head and a Serpent's Tail: Ming China and the First Great East Asian War, 1592–1598* and *The Military Collapse of China's Ming Dynasty, 1618–1644*, as well as numerous articles and book chapters on Ming military, political, and social history. His newest book, *On the Trail of the Yellow Tiger: War, Trauma, and Social Dislocation in Southwest China During the Ming-Qing Transition*, has just been published.

Chapter authors

David A. Bello received his Ph.D. from the University of Southern California and is currently Associate Professor of East Asian History at Washington and Lee University. His main research interest is environmental and borderland history, involving relations between natural systems, ethnic identity, and imperial space during China's last dynasty, the Qing (1644–1912).

Leonard Blussé is emeritus Professor of History of Asian-European Relations, at Leiden University, extraordinary Professor at the Institute of Southeast Asian Studies of Xiamen University and visiting Professor at Huaqiao University (Xiamen).

Jennifer L. Gaynor works on the history of maritime Southeast Asia and its surrounding seas from the seventeenth century to the present. She has held postdoctoral fellowships at the Australian National University, the University of Michigan, Ann Arbor, and at Cornell University's Society for the Humanities. She has published articles in the *Journal of World History*, *Radical History Review*, and *Anthropological Quarterly*, and her book, *Intertidal History in Island Southeast Asia: Submerged Genealogy and the Legacy of Coastal Capture*, is forthcoming with Cornell University Southeast Asia Program Publications.

Xing Hang is Associate Professor of History at Brandeis University. His research focuses on early modern China, overseas Chinese, the East Asian world order, and Eurasian comparative history.

David C. Kang is Professor of International Relations and business at the University of Southern California. His latest book is *East Asia Before the West: Five Centuries of Trade and Tribute* (2010).

Sun Laichen is a Professor of Southeast Asian History at California State University, Fullerton, and joint-appointed Professor in Global History at Osaka University, who specializes in early modern Southeast Asian history and Asian military history.

Paul A. Van Dyke is a Professor of History at Sun Yat-sen University in Guangzhou and author of *The Canton Trade: Life and Enterprise on the China Coast 1700–1845* (2005).

John E. Wills, Jr. taught Chinese history and the history of the early modern world at the University of Southern California from 1965 to 2004. His research into the history of maritime China and its foreign connections, 1500–1800, has led him to archives from Beijing to Madras to Lisbon, and to the sense of an interconnected world expressed in his books and articles.

Acknowledgments

This volume started as a conference in honor of John E. Wills, Jr., in March of 2015 at The University of Southern California, and we wish to thank the many people who participated, including, of course, the contributors to this volume, but also Richard Chu, Bill Deverell, Charlotte Furth, Richard von Glahn, Mark Mancall, Michael Block, Michelle Damian, Richard Dolen, Arline Golkin, Ronald Kadonaga, Janette Brown, Keisha Brown, Duncan Campbell, Alan Freeman, Katrina Leung, Carol Lim, Edwin Perkins, Sally Pratt, James Smith, Terry Seip, Heiwei Liu, Josh Goldstein, Stan Rosen, Gene Cooper, Rongdao Lai, Kazuko Fujii, Lon Kurashige, and Tse-min Fu. These people gave papers or testimonials in honor of Jack. Others, such as Geoffrey Parker, weren't able to be there in person but sent warm remembrances.

We especially wish to thank Paul Van Dyke, who helped us organize the conference, and David Kang, director of the USC Center for International Studies who oversaw arrangements and provided funding. Various departments and centers at USC also lent their support, most notably the USC East Asian Studies Center, the USC History Department, and the USC Korean Studies Institute. Particular thanks go to Grace Ryu for her work organizing the event. David Kang and the USC Center for International Studies also provided funding for the index.

Peter Lorge, who edits the series in which this volume appears, helped inspire us to undertake the project, and his stewardship and enthusiasm greatly facilitated the process of compiling, editing, and writing. Peter Sowden, of Routledge Press, was an early champion of the book and helped move the manuscript swiftly and smoothly into production. Becky McPhee was an exemplary editor, working with assiduousness and alacrity. Communication skills are vital for editors, and she is a wonderful and effective communicator.

Finally, of course, we wish to thank the late Jack Wills himself, who was always unstinting with his time and advice. His mentorship has touched the lives of all of us contributors, and his written work continues to inspire us, serving as a model of deeply-sourced and accessible scholarship. We dedicate this volume to him.

Introduction: Jack Wills and his work and influence

Kenneth M. Swope and Tonio Andrade

John Eliot Wills, Jr. (1936–2017), known to his students and friends as Jack, was a pioneer in historical scholarship, whose contributions have touched many fields and subfields, most notably global history and Chinese history. Long before global history existed as a research field, he was already focused on the maritime interactions that have become one of global historians' key obsessions. His work is exceptional for its ability to understand global encounters in human terms, and for prose that brings those exchanges alive.

He was born in 1936 and grew up in Urbana-Champaign, site of the main campus of the University of Illinois. His father was a professor, who mentored graduate students from all over the world. Jack enrolled as a university student in his hometown and majored in philosophy, but his girlfriend was a student in the history department. She eventually became his wife, and he eventually decided to devote himself to the study of history.

Jack's interest in China was born in an encounter with Confucius. While in the army in San Antonio, Texas, he began reading an English translation of the ancient sage's work and felt an immediate affinity. He connected with Confucius's ethical pragmatism, which eschewed spiritual and metaphysical speculation in favor of concrete action to improve the world. In 1958, after finishing his military service, he enrolled in the MA program in East Asian Regional Studies at Harvard University, a training ground for so many of the leading lights in China studies of the twentieth century. He went on to the Ph.D. program, where his dissertation advisor was the great John King Fairbank.

Fairbank, Harvard's first professor of Chinese history, was fascinated by China's relations with the West, and historians today still grapple with his pathbreaking and lucid descriptions of the "Sinocentric World Order" or "Tributary System." Jack, too, set out to explore Sino-western relations, but whereas Fairbank had focused on the nineteenth century and primarily explored Chinese relations with the Anglophone world, Jack focused on the seventeenth century and explored China's relations with the United Netherlands, or, more specifically with the Dutch East India Company. At the time, it seemed an odd choice, but it turned out to be a fruitful one.

In 1963, Jack traveled to The Hague, Netherlands, and began researching in the Dutch National Archives (then known as the Algemeen Rijksarchief). During the morning and afternoon coffee breaks – a ritual that fellow researchers in the Dutch archives will recognize – he made friends with other scholars from around the world, including Indian historian Om Prakash and Africanists Kwame Daaku and John Fynn. He also discovered the incredible richness of those records, which, when paired with Chinese sources, allowed him to make minute reconstructions of voyages, parleys, and exchanges of delegates and letters.

This ability to look at both sides of the story is the most important hallmark of Jack's work. In fact, one should say *all* sides of the story, because his linguistic expertise was not limited to Dutch and Chinese. He also used sources in Spanish, Portuguese, French, Japanese, and, as the Dutch say, *noem maar op*. He was a historian's historian, and his meticulous readings and stunning range of experience made for authoritative accounts.

The result of his fieldwork was a 700-page dissertation on Dutch-Qing relations, which became the basis for his two seminal monographs, *Pepper, Guns, and Parleys* (1974), and *Embassies and Illusions* (1984). At the time, they were well received by specialists, who appreciated the way they both built upon and challenged the Fairbank Tributary model, but it was only later that they took on their iconic status as pioneering studies in global and maritime history.

What has given these books their unusual staying power? For one thing, they are painstakingly researched, drawing on an immense corpus of primary and secondary sources in many different languages. Yet, Wills wore his scholarship lightly. The books are a delight to read: vivid, compelling, and, most important of all, human. Wills understood that it was difficult to communicate across vast cultural gulfs and treated his historical actors with understanding and compassion. There are few villains in his work, just confused humans struggling with their roles in life. Historian Kenneth Swope remembers seeking advice from Jack about the late Ming military figure Mao Wenlong and whether he should be seen as a Ming loyalist or traitor. Jack said, "It's not really about heroes and villains. It's about people finding a way to get by within their respective frameworks of action."

This humanistic insistence on balance is a key reason that his work has had such resonance among younger generations of scholars, particularly as global history emerged as a research field. Jack got there first and has been an example to all who followed. His focus was always on interaction and exchange.

His first two monographs were accompanied by numerous articles, including two influential chapters for the monumental *Cambridge History of China* and a seminal chapter in a volume he co-edited with his friend, Jonathan Spence: *From Ming to Ch'ing* (1979). That chapter explores China's peculiar relationship to the oceans, hypothesizing that official attitudes toward maritime commerce were shaped by China's geography. Whereas certain maritime regions – such as the Baltic, the Mediterranean, and large parts of current-day Malaysia and Indonesia – had maritime bottlenecks, where local polities could control and tax maritime trade, China had a vast and open coastline. "Maritime China," he wrote, "offered only meager opportunities for … positive interactions between profit and power." Another prominent piece was a review article for *The American Historical Review*, "The Interactive Emergence of European Domination," whose thesis remains as compelling today as it was when it was first published in 1993: European dominance in maritime Asia emerged gradually after 1500, and it was based on close interactions with seafaring Asians and their polities. This paradigm helped lay the groundwork for dozens of dissertations and books and is still widely cited.

Jack also published three books for more general audiences. *Mountain of Fame*, whose first edition appeared in 1994, is an accessible introduction to Chinese history and historiography by means of biography. In short sketches, some no more than ten pages in length, he provides a sweep of China's long history, from the mythical Yellow Emperor to Mao Zedong. In *1688: A Global History* (2001), he took the opposite approach, painting a picture of one year in global history. It's a delightful and pioneering book, filled with sympathetic portraits of individual humans: a Congolese king writing in Portuguese to an Italian priest; a fifteen-year-old girl and her suitors in Potosí, Peru; the King of Siam sending emissaries to Louis XIV of France; and the Jesuit Ferdinand Verbiest negotiating the court of China's Kangxi emperor. In *The World from 1450 to Today*, Jack traced the increasingly dense connections that bound together the societies of the world during the early modern period, and also the odd parallel developments that occurred in far-flung regions. This book, too, was praised for its vivid prose and its focus on human stories and global connections.

Connecting was something Jack did well in his personal and professional life, too, forging close and enduring friendships with people he met during his many trips throughout the world: Om Prakash, Kwame Daaku, John Fynn, Leonard Blussé, Ts'ao Young-ho, Geoffrey Parker, C.R. Boxer, Jonathan Spence, and many, many more. As a faculty member at the University of Southern California, he built up its Asian and global curricula, working closely with his colleagues, most notably Peter Mancall, Charlotte Furth, and Gordon Berger, the latter two recruited by Jack himself. He was an active administrator as well, founding USC's East Asian Studies Center and organizing meetings and symposia. He particularly enjoyed conferences, keeping an active presence in them to the very end of his life. Similarly, his scholarly production didn't flag after his retirement in 2004. He went on to publish three books and many articles.

Throughout his busy life, he always made time to mentor younger scholars, many of whom were not even his own students, and the essays collected in this volume are a testament to his deep influence. They cover many topics – war, drugs, trade, shipping, politics, diplomacy – but each follows Jack's example, combining rigorous scholarship with a focus on individual human experience.

The volume opens with David Bello's chapter on the opium trade in Qing and Republican China, tracing how domestic consumption patterns, internal politics, and foreign relations and policies interacted to create a "drug infra-structure" in China. Despite its obviously deleterious effects on the population, opium was an attractive product from a revenue standpoint, and successive regimes within China relied upon it to sustain themselves financially, illustrating an unintended consequence of the intersection of war, commerce, and cultural exchange.

Bello also draws our attention to the interrelationship between trade and ecological activities, reminding us that the two were often intimately connected. This in turn reminds us of the ecological consequences of endemic warfare, a theme that comes to the fore in later chapters by Kenneth Swope and Xing Hang. Ironically, Qing success, at least in a relative sense, in rooting out opium traffickers in urban areas had the unintended consequence of stimulating rural domestic production. And as the Qing state was increasingly desperate for revenue to maintain order, counter foreign threats, and put down domestic uprisings, officials realized that revenues from opium were far more profitable and reliable than those from other sources. This marks yet another unexpected intersection of war, commerce, and cultural exchange.

As new local institutions evolved to take advantage of Qing policies, the Qing itself resorted to using such revenues for its modernization efforts, particularly in the military sphere. In effect, the symbol of Qing decay became a means of its survival, at least for a while. But in the end, the opium trade, like so many other aspects of the late Qing reform state, contributed to the dissolution of centralized power and helped create the conditions that fostered warlordism in the twentieth century. By tracing the relationship between the opium trade and warlordism, Bello highlights the importance of historical contingency as it intersects with local human agency, ecology, and even physiology.

Chapter Two, by Kenneth Swope, offers a reappraisal of the short and bloody reign of Zhang Xianzhong (1606–47), the "King of the West" in China's Sichuan Province. Zhang is one of the most significant and understudied figures in the Ming-Qing transition period. Known as the Butcher of Sichuan, he was long blamed for the massive depopulation that affected southwest China during the mid to late seventeenth century, and Swope shows that, although Zhang cannot be completely exculpated from blame, the story was much more complex than many historians have recognized. Many actors were involved – Zhang's forces, Ming loyalists, warlords of various stripes, local bandits, and Qing armies – all of them contending for control of the region for several decades. Compounding this endemic warfare were a series of natural disasters and epidemics, some of which have been reliably linked to global climate anomalies that historians have dubbed the Little Ice Age, or the Global Crisis of the seventeenth century. Textual, archeological, and climatological evidence suggests that China was the region of the world most affected by these calamities and it appears that southwest China suffered the worst and the longest. Thus, this chapter, like many of the others, helps to situate developments in China within a global framework.

Following Jack's inspiration, Swope plumbs his rich sources to offer a sobering representation of the effects of warfare on society, as families were ripped apart, villages and cities destroyed, crops ruined. Amid constant pressures, society unraveled, and people banded together for security or simply fled into the wilderness, many never to return to their homes. All the while, those above them played their game of thrones, with some trying to bring order to the chaos and others seemingly only wishing to extend it for their own gain. And yet even here we find Jesuit missionaries trying to spread their faith and bring elements of their culture to the Chinese. In the present case they were, of course, less than successful, but the accounts left by Jesuit missionaries at Zhang's court remain some of the most fascinating documents from the era. They allow us to reassess some of the most lurid tales of his reign while also serving as a testament to the widespread suffering of the common folk. Chinese accounts corroborate certain aspects of the Jesuit accounts, while providing culturally significant representations of the effects of warfare upon society and the natural order. The proliferation of tiger attacks, for example, was seen as a manifestation of Heaven's disfavor and the government's inability to properly order the realm. Likewise, tales of cannibalism and humans going feral indicated what might happen if chaos was not checked by proper authorities. The writers of such accounts did not merely describe events – they cast judgment, deciding who deserved the blame for the disorder under Heaven. Finally, the essay touches upon the subject of historical and cultural transmission, as tales of Zhang Xianzhong and his exploits continue to regale Chinese audiences today, both in print and on the Internet.

Chapter Three similarly honors Jack's legacy by combining Western and Chinese sources: Leonard Blussé explores the rich records of the Dutch East India Company to illuminate the complex relationships between Dutch colonists and Taiwanese (Formosan) aborigines, again demonstrating that native peoples were not merely hapless victims of Western imperialism. In Taiwan, for example, the natives could and often did manipulate the Dutch for their own ends and used their cultural exchanges to advance personal aims, including drawing the Dutch into local conflicts in a pattern that would be familiar to students of colonial American history.[1] Likewise, the key roles played by cultural intermediaries, often female (again as in the Americas), demonstrates the sophistication of these early interactions and the ways in which commerce drove much of the intercourse between the peoples.

Furthermore, we see how political unrest on mainland China stimulated immigration into neighboring lands. In the case of Taiwan, this presaged the eventual annexation of the island by the expanding Qing empire. Nonetheless, the limitations of colonial power are also amply illustrated in Blussé's treatment. Indeed, as he notes, "colonial projects were negotiated, received, and manipulated at the local level with frequently unforeseen, but often significant consequences." Notably however, the locals were better able to keep the Dutch at arm's length than they were the Chinese, who had the advantages of proximity and numbers to aid their colonization of the island, a process traced in the work of Tonio Andrade.[2]

Jack's work focused on China, his primary geographic area of expertise, but it also extended outward, touching especially on Southeast Asia, and Chapter Four, by Jennifer Gaynor, helps fill some of the surprising lacunae in maritime studies of island Southeast Asia. In the process, she reminds us that conflicts in the maritime realm were an integral aspect of politics in the seventeenth century and that maritime-oriented peoples were often closely allied with land-based realms. Moreover, as seen in other pieces in the present volume, these supposedly stateless people often had a direct stake in the concerns and activities of the states in their midst. They also frequently played key roles in thwarting European efforts to dominate trade in the region.

Gaynor's research, like Blussé's, brings actively engaged Asians back into the colonial picture. At the same time both authors make the important point that, in some cases, European sources must be used to get a better sense of local dynamics owing to the paucity of sources from the native perspective. The key is reading them with a proper sense of perspective. Gaynor also draws our attention to the issue of "terracentric biases" inherent in many of the contemporary sources.[3] But as amply demonstrated by multiple essays in the present collection, oceans and waterways linked as much as they divided, certainly in the trade-dependent realms of East and Southeast Asia.

Continuing the spirit of ongoing scholarly debate and inquiry, in Chapter Five Tonio Andrade reassesses the now ubiquitous belief that China "failed to perfect" firearms because the primary threat to China was posed by mounted nomads, whose mobility supposedly countered the efficacy of clumsy early guns. Andrade shows that the Chinese did in fact regularly deploy guns in battles against mobile steppe foes, while also noting that the nature of such warfare created a particular challenge–response dynamic that helped push firearms development in a different direction in northern China. Moreover, following many other authors in the present volume, Andrade stresses the importance of maritime connections for China's military development. After all, contact with the Portuguese and other Europeans helped spark a revival of the mid-Ming military. Although the steppe might be regarded as posing the core strategic problematique of Chinese empires, the maritime regions of China were a "key locus of innovation." Moreover, as Andrade demonstrates elsewhere in more detail, throughout much of the early modern era (c. 1400–1750) at least, China remained at the forefront of a Eurasian-wide process of firearms innovation.[4] So again we see the interplay between war, commerce, and cultural exchange.

Andrade's essay also reminds us of the danger of adopting Eurocentric perspectives when it comes to warfare and military effectiveness. Just because Chinese used firearms in different ways than Europeans does not mean that they were less proficient in their use or less interested in their applications. Like people everywhere, they were adapting firearms to their own strategic needs and circumstances. The clever ways that Ming military officials adapted guns to fight against mobile steppe warriors illustrates this point well, as do the innovations of Qi Jiguang (1528–88) in southern infantry warfare. Moreover, China's military innovations influenced other lands, as for example, Qi Jiguang's practices and theories were disseminated to Korea in the 1590s, and thence to Manchu conquerors of Korea, yet another example of cultural exchange cum technological diffusion that has been underappreciated until recently.

The following essay, by Sun Laichen, is a detailed – and brilliant – analysis of the cauldron of military innovation that was China's maritime littoral, focusing on the anti-pirate campaigns in southeast China during the mid to late Ming. Whereas previous studies have focused largely on the political and economic aspects of these campaigns (and to a lesser extent the training innovations of Qi Jiguang in the 1560s), Sun highlights the important role of matchlock muskets in these operations. Interestingly enough, his piece also indicates the multinational character of the pirate groups operating in the south seas and illustrates the fact that the pirates themselves eagerly adopted firearms of all kinds, belying traditional assertions that only Europeans or Japanese made adept use of such weapons in battle, and thereby squeezed out local competitors.

This also draws attention to the burgeoning international arms market in Southeast Asia, something manifested in Jennifer Gaynor's study as well. While much attention has heretofore been directed toward such markets in Europe and the Mediterranean world, it is a welcome change to see Asianists also contributing to these explorations of arms flows. In the immediate sense, such flows served the important role of bringing more weapons and ships into Chinese hands. As Sun notes, these ships and guns would play key roles in China's military life for centuries, providing yet another example of the unforeseen consequences of technological transmission.

Turning to the latter issue, Sun's chapter also alerts us to the multiple lines of transmission and exchange throughout the imperial era. Historians of earlier periods in Chinese history tend to emphasize the overland silk routes of Central Asia whereas historians of the late imperial era tend to pay more attention to maritime routes as key loci of trade and cultural exchange respectively. But Sun reminds us that both routes remained viable, and the Ming entertained envoys and adopted technologies from both the Ottomans (at least according to Sun's research) and the Portuguese, suggesting that this was an empire cognizant of the need to maintain its military edge by borrowing and adaptation. And, as Tonio Andrade also indicates, officials quickly appreciated the efficacy of the new weapons and encouraged their manufacture and deployment.

Yet another point that bears mentioning with respect to Sun's chapter is the process of cross-fertilization and continuous adaptation he describes. Asians were not content simply to copy foreign weapons wholesale; they often made significant modifications such as the breech-screw plugs referenced by Sun as having been adopted by the Japanese, or the changing barrel lengths for cannons discussed by Andrade in his chapter. In other words, they adapted these technologies to suit local needs and conditions, a process that fascinatingly mirrors the one traced by Bello for opium cultivation. Placing guns on coastal patrol and fishing boats is another example of this principle in practice, which brings us to Xing Hang's fascinating examination of piracy in China and Southeast Asia in the seventeenth century.

In the seventeenth century, Guangdong's importance in transnational trade grew as global patterns shifted toward Southeast Asia. This was an example of how global trends impacted regional developments. In this case, Indian textiles and natural resource flows supplanted silver from the New World as the key engines of global trade, also interfacing with the seventeenth-century crisis mentioned above. In this particular instance, the ability of the Zheng clan to take advantage of circumstances provided by the decline of the Ming and shifts in international trade patterns is a fine example of how individuals and organizations could adapt to systemic crises and changes and even profit from them.

Complementing Gaynor's work, Hang's chapter also offers a perspective on how independent political actors could take advantage of fluid political situations, in this case the ongoing Ming loyalist movement. At the same time, those willing to cross boundaries and take a catholic approach toward political loyalty could turn a tidy profit. And those with trade connections and/ or military skills could market their services to the highest bidder as we see with the Leizhou commanders from China who served the Ngúyen against the Cambodians. This situation is a perfect example of the unintended consequences of extended political and societal unrest.

Furthermore, Hang situates the Guangdong pirates of the Ming-Qing transition within a longer tradition of "politically autonomous maritime Chinese states," challenging facile generalizations about overseas Chinese as stateless outsiders, ripe for exploitation. It also indicates that the simple fact that imperial China did not (with a few notable exceptions such as during the Song and the early Ming) generally maintain a large formal navy, does not mean that it did not have significant and ongoing interests in the maritime realm. Nor were maritime Chinese actors unwilling to use military force or the threat of it to obtain their goals.

Chapter Eight explores the further development of maritime China in the eighteenth century. Paul Van Dyke's richly detailed study presents yet another example of the relationship between individuals and broader commercial networks and processes and the often unforeseen consequences of these connections. While much has been said about the experiences of Westerners sailing to Asia in the period under consideration, far less is known about movement in the other direction, which has, in many respects, proved more enduring, judging from the flourishing of Chinese diasporic communities around the globe. Van Dyke examines not these individuals, but rather the intrepid, or perhaps desperate, Chinese sailors who sailed from China to Europe and back. Driven by the erosion of the traditional junk trade in Southeast Asia, these men took advantage of new opportunities to try and build better lives.

In a process that may be familiar to modern readers, changes in the nature of trade impacted labor flows as well, and the poorest and most marginalized elements of society were often the first and most negatively affected. The sailors that are the subjects of Van Dyke's study took advantage of their unique skills and knowledge to find their way. As we become increasingly aware of such flows today, as the result of government policies and popular responses to them, it is instructive to consider how earlier governments, companies, and individuals navigated such choppy waters, literally and figuratively. The study also provides a useful case study of the local consequences of global processes as seen in Van Dyke's discussion of how increased competition between trading companies, occasioned by the expansion of private trade, opened up new opportunities for recently displaced Chinese seamen. Finally, while underscoring the key role played by these common seamen in facilitating the China trade, Van Dyke admits that we can only speculate upon their impact on the places they visited or how they perceived these vastly different lands and cultures. Perhaps a seaman's diary remains to be discovered in a moldering sea chest in Macao or Guangdong.

Bridging the gap between history, political science, and international relations, David Kang offers an apt critique of the "presentist" Eurocentric focus of international relations theory today, a state of affairs rendered even more problematic by the growing importance of Asian nations in the international arena. Kang points to the extensive literature on pre-modern East Asian international relations produced by both historians and political scientists as particularly useful for analyzing alternative frameworks of diplomacy and international discourse. The volume and diversity of surviving primary source materials make this fertile ground for study and, as Kang notes, offer much promise for bringing historians, political scientists, and international relations scholars together in conversation to the mutual benefit of all.

Kang's central argument, building upon his earlier work, is that East Asia's specifically hierarchical system of foreign relations, popularly known as the tributary or tribute system, was more effective in maintaining regional peace and stability than the so-called Westphalian system of Europe, which was based upon the implicit notion of equality between states and the explicit idea of a balance of power between them.[5] What is crucial here is that, according to Kang, the system in question managed to maintain peace and stability for centuries, in contrast to the European system, which eventually emerged as the global model and has generally been assumed by political scientists and international relations scholars to be the objective standard according to which other systems of foreign relations are judged.

In fact, one of Kang's key insights is that much of the system's success can be attributed to its flexibility, a point often overlooked by its critics, but one that Jack Wills recognized decades ago in his writings. Nonetheless, the fact that it operated by different norms meant that there was bound to be friction with the full-scale arrival of the Western imperialist powers in the nineteenth century. In the clashes that followed, of course, the tributary system was supplanted, but that should not erase its appeal as a subject for comparative study. Most significant is the recognition that East Asia had a viable international system. As amply demonstrated by the contributions of this volume, it was not a mere collection of xenophobic, isolated states clinging to "tradition" and unwilling to admit outside influences or change with the times. These states and their subjects, not to mention those who operated outside and between the states, interacted pragmatically, pursuing their own agendas. The China-centered hierarchical order represented an abstract ideal, one that multiple states deployed for their own benefit. One must be careful to not let the rhetoric obscure the reality.

We conclude the volume with a brief interview Jack did for the journal *Itinerario* in 2006. As Jack himself noted in a postscript he prepared for the present volume, "I am struck by the ways personal encounters with people and places add enormously to the insights of the student of history... The concreteness of lived experience of persons and places remains one of the main sources of the humane power of the study of history." Indeed, this volume itself was born in a conference we put together in Los Angeles in 2015 to honor Jack. He was truly touched by the experience and it embodied his belief that even in an era of easy, instant communication, personal interaction in the non-virtual world "remains essential to the intellectual vitality of our calling as historians."

We wholeheartedly agree. We are deeply saddened that Jack is no longer with us to witness the fruit of his guidance and inspiration, and we hope that the essays in this volume will help serve as a testament to his enduring influence.

Notes

1 See, for example, Wayne E. Lee, "Peace Chiefs and Blood Revenge: Patterns of Restraint in Native American Warfare, 1500–1800," *Journal of Military History* 71.3 (October 2007), pp. 701–41.
2 Tonio Andrade, *How Taiwan Became Chinese: Dutch, Spanish, and Han Colonization in the Seventeenth Century* (New York: Columbia University Press, 2008).
3 On terracentrism, see Markus Rediker, *Between the Devil and the Deep Blue Sea: Merchant Seamen, Pirates, and the Anglo-American Maritime World, 1700–1750* (Cambridge: Cambridge University Press, 1989).
4 See Tonio Andrade, *The Gunpowder Age: China, Military Innovation, and the Rise of the West in World History* (Princeton, NJ: Princeton University Press, 2016).
5 See David Kang, *East Asia Before the West: Five Centuries and Trade and Tribute* (New York: Columbia University Press, 2010).

1 Qing opium dependency and Republican opium autonomy

David A. Bello

The Sino-British global drug traffic was a development of what John E. Wills Jr. has called "the interactive emergence" of European domination of "the modern world system" in maritime Asia. This interaction, as shaped by regional "patterns of production, trade, and governance," subsequently "emerged in highly contingent and specific ways from ... mutual adaptations" between European and Asian actors. The invention of opium paste is one such contingent emergence because it was the largely fortuitous result of a semi-conscious collaborative transnational enterprise between Chinese smokers of Qing China and its Southeast Asian diaspora, the poppy cultivators of British India and the free-trading smugglers of Great Britain and their monopolist opponents. The outcome of this collaboration proved very difficult for any state to fully control, at least in part because opium constituted an unprecedented concentration of the essence of state power itself, in an all too easily reproducible and exploitable form. The emergence of what is arguably the world's first modern drug problem challenged state centralization through its potential for converting mass drug consumption into the economic basis for regionalized sovereignty. Through the process of mutual adaptation, the physical drug dependency of individuals could abet regional economic, and ultimately political, autonomy.

In China, such autonomy came about through the interplay of complex factors, which include those that can be categorized quite broadly as "natural" and concern the mutually conditioning effects of ecology, human physiology and poppies. Anthropogenic factors can be subdivided into domestic administrative structures, which concern indirect rule and revenue problems as well as related domestic obstacles to prohibition and monopolization. The other subdivision is foreign relations, which concerns Qing diplomatic and economic interactions with British India as well as the Inner Asian Khanate of Kokand. The Raj and the Khanate were effectively sponsors of the drug traffic on the Qing empire's southeastern and northwestern frontiers, respectively. These natural and anthropogenic factors combined to create a Qing drug infrastructure in three basic dimensions, which were to some extent, ethnically distinct. The production dimension was grounded in borderland domestic poppy cultivation by mainly minority growers in northwestern and southwestern China. The consumption dimension was centered in urban regions of largely Han, or ethnic Chinese, residence in China proper. The distribution dimension, encompassing both foreign and domestic subsections, connected producers and consumers across the empire and beyond, mainly via South Asia, Inner Asia and maritime Europe.

Full-blown opium-enabled political autonomy emerged only during the first half of the twentieth century, most notably during China's warlord period which, strictly speaking, lasted from 1916–26. Nevertheless, China, despite the official establishment of the Republic in 1911–12 and its substantial consolidation after 1926, was never a fully unified nation-state during the eponymous Republican period up to 1949. Republican China saw the emergence of many warlord states that drew critical portions of their revenues from opium.[1] The foundation of this opium autonomy had been laid during the preceding Qing Dynasty (1644–1912).

While the Qing origins of Republican opium dynamics are generally recognized, most studies tend to focus on one regime or the other. Opium control problems within China and within British India, as opposed to the drug traffic between them, are likewise almost always treated separately. Even work that does try to encompass both usually does not cover Qing events in detail before the late nineteenth century and beyond the southeast coast.[2] Finally, little current material on poppy ecology and opium effects on human physiology is integrated into any of the historical literature. This chapter addresses these critical gaps through the additional examination of the longer Qing record prior to the 1830s in a more global context. It will also outline the significance of ecological and physiological, as well as anthropogenic, factors characteristic of the Qing drug dependency that produced Republican opium autonomy. I emphasize the appearance of opium paste smoking in the context of regional dynastic administration to take the empire's western borderlands into greater consideration. Where possible, I also briefly consider the comparative implications of opium control for China and for British India, the two imperial states that formed the axis of what I consider the first modern global drug traffic.

Some global considerations

The Qing predecessor, the Ming Dynasty (1368–1644), was the first Chinese society to encounter early modern globalization within the context of maritime Asia's interactive emergence. The Ming experienced the early stage of globalization primarily through "exchanges of trade goods, food plants, diseases, people, and ideas" that were situated within "a very special set of environments dominated by a very distinctive variant of Chinese culture, economy, and politics: that of the maritime Han Chinese."[3]

In the sixteenth and seventeenth centuries, maritime East and Southeast Asia were subject to considerable economic and political instability and conflict as a succession of European rivals, first the Portuguese, then the

Spanish, then the Dutch, aggressively shoved their way in among an already unruly, heterogeneous indigenous populace. Illicit practices, which could encompass whole rafts of commodity traffics and islands full of unauthorized settlement, were endemic, if not ubiquitous. Melaka, Macao, Manila, the Penghu Islands, the Zhoushan Archipelago and Taiwan all became, at one time or another, shady sites of commercial and military clashes between a bewildering array of contenders.[4] By the nineteenth century, the regional contest among the European maritime powers had been settled in favor of Great Britain, but maritime Asia did not exactly settle down. The global drug traffic was one contemporary result of "the changes that ended around 1800 with Europe dominating all the world's seaways." This conclusion, however, did not end conflict with China, but actually exacerbated it. Moreover, European maritime power could not have prevailed without the active participation of non-Europeans. Indeed, Indian cultivators and distributors, along with their Chinese counterparts continued to participate in support of a British early modern seaborne drug trade between the two Asian countries well beyond 1800.[5]

Yet, there was resistance as well, arising in part from different early modern experiences with opium in India and China. From the perspective of India's rulers, the Qing state had a rather belated, schizophrenic socio-political relationship with poppy (*Papaver somniferum*) cultivation for opium. A legacy of the Mughals, the drug monopoly played a critical role as a legitimate source of revenue for virtually the whole period of British rule in India. During the nineteenth century, it has been estimated that, at its peak, the opium monopoly generated 16 percent of total state revenues.[6] Such an official relationship did not initially exist in China, despite its society's familiarity with various poppy products, including a comparatively crude form of edible opium, since the Tang dynasty (618–907 CE).

In Indian terms, the Chinese state was indifferent to the economic potential of poppy. China's first formal opium prohibition did not even emerge until 1729, and was not strongly enforced until the nineteenth century.[7] Heavy public censure continued even during the qualified Qing legalization of the drug between 1858 and 1906, which, among other things, prevented the full legalization of domestic poppy cultivation until the 1880s. Equally intense private consumption and burgeoning cultivation, which persisted during corresponding periods of dynastic prohibition, effectively existed side by side from the late eighteenth century on. Genuine intensification of both opium consumption and prohibition during the Qing began only after the transformation of the drug from edible substance to smokeable paste, which occurred around 1800.[8] The rough chronological coincidence of a polarization in attitudes to opium and a transformation in the drug's mode of consumption suggests a link between the two at a formative stage in the Chinese historical context. Opium paste smoking, rather than generalized opium consumption, substantially and characteristically conditioned the responses of both Qing state and Qing society to opium.

The vast majority of historical studies of opium have focused on its purely socio-economic and socio-political effects, whose significance is certainly indisputable. However, as Flynn and Giráldez have convincingly argued,

> trade and ecological activities are components of a single global network. It is dangerous and misleading to analytically bifurcate this global network into separate economic and ecological components because in doing so one risks losing sight of the global unity of the general system.[9]

The introduction of New World crops into early modern China during the Ming, which radically expanded arable land into previously inaccessible highland areas to boost food supply and ultimately population, is a classic example of what I would call this econo(mic)-ecolo(gical) synergy.[10] The prevailing assumption in the mainly socio-economic analyses of the opium traffic is that only human interaction matters. This anthropocentric perspective tends to "restrict conceptualization of globalization to the sphere of economics alone," without recognizing that "global economic forces have evolved in a deep and intimate intermix with noneconomic global forces over the past five centuries."[11]

Poppy, however, is an Old World crop, indeed one of the oldest and most valuable. Opium's commodification, preceded by tea, actually displaced the two previous silver cycles that Flynn and Giráldez see as the main stuff of "global economic unity" from the sixteenth into the eighteenth centuries. The onset of what they call "the tea and opium cycle" produced "a sea change in foreign commerce in the middle of the eighteenth century in Asia" when "silver-based trade at the global level was in trouble." In this process Old World crops replaced New World minerals as the most important commodity manifestations of globalization. In the geographic terms that Wills has stressed, there was likewise a shift from the Pacific to the Indian oceans. This does not mean that silver was no longer relevant to the global economy by the second half of the eighteenth century, but that its role became "complementary in terms of profitability" to that of tea and opium.[12] By this time Old World and New World commodities had become cyclically integrated. New World products were unquestionably profound agents of global transformations, but, to slightly reorient Wills' core argument, they cannot be privileged through "an analytic separation" of New World "intrusion" and Old World "response."

Whatever change in globalization trends produced by these crops and minerals was not purely "economic," but related to physiological and ecological conditions to which humans could adapt, but not fully control or understand. Globalization, as manifested in historical formations like the Sino-British opium traffic, cannot be defined in purely economic terms as "a free market," etc. These narrow parameters rigorously exclude the extra-economic conditions for the emergence of globalized market relations. In more specific terms of the traffic, they cannot alone explain why state-building and state-destabilizing levels of mass consumption of opium arose, but mainly how they did so in largely quantitative terms.[13]

Some environmental considerations

The Sino-British opium traffic was a highly contingent and specific maritime "interactive emergence," born not only of "mutual adaptations" between Europeans and Asians, but between people and cultivars in an econo-ecolo synergy of globalization. It is therefore necessary to understand some of the basic physiological effects of opium, along with the ecological factors that produce them as a part of poppy botany. This perspective does not just maintain the global unity of the general human system, but redefines that system to appropriately expand its confines toward a genuinely world scale in environmental (i.e. interpenetrating cultural and ecological) terms.

Smokeable opium, in its initial, diluted form of *madak/madat* (tobacco soaked in an opium solution) and later as a much more powerful paste extract, was a poppy product of unprecedented psychoactive power in China, and probably the world as well. Prior to the emergence of *madak* some time during the closing years of the Ming Dynasty in the 1500s, medicinal poppy products were eaten in largely unrefined forms that much less effectively tapped opium's primary psychoactive alkaloids of codeine and, above all, morphine.[14] Complex conditions still incompletely understood, brought together consumers, distributors and producers in Southeast Asia, diasporic Chinese among them, to forge a new synergy between the New World crop of tobacco and Eurasian poppy sap. This kind of synergy was typical of how "drug foods" or "addictive consumables" were developed, particularly for mass consumption, the classic combination being sugar added to caffeinated drinks like tea and coffee.[15] The "tea and opium cycle" of Flynn and Giráldez is really an addictive consumables cycle in econo-ecolo terms.

The combination of New World tobacco and Old World poppy sap yielded "global" *madak*, which created a commensurately mass market for opium consumption. *Madak*'s wider appeal arose mainly from its affinity for volatilization, which introduced psychoactive alkaloids into the body much faster than any other combination of poppy product and consumption technique. Opium's most potent alkaloids, morphine and codeine, are absorbed comparatively slowly through the digestive tract, but quite rapidly when inhaled into the lungs. While the effects of smoking opium are much more ephemeral than eating it, their onset is much quicker, taking only a few seconds to reach the brain. Volatilizing inhalation, however, also burns away a considerable amount of morphine content as smoke.[16]

More efficient consumption of opiate alkaloids through practices like smoking generally produces a physiological dependency, indicated by the onset of withdrawal symptoms, quite easily. Euphoric effects of such consumption cause dopamine neurotransmitters to stimulate neural pathways, normally less intensively triggered by food and sex, that have evolved as part of the human survival mechanism. Dependency, however, is distinct from addiction, whose nature and mechanics remain subject to considerable scientific uncertainty. Recent research nevertheless suggests that addiction may be connected to increased dopamine levels that are now understood to stimulate pathways for motivation, or "salience," rather than for reward. This is why some addicts continue to use drugs even when they no longer experience any rewarding effects. Some recent imaging studies, moreover, suggest addiction may be a brain disease that would probably seriously disrupt any volitional consumption through impairment of brain areas responsible for inhibition and salience. Subjective responses to a wide range of environmental factors, including "persons, places and situations," also remain critical, in addition to neurological factors.[17] In general, it can be concluded that smoking paste, as opposed to eating opium or mixing it with tobacco, engaged more of the neurophysiology of more people more intensively to form either dependency or addiction.

The way opium was smoked also mattered. The introduction of paste smoking eliminated tobacco along with many other extraneous impurities, particularly various forms of vegetable tinder necessary to ignite *madak*. Paste constituted a qualitative change in the drug for it refined poppy sap into a more concentrated alkaloid substance with fifty times the morphia content.[18] Techniques of refinement and consumption also engendered consumer preferences, and consequently various cultures of consumption, as it became clear that some kinds of opium were more palatable than others. Such preferences were responses to a range of chemical variables that production could not entirely control and were incompletely understood, so that "the only thing consistent" about all opium products from all poppy producers "was the variability of inherent alkaloids."[19]

Opium potency could be affected by variance in natural, processing and consumption conditions. The opium poppy's main agro-botanical distinction from other poppy species is its production of certain alkaloids, especially morphine, which may be a repair response to physical damage like incisions. The latex extracted from precise slices in the poppy capsule under the proper seasonal and harvesting conditions contains an alkaloid content of about 6 to 10 percent, most of which is morphine.[20] Species diversity, divergent ecologies and production variation all influence the alkaloid potency of opium extracted from different types of poppy and even from different "vintages" of raw opium latex from the same type of poppy. Turkish opium sown in fall, for example, generally has higher morphine content than that sown in spring. One 1965 study even demonstrated that clay pots used by Indian cultivators to collect and store raw opium latex were leaching about 8.5 percent of its morphine content. These earthen containers were cheap to use, and their porosity intentionally facilitated the removal of excess water, which contained water-soluble morphine, from the latex. Even this rate of denaturing was inconsistent because the porosity of the pots was not uniform. Such an incidental aging process probably contributed to the "mellow" quality of Indian opium in comparison with types of higher morphine content like Turkish opium.[21] The nineteenth-century emergence of Chinese regional brands, like "Tai juice" (opium from the poppies grown in the southeast China coastal locale of Taizhou (台州) decocted in alcohol), is both representative of such intersections of human and ecological processes and evidence of ongoing synergy.[22]

Botanical and physiological factors came together as critical for the socio-economic rise of the paste traffic between British India and Qing China. The organic composition of the Indian poppy generally contained just enough of the right alkaloid because it "provided sedation without the lethal effects of too much morphine" when smoked, which probably further reduced morphine content through volatilization.[23] In effect, Qing opium paste was first produced from a transnational intersection of the Southeast Asian-Chinese consumption technique of smoking with the raw material of Indian poppy sap as semi-intentionally refined by British techniques of mass production and limited quality control conditioned by a regional environmental context.

The dual revolution in the processing and consumption of poppy sap was completed around 1800, when paste smoking unambiguously emerged in China. Contemporary accounts describe paste's comparatively elaborate and distinctive preparations revolving around its formation into pills and volatilization by a special lamp. Some also describe the formation of a physical dependency such that "if one does not smoke daily on a regular basis, illness results. This is commonly known as 'craving' (*yin*癮), which in extreme cases causes tears and mucus to flow and so debilitates the limbs that they cannot be raised."[24]

Paste smoking of opium trafficked from India was a distinctively Chinese form of consumption that arguably made China the first country in the world confronted with a recognizably modern global drug problem. I have explored the development of opium as a global commodity over the past four hundred years elsewhere in detail. Its complexities into the nineteenth century encompassed Euro-American traffickers running various types of South Asian and Turkish opium, of various degrees of legality across a number of state jurisdictions, into China, which also maintained its own illicit domestic production, distribution and consumption network.[25]

The general exponential increase in Qing paste's socio-economic and physiological manifestations made "opium" undergo a series of quantitative changes so vast they amount to a qualitative one. It is unlikely that *madak*, given its comparatively adulterated condition and consequently milder effects, could have created such a complex, conflicted network.

Qing domestication of opium

Qing opium paste soon manifested another characteristic of a modern drug, macroeconomic power on an interstate scale. By 1819, Chinese consumption of Indian opium had shifted the balance of trade from China in favor of Britain, with the first major opium boom coming during the late 1820s.

In comparison with the previous decade's annual average, opium imports to China more than doubled from 4,568 to 10,361 chests. During the 1830s, the average jumped to 26,003 chests, and over the 1840s, 40,484 chests were moved to China in an average year. In the 1850s, many aspects of the trade were legalized, and in the year 1858, 68,607 chests entered China. It has been estimated that as early as 1830, Indian opium was probably the single most valuable commodity, in terms of total trade, of the entire nineteenth century.[26] The late 1820s' watershed in the smuggling traffic was instrumental in convincing the dynasty to actively enforce previously weak opium prohibition. Awash in opium, authorities eventually pursued what I have called "absolute prohibition," namely, capital punishment for producers, consumers and distributors in 1839.[27]

Of course, strictly speaking, these changes were triggered by the Sino-British-Indian construct of opium paste, which was more than simply opium. This is an important point in a number of respects. From a comparative perspective, it explains why a modern drug problem did not also immediately arise in India itself, where opium eating was the traditional norm as it had been in pre-Qing China. Indeed, opium smoking was identified as a Chinese import to India by informed observers like Raj financial official George Watt.[28] India was not yet dealing with a modern drug problem because Indian consumers did not smuggle and smoke foreign paste that could engender much deeper physical dependency. Moreover, the development of such a problem was inhibited, both in India and in Britain where opium could be legally ingested, by smoking's stigma as a "Chinese" or "oriental" vice.[29] Paste smoking was ethnically marked in negative terms in both India and Britain.

In China, on the other hand, it was also so marked, but in a more complicated way. The practice of smoking itself had been nativized within a few decades after the introduction of tobacco some time around 1560. By the eighteenth century the raw material needed to produce paste, namely crude opium, was an exclusively foreign import initially from Southeast Asia, but mainly from British India. Consequently, and in contrast to British and Indian views, the Chinese considered paste itself to be of ultimately foreign, specifically Euro-American, origin. This view was never entirely abandoned by Chinese public discourse, even when domestic production surpassed that of British India in the latter half of the nineteenth century.[30] The increasingly historical origins of the premier, but no longer sole, article of consumption for paste smoking were discursively preserved.

One of the most important concrete effects of this selective conceptualization was a Chinese state prohibition policy centered on the suppression of an article of foreign contraband that by the 1830s, the height of Qing prohibition, was no longer exclusively, and by the 1870s no longer mostly, foreign. The first period of large-scale state prohibition in the 1830s targeted coastal smugglers who were based in the foreign trade hub of Guangzhou (Canton) and who served as the main conduit of opium into China. The Qing state tended to ignore or downplay domestic poppy cultivators who had emerged in the southwestern provinces of Yunnan, Guizhou and Sichuan, as well as in the extreme northwestern Inner Asian territory of Xinjiang, along with some lesser producers in a few coastal provinces. This was probably not simply because these sources produced much less opium, but also because the state was reluctant to disrupt relations in sensitive borderlands. Opium distribution was the only criminal drug offense until 1813, when consumption was likewise prosecuted.[31] By the time cultivation was formally criminalized in 1830, however, poppy cultivation for opium production had likely already existed for around a quarter-century in Yunnan, where China's first major poppy center would emerge in the 1860s.[32]

The central government had not entirely ignored domestic cultivation. The first formal, large-scale anti-cultivation operations in Chinese history had been initiated in 1830. The state, however, soon found that its local, urban-based administration was unable to project sufficient power into the countryside to eradicate poppy. This problem was particularly acute in the Qing empire's southwestern and northwestern frontier areas, where large majorities of non-Chinese indigenous populations were administered indirectly on behalf of the throne by their own leaders and organizations. Regular dynastic officials in the southwestern provinces and in Xinjiang openly admitted their inability to extend prohibition operations into areas under the indirect rule of Southeast Asian indigenous peoples and Inner Asian Muslims, respectively.[33] These political conditions, in combination with congenial environmental factors, ensured many frontier zones would become relatively inviolable areas of illicit poppy cultivation.

Consequently, the way that the production, distribution and consumption of opium paste was constructed by the Qing Chinese state ensured that its resources would be devoted almost entirely to stopping foreign coastal smuggling, and secondarily domestic consumption, rather than domestic cultivation. This approach was predicated on the questionable assumption that arresting coastal traffickers, and later domestic consumers, would automatically eliminate all other offenders by blocking the main source of smokeable opium.[34] Senior provincial officials in Yunnan had already refuted this logic in 1832. They correctly identified the inverse relationship between imported and domestic opium demand, stating that local production of cheaper poppy was the main reason for the local decrease in more expensive Indian opium smuggled in from the coast. They believed demand for the coastal product would resurge if domestic supplies were suppressed.[35]

Much of the impetus for anti-trafficking and anti-consumer policies came from the inherent urban-centric limitations of Qing local administration, as well as from the initial conceptualization of opium as a problem of foreign contraband. Urban distributors and smokers were much easier to get at than rural cultivators. The implementation of this policy, however, failed to stop trafficking and consumption. It also promoted the development of nearly inviolable enclaves of production, particularly in southwest China, that the

Qing state could not control even after it relaxed prohibition and legalized imported opium in 1858.

The roots of Qing opium dependency

Such enclaves were not limited to areas of non-Chinese settlement. Evidence from the late eighteenth and early nineteenth centuries indicates that a number of sub-provincial local administrations, some coastal, most in the southwest, were dependent on poppy cultivators to meet their tax collection quotas and local expenses. In 1840, Metropolitan Censor Lu Yinggu (陸應穀; d. 1857) summarized the problem most explicitly. Lu had served in Yunnan where he had heard there was extensive illicit poppy cultivation throughout the province. He questioned how local officials could be entirely ignorant of such vast areas, whose fields, which had previously produced beans and rice, were now producing poppy. Lu concluded that poppies were so profitable that tax quotas could be easily and quickly fulfilled, to the immense relief of local officials, who were responsible for both the smooth collection of revenue and strict enforcement of opium prohibition.[36] In Yunnan, the local state had already become dependent on opium.

Tax quota pressure arose mainly because the central government gained control of almost all local revenues as a result of fiscal reforms in the early decades of the eighteenth century. Consequently, locales were impelled to search for "informal networks of funding" to maintain themselves, and opium, which could generate ten times the revenue produced by staple crops, proved to be one of the most effective among such networks for many areas.[37]

It was in the empire's western frontiers where the dependency of local governments on opium production was particularly acute. The first province to tax opium after legalization in 1858 was Yunnan, rather than any locale on the southeast coast where Indian opium smuggling was centered. In 1877 Board of War Senior Vice Minister Guo Songtao (郭嵩燾; 1818–91) confirmed that illicit taxation remained a staple of local official revenue in western China, flatly stating that, "in Sichuan, Yunnan, Gansu, and Shaanxi, the primary motive for cultivation is tax revenue." These locales collected "an illicit tax on crude opium, which also is many times greater than regular tax revenue. Since both official and commoner profit thereby, opium spreads everywhere."[38]

Guo's characterization of the western region's opium dependency, at a time when domestic poppy cultivation was still technically illegal, is significant in terms of its units of measure, namely the southwestern provinces of Sichuan, Yunnan and the northwestern provinces of Gansu and Shaanxi. There were also contemporary and contrasting official arguments promoting poppy cultivation as the best crop per unit area to develop such agriculturally deficient provinces.[39] These views are some of the many late Qing portents of the political fragmentation of the empire into provincial- or multi-provincial-sized warlord mini-states after the fall of the dynasty in 1911. This fragmentation was often abetted or sustained by opium revenues and such trends continued into the twentieth century. In Sichuan, commercial drug dependency was obvious to British colonial authorities by 1901, when one consulate official observed that opium had become "the province's most valuable developed asset ... to Szechwan opium is money."[40]

Conditions on the coast were no better. Allegations of the illicit taxation of contraband opium by Canton's superintendent of maritime customs surfaced as early as 1822. Seven years prior in 1815, the city's foreign, and largely British, merchant community had already privately established what they bluntly termed a "corruption fund" to defray the quasi-official costs of dealing in opium. Official concerns over revenue became more overt in the wake of the Opium War and were clearly decisive for the informal taxation of opium appearing in various coastal ports in the years immediately before legalization in the late 1850s.[41] Regardless of its ultimate origins, opium had created substantial dependencies in certain local administrations, both on the coast and in the interior, before formal legalization of imported opium was promulgated in 1858. By this time there were already quasi-official apparatuses to tap opium revenue, but they were deliberately concealed from central government oversight.

One reason for this ongoing concealment was the continuing hostility of senior Qing central officials to opium in all its manifestations, and such officials even included advocates of legalization. One of the most prominent and famous of these officials, Li Hongzhang (李鴻章; 1823–1901), advocated for the legalization of domestic poppy cultivation in 1874 in order to tax it out of existence. In 1881, in response to questions about the propriety of legalizing domestic cultivation, Li cogently expressed the rationale for the Qing state's contradictory attitude toward opium: "the single aim of my government in taxing opium will be in the future – as it has always been in the past – to repress the traffic, never the desire to gain revenue from such a source."[42] There was undoubtedly much official hypocrisy on this issue, just as there was in British India over the state profiting from what the founder of its drug monopoly, Governor-General Warren Hastings, called "the pernicious article of luxury." There was also, however, genuine, and increasingly nationalist, opposition to opium in all its forms.

Extremist or conflicted reactions to opium issues were conditioned by historical experiences. This is why the chronology of opium's prohibition and legalization in Qing China is critical for an understanding of how nineteenth-century imperial opium dependency engendered twentieth-century warlord drug independence. Failure to suppress domestic cultivation during the height of dynastic prohibition in the 1830s, in combination with the revenue crisis of local administrations, encouraged the formation of covert administrative drug dependencies in many locales, particularly in the southwest. Thus, absolute prohibition abetted a series of local opium regimes, which developed both independently of each other and outside the control of the central government. Legalization did not bring these structures under state control, or did so only in a very illusory and deceptive fashion. The equivocal nature of Qing state legalization permitted these structures to develop unmolested while continuing to provide strong incentives for localities to maintain the autonomy of their opium revenue. This is why the Qing central state could not use taxation to repress the traffic in the way envisioned by Li Hongzhang.

The state's aggrandizing fiscal policies created a major incentive for much nascent provincial opium production to protect local revenues from central government encroachment even after legalization. Consequently, a number of provinces were developing their own individual opium revenue systems that not only could not be overseen by the central government, but were deliberately intended to be independent of it and exist for the sole benefit of provincial, or even sub-provincial administrations. These localized opium revenue systems were in place long before legalization in 1858, and were consequently originally designed for concealment from the center's surveillance. This situation, which arose from a particular approach to prohibition, ensured that the central government would neither maximize its revenue from legalization nor ever be able to impose a comprehensive opium monopoly like that inherited by British India.[43]

The late Qing case of the Hubei Arsenal in Hanyang is a good example of the dependency of Chinese modernization on opium. The arsenal, "one of the key institutions on which the fate of the Ch'ing dynasty hung," had been intended to produce modern weapons as part of the Self-strengthening Movement (*Ziqiang yundong*自强运动). A critical portion of the funding for its initial establishment came from opium revenues, which were captured by the central government's 1906 edict to eradicate opium within a decade, mainly through high taxation. The edict initiated one of the most effective of late Qing reforms, the Anti-Opium Campaign of 1906–11, which was powered by a pervasive spirit of nascent Chinese nationalism. The campaign's genuine accomplishments did not convince all contemporary foreign observers, some of whom felt the center's capture of opium revenues was actually done to increase its own income, not eradicate the drug locally. In any event, the 1906 reform devastated the arsenal's production, which was "financially strapped by the elimination of opium revenues."[44]

It is important to note that provincial fiscal autonomy was inherent in the empire's basic administrative structure rather than an aberration created by the drug traffic. The Qing Board of Revenue (*Hubu*; 戶部) did not have direct fiscal authority over provinces. In its mainly supervisory capacity, the Board simply had "the authority of disposal over taxes" collected by provincial administrations and remitted to Beijing. Provinces routinely excluded substantial portions of this revenue from remission for a variety of reasons.[45] Control of finances was further fragmented by the traditional dynastic practice of dividing revenue set aside for central government administration from that assigned for the emperor's own disposal as the privy purse (i.e. the Imperial Household Department; *Neiwufu*; 內務府). There had always been some degree of fund transfer between the two, with the inner court privy purse more often supplementing outer court Board shortfalls to fund mainly military and public works expenses. The relatively stable and moderate distinction between these main fiscal structures of the inner and outer courts was seriously distorted by the mid-1850s as many privy purse revenue sources were disrupted by political upheavals. As a result, increasingly large amounts of Board funds were diverted to cover mounting privy purse expenditures and deficits. The apportioning of maritime customs revenue was especially convoluted, to the extent that the part of the revenues assigned to the Board for the regular operation of the maritime customs was often in deficit while that part surrendered to the privy purse was often in a surplus that actually exceeded this regular operating deficit.[46] Consequently, when control over commercial revenues was officially and ostensibly transferred to the state bureaucracy, represented by the Imperial Maritime Customs Service (IMCS) in 1861, this did not unequivocally enhance Qing state fiscal strength.

The assertion that these restructured "trade taxes often constituted a valuable new source of revenue for states such as Qing China" must be qualified. The IMCS was established in 1854 by foreign commercial interests to collect maritime trade taxes on behalf of a Qing state administratively crippled by the Taiping Rebellion (1851–64), one of the largest civil wars in world history. Whereas under Inspector General Robert Hart it subordinated itself in many respects to the Chinese Foreign Office (*Zongli Yamen*; 總理衙門) authorities and interests, the IMCS nevertheless "served the interests of British free trade policies" in "the semi-colonial realm" of Qing China. In the 1860s, Britain was interested in strengthening the central government authority, mainly so that the dynasty could meet its unequal treaty obligations. In this respect the IMCS was "'a necessary supplement' to the treaties of 1858 and 1860 for the Qing would otherwise [have] been unable to implement key financial elements of these agreements."[47]

The IMCS was indeed able to sequester comparatively more provincial revenue for Beijing, but these funds were ultimately more useful for servicing foreign loans and indemnities, not for the realization of self-sufficient centralization. During the last decade of Qing rule, the IMCS "had become primarily a debt collection agency for foreign creditors." Post-Taiping Rebellion structural fiscal fragmentation persisted, creating general disparities between provincial revenue collection and amounts reported to the central government by an estimated 100 to 200 percent.[48] In other words, enough revenue was being held back collectively at the local levels, despite IMCS rationalization efforts, to run an empire once or twice over.

The fruition of Republican opium autonomy

Given the combination of structural fiscal fragmentation and the localized opium revenue system, it is not surprising that there was gross under-reporting of opium revenues from the provinces during the legalization period. Under-reporting can be determined by, among other factors, discrepancies between provincial production figures and the corresponding tax revenue collected.

In 1895, for example, Sichuan, then the world's largest producer of opium, was reporting only about 43 percent of its actual revenues. Under-reporting was commonly recognized as a revenue protection strategy of local administrations even by foreign newspapers like *The New York Times* as well as the Qing central government. Contemporary, and not completely disinterested, Japanese observers went even further to conclude that

> China, so-called, is actually not a fully integrated empire. Its twenty-one provinces are seemingly divided into twenty-one states, each with its own semi-independence. Join them up again and this dispersed, undisciplined state is then formed. This view is confirmed by the evident realities of all kinds of administrative matters, most prominently those of fiscal administration.[49]

This long-standing deficiency in centralization was exacerbated by European imperialism. The post-Opium War central Qing state had comparatively less control over its own revenue, especially that increasingly substantial portion derived from foreign trade. It had, as previously noted, ceded considerable portions of its authority over its maritime ports and their tariffs to semi-colonial institutions like the IMCS. Maritime customs was one of the Qing state's three major sources of revenue along with the land tax and the salt tax, which was likewise encroached upon by 1913. Consequently, both Qing and early Republican revenue went to semi-colonial projects like debt servicing, particularly for indemnities incurred after China's defeat by Japan in 1894–95 and the failure of the Boxer Rebellion in 1900. Much was also spent on crippling military modernizations that were central to the Self-strengthening Movement in response to these and other defeats. By the end of the dynasty, debt servicing was accounting for about 20 percent of the Qing state's budget expenditures. Just after the dynasty's fall, debt servicing peaked at 46 percent in 1913, dropping off to around a still imposing 30 percent thereafter.[50] Revenue from opium legalization, another foreign import and therefore under the control of the IMCS, was no exception to any of these conditions; indeed, it was the single largest source of customs revenue.[51]

In sum, the Qing central state was not the sole, and not necessarily even the primary, beneficiary of drug legalization because of its deficiency in fiscal autonomy. The dynasty's inability to exert something approaching full control over its own revenues, which were, moreover, diverted to various foreign and domestic enterprises effectively designed to further dilute central authority, was exacerbated rather than alleviated by legalization.

A substantial portion of this diverted revenue undoubtedly went to foster the growing fiscal independence of provinces, many of which would form the nuclei of warlord governments from the 1910s onward. Given the fact that the Qing state derived an estimated 6 to 7 percent of its total revenues from opium between 1885 and 1905, a figure that jumped to 14 percent in 1906 when these various taxes were consolidated, it is easy to see how critical opium was to the state's fiscal well-being.[52] It is equally clear that such financial power could be used for state formation, albeit on a lesser scale, relying on a readymade system of regional revenue generation.

Drug revenue seems to have been the state-building strategy of a number of Indian Malwa opium states, especially Holkar and Sindia, in the early decades of the nineteenth century (and of Afghanistan today). It was, ironically, the attempt of such states to compete with Company Bengal opium for control of the China market that flooded the Qing empire with both products. This flood, in turn, provoked the absolute prohibition of the 1830s that led to the Opium War and, ultimately, the Qing's own state-preserving legalization strategy in the 1850s.[53] In some sense, the attempt of even Indian native states to assert their autonomy affected the sovereignty of the Qing state. There is no better testament to the intercontinental power of a modern drug trade and its relationship to both state-building and indirect rule.

It would be wrong to attribute the demise of the imperial system and the rise of warlordism solely to the political power derived from commodified, morphine-enhanced smokeable opium. It has recently been argued, for example, that the late Qing military modernization program, itself a product of imperialist pressure and instrumental in concentrating more power in military hands, occurred at a very inopportune time of fiscal crisis. Exacerbated by increased competition for revenue, both between the central government and provincial administrations, as well as within provinces themselves, the problem of military modernization ensured that "the traditional Chinese empire could not make itself into a modern nation-state."[54]

Nevertheless, some Qing officials considered opium uniquely responsible for the continuous crises that arose in the late Qing after 1839. One was Guo Songtao, who considered opium to be "the decisive factor for the stability or disruption of the state" from the 1830s on.[55] Symptoms of an addicted state and society initially appeared during the escalating prohibition campaign of that decade but persisted long after opium production, consumption and distribution had been legalized. It could be argued they persisted beyond the fall of the dynasty and characterized the warlord period.

Guo's statement may be just another example of the hyperbole so characteristic of elite discourse about opium, but drug revenues were genuinely critical for a number of regional polities that arose in the wake of the Qing Dynasty's fall. Seventy-two percent of Yunnan's provincial revenue came from opium before 1926, falling to a still significant average of around 40 percent in the early 1930s.[56] Guangdong's euphemistically-termed "opium suppression tax," a common contemporary method of obscuring opium revenue throughout China, accounted for 25 percent of all state revenues collected by the warlord Chen Jitang's regime from 1930–35.[57] Taxes on opium cultivation or transit amounted to 58 percent of Guizhou warlord Zhou Xichen's total revenue in 1928 alone. The regime of Liu Xiang, one of five warlords who divided up Sichuan between them during the late 1920s and early 1930s, officially declared an average of 23 percent of its total revenues came from opium from 1928–33, while scholarly estimates run as high as 46 percent for the year 1931 alone. The Guangxi regime, which did not even cultivate much poppy, nevertheless was deriving 51 percent of its total revenue from opium in the form of transit dues on the drug as it moved back and forth between areas of coastal consumption and interior production.[58] In addition, regimes in the provinces of Hubei, Fujian, Gansu and Shaanxi all derived at least 30 percent of their respective revenues from opium.[59]

It is clear from these statistics that provinces like Yunnan, Guizhou and Guangxi subsisted largely on opium, while others like Guangdong and Sichuan derived significant portions of their revenue from the drug, which was often their single largest income source. Opium had taken root in all these provinces during the Qing and some of them, particularly the southwestern provinces of Yunnan, Guizhou and Sichuan, had already become major poppy cultivation areas in the dynastic period. Other southeastern provinces like Guangdong and Fujian, had been the empire's major trafficking centers. At the time of the warlord period, these areas had been developing opium consumption, production and distribution for at least a generation and in some cases several generations.

Opium did not cause warlord regimes to spring up in China, but it did make them more economically viable than they otherwise would have been. Indeed, one authority argues that opium was a decisive factor in the continued existence of warlord regimes.[60] It is certainly indisputable that the drug traffic made a major contribution to sustaining many of these regimes throughout China. Moreover, examples of such regimes continue to interactively emerge beyond China, but not beyond the poppy zone, in ways that inhibit centralized state development. The Golden Triangle region, for example, split between Myanmar, Thailand and Laos, produced about 65 percent of the globe's illicit opium at a profit comparable to that of the international arms trade in 1999. Local cultivation was almost certainly stimulated by migrants from China's southwestern provinces, with production accelerated by separatist movements in the Shan States during the 1970s. In the 1990s, the region was far from the centers of state power, allowing "the drug lords of northeastern Burma ... to exercise almost absolute power over their narco fiefdoms."[61]

Afghanistan is another, more recent example that continues the pattern in Asian poppy zones. Integral to the increasing "strength of local power structures in southern Afghanistan has been the recent consolidation of the opiate economy, the evolution of which is a by-product of globalization."[62] As of 2007, Afghanistan was estimated to have produced 93 percent of the world's illicit supply of opium. Between the two of them, Burma and Afghanistan have been the source of about 90 percent of the world's illicit supply in recent decades.[63]

There are, nevertheless, significant variations in interactive emergence. The drug infrastructure in many Chinese provinces was not established by warlords, but by their Qing provincial predecessors in dynamic relations with the individual traffickers, cultivators and even consumers as participants in the interactive emergence of the Sino-British-Indian global drug traffic that was substantially legalized. This infrastructure was a Qing state legacy to warlord successors in China in much the same way as it was a Mughal state legacy to British successors in India. Modern Southeast and Central Asian opium networks have much less legitimized pedigrees within much more ramified structures. Prohibition, like consumption, is now consequently global.

Nevertheless, all such cultural legacies are rooted in human physiological susceptibility and a territory's ecological amenability to opium poppy. The resulting interactive emergences of the Sino-British global drug traffic, Qing (and British Indian) opium dependency, and Republican opium autonomy were all able to indifferently convert drug consumption into state power, if not state longevity. Human consumption of opium continues and poppies keep growing in places where all these states once ruled. In this respect, environmental relations have emerged to outlast political ones.

Notes

1 For the persistent nature of warlordism in the Republican period, see Alfred H. Y. Lin, "Building and Funding a Warlord Regime, the Experience of Chen Jitang in Guangdong, 1929–1936," *Modern China*, 28, no. 2 (April, 2002): 177–78. For warlord regimes and opium, see Zhou Yongming, "Anti-drug Crusades" in *Twentieth-century China: Nationalism, History, and State Building* (Lanham, MD, 1999), 39–92; Edward R. Slack, *Opium State and Society: China's Narco-economy and the Guomindang, 1924–1937* (Honolulu, 2001), chapter 4, "Nanjing's Response to Attacks on Opium Policy, 1924–1937," 86–114.

2 The outstanding exception to most of these limitations is the work of Qin Heping; Qin Heping, *Yunnan yapian wenti yu jinyan yundong* [Yunnan's opium problem and prohibition movement] (Chengdu, 1998) and *Sichuan Yapian Wenti yu jinyan yundong* [Sichuan's opium problem and prohibition movement] (Chengdu, 2001).

3 John E. Wills, Jr., "Maritime Asia, 1500–1800: The Interactive Emergence of European Domination," *The American Historical Review*, 98, no. 1 (February, 1993): 84–85; John E. Wills, Jr., "Relations with Maritime Europeans, 1514–1662," in Denis C. Twitchett and Frederick W. Mote eds., *The Cambridge History of China. Vol. 8, The Ming Dynasty, 1368–1644*, Part 2 (Cambridge, 1998), 333, 373–74.

4 Wills, "Maritime Asia," 336, 340, 341, 344–45, 348, 353–55, 360–61, 366–67, 369, 371, 373.

5 John E. Wills, Jr., "A Very Long Early Modern? Asia and Its Oceans, 1000–1850," *Pacific Historical Review*, 83, no. 2 (May, 2014): 196.

6 John F. Richards, "The Opium Industry in British India," *Indian Economic and Social History Review*, 39, nos. 2–3 (April–September, 2002): 155.

7 *Da Qing lü li tongkao jiaozhu* [Annotated edition of the comprehensive analysis of the great Qing code with substitutes] (Beijing, 1992), 621, 623. An imperial vermilion rescript suggests that the actual year of the promulgation of the prohibition was 1728; *Yongzheng chao hanwen zhupi zouzhe* [The collected Chinese-language palace memorials of the Yongzheng reign] (Nanjing, 1989–91), December 6, 1728 (Yongzheng 6/11/6), 13: 848b–53b. If so, 1729 probably marks the date of the

first case handled under this new prohibition. There were no further unambiguous prosecutions until 1806, although the East India Company did express caution regarding Chinese prohibition regulations between 1750 and 1782; Hosea Ballou Morse, *The Chronicles of the East India Company Trading to China 1635–1834* (Oxford, 1926–29), 1: 215, 288–89, 301, and 2: 20, 77–78.

8 David A. Bello, *Opium and the Limits of Empire, Drug Prohibition in the Chinese Interior: 1729–1850* (Cambridge, MA, 2005), 152–53, 294–96.

9 Dennis O. Flynn and Arturo Giráldez, "Cycles of Silver: Global Economic Unity through the Mid-Eighteenth Century," *Journal of World History*, 13, no. 2 (Fall, 2002): 415–16.

10 For an extended analytical example of econo-ecolo synergy, see Dennis O. Flynn and Arturo Giráldez, "Path Dependence, Time Lags and the Birth of Globalisation: A Critique of O'Rourke and Williamson," *European Review of Economic History*, 8, no. 1 (April, 2004): 95–98.

11 Flynn and Giráldez, "Born Again: Globalization's Sixteenth Century Origins (Asian/Global Versus European Dynamics)," *Pacific Economic Review*, 13, no. 3 (August, 2008): 361, 365.

12 Flynn and Giráldez, "Cycles of Silver," 411. The role of silver, in addition to bronze ("copper"), in the Chinese bimetallic economy was certainly important, but should be qualified, especially from a global comparative perspective. Qing economic problems, especially in the nineteenth century, were not absolutely determined by fluctuations in Latin American supplies of silver, as Lin Man-houng has boldly argued; Lin Man-houng, "Introduction," *China Upside Down: Currency, Society and Ideologies, 1808–1856* (Cambridge, MA, 2006). An excessive emphasis on silver supply ignores complexities of silver demand, critical distinctions between different types of silver (e.g. sycee vs. dollars) and persistent deflation in China even when silver stocks were high, etc; Dennis O. Flynn, "Review: Man-houng Lin, China Upside Down: Currency, Society and Ideologies, 1808–1856," *China Review International*, 14, no. 2 (Fall, 2007): 505–09; Richard von Glahn, "Review: Man-houng Lin, China Upside Down: Currency, Society, and Ideologies, 1808–1856," *Social History*, 33, no. 3 (August, 2008): 375–76. Moreover, Lin's unqualified embrace of silver-based economic factors as the sole explanation for the failiure of Qing opium control, to the exclusion of critical elements like territorial and population expansion, well beyond existing dynastic administrative capacities, is also untenable; Lin, *China Upside Down*, 24. One recent work has concluded that Qing China "simply lacked the means to implement sophisticated fine-tuned policies," an inability rooted in "the [fiscal] incapability of government to tap the country's existing resources." This serious administrative limitation, moreover, was not exclusively determined by narrow economic bounds, but also constrained by spatial and population factors:

> in contrast to what happened in the West, the infrastructural power of China's state, which was weak to begin with, decreased even further during the last third of the very long eighteenth century. Considering the amazingly small number of officials that worked for the central government, the immense empire can never have been ruled from Peking in an effective way. ... The Qing Empire had been an extremely successful ideological and moral construct, but began to lose its effectiveness from the end of the eighteenth century onwards ... The fact that it had expanded its realm

over regions with ethnically differing populations only added to its problems from the late eighteenth century onward.

Peer Vries, *State, Economy and the Great Divergence: Great Britain and China, 1680s – 1850s* (London, 2015), 235, 265, 430. While these assertions might require more qualification, it is clear that the fiscal and monetary weaknesses exposed by the silver drain were, in many respects, not unique to a nineteenth-century dynastic decline. The Qing state was chronically under-supplied with its main monetary metals, silver and bronze, yet left the coinage of silver and the printing of paper in private, and sometimes even foreign, hands while authorizing no uniform circulation of bronze. As territory and people diversified, so did monetary supplies, adding Xinjiang's locally minted and circulating pul, for example, to the Qing monetary mix. In contrast, one nineteenth-century monetary resource that was comparatively uniform, although far from fully standardized was opium, which outlasted the circulation of both dynastic silver and bronze.

13 For an extended refutation of a purely economic analysis, based on commodity price convergence, to historicize globalization, see Flynn and Giráldez, "Born Again."

14 Jonathan Spence, "Opium Smoking in Ch'ing China," in Frederic Wakeman, Jr., and Carolyn Grant (eds.), *Conflict and Control in Late Imperial China* (Berkeley, 1975), 147; Lars P. Laamann, "Pain and Pleasure: Opium as Medicine in Late Imperial China," *Twentieth-Century China*, 28, no. 1 (November, 2002): 4, 7.

15 Sidney W. Mintz, *Sweetness and Power: The Place of Sugar in Modern History* (New York, 1985), 108–17. Bello, *Opium and the Limits of Empire*, 16–21.

16 Jamshid Ahmadi, Mohammadali Babaee-Beigi, Mohammadjavad Alishahi, Iraj Maany, Taghi Hidari, "Twelve-month Maintenance Treatment of Opium-dependent Patients," *Journal of Substance Abuse Treatment*, 26 (2004): 363.

17 Roy A. Wise and George F. Koob, "The Development and Maintenance of Drug Addiction," *Neuropsychopharmacology*, 39, no. 2 (January, 2014): 254–62; Charles P. O'Brien, "Evidence-Based Treatments of Addiction," *Philosophical Transactions: Biological Sciences* 363, no. 1507 (October 12, 2008): 3277–78; Nora D. Volkow and Ting-Kai Li, "Drug Addiction: The Neurobiology of Behaviour Gone Awry," *Nature Reviews Neuroscience*, 5, (December, 2004): 963–65.

18 Spence, "Opium Smoking," 148.

19 Paul C. Winther, *Anglo-European Science and the Rhetoric of Empire: Malaria, Opium and British Rule in India, 1756–1895* (Lanham, 2003), 23–24.

20 Jules Janick and Péter Tétényi, "Opium Poppy (Papaver somniferum): Botany and Horticulture," *Horticultural Reviews*, 19 (July, 2010): 387, 389, 396; Satoshi Morimoto et al., "Morphine Metabolism in the Opium Poppy and Its Possible Physiological Function," *The Journal of Biological Chemistry*, 276, no. 41 (October, 2001): 381–84.

21 V. S. Ramanathan, Kesav Prasad and R. M Gupta, "Absorption of Morphine from Opium by Porous Earthen Pots," *United Nations Bulletin on Narcotics*, 4 (1965): 21–25; A. D. Krikorian and Myron C. Ledbetter, "Some Observations on the Cultivation of Opium Poppy (Papaver somniferum L.) for Its Latex," *Botanical Review*, 41, no. 1 (January–March, 1975): 66–67; Paul Winther, personal communication, April 16, 2004.

22   China's First Historical Archives, Beijing, *Junji jinyan Junji chu, lufu dang, falü dalei, jinyan*, [Grand Council copy archive, legal category, opium prohibition; hereafter, *Junji jinyan*], DG 10.6.24, #1545–46.

23   Winther, *Anglo-European Science*, 22.

24   Quoted in Wang Hongbin, *Jindu shijian* [A history of drug prohibition] (Beijing, 1997), 25–26.

25   David A. Bello, "Opium as a Historical Commodity," *Global Commodities: Trade, Exploration and Cultural Exchange*. (www.globalcommodities.amdigital.co.uk/ FurtherResources/Essays/Opium), Adam Matthew Digital, 2012.

26   Lin, *China Upside Down*, 89 (table 2.7); Frederick Wakeman Jr., "The Canton Trade and the Opium War," in John K. Fairbank (ed.), *The Cambridge History of China*, vol. 10, *Late Ch'ing, 1800–1911*, Part 1 (Cambridge, 1978), 172.

27   For the relationship between the apparent outflow of silver and the intensification of opium prohibition under the Daoguang emperor, see, Li Yongqing, "Youguan jinyan yundong de jidian xin renshi" [A few points of new understanding concerning the opium prohibition movement], *Lishi dang'an*, 3 (1986): 79–80; Ma Weiping, "Qing Daoguang 1838 nian jinyan yuanyin bianxi" [Critical analysis of the reasons for the Daoguang emperor's 1838 opium prohibition], *Zhongshan daxue yan-jiusheng xuekan*, 1 (1990): 75–80; Wu Yixiong, "Guanyu 1838 nian jinyan zhenglun de zai tantao" [A re-examination of the prohibition debate of 1838] *Fujian luntai*, 6 (1985): 59–60; Zhu Jinfu, "Yapian zhanzheng qian Daoguang chao yanguan de jinyan lun" [The pre–Opium War debate on prohibition among the censors at the Daoguang court], *Jindaishi yanjiu*, 2 (1991): 57–66; Inoue Hiromasa, "Shindai Kakei Dōkōki no ahen mondai ni tsuite" [The opium problem during the Jiaqing and Daoguang periods], *Tōyōshi kenkyū*, 41, no. 1 (June, 1982): 72–79.

28   George Watt, *A Dictionary of the Economic Products of India* (Calcutta, 1892), 6: 41.

29   Watt, *Economic Products of India*, 6: 41; Barry Milligan, *Pleasures and Pains, Opium and the Orient in 19th-Century British Culture* (Charlottesville, 1995).

30   W. S. K. Waung, "Introduction of Opium Cultivation to China," *Xianggang zhongwen daxue xuebao*, 5, no. 1 (1979): 211, 217; Lin Man-houng, "Qingmo shehui liuxing xishi yapian yanjiu: gongjimian zhi fenxi, 1773–1906" [A study of the spread of opium smoking in late Qing society: A supply-side analysis, 1773–1906] (Ph.D. diss., Taiwan Normal University, 1985), 189, 192–93, 453.

31   *Yapian zhanzheng dang'an shiliao* [Historical materials from the Opium War archives], Zhongguo diyi lishi dang'anguan (ed.) (Tianjin, 1992), JQ 18.7.10, 1:6; Bello, *Opium & the Limits of Empire*, 181–83, 198.

32   Bello, *Opium & the Limits of Empire*, 249, 300n.

33   *Junji jinyan*, DG 18.12.18, #2321–26 (Guizhou); China's First Historical Archives, Beijing, Neige, xingke tiben, weijin lei [Grand Secretariat archive, routine memorials for the Office of Scrutiny of the Board of Punishments, prohibitions violations category], DG 8.5.22, #10092 (tongben [provincial memorial]) (Yunnan); *Yapian zhanzheng dang'an shiliao*, DG 19.7.27, 1: 678 (Xinjiang); Bello, *Opium & the Limits of Empire*, p. 84.

34   Bello, *Opium & the Limits of Empire*, 137.

35   *Junji jinyan*, DG 12.2.9, #1746–49.

36   China's First Historical Archives, Beijing, Junji diqin Junji chu, lufu dang, diguozhuyi qinlue dalei, diyi yapien zhanzheng [Grand Council copy archive, imperialist aggression category, First Opium War], DG 19.12.17, 267: 11.

37 Zhang Pengyuan, "Luohou diqu de ziben xingcheng: – Yun Gui de xiexiang yu yapian" [Capital formation in an underdeveloped region: Assistance loans and opium in Yunnan and Guizhou], *Guizhou wenshi congkan*, 1 (1990): 55–60; Junji jinyan, DG 18.12.9, #2275.
38 *Guangxu chao Donghua xu lu* [The Donghua records of the Guangxu reign], Zhu Shoupeng (ed.) (1909, reprinted – Beijing, 1958), GX 3.4, 1: 394.
39 Man-houng Lin, "Late Qing Perceptions of Native Opium," *Harvard Journal of Asiatic Studies*, 64, no. 1 (June, 2004): 125–26.
40 Quoted in S. A. M. Adshead, "The Opium Trade in Szechwan, 1881–1911," *Journal of Southeast Asian History*, 7, no. 2 (September, 1966), 96.
41 *Yapian zhanzheng dang'an shiliao*, DG 2.2.12, 1: 37–38, DG 2.2.15, 1: 38–39, DG 2.5.25, 1: 44–45, DG 2.11.23, 1: 46–47; Morse, *The Chronicles of the East India Company*, 3: 323; John K. Fairbank, "Legalization of the Opium Trade Before the Treaties of 1858," *Chinese Economic and Political Science Review*, 17, no. 2 (July, 1933): 232, 258–63.
42 Quoted in Kathleen L. Lodwick, *Crusaders against Opium: Protestant Missionaries in China, 1874–1917* (Lexington, KY, 1993), 28.
43 The efficiency of the British monopoly can be exaggerated. For qualifying statements about its continued vulnerability to smuggling in the late nineteenth century, see Elijah Impey, *A Report on the Cultivation, Preparation and Adulteration of Malwa Opium and Appendix* (Bombay, 1848), 19–21; Watt, *Economic Products of India*; 6: 102–3.
44 Thomas L. Kennedy, "Mausers and the Opium Trade: The Hupeh Arsenal, 1895–1911," in Joshua A. Fogel and William T. Rowes (eds.), *Perspectives on a Changing China: Essays in Honor of Professor C. Martin Wilbur on the Occasion of His Retirement* (Boulder, CO, 1979), 120, 132; Thomas D. Reins, "Reform, Nationalism and Internationalism: The Opium Suppression Movement in China and the Anglo-American Influence, 1900–1908," *Modern Asian Studies*, 25, no. 1 (February, 1991), 122, 132–33.
45 Wang Yeh-chien, *Land Taxation in Imperial China* (Cambridge, MA, 1973), 14–17; Zhou, *Anti-Drug Crusades*, 25–37. Chang Te-Ch`ang, "The Economic Role of the Imperial Household in the Ch`ing Dynasty," *Journal of Asian Studies*, 31, no. 2 (February, 1972): 251, 256–59, 268–71. Contrary to a recent assertion, the Qing state appreciated the substantial sums derived from maritime customs; Richard S. Horowitz, "Politics, Power and the Chinese Maritime Customs: The Qing Restoration and the Ascent of Robert Hart," *Modern Asian Studies*, 40, no. 3 (July, 2006): 558. For evidence, see Preston M. Torbert, *The Ch'ing Imperial Household Department: A Study of its Organization and Principal Functions, 1662–1796* (Cambridge, MA, 1977), 97–103; Bao Shichen, *Baoshi Chen quanji* (Bao Shichen's complete works). Hefei: Huangshan shushe, 1997, 213; Qi Meiqin, *Qingdai Neiwufu* (The Qing imperial household department), (Beijing, 1998), 148. In 1820, Bao estimated revenue from all ports amounted to over two million silver taels annually. Qi cites documentation from the Daoguang reign (1821–50) that the port of Guangzhou alone contributed 300,000 taels to the privy purse annually.
46 Man-houng Lin, "Late Qing Perceptions of Native Opium," *Harvard Journal of Asiatic Studies*, 64, no. 1 (June, 2004): 125–26.
47 Richard S. Horowitz, "International Law and State Transformation in China, Siam and the Ottoman Empire During the Nineteenth Century," *Journal of World*

History, 15, no. 4, (December, 2004): 475; Horowitz, "Politics, Power and the Chinese Maritime Customs, 551, 575.

48 Frank H. H. King, "The Boxer Indemnity: 'Nothing but Bad,'" *Modern Asian Studies*, 40, no. 3 (July, 2006): 665; Hans J. van de Ven, "Public Finance and the Rise of Warlordism," *Modern Asian Studies*, 30, no. 4 (October, 1996): 836.

49 Liu Zenghe, *Yapian shuishou yu Qingmou xinzheng* [Opium revenue and the late Qing New Policy reforms] (Beijing, 2005), 33–34. Note here the emphasis on the significance of fundamental fiscal weakness that forms the core of Vries' revisionist analysis; Vries, *State, Economy and the Great Divergence*, 233–40.

50 Horowitz, "State transformation," 469–70, 473; van de Ven, "Rise of Warlordism," 829–30, 832. For a very crude comparison, US interest payments on its national debt were about 6 percent of the 2013 federal budget (they were over 15 percent in the 1990s). It is instructive for the discussion here to note, however, that over 28 percent of this US debt was actually owed to other US federal agencies (about two-thirds of the US debt is held domestically), Social Security chief among them. China, as the largest US foreign creditor held 7 percent of the debt; Drew Desilver "5 Facts About the National Debt: What You Should Know," (www. pewresearch.org/fact-tank/2013/10/09/5-facts-about-the-national-debt-what-you-should-know/).

51 R. K. Newman, "India and the Anglo-Chinese Opium Agreements, 1907–1914," *Modern Asian Studies*, 23, no. 3 (1989): 525. It is misleading to consider opium as an exclusively foreign import, especially after its legalization. The IMCS report on opium in 1881, for example, estimated that domestic production was roughly equal to foreign imports at that time, and domestic opium was used to adulterate the more expensive foreign product; Bello, "Opium as a Historical Commodity," 17–19.

52 Zhou, *Anti-Drug Crusades*, 30.

53 David Edward Owen, *British Opium Policy in China and India* (Hamden, CT, 1968), 105–6, 110; Amar Farooqui, *Smuggling as Subversion, Colonialism, Indian Merchants and the Politics of Opium* (New Delhi, 1998), 38, 42.

54 Van de Ven, "Rise of Warlordism," 829–68.

55 *Guangxu chao Donghua xu lu*, GX 3: 49, 1: 397.

56 Qin Heping, *Yunnan yapian wenti yu jinyan yundong* [Yunnan's opium problem and prohibition movement] (Chengdu, 1998), 142–43.

57 Lin, "Funding a Warlord Regime," 192

58 Zhou, *Anti-Drug Crusades*, 88–89; Gao Yanhong, "Xi'nan junfa yu yapien maoyi" [Southwestern warlords and the opium trade], *Xueshu luntan*, 2 (1982): 74–76; Li Longchang, "Luetan Guizhou de yanhuo" [A brief discussion of Guizhou's drug disaster], *Guizhou wenshi congkan*, 2 (1983): 21–26; Yang Kaiyu, "Jindai Guizhou de yapien liudu" [The venomous course of opium in Guizhou during the Republican period], *Guiyang shiyuan xuebao, sheke ban*, 1 (1984): 34–40; Lin Shourong and Long Dai, "Sichuan junfa yu yapianyan" [Sichuan warlords and opium], *Sichuan daxue xue-bao*, 3 (1984): 101–06; Wu Xiaogao, "Zhengshou yapien teshui de neimu" [The real story behind the special opium tax levy], *Guizhou wenshi ziliao xuanji*, 15 (1984): 169–75.

59 Jiang Qiuming, *Zhongguo Jindu Licheng* [The historical stages of China's drug prohibition] (Tianjin, 1996), 240.

60 Qin Heping, *Sichuan Yapian Wenti yu jinyan yundong* [Sichuan's opium problem and prohibition movement] (Chengdu, 2001), 208.

61 Alan Dupont, "Transnational Crime, Drugs, and Security in East Asia," *Asian Survey*, 39.3 (May–June, 1999), pp. 439–40.
62 Justin Mankin, "Gaming the System: How Afghan Opium Underpins Local Power," *Journal of International Affairs*, 63, no. 1 (Fall/Winter, 2009): 199.
63 Pierre-Arnaud Chouvy, *Opium: Uncovering the Politics of the Poppy* (Cambridge, MA, 2010), 13.

2 Rivers of blood & roads of bones

Sichuan in the Ming-Qing Transition

Kenneth M. Swope

It has been more than thirty-five years since Jack Wills and Jonathan Spence published their classic edited volume *From Ming to Ch'ing: Conquest, Region, and Continuity in Seventeenth-Century China.*[1] That volume grew out of a conference held five years before that brought together a variety of scholars at all levels of their careers, all of whom turned out to be leading lights in the field of what has subsequently morphed into late imperial Chinese history. In addition to the quality of the essays and breadth of knowledge displayed therein, it was typical of Jack's enthusiastic and unselfish support of younger scholars in the field, a support that continued throughout his distinguished career and is reflected in the contributions in the present volume. In the preface to that volume the editors noted how the state of knowledge about this critical period in Chinese history was still in its relative infancy in the West and how scholars were just starting to understand its broader ramifications for the study of world history.[2] They were, of course correct and much has changed since the publication of that book in terms of our knowledge about the Ming-Qing transition and its broader historical significance. Part of that is due to the fact that most Western scholars now have ready access to resources and archives in the People's Republic of China in addition to the huge volume of Ming and Qing primary sources that have been collected and reprinted in the ensuing decades. That has facilitated the publication of a great number of important scholarly monographs, many written by the same young scholars included in the aforementioned volume. But it must also be said that the work of Jack Wills set the standard and blazed a trail for the next generation in terms of creative approaches to the study of China's past and in integrating the history of China within the broader processes of world history and vice versa. The present essay is merely one way in which my own work has been informed and inspired by Professor Wills' example.

Significantly, our story begins with a simple episode whereby China's past intersected with its breakneck rush toward the future, a path some believe was derailed in part by the Qing defeat of the Ming in the seventeenth century.[3] In 2002, workers were undertaking excavations as part of the municipal government's renovation of the south gate in the Sichuanese city of Chengdu, when they discovered masses of very old scattered bones. The local news was abuzz with accounts of the "10,000 person grave." It was eventually determined that the bones dated from the Ming-Qing transition and were from one of Zhang Xianzhong's (1606–47) great massacres while he ruled the city as King of the West.[4] Zhang had occupied Chengdu in the eighth month of 1644, some three months after the fall of Beijing to the Qing, and declared it his Western Capital (*Xi Jing*). Over the next three years, Zhang's atrocities would allegedly multiply as his enemies closed in and his paranoia increased. According to surviving accounts, he would massacre hundreds of thousands – hundreds of millions according to the most lurid versions of the story.[5] In some cases, even dogs and chickens were not spared. His generals were rewarded and promoted, based upon the number of severed hands, feet and heads they turned in. It was said that severed hands, arms, and heads "piled up outside Zhang's palace like Mount Fenghuang."[6] Zhang's paranoia grew to such a state that he eventually resolved to kill all the people of Sichuan, thereby "cleansing" them from the earth in accordance with directives he received from Heaven. By the time he was killed by Qing forces in 1647, the population of the entire province of Sichuan was allegedly less than the population of Chengdu alone prior to his arrival.

Furthermore, in the wake of these systematic programs of terror, some accounts maintain that people reverted to a feral state, growing coats of hair and waylaying travelers to consume their flesh.[7] As one contemporary account of Sichuan in the time after Zhang's death relates, "Villages were empty and for hundreds of *li* there were no people. Subjects fled deep into the mountains. Those who could not eat [to survive] piled up in ravines. Some ate grass and leaves and those still alive became wild people, living in forests and growing coats of white fur. If they happened to meet someone along the road they would kill them and drink their blood."[8] It was said that only tigers, wolves, and leopards flourished due to the widespread availability of decaying human flesh. This essay will examine not only accounts of Zhang's bloody reign of terror, but also consider the actions of other groups and analyze the social and environmental implications of the Ming-Qing transition in Sichuan. But we begin with the man blamed, perhaps somewhat unfairly, for the devastation wreaked upon the hapless residents of the province.

The name Zhang Xianzhong, aka the Yellow Tiger, the Butcher of Sichuan, and the Eighth Great King, has become synonymous with butchery and chaos. Though often considered alongside his contemporary Li Zicheng (1605–46), aka the Dashing Prince, as a champion of the "people's movements" (*minbian*) or "righteous peasant uprisings" (*nongmin qiyi*) of the late Ming, Zhang's historical reputation has been, on the whole, much less positive than Li's.[9] For example, in a 1950 *Time* magazine article on the Korean War, Zhang was the murderous yardstick by which Mao Zedong was judged with respect to the devastating human wave attacks and mass butchery perpetrated by America's "Godless" communist foes. As the article claimed, "No warlord has left a more gory trail of death than Mao, not since the mad General Zhang Xianzhong, who slaughtered 30 million in Sichuan during the Ming

Dynasty."[10] A recently published compilation of source materials from the Ming and Qing, pertaining to Zhang's tenure in Sichuan, portrays the rivers of Sichuan running red with blood on its front cover and on the back boldly proclaims "The Eighth Great King massacred Ba" and "the thirteen houses drenched all of Shu in blood."[11] Zhang's official biography in the *Ming shi* notes, "He was of a fierce disposition and he liked killing people. If a day went by and he had not killed someone, then he became really, really unhappy."[12] Following this lead, many modern scholars continue to blame Zhang for everything from depopulation to destroying the formerly vibrant literary culture of Sichuan, leading to the collapse of learning in the province, among other things.[13]

Nonetheless, like other great villains in history, Zhang continues to fascinate. While most scholars do not go quite so far as Hu Zhaoxi, who has been dubbed "an enthusiastic apologist for Zhang" by Yu Li, reappraisals of Zhang's tenure in Sichuan and of his actions in general are starting to appear.[14] Wang Xingye's *Jiaoxiaode Zhang Xianzhong* (The Crafty Zhang Xianzhong) emphasizes Zhang's bitter youth as helping to form his worldview and credits Zhang for his bravery and intelligence, even as it chronicles his savagery and many personal excesses.[15] Wang concludes that in fact Zhang Xianzhong was not inferior to Li Zicheng on the whole and that in certain areas, such as battlefield command, Zhang was probably superior to his more famous rival.[16] Zheng Guanglu's meticulously documented *Zhang Xianzhong jiao Sichuan zhenxiang* (A True Look into Zhang Xianzhong's Massacres in Sichuan) offers a balanced account that seeks to put Zhang's actions into their full context by examining the full array of primary and secondary source materials, including accounts left by Jesuits who served at Zhang's court.[17] Yingcong Dai also questions the veracity of contemporary and especially, Qing accounts of Zhang's massacres, noting that, "While all these records exaggerated Zhang's killings, they neglected the important fact that there was a hiatus of more than a dozen years between Zhang's death in 1647 and the complete Qing conquest in the early 1660s. The delay of the Qing conquest gave rise to an optimum environment for the outgrowth of bandits and warlords who would render further, more serious devastation in Sichuan."[18] Earlier, the Chinese scholar Sun Cizhou also questioned the veracity of early Qing accounts that blamed Zhang and the peasant rebels for widespread slaughter and rape, suggesting that most civilian deaths were caused by rapacious and incompetent Ming and Qing officials, though the political climate in which Sun wrote his piece (in the mid-1950s) might lead one to question his attacks on the gentry class.[19] Robert Entenmann, countering Qing assertions to the contrary, suggests that population levels in Sichuan were restored to Ming levels "within a few decades" of the conquest, though he also puts much of the blame for the depopulation on Zhang.[20]

As fascinating as these historical debates are, in and of themselves, they also have the potential to shed new light on the course of the Ming-Qing transition in general and on the complex, multifaceted relationship between war and society in seventeenth-century China. For as eminent historian Lynn Struve has observed, the Ming-Qing transition "involved just about every-thing that took place in China during the seventeenth century" and "sig-nificantly affected subsequent Chinese views of their culture, society, and polity."[21] Moreover, perhaps no region of China was as continuously and pro-foundly affected as the southwest in general and Sichuan in particular. If one were simply to date the times of strife from the first entry of the wandering bandits (*liukou*) into Sichuan in 1633, the province endured nearly five dec-ades of constant warfare until the suppression of the Three Feudatories revolt in 1681. But some contemporary sources date the troubles from earlier, going back to the massive "Miao" uprisings of Yang Yinglong (1587–1600) and She Chongming and An Bangyan (1622–29), which disrupted large swathes of the province and undermined administrative effectiveness prior to the rise of peasant rebels in the region.[22] Viewed in this light, the problems experienced by the hapless residents of Sichuan lasted nigh on a century.

Thus, as Li Furong noted,

Nowhere was the poison of the bandits more severe than in Sichuan. And, in the wake of the bandits came tigers and wolves, famine spread everywhere and as a result, epidemics broke out. Thus, bones piled up like mountains and blood flowed like rivers. Although it is said that there are heavenly spirits, who can say where they go in the face of such calamity and chaos?[23]

Peng Zunsi agreed, stating,

In the late Ming the wandering bandits arose in the four directions and their poison spread across all within the seas; of all the places where their calamities spread, it was most dire in Sichuan. The land was red [with blood] for more than a thousand *li*.[24]

Likewise, Ouyang Zhi observed,

The people of the former generation said when disorder had not yet erupted [elsewhere] in the empire, Sichuan was already in chaos. When [the rest of] the empire had already been brought to order, Sichuan was then brought to order.[25]

Indeed, given the vast scale and duration of the catastrophes in question, it's a wonder that anyone survived to tell their tale.

As unfortunate as these events were for those who experienced them, how-ever, luckily enough for later historians, a few at least apparently not only survived, but managed to preserve their own personal accounts or those of relatives or friends. Taken together, these works offer a fascinating window into how war, trauma, and social dislocation affected the lives of Chinese at all levels of society in this turbulent era. This, in turn, can help us better understand not only the processes and ramifications of the Qing consolidation of power, but also the ways in which war impacted society in the long seventeenth century of crisis on a global scale, for virtually no contemporary society is as rich in surviving source materials as China. Thus we are offered glimpses of the mentalities of the conquerors and the conquered, the survivors and the slain. In reading these accounts we can therefore get a better sense of what their authors valued and held dear and how they remembered these traumatic events. While many of the details are culturally specific, such as the plethora of stories about Confucian-style loyalist martyrdom by both men and women, others, like the graphic descriptions of starvation and desperate cannibalism, have more universal resonance.

Before providing a few representative examples from the sources themselves, a few general comments about the types of sources examined is in order. As noted above, we are fortunate in that a great number of primary and secondary sources (from the early Qing) have survived. Furthermore, the diversity in scope and coverage is also impressive and allows the researcher to read between the lines for biases and discrepancies based upon the perspective of the author in question. The most immediate accounts are the diaries and personal chronicles of those who either witnessed the events themselves or heard about them from family or friends. These sources are useful in that they often provide visceral emotions and immediate reactions to events and policies, though one might question certain details in the case of sources compiled years or decades later from memory. They also sometimes suffer from the limitations of local perspective, though some authors made significant efforts to consult with each other and with more official sources to contextualize their personal accounts. In some cases, however, perspective can shift with dizzying frequency as the author in question is buffeted by the winds of fortune. To use the most extreme example, Ouyang Zhi, author of the *Shujing lu*, served successively under Zhang Xianzhong, the Ming loyalist generals Zeng Ying and Yang Zhan, the Qing Supreme Commander Li Guoying, Zhang Xianzhong's former lieutenant, Liu Wenxiu, Liu's adoptive brother and rival Li Dingguo, and the last Southern Ming Emperor Yongli (r. 1647–62)! Such mobility is a testament to both Ouyang's survival skills (or political opportunism) and to the cache that literacy and bureaucratic experience represented for these contending regimes.

The next category of sources encompasses the official and semi-official accounts of the conquest produced by the Qing and Southern Ming regimes. The former tend to be straightforward accounts of campaigns, battles, requests for supplies, and discussions of strategy and policy. These provide a good official version of events and give a sense of the bigger picture. They also alert researchers to the kinds of challenges faced by the Qing, particularly in the realms of logistics and military exchanges. The Southern Ming sources, by contrast, are much more clouded with extended discussions of factionalism that reveal the underlying weaknesses of the regime. Even when the tide was turning in favor of the Ming loyalist movements, it was obvious that their many petty personal rivalries and disagreements were likely to undermine cooperation. Indeed, in the face of such problems, it is somewhat surprising that the Ming loyalists survived as long as they did. One might also add local gazetteers to this category, as they often provide a sanctioned local perspective that gets incorporated into regional lore. Though quite useful for the bigger picture, I am not relying on these sources much for this chapter.

The next category of sources consists of the general accounts of the late Ming peasant rebellions and their leaders, the so-called "wandering bandits." These are useful in that they put bandit actions, behaviors, and strategies into a broader perspective. One can often find antecedents for particular policies and actions such as Zhang Xianzhong's massacres of scholars in Chongqing and Chengdu. They also serve to illuminate the wider social effects, interpersonal relationships between rebel leaders, and general reactions to the wandering bandits. Particularly interesting in this respect is the transition from being rebels who helped overthrow the Ming to loyalists, who battled the Qing to the bitter end on behalf of the Southern Ming court. Some sources suggest that Zhang Xianzhong told his lieutenants before his death that he wished to revert to Ming allegiance rather than submit to barbarian rule, but this seems unlikely. It does seem evident, however, that Li Dingguo, at least, was sincerely devoted to the Ming cause from the early 1650s until his death in 1662.[26]

Finally, we have a few Jesuit records and other sources by outside observers. Of the former the most valuable are the accounts of a pair of priests who served at Zhang's court, Gabriel de Magalhaes, and Louis Buglio.[27] While noting Zhang's many excesses and eccentricities, they also point out that he was in fact quite intelligent, and particularly interested in astronomy and Jesuit science.[28] While they claim he had some interest in their religion, that seems highly unlikely, given his persecution of several religious groups, though it is possible he equated their stories of the Christian God with the Lord of Heaven who bestowed visions upon him in the kind of syncretism that many Chinese of the era practiced. They also suggest that Zhang, at least initially, took measures to govern wisely and keep order among the people in his kingdom, though the Chinese sources overwhelmingly dispute this. Nonetheless they also provide verification of many of Zhang's excesses, including his purges of the literati.

Overall, in terms of assessing the sources, one can discern pro-Qing or pro-Ming biases in most of them, depending upon the position and perspective of the author. Some clearly seek to support the Qing project of a reconstructed order. Others are much more in the Ming loyalist vein. But few of the contemporary sources can be described as pro-Zhang, though Li Dingguo usually comes off quite well. What is perhaps most fascinating, however, are the extremely graphic accounts of starvation, cannibalism, and the reversion to various states of savagery by the residents of the region. These certainly speak to broader cultural fears about the loss of civilization and advent of barbarism. But though the details are often culturally specific, the general idea that prolonged time in the wilderness could lead to a descent into a more animalistic state is not uniquely Chinese of course.[29]

Likewise, the widespread fears and often lurid accounts of humans being eaten by tigers are not specific to China, though scholars have found that in fact, in marked contrast to most other regions of the globe, man-eating tigers had long been a problem in South China, suggesting that the particular sub-species native to southwest China, the South China tiger (*Panthera tigris amoyensis*) was unusually predisposed toward attacking humans either due to biology or proximity of habitat.[30] But even in places as far away as Victorian England, perhaps because of their knowledge of tigers in India, tigers had an unsavory reputation due to their reputed fondness for human flesh.[31] But the sheer number of accounts pertaining to tigers and other animals attacking and eating humans remains nonetheless striking. Yet given the frequent popular usages in the Chinese language wherein times of strife and difficulty are referred to as "being in the tiger's jaws," or "riding the tiger," perhaps we should not be surprised to find so many accounts of ferocious man-eating tigers in the primary sources. Interestingly enough, some authors even question the veracity of some claims, suggesting that stories were being spread for effect and perhaps to push underlying agendas.[32]

In any case, this is still remembered as one of the most harrowing and destructive eras in all of Chinese history and certainly adding wild animals to the mix serves to highlight the savagery and offer a stark contrast with the normal order. As Charles Hammond notes,

> in traditional China the tiger was the most savage beast one could expect to meet. Its terrifying aspect led people to interpret its appearance often as an evil omen, or as a signal of bad government. Some would interpret a tiger's behavior towards humans as heaven's just punishment, making the animal itself a symbol of justice or righteousness.[33]

Turning back to Zhang Xianzhong himself, it is worth noting that when he finally decided to make Sichuan his base of operations and the center of his kingdom, it was not the first time he had ventured into the province. Over the previous decade he had alternately raided and sought refuge from his enemies in Sichuan and had therefore come to appreciate what the province had to offer in terms of a strategic base area.[34] But Sichuan was not the first locale where Zhang had ensconced himself and tried to build an administration. In 1643, reacting in part to Li Zicheng's success, Zhang established successive regimes in Wuchang and Changsha, respectively, but had been forced to abandon both before he could accomplish much administratively. In fact, however, Zhang had been more or less forced to move west by pressures from a variety of Ming units in late 1643, most notably those of his old rival, Zuo Liangyu (1598–1645), who had nearly killed Zhang on two separate occasions.[35] He considered moving south into Guangdong or even trying another thrust north toward Nanjing, but feared engaging both the Ming forces and those of

Li Zicheng. Sichuan had the advantages of rugged terrain and a fair resource base but it was also strategically close enough to the Central Plain that Zhang could strike there once he marshaled his strength. So he headed west early in 1644, just as Li Zicheng was setting out from Xi'an toward Beijing.

Sources relate a number of ominous portents associated with Zhang's advance. A mysterious shooting star appeared in the western skies over Sichuan, allegedly being visible for three years until Zhang's heavenly ordained punishment by the Qing. A giant turtle appeared in the Jin River in Chengdu and over the next three days hundreds of small turtles left the river, fleeing the city. This supposedly referred to a portent from the Qin period (221–206 BCE) that maintained when turtles flee a city, its destruction was assured.[36] Such portents litter the late Ming sources with respect to the dynasty's fall and other calamitous events and are often recounted in later compilations, though the degree to which people actually believed these signs is a matter of conjecture.[37] But they are noteworthy in how they provide a sense of the rumors and beliefs that permeated different levels of the populace as well as how they were used and manipulated by all manner of actors to contextualize the significance of events within a broader historical framework. Some sources explicitly mention the impending loss of the Mandate of Heaven or similar catastrophes whereas others are equally strident in noting the cynical manipulation or fabrication of portents for personal gain by one actor or another.

In any event, after capturing Xiangyang in western Huguang, Zhang camped and took dozens of towns in the vicinity. His troops seemed poised to overrun Sichuan and rumors circulated that he had an army of 400,000 ready to sweep into the province. He moved into Wanxian in eastern Sichuan at the start of 1644 and his forces occupied it for three months, delayed in part by heavy spring rains. They lured refugees out of the mountains by promising not to kill them, but then allegedly slaughtered the returnees and tossed their corpses into the nearby Yangzi River.[38] Meanwhile, the Yao-Huang bandits stepped up their operations as the space afforded for them by Zhang's incursion into Sichuan offered them more freedom of action as the remaining Ming units scrambled to counter Zhang's new thrust. In Chongqing the Prince of Rui and Grand Coordinator Chen Shiqi ignored the advice of prefect Shen Yunzuo of Chengdu concerning the proper defense of the province and the city itself and the Ming units failed to properly garrison strategic chokepoints, most notably Tongluo Gorge, which guarded the river approach to the city.[39] Chen was replaced by Long Wenguang but remained at his post for the time being. The Prince of Rui, who was notoriously wealthy despite being a devout Buddhist, was chastised by an official who compared him unfavorably to his cousin, who had dipped into his own coffers in the heroic defense of Kaifeng two years previously.[40] The prince's recalcitrance and stinginess is even more surprising when one learns that he had originally fled to Chongqing from Hanzhong years earlier in fear of the peasant rebels.[41]

Though a few efforts were made to hold key points, in general the Ming troops were ill-disciplined, unevenly led, badly equipped, and low on morale.

They put up token resistance and even thwarted Zhang's units in a couple of battles, but they were eventually driven further into the province and some of their leaders were even refused entry into fortified cities like Baoning by suspicious residents. This, in turn, led to widespread looting by erstwhile Ming units, further undermining their popular support. To make matters even more complicated, Li Zicheng's forces were pushing into northern Sichuan as well and they occupied Baoning in the summer of 1644.[42] Further south, Zhang dislodged the Ming defenders Zeng Ying, Yu Dahai, and Li Zhanchun, who fled to southern Sichuan and the route to Chongqing was open.

Sending deputies upriver to make floating bridges and scout out the approaches to the city, Zhang sailed toward Chongqing at the head of a fleet of a hundred boats with great yellow banners that read "Quelling the Disturbances in [Si]chuan."[43] Other units advanced along the riverbank on foot and on horseback, their lines stretching for some 40 *li* and their banners "looking like a forest."[44] Zhang dispatched an envoy to try and convince the defenders of Chongqing to surrender without a fight. The officials asked him what Zhang's intentions were. The envoy replied, "He wants to take Sichuan as the root and afterwards mobilize armies to pacify the realm. If you hand over the town not a blade of grass or a single tree will be disturbed but if you resist, not even the old and young will be left [alive]."[45]

Despite these threatening words, the Ming officials present resolved to hold out and ordered the execution of anyone who advocated surrender. So Zhang then moved quickly and attacked Fotu Pass, located southwest of the city, and took it, albeit with significant casualties, while the main body of his force proceeded up the Yangzi.[46] A great storm arose in the middle of the night and people in the princely palace were terrified, with some saying Li Zicheng was coming and others, Zhang Xianzhong. Half the prince's retinue fled in the night and he was of a mind to flee too, urging Chen Shiqi to join him, particularly since Chen had already been relieved of his post.[47] At this juncture Chen said, "The bandits have entered Sichuan because of me. How can I face my lord father [in the afterlife] if I flee? It is the duty of the righteous to survive or die with the state."[48] The rebels reached the city late in the sixth lunar month of 1644. As they arrayed their forces around the city, the residents were in a panic.

The fighting was fierce initially, with the peasant army sustaining sufficient casualties as Chen Shiqi led the defense himself from atop the walls. But learning of a weak spot near the Tongyuan Gate in the northwest corner of the city, the rebels concentrated their attacks there, then mined underneath the wall and planted gunpowder charges. As the walls fell and the attackers "swarmed in like ants," the Ming vice-commander tried to mount a defense and a bloody street fight ensued but he was cut down. The victorious rebels rounded up the surviving officials and the prince and his retinue for execution. As Zhang was killing them, a vicious storm erupted as thunder clashed and lightning strikes allegedly came down upon Zhang's units, causing him to curse at Heaven and turn his cannons at the sky shouting, "What business is it of Heaven if I kill people?"[49] It was said more than 10,000 residents of the prince's compound alone were executed, in addition to the high Ming officials. But this was not the end of Zhang's policy of terror. Zhang's men then supposedly severed the (right) sword arms of some 37,000 troops captured in the city, though others who submitted peacefully "merely" lost ears, noses, or hands.[50] Some accounts add that Zhang severed the left arms of large numbers of women so that couples would have a matched set.

Zhang's forces then fanned out and attacked the localities, meeting resistance in a few places such as Luzhou, located southwest of Chongqing. In most places people fled into the mountains. Some of them hid in caves for months while others built their own mountain stockades, some of which would remain standing for decades against all manner of human and animal predators. But for the time being Zhang could afford to ignore these forces because they were ill-coordinated and not much of a threat. He set his sights on Chengdu, which would become the capital of his new realm. As Zhang's armies advanced they stripped the surrounding towns of all supplies. His armies reached the city on September 5, 1644 and surrounded it with twenty divisions.[51]

The Prince of Shu at Chengdu had also vacillated and failed to properly prepare defense of his city. Back when word came in that Beijing had fallen to Li Zicheng, the panicked prince ordered Ming units to rush to his aid, while Wu Jishan, the Prefect of Chengdu, urged him to oversee defensive measures to seal off the province by stationing crack troops at key passes and ordering all officials and troops to rush to the defense of the city. He also urged the prince to dip into his own considerable personal funds, which were allegedly "piled as high as a mountain" within his residence to pay the troops and provide food and aid to the starving populace.[52] Wu recommended tax amnesties for the common folk and the raising of additional mercenary units for defense. He argued that if the prince rectified internal matters, "it would be easy to turn peril into security and transform calamity into good fortune" as news of his achievements spread and people rallied to the Ming cause.[53] Though he initially ignored even pleas from his cousin, the Prince of Taiping, the Prince of Shu was eventually moved by these words and released 30,000 taels for special rewards for the troops. Still, upon hearing of the fall of Chongqing, the prince wanted to flee to Guizhou but was stopped by the intervention of Regional Inspector Liu Zhibo.

Meanwhile, other funds were raised by the efforts of officials such as Shen Yunzuo, who supposedly managed to assemble an army of 1800 defenders paid through private contributions, though training and equipment were both sub-standard.[54] Nonetheless, Liu Zhibo tried to improve morale by organizing the defenders into various brigades with names like the "Awesome Martiality Brigade" (*weiwuying*) and with the help of the military officials Liu Jiachong and Yang Zhan, they assembled a defense force of just under 10,000.[55] They also set about repairing walls and digging new moats.

Just like they had at Chongqing, the rebels initially sent forth emissaries to negotiate a peaceful surrender. Liu Zhibo and his associates killed all of them. As was the case in Chongqing, the initial fighting was fierce and Ming units under Liu Zhibo and Yang Zhan repelled a simultaneous assault on multiple walls, even driving the attackers back some two to three *li*. Yang then led the Ming forces out in a sally, killing some twenty more before falling back into Chengdu in part because a heavy rainstorm had erupted. Another rebel assault was turned back, the sound of the cannons thundering across the mountains for hundreds of *li* according to one account.[56] So the rebels again decided to try and mine a weak area in the wall with gunpowder and great levers.[57] They were successful and as the gunpowder detonated, smoke filled the sky and several dozen *zhang* of the wall collapsed. The bandits clambered through the breach and the prince and his household drowned themselves in wells. Other officials took poison or jumped into the Jin River.[58]

The rebels assembled the surviving officials in a central park in the city. It appears that, initially at least, Zhang attempted to get some of them to join his cause. Playing on the fact that they were from the same hometown not to mention his admiration for his spirited defense efforts, Zhang offered a position to Liu Zhibo. According to one account Liu allegedly replied, "Die bandits! How could I ever join you?" In another version of the story Liu allegedly replied, "I am a court appointed minister. How could I surrender to rebels? If you want to cut me up with a knife it will make my death resound amongst the populace!"[59] They then tied him to a gate and fired arrows at him. Liu remained defiant, shouting, "Shoot me as much as you want so long as you don't harm a single commoner!"[60] His corpse was subsequently cut up by Zhang's lieutenant, Liu Wenxiu.

They also supposedly offered a position to Shen Yunzuo, along with a bowl of food, to which Shen replied,

> I want to eat bandit flesh! How can I eat your rice? Since our troops were defeated I haven't eaten anything in the hope that I will die. But if I don't die can you kill me quickly? How could I possibly help nation-destroyers like you?[61]

The bandits were furious and killed Shen alongside Liu and the others.

The most dramatic account pertains to the capture of General Yang Zhan. He was also apprehended and offered a post but refused so, for reasons not specified in the sources, Yang was led outside the city to be executed. Yang was wearing fancy armor and apparently the rebels asked him to remove it so they could have it. Yang replied, "I don't care about my life so why should I care about my clothes? You can have my armor when you fish my body out of the river." As they moved to forcibly remove his armor, Yang grabbed a dagger from one of his captor's hands, stabbed the man and made his escape by diving into the Jin River.[62] Ming military official Cao Xun made a similar escape by diving into the river. Yang would subsequently become the leading figure of the Ming restoration movement in Sichuan until his treacherous assassination at the hands of allies in 1649.

Zhang then moved into the recently deceased prince's palace and held a victory celebration where one official who had apparently surrendered hit him in the head with a silver bowl. Zhang had him cut to pieces for his insolence.[63] He would be far from the last person Zhang treated in such a fashion. It must be admitted that there were those who chose to cast their lot with the rebels, whether out of opportunism, under duress, or out of a sincere belief that they might be able to do some good for the realm. But the sources have tended not to treat such individuals particularly well. Indeed, some are held up by children or spouses as negative examples in the face of superior moral behavior. Former Ming Grand Secretary Liu Yuliang, for example, accepted a post from the rebels and when he returned home to tell his wife, a woman of the Wang clan, she exclaimed, "If you wish to be a bandit official, you can do so. But I'll not be a bandit's wife!"[64] She promptly hung herself. The primary sources are full of similar accounts attesting to the cardinal Confucian virtues of loyalty and righteousness and so they must be read with that in mind, but such tales certainly lend a specificity to the historical record and shed light on the orthodox mindset of the seventeenth century. Significantly enough, one finds far fewer of these accounts in Maoist-era scholarship concerning the peasant rebels, but there is a full complement of accounts of venal and greedy officials.

Returning to Chengdu, it seems that Zhang carried out a systematic massacre for three days following his occupation of the city though the numbers killed are very much in dispute.[65] A few hapless surviving members of the princely family were killed, along with some 1000 monks at the Daci Temple, who were seen as supporters of the prince.[66] The other massacres were primarily carried out at the Wanli Bridge outside the south gate of the city or outside the east gate. Bodies were dumped into the river or simply left to rot, depending upon which source one reads, though both seem plausible. Nonetheless it is said that some of Zhang's lieutenants questioned the utility of such actions, given that Zhang hoped to use Chengdu as a springboard for the conquest of the empire. What use was a base without resources? Supposedly Li Dingguo, Ai Nengqi, Liu Wenxiu and Sun Kewang, among others, were moved to weeping by the plight of the common folk and this forced Zhang to relent.[67]

Upon occupying Chengdu, Zhang issued strict regulations regarding sedition and limiting movement within the city with curfews and overlapping systems of mutual surveillance and responsibility. Families were organized into units of ten, the traditional mutual security arrangement known as *baojia*. People were forbidden from using terms like "Great Ming" or "Great Shun" (Li Zicheng's dynastic title). The latter was an especially reviled target as Zhang had always been irked at having to play second fiddle to Li. Zhang said, "The Zhang family is tall and the Li family is short" and "Li flees before Zhang's triumphs," and commoners were encouraged to adopt and propagate similar slogans.[68] They were stopped in the street and asked who was greater, Zhang or Li? Those who answered Zhang were declared "good subjects" (*liangmin*) and rewarded.[69]

People were not allowed to go out at night or leave the city without permission and they had to carry passes. People had to report to their local *baojia* representative and say where they were going and when they were returning.[70] Every neighborhood had a stele erected where the Ming reign years were replaced by those of Zhang Xianzhong and his prescriptions were engraved. If someone was found guilty of violating these prescriptions their entire family and the ten households residing to their right and left were all executed and those killed were not even told the reason.[71] Those who spoke seditious thoughts were similarly dealt with. Police regularly patrolled the streets looking for enemies of the regime and hauled suspicious people into the palace.[72] But far from merely executing his victims, Zhang was prone to extreme acts of cruelty and terror.

Perhaps most gruesome was Zhang's habit of flaying his enemies and perceived foes of his regime. Contemporary writers suggest that Zhang's predilection for flaying victims came from precedents set by the august founder of the Ming Dynasty, Emperor Hongwu (r. 1368–98), a peasant rebel himself, who allegedly flayed someone convicted of sedition. Zhang apparently liked this so he decorated his own palace in Chengdu (not unlike the fictional character Roose Bolton in George Martin's *Song of Ice & Fire* series) with the flayed skins of his enemies as an example to future wrongdoers.[73] Moreover, Zhang's executioners were grim masters of their craft. Some victims were kept alive for days and beheaded later. Others were simply left to die slowly of exposure. A minister who opposed this treatment was himself killed by flaying and exposed in public as an object lesson.[74]

The lowest offenses were punished by a hundred strokes of the rod, which in itself could be fatal. Zhang's Minister of Rites was subjected to this punishment after protesting his lord's harshness. He subsequently hung himself in shame.[75] The next most serious offenses were punished by cutting off noses or ears, the next by severing hands or feet. After this came decapitation, then death by slow slicing, then dismemberment by filleting (up to 500 cuts) and the complete dicing of the corpse up to the total removal of the skin, which was for the most severe crimes.[76]

Amid this growing reign of terror Zhang would declare himself Great King of the West with the reign title (ironically) Da Shun on the eighth day of the tenth month of 1644. He made the wife of a deceased Ming grand secretary killed by Li Zicheng his empress and his adopted sons were all elevated to the rank of prince and given charge of his armies to conquer in the four directions. He created a skeletal civil administration and appointed ministers, the most prominent of whom was his long-serving aid, Wang Zhaolin, a petty Ming official with a reputation for cruelty, who seems to have encouraged or even stoked Zhang's murderous inclinations more than anyone else. At the same time Zhang sent out his agents to exact tributes of beautiful girls for his harems, money for his coffers and to plunder temples for artifacts to melt down so he could recast them into coinage. Commoners were instructed to use his *Da Shun tongbao* to demonstrate their loyalty to his government. Buddhist images that were not melted down were discarded and in the early Qing a cache of these was found outside the north gate of Chengdu and dubbed "The Buddha's Grave."[77]

It was not long, however, before things began to turn against Zhang, including omens portending his own demise. Shortly after ensconcing himself in Chengdu he noticed a nearby pagoda outside the city proper that looked like an arrow pointing at his palace, thereby spreading pernicious *fengshui* his way. Zhang had the offending pagoda destroyed but when his men did so they allegedly found an inscription on a stone that read,

> This pagoda was restored by Yu Yilong in the Wanli reign and will be destroyed by Zhang Xianzhong. Over the years from 1644–1647 this land will be drenched red with blood, sorcery will spread in northern Sichuan and the poison will envelope eastern Sichuan. A flute without bamboo will fire an arrow into [Zhang's] stomach.[78]

Meanwhile, Zhang continued to try and assert his authority in the countryside, which was lawless and occupied by multiple contending powers. Contemporary accounts speak of the wilderness south of Chengdu being littered with thousands of naked rotting corpses.[79] These, in turn, invited packs of wolves, wild dogs, and tigers to feed. The bandit armies did little to alleviate these problems, being wont to raid and plunder in the night, taking whatever they wished. This led many to flee into the mountains for safety, which, in turn, prompted the Shun regime to issue proclamations saying things such as

> All who wish to stay in the towns and be loyal subjects, don't be afraid. Those who give the Da Shun government money won't be killed, but those who flee into the mountains and turn to banditry will all be utterly exterminated.[80]

Nonetheless, despite the horrors perpetrated upon the residents of Chongqing and Chengdu and the repressive policies of Zhang's government in general, for the first few months there does not appear to have been that much outright resistance to his government. Most people simply fled or acquiesced to varying degrees. And some did accept local posts under his government and as late as the ninth month of 1645 thousands showed up for one of his recruitment exams, only to be slaughtered as part of his program to wipe out literati opposition, which he deemed critical in undermining support for his efforts in properly governing the province.[81] But by the early months of 1645 it seems that more and more people took to outright opposition. Initially this was primarily in the form of people erecting and occupying fortified stockades in the mountains as noted above. But subsequently it also included attacking cities held by Zhang's appointees and waylaying and ambushing his troops and officials.

Predictably, given his volatile personality and already sharpened sense of paranoia, these activities spurred Zhang on to greater acts of cruelty as he came to articulate a bizarre divine mission to slaughter, which was relayed to him by various means and mediums, depending upon the story. In its most famous incarnation, Zhang composed a poem that read "Heaven bestows myriad things upon man but man gives nothing to Heaven. Kill! Kill! Kill! Kill! Kill! Kill! Kill!" Zhang supposedly had the poem erected on a stele.[82] Another story has Zhang receiving a divine mission to kill at the famous Mount Wudang in Huguang.[83] In a story similar to the account of Zhang's slaughter at Chongqing, during one massacre a thunderstorm erupted and Zhang shouted at the sky, "You sent me down to the world to kill people. How dare you thunder at me!"[84] He then fired his cannons back at the sky. On another occasion when a storm broke out Zhang shouted, "Heavenly father! You want me to kill on your behalf!"[85]

As for Zhang's personal religious beliefs and their connection to his murderous predilections, they are somewhat difficult to ascertain. At times he visited temples dedicated to various popular folk deities such as Guan Yu, the God of War, and made offerings. As seen in the excerpt above, he also often attributed his bloody purges to messages received from Heaven, or the Lord of Heaven. He also claimed to have books that transmitted messages that only he could understand. In fact, later in his career he threatened to kill the Jesuit missionaries because he believed they had stolen one of these books from him. Zhang ranted,

> There are too many commoners in China and their wickedness is unchecked. Therefore the Lord of Heaven has sent old Zhang to the world to kill people. … I want to fulfill the charge of Heaven so my plan is to kill all the evil people in China.[86]

He further admonished the folk of Sichuan to cleanse themselves lest he be forced to do it for them, stating, "His majesty is truly acting on behalf of Heaven. All of you, officials, and commoners alike, must wash your hearts and cleanse your thoughts in order to avoid Heaven's wrath."[87] But it is impossible to identify coherent religious beliefs or practices in Zhang's actions. Rather, it seems that his paranoid delusions shaped his religious interpretations of his actions. Interestingly, however, at least some sources credit Zhang's divine mission to slaughter with a visit to the famous Mount Wudang.[88]

While he would later go after many different groups, it seems that Zhang first directed his special wrath toward literati. We have already seen how he allegedly executed thousands at an exam in Chengdu in 1645. At the time the Literary Temple caught fire seemingly without reason, prompting Zhang to say, "The Confucian sages don't like me killing their little brothers huh?" [Wang] Zhaolin replied, "The literati have now been exterminated, that's the reason [for the fire]."[89] On other occasions Zhang would call exams and threaten those who refused to sit for them with the execution of their children.[90] Then, when the hapless candidates arrived, Zhang would have them enter the exam grounds from the east and exit from the west, killing them as they emerged, in a tactic he had practiced before in Huguang. In another slaughter outside the Qingyang Temple some 17,000 were killed and their writing brushes were piled into a mountain.[91] In one sense Zhang's hatred (fear?) of the gentry makes a good deal of sense. They had the connections, knowledge, local prestige and potential alternative loyalties to cause him trouble. And the fact that relatively few of them willingly joined his regime certainly would have been cause for concern.

But the sources indicate another deep-seated childhood reason for Zhang's hatred. Supposedly, when he was young Zhang accompanied his father on a business trip. His father stopped outside a literati's house and tied up his donkey on a post while he conducted business nearby. The donkey subsequently relieved himself. When the home's owner came out he was enraged and he started beating Zhang's father and then made him clean up the feces with his bare hands. Witnessing this humiliation, Zhang allegedly vowed revenge upon all gentry and the people of that town, whom he incidentally later massacred.[92]

Whatever the reasons, as Zhang's defeats mounted and his enemies closed in, the scale of his massacres increased. By mid-1645 Yang Zhan in particular had emerged as a symbol of resistance and people flocked to his banner.[93] He soon amassed a force of over 100,000 refugees and Ming loyalists of various stripes and his popularity was growing by the day as he seemed to be the only person in Sichuan capable of restoring order and feeding the hungry masses. In response, the people gained morale and they started killing Zhang's appointed officials. Eventually Zhang's men did not dare venture into southern Sichuan after repeated attempts to dislodge Yang had failed. It was around this time that Zhang dispatched his chief lieutenants in all four directions with orders to kill everyone and everything.

Zhang also apparently wanted all the wealth of the province brought back to him and all the Sichuanese killed for betraying him.[94] Another indication that Zhang's mental condition was worsening is that around this time he started seeing apparitions when sitting on his throne and hearing mysterious cries in the palace. One time he claimed to hear the mournful howls of hundreds of dogs that shook the earth yet no one around him heard a thing. Another time he heard a noise from the back of the palace and went to investigate only to find a troupe of headless musicians. Another morning while he was eating breakfast, thousands of disembodied hands grabbed at his food. Zhang tightened his prescriptions on night travel further and feared to walk alone in his own palace.[95]

In a subsequent banquet early in 1646 Zhang declared his intention to mount a northern campaign and recover Hanzhong, presumably en route to conquering the empire, referencing the Three Kingdoms era in considering this region the fulcrum of empire. Zhang then articulated expansive plans to crush his rivals but they were soon dashed when one of his armies was shattered by a much smaller force commanded by one of Li Zicheng's former subordinates.[96] Still, Zhang intensified his purges, offering rewards for submitted heads, feet, and even fetuses, according to some accounts.[97] People died by the thousands and entire towns were filled with nothing but moldering corpses. It was said that if smoke was seen coming from someone's house they were assured of dying that night.[98]

Zhang's main commanders supposedly competed in submitting massive numbers of these grisly trophies, though the outrageous figures given in some sources are impossible to believe. But to give a couple examples, Liu Wenxiu supposedly killed over 10,000 commoners and 1000 monks at Qiongzhou. People who fled into caves in the mountains were smoked out and killed. The lands around Qiongzhou were "covered in blood and flesh for 200 *li*."[99] In another place the bodies were thrown into a river and they were piled so high that they were level with a bridge going into the city and the water flow was blocked for days. Zhang intensified his attacks on scholars and artisans so that "not a single scholar or artisan was left alive" according to one account.[100] The rebels also started rounding up women and children and killing them as well. Rebels would bet on the sex of fetuses then rip them out of the womb.[101] Children would be rounded up into a circle and stabbed to death with spears. Allegedly, when people came in with their reports and trophies Zhang would send them back out, saying, "The people of Sichuan still aren't all dead yet."[102]

Mountains of hands and feet piled up outside Zhang's palace in Chengdu "like Mount Fenghuang" and rotted without even rain to wash them away for nearly three months.[103] Heads, feet, hands, ears and noses would be stacked in separate piles. Zhang would supposedly sometimes gather the severed heads together for banquets *à la* Idi Amin.[104] Promotions and ranks were based on the number submitted. Two hundred pairs of hands and feet got one a rank of squad commander. One could be promoted from vice-commander to commander by submitting 1700 pairs.[105] If one soldier killed hundreds in a single day they could be promoted to supreme commander. Only adults could be counted for the quotas and women were only half as valuable as men.[106] Supposedly, after Zhang instituted this program his ranks were filled with earls, dukes, marquises, and other nobles. According to Shun records between the first and fifth months of 1646 alone Sun Kewang, Liu Wenxiu, Ai Nengqi, and Li Dingguo each killed around 10 million people![107] Zhang then started killing "disloyal" soldiers and more suspect civilians, allegedly killing a million more soldiers and 330,000 civilians in the summer of 1646. It was said that the trail of corpses extended for 70 *li* north and south of Chengdu.[108]

Zhang became angry that the traitors in his midst seemed to be multiplying. He even grew nostalgic for his early days as a simple local wandering bandit, remarking,

> When I first arose from the marshes I had only 500 followers but none dared resist me. Now I have many more and yet last year we were defeated by He Zhen at Hanzhong and now my generals neither appreciate my

favors nor listen to my orders and now the soldiers are all covetous and evil and have duplicitous hearts.

In response to this Wang Zhaolin urged another purge, but only after Zhang got his men thoroughly drunk. He allegedly did so and killed 100,000 more in short order, in less than a day according to some accounts.[109] At this point, however, the writing was on the wall and Zhang's forces began deserting in ever larger numbers, prompting more executions of even high level military officials on Zhang's part.[110] Bodies were sometimes burned and other times thrown into the river. Even animals were targeted in Zhang's later purges until the land was empty and "no birds sang in the forests."[111] Zhang then started encouraging his men to kill their wives and concubines, apparently so they would have fewer mouths to feed once they left Chengdu but also perhaps as a test of loyalty.

Zhang also became even more concerned about "private" hoarding of wealth, perhaps because he thought he needed funds to pay troops for future campaigns. If someone was found with even 1–2 *liang* of silver, their whole family would be executed. If caught with 10 *liang*, they would all be skinned alive. So people resorted to hiding wealth in the ground and in wells, while others informed on their neighbors in hopes of currying favor with the rebels.[112] Zhang allegedly had some of the plundered wealth buried near Chengdu and executed those who dug the pits.

Finally, the resources of Chengdu were exhausted and Zhang readied to depart. As he loaded his hoarded wealth on hundreds of boats, Yang Zhan advanced from the south and engaged Zhang and Jiangkou, southeast of Chengdu. Yang smashed the armies of the erstwhile King of the West and put him to the run toward the northeast. He recovered most of Zhang's plundered wealth and used it to supply his own armies, though much was lost at the bottom of the river where some of it possibly still remains. Zhang's men torched Chengdu in an orgy of destruction, lashing vines to the buildings and dousing them with oil so they would burn longer.[113] The city allegedly smoldered for three months. The devastation was so complete that as late as the Qianlong reign (1736–95) the Manchu governor Fukangan asked the emperor to send him 600,000 taels for restoration work.[114] Yang's army pursued the rebels briefly but abandoned the chase, allegedly because they were bewildered by the sheer number of bones they saw scattered along the roads.[115]

For his part, as he headed northeast Zhang still hoped to weed out the undesirables in his army, which meant purging all the Sichuanese and other newer troops. Zhang thought a return to his Shaanxi roots would reinvigorate his efforts and he boasted that he could take the whole empire from the Qing with just 3000 troops. When another storm erupted Zhang said,

> Heavenly father, you want me to kill for you. From now on the only ones left will be my old commanders and soldiers but since you're watching every day, I'll report to you with ten or more people put to death.[116]

Figure 2.1 Gravesite of Zhang Xianzhong, Xichong, Sichuan Province

As things turned out, Zhang would skirmish with remnants of Li Zicheng's armies through the fall of 1646 inconclusively. But his biggest mistake was his decision to kill his subordinate Liu Jinzhong. Liu and Zhang had clashed before, over both defeats Liu had suffered and over Liu's opposition to Zhang's purges. It came to Liu's attention that Zhang was going to target him so Liu fled and defected to the Qing commander Haoge, who was a few hundred miles to the east of Zhang's position.

Liu told Haoge of Zhang's exact location and even offered to lead him right to Zhang's position. The combined armies traversed over 1400 *li* in just three days and came upon Zhang by surprise. Hearing there was a force in the area Zhang emerged from his command tent, grabbed a spear and mounted a horse to go investigate with just a handful of men. When he galloped into view Liu pointed Zhang out to Haoge's men. Someone fired a single arrow, which caught Zhang in the stomach. He fell dead from his horse and his body was recovered and decapitated by Haoge.[117] Haoge's official title was Prince Su (肅王), which is, of course, a flute (簫) without bamboo. When Zhang's body was cut up he allegedly had a heart that was as black as ink and no liver. In the place he was buried thorns grew everywhere and a black tiger guarded the gravesite and attacked anyone who came near.[118] Incidentally, for his part, Liu Jinzhong continued to serve the Qing, aiding them in their attack on Zunyi the following year that dislodged Sun Kewang's forces, albeit temporarily, from southern Sichuan.[119]

These tales served to further spread the legend of Zhang Xianzhong and certainly helped the Qing conquerors, who could place much of the blame for Sichuan's continuing woes firmly upon Zhang's shoulders. Indeed, Zhang's terroristic policies, exaggerated or not, fit perfectly with the Qing's stated program of avenging the Ming's defeat at the hands of the peasant rebels. Likewise they could easily point to Zhang's other rivals in the province, many of whom were connected to the former Ming state and/or were Ming loyalists of various stripes, as rebels themselves. And the fact that Zhang's lieutenants, whether out of opportunism (as in the case of Sun Kewang) or genuine change of heart (as with Li Dingguo), threw in their lot with the Ming loyalist government, further enabled the Qing to pose as avengers, this time on behalf of the ravaged people of Sichuan. Yang Zhan's untimely death at the hands of one of his erstwhile allies aided the Qing further by removing the one truly competent Ming military figure who had virtually no prior connection to the peasant rebels.

As significantly, despite the demise of the Yellow Tiger, his legacy would live on and unhappily the folk of Sichuan and the southwest would endure many more years of strife at the hands of Zhang's former lieutenants, the Qing conquerors, various Ming loyalist groups, the Yao-Huang bandits, the Thirteen Families, and the Three Feudatory princes. Indeed, warlords, bandits, and militarists of all stripes proliferated in this rugged border region, aided by the terrain and the multiplicity of political options under which one could cloak their activities in the guise of legitimacy. Early Qing records often note how Ming loyalist groups and officials made common cause with aboriginal (*tusi*) officials and at times the Yongli emperor seemed to just be doling out titles of nobility like candy, probably because he had little else to offer his would-be followers.[120]

The province would thus sink further into savagery and disorder. Disease was rampant and Qing accounts, in particular, note that epidemics severely curtailed their fighting capability. As early as the spring of 1648, barely a year after they killed Zhang Xianzhong, some Qing units were down to 20 percent of their original strength due to the combination of combat losses, malnutrition, and disease.[121] Yet they were beset on all sides by local bandits, Ming loyalists, former peasant rebels, and armed locals. This state of affairs eventually forced the Qing governor-general, Li Guoying, to withdraw to Baoning in the north of the province in the sixth month of 1648 to await rations from Shaanxi and other locations in the north. At the time, Li confidently predicted that when the provisions arrived, "the bandits will not be hard to crush and Sichuan would not be hard to recover."[122] But even as Li wrote these words the Qing were trying to bolster their strength by recruiting mercenaries from among the folk of Sichuan because so many of their original troops were deserting on account of the food shortages. And Li admitted that all of Sichuan outside of the northern area of Baoning was still "crawling with bandits."[123]

Because of the endemic warfare the fields were destroyed and no one could grow crops for food. As Li Guoying noted, nine out of ten fields had been ruined by drought and warfare. And on account of these natural and man-made calamities barely one in ten people survived.[124] The number of officials present to help had declined precipitously and the starving resorted to eating leaves, bark, and even pearls for food. Li wanted to implement the *tuntian* policy to at least feed the troops but he was concerned about the productivity of the land. So he begged the emperor to send relief funds and food with all due haste to support the starving troops in order to maintain morale and keep them from further preying on the hapless locals.[125]

Out of sheer necessity Li Guoying adopted somewhat of a wait and see approach with regards to engaging the Qing's foes in combat. This policy had mixed results for the Qing and certainly did not help the local commoners as the various warlords alternately banded together to resist the Qing and then turned on one another when the political winds shifted. As the different commanders died or killed one another, they tried to absorb the troops of their defeated enemies with varying levels of success. By 1650 Li Guoying felt he would soon be able to sweep in and bring order to the chaos, though he again requested more troops and supplies from the Qing court as the ongoing drought had hampered his efforts to establish military farms. Still, once he had sufficient supplies, Li told the emperor he could "sweep through the remaining rebels as if he was chopping bamboo."[126]

Li also made numerous proposals for inducing the local *tusi* officials to renounce their ties to the Ming and support the new regime, though the battle for minority hearts and minds would rage well into the 1660s and even beyond in some cases.[127] Indeed, Li was frank in noting the origins of local officials and power brokers in the late 1650s, which included Eight Banner troops, former Shun rebels, those who had pledged allegiance to the Qing, and those who were mere refugees. So it was important from Li's perspective to investigate the background of would-be officials and determine their fitness for service. But it was also vital that general order and agricultural productivity be restored as soon as possible. Given that this memorial was composed nearly a decade after the death of Zhang Xianzhong and several years after the defeat of a major expeditionary force led by Zhang's former lieutenant Liu Wenxiu against Baoning, it is illuminating concerning the ongoing disarray in Sichuan.[128] In fact, in 1655, Li Guoying and Wu Sangui had memorialized the court, complaining that they lacked the troops and resources to make progress in Sichuan but if these were granted, they could retake Chengdu and use it as a base to recapture the rest of Sichuan and then push into Yunnan and Guizhou, where the Southern Ming forces were then ensconced.[129] But Li admitted that Sichuan was still devastated and "no smoke [from cooking fires] can be seen for 1000 *li*," and local bandits, allegedly from the minority groups in the region, continued to aid the Ming cause, at least nominally. So it was tough to revive the agricultural base but Li felt that if Manchu troops were brought in, the Lolo raids could be curtailed and order could be restored as the fields around Chengdu were re-cultivated.[130]

Moreover, in addition to the difficulties with growing crops, Zhang Xianzhong's policy of appropriating animals had removed most of them too. So the province experienced years of famine. As one source chillingly recounts, "Because of the long period of disorder the cattle were all gone so people replaced cattle [as food]."[131] A peck of rice sold for 10,000 cash. Because there was nothing to eat in the wilds, when bandits spotted a person they ate him. And because fires could be seen a great distance at night and people would sneak up to ambush and eat you, people started eating without using cooking fires.[132] Some feared to enter dwellings for fear they'd be ambushed and eaten. Parents, children and spouses would make meals of deceased relatives.[133] For protection people lived in tight-knit communities in mountain stockades.[134] Others supposedly went feral as described above. For example, people near Xuzhou fled into the mountains and learned to walk with such light steps it seemed as if they were flying. Their bodies became covered with light fur and they lived in the tress.[135]

More realistically perhaps, and as many contemporaries noted, tiger and leopard attacks proliferated. Tigers and leopards climbed through windows into houses and the former even swam and attacked people in boats![136] So people resorted to living in elevated compounds and traveled in well-armed groups as tigers would enter cities even in broad daylight. There were daily reports of tiger attacks and in some districts not a single person survived. Over time, towns became overrun by forests and were occupied by packs of ravenous dogs that had acquired a taste for human flesh from eating the copious numbers of dead bodies.[137]

A report from the Pacification Commissioner of Sichuan, Zhang Chun, from the sixth month of 1650, offers an excellent example of contemporary reporting on the problems in the province. Zhang begins by describing Sichuan as a den of tigers and haven of chaos caused by the Yao-Huang bandits.[138] After noting that one could traverse a great distance without even seeing smoke from cooking fires, Zhang asserts that only 2 to 3 percent of the population in Sichuan still lived. And while he blames that destruction primarily upon the depredations of the Yao-Huang bandits (conveniently exculpating the Qing from blame), he then relates information about reports of man-eating tigers that came to his attention when he took up his post at Baoning. Zhang notes that people feared to travel because of the prevalence of tigers. In one district, out of a previous population of 506, 228 people were killed by tigers and another 55 died of illness, leaving just 223 alive. In another place, forty-two out of seventy-four inhabitants were allegedly eaten by tigers. Some people were reportedly eaten by tigers in broad daylight while working in their fields. So many people escaped the clutches of bandits only to end up in the mouths of tigers, as Zhang put it.[139]

Zhang's observations were further supported by those of Wu Sangui, who finally launched his portion of the assault against the Southern Ming from

Map 2.1 Warlords in Sichuan Province, c. 1648

Hanzhong in early 1658, after Sun Kewang had been defeated by Li Dingguo in a power struggle and had defected to the Qing. As had been his original plan, Wu was to secure Sichuan first and then proceed south. Advancing by land and water, Wu's troops were able to move surprisingly fast because "the war ravaged land was filled with nothing but ghost towns."[140] As Wu and his men approached Chongqing, "corpses and bones were strewn alongside the road and only mountain flowers grew and the only sound emanating from the eaves of the houses was the sound of cuckoos calling." As Wu himself noted, "In the empty mountains there are only the tearful cries of the cuckoo while the leftover houses cannot even sustain swallows' nests."[141] Given such a state of affairs it is no wonder that dangerous animals might have flourished, though again one must be wary of taking all the primary sources at face value.

Nonetheless, modern accounts suggest that such circumstances can lead to a rise in aggressive predatory behavior on the part of animals. In Burma during World War II, tigers that fed on human corpses subsequently attacked living humans.[142] In India, tigers even attacked soldiers on guard duty. Experts also note that leopards also occasionally take to man-eating, particularly targeting children. Moreover, a leopard will not necessarily shy away from attacking a group, but will simply go after what it perceives as the most vulnerable member.[143] These observations suggest that at least some of the tales in the primary sources are plausible, even if there is exaggeration and/or hearsay involved.

Additionally, as noted above, tigers could function as symbols of both oppressive government and as agents of righteousness, the latter aspect making them somewhat akin to lions in the Western world.[144] Most commonly the presence of man-eating tigers was seen as a manifestation of bad government or an inability of the ruler to order the world, though some writers argued that man-eating was simply a natural behavior for tigers.[145] As representatives of the emperor, officials were responsible not only for ruling the people, but also controlling natural phenomena. So tigers were theoretically under their purview as well. In any case, it is striking that the accounts of man-eating tigers decrease drastically after the first several decades of Qing rule. While this could be explained by the general restoration of order and repopulation of the province, it might also be a manifestation of the acceptance of Qing rule.

In a broader cultural context the emphasis upon the spread of man-eating animals, not to mention cannibalistic humans, who also appear in great numbers in the sources, speak to general fears about the decline of civilization and its values. Crocodile biologist Alistair Graham posited "One of civilization's imperative taboos is against cannibalism; little else arouses such fear or loathing. And we do not distinguish emotionally between a human eating a human and an animal eating a human."[146] While I would differ with this last assessment, I do agree that such accounts are designed to warn against the dangers of the loss of civilization and its values. These become especially striking when one considers the emphasis upon Zhang's purges of the literati in the sources. They were the traditional guardians of culture and civilizational values and their systematic eradication, viewed against the backdrop of invasion by a foreign barbarian people, was certainly distressing for the members of the literati class who managed to survive these traumatic events. And the fact that Zhang himself was known as the Yellow Tiger only further highlights the links between the descent into savagery and the loss of moral order. Zhang could be seen as both the destroyer and the manifestation of lax government on the part of the Ming. But he remained an ambiguous figure, for while the Qing could point to his destruction as proof of their ability to bring order, the fact that his lieutenants became the leading military figures in the Ming resistance movement adds an element of righteousness and loyalty to his memory. And, as Li Furong noted, "Chaos is not born from chaos, but is born from order; order is not born from order but is born out of chaos. Without great chaos, one cannot have great order."[147] Thus, in reading the disparate accounts of the Ming-Qing transition in Sichuan and southwest China one gains tremendous insight into the cultural and socio-political ramifications of endemic warfare at the local level. We can then profitably apply these insights to contemporary conflicts elsewhere, in a manner that does justice to the pioneering efforts of Dr. John E. Wills, Jr.

Notes

1 Jonathan D. Spence and John E. Wills, Jr. (eds.), *From Ming to Ch'ing: Conquest, Region, and Continuity in Seventeenth-century China* (New Haven, CT: Yale University Press, 1979).

2 See Spence and Wills, *From Ming to Ch'ing*, xi–xii.

3 On the Qing conquest as a contributing factor in China's supposed delinquency in "modernizing" see Chun-shu Chang and Shelley Hsueh-lun Chang, *Crisis and Transformation in Seventeenth-Century China: Society, Culture, and Modernity in Li Yü's World* (Ann Arbor, MI: University of Michigan Press, 1992), 298–303.

4 See Yu Lizi, *Ming-Qing shi jiang gao* (Jinan: Jilu shushe, 2008), 51–52.

5 The *Ming shi*, for example, following Fei Mi's *Huangshu* and Mao Qiling's *Houjian lu*, gives the outrageous death toll of 600 million! See Zhang Tingyu et al. comps., *Ming shi*, 12 vols (Taibei: Dingwen shuju, 1994), 7976. Hereafter *MS*. On the propensity to exaggerate the numbers killed by Zhang with a discussion of the sources from whence these numbers are derived, including specific numbers allegedly slaughtered by Zhang's main lieutenants, see Hu Zhaoxi, *Zhang Xianzhong tu Shu kaobian: jianxi Huguang tian Sichuan* (Chengdu: Sichuan renmin chubanshe, 1980), 4–9. Also see Sun Cizhou, "Zhang Xianzhong zai Shu shiji kaocha," *Lishi yanjiu*, 1, (1957), 47–57.

6 Liu Jingbo, *Shu guijian* in He Rui et al. (eds.), 282. Hereafter, *SGJ*.

7 See, for example, *MS*, 7977, and Wang Fuzhi, *Yongli shilu* (Beijing: Beijing guji chubanshe, 2001), 127. Hereafter, *YSL*.

8 *YSL*, 127.

9 In the military museum in Beijing, for example, there is a portrait of Zhang, looking fierce and sporting a great beard, leading an attack on the city of Xiangyang, alongside one of Li Zicheng, who is characteristically represented on horseback, as befitting his dashing image. There are many biographies of both these peasant rebel leaders, though Li gets far more coverage in general, in large part because it was his armies that seized Beijing from the Ming in 1644, even if they only held it for a few weeks. For brief English-language biographies of Zhang and Li respectively, see Arthur O. Hummel, *Eminent Chinese of the Ch'ing Period*, 2 vols (Washington, DC: Library of Congress, 1943), 37–38 (under Chang Hsien-chung), and 491–93 (under Li Tzu-ch'eng). Hereafter, *ECCP*. For a more recent short English biography of Li, also see Kenneth M. Swope, "Li Zicheng," in Kerry Brown (ed.), *The Berkshire Dictionary of Chinese Biography*, 4 vols (Great Barrington, MA: Berskshire, 2014), vol. 2, 942–52. For a modern Chinese account that treats the rebellions as a whole as "people's movements," see Li Wenzhi, *Wan*

Ming minbian (Shanghai: Zhonghua shuju, 1948). For an account that emphasizes the links between the late Ming peasant rebellions and the Qing invasion, see Li Guangtao, *Mingji liukou shimo* (Taibei: Zhongyang yanjiuyuan lishi yuyan yanjiusuo, 1965). The standard English-language treatment remains James Bunyon Parsons, *Peasant Rebellions of the Late Ming Dynasty*, reprint (Ann Arbor, MI: Association for Asian Studies, 1993). For a recent account that places the peasant rebellions within the broader context of the fall of the Ming, see Kenneth M. Swope, *The Military Collapse of China's Ming Dynasty, 1618–1644* (London: Routledge, 2013). On comparisons between Zhang and Li in Ming-Qing records, see Li Guangtao, "Zhang Xianzhong shi shi," in Li Guangtao, *Ming-Qing dang'an lunwenji* (Taibei: Lianjing chuban shiye gongsi, 1986), 567–74.

10 See "War in Asia," *Time* (December 11, 1950), 33. Original Romanization changed to pinyin.

11 This book is the He Rui text. The moniker "Eighth Great King," (*ba da wang*) sometimes rendered as "Eight Great Kings" in English scholarship, seems to be connected to the Buddhist term *"Ba Da Ming Wang,"* and appears to reference bodhisattva guardians of Vairocana, who were represented as fierce and destructive. See James B. Parsons, "Overtones of Religion and Superstition in the Rebellion of Chang Hsien-chung," *Sinologica: Review of Chinese Culture and Science*, 4 (1955), 174. The full title is also sometimes rendered as "Eighth Great King of the Western Camp" (*Xi ying ba da wang*). See Dai Li and Wu Qiao *Liukou changbian*, 2 vols (Beijing: Shumu wenxian chubanshe, 1991), 76. Hereafter *LKCB*. This source is also known as *Huailing liukou shizhong lu*. For a fanciful fictionalized account of how Zhang acquired the nickname from his stepmother in his youth, see the novel by Ren Naiqiang, *Zhang Xianzhong*, 2 vols (Xi'an: Shaanxi renmin chubanshe, 1995), 29. The "thirteen houses" refers alternatively to either the remnants of Li Zicheng's forces or to the so-called Yao-Huang bandit leaders, who ravaged the Sichuan-Huguang border regions for nearly three decades before their final commander, Li Laiheng, immolated himself in the face of a Qing assault on his mountain stronghold in 1664. Their original designation derived from the surnames of their two most prominent early leaders, Yao Tiandong and Huang Long. However, records vary as to whether these two survived very long as Ming commanders claimed to have killed them on multiple occasions and it is likely that others assumed their identities for the purpose of attracting followers. On their depredations, see Li Furong, *Yanyu nang* in He Rui et al. comps., *Zhang Xianzhong jiao Sichuan shilu* (Chengdu: Bashu shushe, 2002), 32–35. Hereafter *YN*. For a modern Chinese study of the group, see Gu Cheng, *Li Yan zhi yi: Ming-Qing yidai shi shi tanzheng* (Beijing: Guangming ribao chubanshe, 2012), 296–310.

12 *MS*, 7976.

13 See Yu Li, "Social Change During the Ming-Qing Transition and the Decline of Sichuan Classical Learning in the Early Qing," *Late Imperial China*, 19.1 (June 1998), 26–30.

14 See Yu Li, 27–28. Hu Zhaoxi's work is cited above.

15 See Wang Xingye, *Jiaoxiaode Zhang Xianzhong* (Beijing: Zhongguo shehui kexue chubanshe, 2008).

16 For Wang's overall appraisal of Zhang, see 204–08.

17 See Zheng Guanglu, *Zhang Xianzhong jiao Sichuan zhenxiang* (Chengdu: Sichuan minzu chubanshe, 2010). For more on the Jesuit perspective, see Erik Zurcher, "In

the Yellow Tiger's Den: Buglio and Magalhaes at the Court of Zhang Xianzhong, 1644–1647," *Monumenta Serica*, 50 (2002), 355–74.

18 Yingcong Dai, *The Sichuan Frontier and Tibet: Imperial Strategy in the Early Qing* (Seattle: University of Washington Press, 2009), 19.

19 See Sun Cizhou, 51–53. Interestingly, Sun also references Jesuit accounts and concludes that Qing pacification efforts and the subsequent Three Feudatories Revolt caused far more social disruption than Zhang's actions and goes out of his way to contrast incidents of good behavior by Zhang's forces with rapaciousness on the part of the Ming or Qing units.

20 Robert Entenmann, "Sichuan and Qing Migration Policy," *Ch'ing-shih wen-t'i*, 4.4 (1980), 35. Also see Robert Entenmann, "Migration and Settlement in Sichuan, 1644–1796," (Ph.D. Diss., Harvard University, 1982), 23–24.

21 Lynn A. Struve, *The Ming-Qing Conflict, 1619–1683: A Historiography and Source Guide* (Ann Arbor, MI: Association for Asian Studies, 1998), 1.

22 See, for example, the discussions found in *SGJ*, 209–15, and *YN*, 31. The uprising of Yang Yinglong and the so-called She-An rebellion are well chronicled in Ming sources. For good summary accounts of both in Chinese, see Gu Yingtai, *Mingshi jishi benmo*, reprint in *Lidai jishi benmo* (Beijing: Zhonghua shuju, 1997), 993–1003, and 1109–25, respectively. For a modern English-language account of the suppression of Yang Yinglong, see Kenneth M. Swope, "To Catch a Tiger: The Suppression of the Yang Yinglong Miao Uprising (1587–1600) as a case study in Ming military and borderlands history," in Michael Arthur Aung-Thwin and Kenneth R. Hall (eds.), *New Perspectives on the History and Historiography of Southeast Asia* (London: Routledge, 2011), 112–40. On the She-An Rebellion, see John Dardess, *Ming China: A Concise History of a Resilient Empire, 1368–1644* (Lanham, MD: Rowman & Littlefield, 2012), 9–10; and Swope, *Military Collapse*, 42–44. Interestingly enough, Ren Naiqiang's biographical novel of Zhang connects him to the She-An Rebellion too, maintaining that his father was tasked with helping supply mounts to the army sent to crush the revolt. See Ren, 28.

23 *YN*, 31.

24 Peng Zunsi, *Shubi*, 127, in He Rui et al., comps. Hereafter *SB*.

25 Oyang Zhi, *Shujing lu* in He Rui et al., comps, 184. Hereafter *SJL*. This version of the work includes both the *Shuluan shimo* and the *Ouyang shi yishi* discussed in Struve, 310.

26 In fact, one modern scholar argues that Li Dingguo's overriding goal in the last fifteen years of his life was to erase the shame of having been a "wandering bandit" from his name. See Teng Shaozhen, *San fan shilue*, 2 vols (Beijing: Zhongguo shehui kexue chubanshe, 2008), 691. Li was certainly regarded as a dashing figure by contemporary friends and foes alike and his legend continues to survive. There is even a regional cubed chicken dish named in his honor in Kunming. For the most complete modern account of Li's exploits, which includes numerous excerpts from traditional accounts, see Guo Yingqiu, *Li Dingguo jinian* (Beijing: Zhongguo renmin daxue, 2005). This is a reprint of an older work.

27 Most notably, see Gabriel de Magalhaes, "Yellow Tiger," trans. by Joseph Costa, SJ, ARSI JS 127ff, 1–35; digital manuscript copy held in the archives of the Ricci Institute of the University of San Francisco. The Portuguese original is held in the Jesuit archives in Rome.

28 See, for example, Magalhaes, 37–38 and 93–94.

29 In a fascinating parallel, the Tlingit tribe of Native Americans, who occupy what is today southeast Alaska, believe in *kushtakaas*, identified as akin to sasquatches, who are supposedly the descendants of ancestors "gone wild." According to popular lore, over the centuries they grew long hair for protection and developed other animalistic traits. They are seen as connected to both humans and totemic animals, particularly otters. Similar legends date back to earlier periods of Chinese history as well and apparently continued to circulate during the Ming-Qing era. The Qing writer Yuan Mei (1716–98), for example, includes a short story about the "hairy people of Qin," refugees of the projects to build the Great Wall under the first emperor of China who still supposedly lurked in the mountainous border between Hunan and Guangdong in his own day. These people sound suspiciously like those referenced in some of the sources discussed herein, not to mention the *yeren* (wild man) reputed to haunt the Shennongjia region of western Hubei today.

30 On the propensity for man-eating among Chinese tigers, see David Quanmen, *Monster of God: The Man-eating Predator in the Jungles of History and the Mind* (New York: W.W. Norton, 2003), 386; and Charles McDougal, "The Man-eating Tiger in Geographical and Historical Perspective," in Ronald Tilson and Ulysses S. Seal (eds.), *Tigers of the World: The Biology, Biopolitics, Management and Conservation of an Endangered Species* (Park Ridge, NJ: Noyes, 1987), 436–43. On the sub-species of tigers found in China, see Susie Green, *Tiger* (London: Reaktion Books, 2006), 12.

31 Harriet Ritvo, *The Animal Estate: The English and other Creatures in the Victorian Age* (Cambridge, MA: Harvard University Press, 1987), 28.

32 See Liu Jingbo, *Shu guijian* in He Rui et al. comps., 290–91. Hereafter *SGJ.*

33 Charles E. Hammond, "An Excursion in Tiger Lore," *Asia Major*, 4.1 (1991), 87.

34 For an overview of Zhang's earlier activities in Sichuan, see Yu Duanzi, *Zhang Xianzhong xian Luzhou ji*, in He Rui et al. (comps.), 2–28.

35 For a short biography of Zuo, see *ECCP*, 761–62.

36 *SGJ*, 247. This incident is from whence this source (*Shu guijian*) takes its name.

37 For example, many sources record a solar eclipse at the start of 1644 foretelling the demise of the Ming. See Xia Xie (comp.), *Ming tongjian*, 5 vols (Taibei: Xinan shuju, 1982), 3529. Hereafter *MTJ.*

38 *SGJ*, 249 and *YN*, 49.

39 See *SGJ*, 251–52, and *SB*, 142–43.

40 *SGJ*, 252.

41 *SB*, 143.

42 *YN*, 53.

43 *YN*, 54.

44 *YN*, 54–55 and *SGJ*, 254.

45 *YN*, 55.

46 Incidentally, today Fotu Pass is located in a park in the center of the city. A pagoda in the park offers a commanding view of the city along the Yangzi and Jialing rivers, demonstrating why it was so strategically important in the seventeenth century, when the city was much smaller.

47 *SGJ*, 254.

48 *SB*, 143.

49 See Shen Xunwei, *Shunan Xulue* in He Rui et al. (eds.), 101. Hereafter *SX.* Shen was the son of Shen Yunzuo, mentioned above. Also see *SGJ*, 255, and *YN*, 55.

50 *SB*, 143, and *SGJ*, 255.

51 *YN*, 56.
52 *MTJ*, 3529.
53 *YN*, 52.
54 *SX*, 101.
55 *YN*, 56.
56 *YN*, 56.
57 *SX*, 101.
58 *SX*, 101, and *SGJ*, 256.
59 *YN*, 56.
60 *SB*, 145.
61 *SX*, 102, and *SB*, 145. For lists of the notables killed at Chengdu, see *SGJ*, 256–57, and *SB*, 145–46.
62 *YN*, 57, and *SGJ*, 257.
63 *SGJ*, 256.
64 *SB*, 146.
65 See the discussion in Hu Zhaoxi, 17–19, who contends that since the sources only list the names of the prince and high officials, Zhang likely did not kill many more people than that. He also contends that the fact that Zhang issued so many regulations for life in Chengdu later proves that his killing was restrained.
66 *SGJ*, 259.
67 *YN*, 57.
68 *SGJ*, 259.
69 *YN*, 59.
70 *SB*, 150.
71 *SX*, 102–03.
72 *SJL*, 190.
73 *SGJ*, 259 and *SJL*, 188.
74 *SB*, 158.
75 *SB*, 158.
76 *SGJ*, 259.
77 *SB*, 150.
78 *YN*, 58.
79 *SX*, 103.
80 *SX*, 103.
81 *SX*, 106.
82 *SGJ*, 265. For more discussion of the poem and variant versions, see Parsons, "Overtones of Religion and Superstition," 171–72.
83 *SGJ*, 267.
84 *SGJ*, 267.
85 *SJL*, 192.
86 Zheng Guanglu, 189. On the question of Zhang's visions, see Wang Xingye, 171–72.
87 Zurcher, 365.
88 *SGJ*, 267, and Zurcher, 367.
89 *SX*, 106. Jesuit observers attest to this slaughter. See Parsons, *Peasant Rebellions*, 177.
90 *SB*, 158.
91 *SB*, 159. Oyang Zhi was allegedly one of only two people to survive this slaughter.

92 *SB*, 159. Some modern Chinese accounts use this story to illustrate the righteousness of class struggle and the arrogance of the traditional gentry class, thereby
justifying Zhang's actions, at least to an extent.

93 *YN*, 60.

94 *SJL*, 191–92 and Magalhaes, 102–03.

95 *SGJ*, 272, and *SJL*, 191.

96 Li had been killed in the summer of 1645.

97 *SX*, 106.

98 *YN*, 63.

99 *SB*, 160.

100 *SB*, 161. This same account claims that Sun Kewang saved thirteen artisans and
took them with him to Yunnan.

101 *SB*, 162. For what it's worth this story is oft-repeated in late Ming accounts of
peasant rebels and it may well be just another way of accentuating their supposed
savagery and barbarism.

102 *SB*, 162.

103 *SGJ*, 282.

104 *SB*, 167. For a fictionalized version of this practice by Idi Amin, see Giles Foden,
The Last King of Scotland (London: Vintage Books, 1998), 299.

105 *SJL*, 189.

106 *SB*, 162.

107 *SB*, 162. As outrageous as these figures are, they pale in comparison to the 600
million figure given in the *Ming shi* and some other accounts. See Hu Zhaoxi,
4–5. Yet the sources also note that Zhang's principal lieutenants, especially Li
Dingguo and Sun Kewang, tried to restrain him from his excesses.

108 *SB*, 162–63.

109 *SB*, 163. Note the reference to the novel *Water Margin* in the passage, which
might well indicate dramatic license on the part of the author.

110 *SB*, 163.

111 *SGJ*, 282.

112 *SB*, 164.

113 *SJL*, 192.

114 *SGJ*, 284.

115 *SB*, 168 and *YN*, 63.

116 *SGJ*, 285.

117 *YN*, 65.

118 *SB*, 168–69. Having visited the gravesite, I can attest that it is remote and hard to
find, though there were joss sticks placed in the ground before it when I was there
in the summer of 2015.

119 See Cao Yuanpei et al. (comps.), *Ming-Qing shiliao*, 15 vols (Taibei: Zhongyang
yanjiuyuan lishi yuyan yanjiusuo, 1972), *jia* 223a. Hereafter *MQSL*.

120 *MQSL jia*, 223a.

121 *MQSL jia*, 223a.

122 *MQSL jia*, 229a.

123 *MQSL jia*, 229a.

124 *MQSL jia*, 229a.

125 *MQSL jia*, 229b.

126 *MQSL jia*, 258b.

127 See *MQSL bing*, 940b–42b.

128 Concerning the offensive of Liu Wenxiu in 1652, which involved some 50,000 troops on the Southern Ming side and nearly expelled the Qing from Sichuan entirely, see *MQSL jia*, 295a–b, and *MQSL ding*, 701a–702a, and Zhongguo renmin daxue history department (comps.), *Qingdai nongmin zhanzheng shi ziliao xuanbian*, 3 vols (Beijing: Zhongguo renmin daxue chubanshe, 1984), 225–31. Hereafter *QNZS*. Also see Li Zhiting, *Wu Sangui da zhuan* (Nanjing: Jiangsu jiaoyu chubanshe, 2005), 207–14.

129 See Li Zhiting, 218–19, and *MQSL bing*, 897a–b.

130 See *QNZS*, 233–34.

131 *SGJ*, 292.

132 *SGJ*, 292.

133 *SGJ*, 292.

134 On the creation of these mountain stockades, which were often bristling with cannon and other firearms, see reports from Li Guoying and Hong Chenchgcou in *MQSL jia*, 520a–21b, and 540a–b.

135 *SB*, 169.

136 *SGJ*, 290. Tigers are incidentally the only great cats that are fond of swimming.

137 *SGJ*, 290. This phenomenon is still observed today in places such as Afghanistan where packs of man-eating feral dogs remain a serious problem in the wake of the ongoing civil war. These aggressive animals have developed a taste for human flesh owing to the huge numbers of corpses left rotting in the desert (personal communication with Colonel Joel Bius, USAF). In fact, this has been the case since the civil war with the Taliban began in the mid-1990s. See Ahmed Rashid, *Taliban: Militant Islam, Oil and Fundamentalism in Central Asia* (New Haven, CT: Yale University Press, 2000), 73.

138 *MQSL jia*, 519a. The Yao-Huang bandits are the aforementioned "13 Houses."

139 *MQSL jia*, 519a.

140 Ji Liuqi, *Mingji nanlue* (Beijing: Zhonghua shuju, 1984), 475.

141 Li Zhiting, 229.

142 McDougal, 436.

143 Quanmen, 61.

144 See Hammond, 87–88.

145 Hammond, 88.

146 Quanmen, 132.

147 *YN*, 29.

3 Dueling wills

Dutch administration and Formosan power, 1624–68

Leonard Blussé

After founding Zeelandia Castle in 1624 at the entrance of the bay of Tayouan (near present-day Tainan city) the Dutch East India Company (VOC) came to govern over a large part of Taiwan before it was dislodged from the island by the Chinese Ming loyalist Zheng Chenggong on 1 February 1662 after an eight-month siege.[1] During their thirty-eight-year rule on Formosa (as Taiwan was called at the time) the Dutch merchants amassed, in the course of their daily pursuits, a wealth of archival data about East Asian overseas trade and about the island and its native Austronesian languages speaking peoples. Until quite recently the few Chinese scholars of the Dutch period in Taiwanese history rarely used these archives and instead drew on the selection of contemporary records published in William Campbell's 1903 *Formosa under the Dutch.*[2] Since the appearance of important source publications concerning the VOC on Taiwan, such as the *Dagregisters van het Kasteel Zeelandia* (The Diaries of Zeelandia Castle), *De VOC en Formosa 1624–1662* and *De Missiven van de VOC-gouverneur in Taiwan*, first in Dutch and then in Chinese translation, the study of pre-modern Taiwan has made a dramatic leap forward.[3] Drawing on these newly published data from VOC records various PhD theses have been published in English about Sino-Dutch colonization, the colonial 'civilizing process' of the indigenous population, and the Zheng family.[4]

When on the request of the *Shung ye museum of Formosan aborigines*, Natalie Everts and I began to assemble archival data on the aboriginal population of Taiwan from the VOC archives, we chose *The Formosan Encounter, Notes on Formosa's Aboriginal Society* as the book title of the collection of documents we selected, translated and edited.[5] The selections in that multi-volume source publication reflect not just the various ways in which the servants of the Dutch East India Company perceived indigenous peoples, but also the different types of encounters, and the multiple relationships that were fashioned between the Company and the various tribal communities of Taiwan during the more than forty years of Dutch presence on the island (1624–68).[6] In these sources the Formosan protagonists of the pre-modern past are seen not only thinking and acting independently, but showing notable skill in manipulating their Dutch antagonists. Apart from the proverbial colonial submissiveness of the villagers living in the shadow of the imposing

Zeelandia Castle, one finds in the encounters with the other aboriginal tribal people considerable dynamic agency.

Any encounter between people of different cultural background tells something about differences in norms and values of the interacting persons. In the many testimonies of VOC servants concerning their encounters with native Formosans, a wide range of actions and reactions can be found. Trust, distrust, sympathy and disgust alternate. The deeper one delves into the archival collections of Dutch letters, travel accounts and reports, the more one learns about open and hidden aims and agendas of both sides of the encounter, the important role of those who acted as go-betweens in the cross-cultural traffic, and their aims and agendas in turn.

Surprise encounters

At their first encounter with native Formosans at Soulangh (today's Jiali, north of Tainan) in November 1623, the Dutch merchants Jacob Constant and Barend Pessaert and their indigenous hosts were equally flabbergasted. It was in all respects an "observe, touch and feel" event. The two merchants in the service of the VOC had been sent on a reconnaissance mission from the nearby Pescadores (Peng-hu) archipelago where a fleet had been stationed to open up trade with China. After stepping out of a Chinese sampan, which had taken them a few miles up a river estuary, the two visitors discovered, almost hidden in the bush, a widely laid out town

> with such exquisite buildings that you should take every house for a temple, fenced as they are by whole bamboos on all sides ... So artfully and neatly these houses were shaped, looking like ships turned upside down, that one might believe them built by European master craftsmen rather than by uncivilized people.

The stark naked Soulangh men and women, "a very sturdy and well-built people, taller than our average men by a head and a neck," were not shy at showing their surprise at the appearance of the two neatly dressed Dutchmen: "they opened up our clothes, doublets and trousers to inspect what was inside."

"Nay," adds Constant,

> to put it bluntly, they even had a smell of it and as a result there was hardly any part of our naked body that they did not want to see and smell, both women, young girls and men, without showing any respect, shame or giving it a second thought.

Emphasizing the absence of shame among his hosts, he continued:

> They do not appear to be very jealous of their wives, nor do they think prudishly of the act of procreation, because it so happened that a man

used his wife in a natural way (to put it in decent language) in our presence, whereupon he took her by the hand and led her to us inviting us to commit the same act and replace him at his work. To their amazement we refused, deeming this behaviour unfitting for a Christian.[7]

In short it was all surprise and merry laughter and a bit of embarrassment during that first encounter.

A few weeks later, when the Dutch started cutting timber in the forest near the village of Matauw in order to build a wooden stockade by the sea, the inhabitants of this settlement showed themselves to be neither amused nor tolerant. A large crowd of armed warriors made a surprise attack on the Dutch woodcutters, several of whom were killed. It turned out that the "giants" of Matauw had been jealous of the Dutch amity with the inhabitants of the neighbouring villages with whom they were involved in chronic warfare.

In the following summer of 1624 the Dutch fleet at Penghu, facing a large Chinese invasion force, reached an armistice and retreated to Formosa. On a sand dune at the outer end of a spit of land on the bay of Tayouan, work was started on the construction of Zeelandia Castle, which was to serve as a rendezvous and entrepôt in the VOC's triangular trade between Siam, China and Japan.

Real Politik

In the years that followed, the Dutch were drawn bit by bit into internecine feuding among the headhunting peoples of the southwestern plains of Formosa. On the one hand, the Governor and his council based at Zeelandia Castle sought to prevent quarrels among their headhunting neighbours, but on the other hand they were expected to protect allied communities. Thus the Company gradually created around Zeelandia Castle a colonial state of sorts.[8]

A set of more or less problematic relationships developed, varying from the colonial vertical relationship between the Company as local ruler and its loyal subjects, the allied indigenous villages in the direct vicinity, to a wide variety of relations between ruler and vassal in the more remote regions to the south and the north in the western plains. In the eastern part of the island hidden behind the high central mountain ridge, cross-cultural contacts amounted to little more than occasional ad hoc visits or haphazard attempts to establish trade relations.[9] One fascinating element common to all these various encounters is that, throughout the archival documentation, one can witness the independent agency of highly autonomous indigenous populations at work.

Taiwan's geography determined to a large extent the limitations of Dutch domination over the tribal peoples that were widely, but sparsely spread about the island. Taiwan consists of a long watershed of mountain ridges stretching from north to South, with a large plain on the western side and some smaller plains bordering the Pacific Ocean. It is thus not surprising that the

indigenous people, with whom the VOC entered into more or less stable relationships, lived on the western plains and in the foothills along the strategic
thoroughfares connecting the north and south of the island. The Dutch never
had formal contact with the indigenous groups living in the inner recesses of
the central mountain massif.

Little is known about the pre-modern Formosan "people without history"
from records other than the VOC archives.[10] The observations recorded by
Dutch outsiders early in the seventeenth century provide remarkable insights
into the social structure and customs of the Austronesian languages speaking
people of Taiwan. One finds that these peoples, who varied in political organization and spoke different languages (albeit from the same language family),
were most adept at politics and diplomacy. The Reverend Candidius, after
observing tribal gatherings at Sincan in the late 1620s, wrote:

> When someone is speaking at a village meeting, the others will all be
> silent and listen, even though they are in their thousands. Their elo-
> quence and talent for orating are such that I was extremely surprised by
> them and I think Demosthenes himself could not have been more elo-
> quent and more fluent with words.[11]

Given the great variety of contacts, the people of Sincan considered the VOC
to be a "Stranger King" who could provide protection and solve disputes,
while the villagers of Matauw saw the Dutch as deadly enemies.[12] Others
kept some distance but sought to lure the Company into offering assistance
in conflicts with local enemies. In the case of the Basay of North Formosa,
with whom the Dutch came into contact in the early 1640s, it was even more
complicated: to them the Company was both a rival in trade and a potential
milk cow.

Go-betweens

Human intermediaries, the men or women who made the early cross-cultural
encounters possible and in some respects shaped them, are a key part of the
Dutch colonial narrative. One familiar kind of intermediary in early colonial encounters was the female interpreter, such as Pocahontas in Virginia
and Krotoa alias Eva on the Cape of Good Hope. In the Formosan encounter, young women also played crucial mediating roles. Pieter Nuyts, one of
the first Dutch governors, was smitten by a local belle named Polcke who
kept him informed about local developments. Johanna, discussed later in this
chapter, helped open up relations with the Kavalan people of the Ilan plain.

Other intermediaries included the first two Dutch missionaries on Formosa,
Candidius and Junius. Georgius Candidius took up residence in the village of
Sincan close to Zeelandia Castle. He produced the first detailed anthropological
account of the Siraya people on the request of governor Nuyts, and unwit-
tingly started the process of Dutch territorial expansion on the island. After

this pastor had spent several months in the village preaching the Gospel to little result, the council of village elders agreed that for experimental purposes several families should turn Christian so that after a year or so it could be judged whether this made any difference. To Candidius' relief, that judgment was made in short order, but in a different way than he had imagined. When the village of Sincan was suddenly overrun by neighbouring villagers, the Company was forced to send soldiers to punish the attackers and protect the settlement henceforth because of the presence of Candidius and his Christian flock in its midst. This opened the eyes of the other inhabitants to the benefits of the Christian religion and from then on they willingly converted en masse. The Reverend Robertus Junius, a more martial figure than his confrater Candidius, led the indigenous "Christian allies" of the VOC on several punitive campaigns against local enemies and thereby quickly extended Company rule over a large part, perhaps too great a part, of the island.[13]

As for other intermediaries, we may think of "men on the spot," such as Johan Van Linga and Maarten Wesseling, pioneering individuals who were sent on expeditions in search of the fabled gold mines of Terraboan, on the eastern side of the island. Another key person was the Spanish-speaking interpreter Theodore, a member of the Basay tribe in North Formosa who became the Company's main contact person after the Spaniards left. The Basay as a group were important intermediaries too, because these able traders were in full control of all the trading routes and networks in the northern part of the island.

Ethnic Han Chinese (sojourners from nearby Fujian province) were likewise involved in many local encounters, not only as interpreters but also as route guides. As pedlars, some of them had already visited several places on the West coast, and in the north and the south of the island prior to the arrival of the Dutch. Only the Pacific side of the island, which they called *hou shan*, remained unknown territory to the Chinese. When the Dutch sought to cross the southern foothills of Taiwan on their way to the east coast, a Chinese interpreter played a crucial role in negotiations with a man known as Tartar, ruler of the kingdom of Lonqiaow. Constant and Pessaert, whose reception at Soulangh is described above, had been introduced by an escort known as "Captain China," in actuality one Li Dan, head of a Chinese smuggling ring with an overseas trading network that ranged from Hirado in Japan to the north to as far as Luzon in the South.[14] This same person played an instrumental role in moving the Dutch from Penghu to Formosa in the summer of 1625.

The variety of colonial relations

Although the Dutch wished to concentrate on developing their trade in the East and South China Seas, they were gradually drawn into the local feuds between Formosan villages and piecemeal interventions in local struggles and impositions of sovereignty. This was generally done peacefully but when local resistance arose, armed force was employed. By contrast with the recent past in which local village feuds had been settled with the taking of a few heads, the arrival of the Dutch with their advanced weaponry changed the rules of the game. Clashes between VOC forces and their opponents often resulted in mass killings and in a few cases even in the complete annihilation of set-tlements.[15] Once a domain of allied villages had been assembled, the VOC appointed representatives in each village who were provided with a hat, a stick and a Dutch flag and, if necessary, with a few Dutch soldiers to support their authority in the village. Dutch schoolmasters and clergymen were stationed throughout the Company's domain. The protestant clergy originally also acted as political residents but were later replaced by specifically appointed political administrators.

In matters of religion, the Dutch missionaries, although they initially met with much opposition from native female priestesses, were ultimately quite successful in converting villagers to Christianity, and in teaching them to read and to write in their native languages.[16] In an effort to bring together a growing collection of village domains, the governor of Formosa organized so-called *landdagen* or diets, convened every year or two in the west, north, south and east of the island. Representatives from allied villages were received by the governor and his councillors at these gatherings, where they were wined and dined and exhorted to keep peace with one another and to renew their allegiance to the Company.

While the Company was successful in suppressing internecine strife and concomitant headhunting practices in the villages of the western plains that acknowledged its rule, it was never able to achieve such peace in the more remote parts of the island. In these areas, their vassals resisted Dutch attempts to formalize colonial administration by introducing a uniform system of trib-ute and taxation. Especially in the north, the reactions of villages ranged from reluctant cooperation to open resistance. Under orders issued by Governor-General Antonio van Diemen (r. 1636–45) in Batavia, the allied villages were directed to reciprocate "the blessings of colonial rule" by delivering tribute in the form of deerskins or rice supplies. As it gradually became clear to the vassals that the Dutch could not possibly contain the occasional raids by still unpacified hill tribes, they refused to deliver apportioned tribute because they were not receiving the protection against those raids that had been promised. Since the *quid pro quo* formula did not work, the imposition of a colonial state organization throughout the north of Taiwan failed and finally was given up. Ironically, locally stationed VOC servants ended up handing out small gifts to village heads to ensure their loyalty.

After the countryside on the southwest coast, in the neighbourhood of Zeelandia Castle, had been pacified, large numbers of Chinese settlers were encouraged to move to Formosa from Fujian. These migrants set their hands to the plough and within twenty years the countryside of the southwestern plain had been transformed from hunting fields into extended rice paddies and sugarcane plantations. The VOC assured profitable revenues by farming out the taxation of the indigenous villages to Chinese tax farmers. This enterprise failed in 1652 when the mutual trust that had existed between the Dutch administrators and the Chinese settlers collapsed. One of the Chinese headmen, Guo Fayi (*Fayett*), raised a rebellion that was bloodily suppressed with the assistance of indigenous tribesmen. Suddenly the Formosans were allowed again to hunt (Chinese) heads and were even rewarded for this.[17]

VOC documents produced at various levels in the Company hierarchy, from the Gentlemen XVII, the Directors of the VOC in the Dutch Republic, to the Governor General in Batavia, and from there to the Governor of Formosa, show how "native policy" was continually discussed and shaped by different administrators. Time and again the directors in Holland admonished their personnel to behave in a restrained way in their dealings with the native populations of Taiwan. In 1655 they wrote:

> The inhabitants over there should be treated well and shielded and protected from molestation and injustice [...]. We should bear in mind that we did not come to Formosa, nor have we taken domicile there, in order to rule over the inhabitants and dominate them, much less terrorize them. We see – God forbid – this is only too often being committed by our people. Instead we should only shield and protect them from all violence, be it from within or without and consequently allow them to lead a peaceful life under us.[18]

Much surviving documentation shows the many difficulties experienced by VOC servants in attempting to apply this facially proper directive from on high.

Gold fever

The Company administration in Zeelandia Castle felt strong enough by 1641 to replace the Spaniards as colonial rulers in the northern part of Taiwan. In the following year the Spanish fort of San Salvador in Quelang (Jilong) was forced to surrender without much effort. One reason the Dutch were so keen on removing the Spaniards from the north was that they still believed in the existence of fabled gold mines at a place called Terraboan, somewhere on the unexplored eastern side of the island. In the late 1630s, attempts had already been made to find a way to the other side of the island via the South. With the Spanish now out of the way, it was time to approach the legendary gold fields from the north and south.

Explorative expeditions were mounted from the 1640s onwards. Some proceeded in part by ship and in part by land along the rugged rocky east coast from Jilong down to the south, and some proceeded from Zeelandia Castle in an eastern direction via the foothills of the southern promontories where the kingdom of Lonqiouw was located. In order to follow the latter route, a treaty had to be negotiated with Tartar, the king of Lonqiouw, to permit expeditions to cross his territory. Another treaty had to be reached with the Puyuma tribe at Pimaba (in the area of today's Taitung City) on the East coast before the Dutch could proceed northwards to the Terraboan region where the gold mine was said to exist. The encounters with these rulers, and the means by which they bent the Company's desires to their own agendas, deserve attention.

In contrast with the southwestern plains, where the Company dealt with acephalous societies (tribal peoples that, except for age groups, do not have hierarchical rulers), the VOC encountered in the south in Lonqiouw a kingdom governed by the aforementioned ruler called Tartar. Before an expedition could be sent to the East coast of the island, permission for free passage had to be sought. In 1636, a Chinese pedlar who spoke the local language, called Lampack, was sent to Tartar with presents and the request for a treaty with the Company. The messenger explained his good intentions, and Tartar replied: "If the Dutch desire to live at peace with us, it is well; if not, it is also well." Clearly the proud ruler was not much impressed by the foreigners. When he was told that the VOC possessed a strong army to be reckoned with, he shrugged his shoulders and replied, "the Dutch would not be able to climb the high mountains and if they did and proved too powerful for him, he would flee and climb still higher."[19]

After lengthy negotiations, Tartar agreed to let his brother make a personal visit to Zeelandia Castle where he was received with cannonades, blares of trumpets and pomp and circumstance. Now impressed by reports of the Dutch show of arms, Tartar signed a peace treaty allowing free passage through his territory but also providing him with protection against his enemies. It soon dawned upon the Dutch why the Lonqiouw ruler changed his mind and signed the treaty. In offering himself as intermediary for the encounter with Pimaba, Tartar expected to march with Company soldiers to the eastern part of the island and to join an attack on Pimaba, which he considered a mortal enemy. This objective was not shared by the Dutch commander who wished to strike an alliance with Pimaba. Consequently, he decided to mount, even if against Dutch interest, a joint expedition with Tartar against another enemy of his, to satisfy the latter's wishes and temper his bellicose attitude towards Pimaba.

When, in 1638, Johan Van Linga, at the head of 150 Dutch soldiers and some 500 Lonqiouw warriors under the command of Tartar, finally marched to the east coast, they were met at the other side of the mountains by Magol, the local chief of Pimaba, and a phalanx of fighters ready to defend themselves. All kinds of peaceful gestures were made by Van Linga, whereupon he was suddenly cordially embraced by the Pimaba headman, who dramatically took his crown from his head and placed it on Van Linga's, saying, "May this hat, which I have inherited from my ancestors … serve as a sign of our union through which my people will find out that we have become the Company's allies and that you have become my friend." The astonished Van Linga in turn placed his own hat on Magol's head and answered perhaps a bit prosaically

"I bestowe on you the uppermost cover of my body which is held by my own troops in high esteem."[20]

In the years that followed it turned out that Magol, the ruler of Pimaba, was also shrewdly capitalizing on the Dutch presence in his territory in order to enlarge his regional power. In his village he created room for a small VOC trading lodge and gave the local VOC representative Maarten Wesselingh authority to make peace with traditionally hostile neighbouring villages so that the path to the fabled Terraboan gold mines might be opened. By the time it had been ascertained that there was no such gold mine but that gold dust was sifted from the river in the vicinity of Terraboan, and Wesseling had been murdered during a drunken brawl, the ruler of Pimaba had, thanks to his use of the Dutch diplomatic intervention, tripled his domain in all directions. This skillful maneuvering one may call statesmanship and it certainly belies standard representations of supine, exploited indigenous peoples.

Heading North

In the north the Dutch faced a completely different challenge. This was not "virgin territory." Since 1626, the Spaniards had been occupying Danshui (Tamsuy/Tamsui) on the northwest and Jilong on the northeast coast where they had built respectively a gun tower and a castle. Spanish missionaries were active in the region and had converted a large number of people, especially among members of the Basay tribe who moved to the direct vicinity of the strongholds in order to provide the Spaniards with needed supplies. As a result, the Dutch encountered some people who spoke Spanish and knew how to get along with Europeans. Despite this the VOC servants who were stationed at Danshui and Jilong after 1642 were baffled by the uneasy relations with local peoples. For their part, the locals quickly realized that the Dutch garrisons, especially at Danshui, were so small that the Dutch could not possibly control the region. In the autumn of 1655, Junior Merchant Thomas van Mildert complained that he was unable to punish a group of ruffians who upon killing all his cattle had tried to assault his redoubt at Danshui. His men were "trapped like mice" in their stronghold, and hardly dared to venture outside the gate. "Hence the Formosan is playing the master and we, who seem to have supreme power, have to content ourselves with fawning instead of using force," Van Mildert sighed in despair.[21]

This state of affairs stirred up recalcitrant behaviour among the inhabitants including some revival of headhunting. Young men in the allied villages rose to challenge the authority of their own village chiefs, who ruled in the name of the Company. Van Mildert reports that one day the *cabessa* (chief) of the village of Chenaer and his family came to see him "with tears in their eyes," complaining about obstinate men in their village who brandishing bow and arrows and slapping their behinds were shouting abusive slogans like: "What is the Company and what kind of people are you, who are under its obedience? If we want to, we could shoot you down right away…"[22]

This was not just an isolated incident. Various documents manifest the ire of indigenous peoples provoked by what they felt to be the overbearing behaviour and unreasonable demands of locally stationed soldiers of the Company. Commenting on this, Governor Cornelis Caesar wrote that the people living in the neighbourhood of Danshui and Jilong were "much more civilized" than the inhabitants to the south thanks to the former efforts of the Spanish missionaries. He advised the chiefs of the northern outposts that:

> for that reason you must treat them very courteously and not call them dogs, scoundrels and the like. For they have to some extent absorbed the Spanish nature of containing themselves whenever they are being scolded, but will not hesitate to take their revenge if an opportunity arises later on, even if it cost them their lives.[23]

In all colonial societies go-betweens helped facilitate relations between the colonial ruler and the ruled. That role was played in the southwestern plains of Formosa by Dutch missionaries or by ethnic Han Chinese, who collected taxes and often acted as interpreters or guides for the colonial administration. In its northern establishments, VOC garrisons relied heavily on the services of the Basay people, who lived scattered among various villages. The Basay village of Tappare (Tapparij) adjoined redoubt Anthonio at Tamsuy, on the East side of the island. North of Jilong was situated the Basay village of St. Jago. The larger Basay village of Kimaurij was located across the bay.

The Basay people monopolized the river and the coastal trades of North Formosa from their river mouth settlements. Their strategic position was similar to that of the Malays in the Indonesian Archipelago, whose language functioned like Basay in North Formosa as the *lingua franca* of regional trade. The Basay were able to move freely through the territory of other and even hostile tribes, because local villagers knew it would be foolish to kill these providers of staple goods and services.

The two northern VOC garrisons were thus completely dependent on the Basay, who were their primary sources of information, as well as providers of essential food supplies, which were purchased from tribal villages in the Danshui River Basin. Thomas van Iperen, *opperhoofd* of the VOC Tamsuy redoubt, wrote that Basay interpreters provided him with local knowledge and information about the past by consulting "the archives of the villages, namely the memories of the most elderly." Because of their instrumental role in providing vital supplies to the Dutch garrisons, the Basay were able to control markets, forcing up the price of foodstuffs as they liked.

In addition to their business pursuits, the Basay were involved in coal mining and the forging of iron. While engaged in mining coal for the VOC, they regularly requested iron implements from the Dutch to replenish their stocks. It gradually came home to the Dutch that the Basay miners and blacksmiths were actually using the iron pinch bars and chisels for other purposes than mining. Parts of the iron implements were being resold at a high price to neighbouring tribes in the mountains who used them to fashion arrow heads and spear points. The VOC archives brim with complaints about the unreliability of the Basay.

The Dutch also relied on the Basay for local travel. They commuted in Basay canoes between Danshui and Jilong via the Danshui and Pinnerouan Rivers, a strenuous trip which took at least 24 hours, including crossing the mountain watershed that separated the two rivers. Via the coastal waters, the Lan Yang plain and, even farther south, the territory of Terraboan could also be reached by seagoing Basay canoes or *proas*.

The only lowland area of Formosa that remained little known to the Dutch for a comparatively long time was the homeland of the Kavalan tribe, the Lan Yang (or Ilan) plain on the northeast coast, hemmed in by high mountains and the sea, and situated between Jilong to the north and Terraboan to the south. This fertile plain was difficult to reach until very recent times. Han Chinese settlers came into this region as late as the nineteenth century, driving out the Kavalan in the direction of present-day Hualian. Yet it was not simply the inaccessible geographical situation that kept the VOC out of the Lan Yang region. The principal reason the Dutch gained little grip on the Kavalan people had to do with existing trading networks that the Basay people manipulated and actively sought to preserve. Heavily relying on the Basay as informants and purveyors of foodstuffs from the Kavalan people, it took some time before the Dutch realized that instead of serving the needs of the Company, the Basay were actually interfering to their (undisclosed) private benefit.

In September 1644, Captain Pieter Boons, who was stationed with his troops at Jilong Castle, was sent by the governor of Formosa to "The Bight of Kavalan" (Lan Yang plain) to proclaim to the forty villages of *Cavalangh* that the Company had taken possession of the whole island of Formosa and that all the inhabitants (except for some rebels) were showing obedience. The Kavalan people were invited to follow and pay a yearly tribute, in exchange for which the Company would protect them from their enemies.[24] Thirty villages sent representatives and promised tribute. Fourteen villages did not appear. Two – Sochel-Sochel and Kakitapan – refused

> in a mocking and despicable way, knocking on their heels saying that they were not the ones to ask for the Dutch [to come]. But if the Dutch wanted to meet with them they could come freely, as they were strong enough to withstand them.[25]

Boons responded by attacking the two villages, and setting fire to their dwellings, including granaries stocked with rice. Yet in the years that followed, few villages were willing to pay tribute, especially when they realized that the VOC was either unwilling or unable to station soldiers in the region and to maintain order and give them protection. This early attempt to cause the Kavalan people to pay tribute to the Dutch in Jilong thus failed miserably.

Boons' expedition and succeeding attempts to contact the Kavalan people always relied on Basay helpers. Throughout the 1640s and the early 1650s trade with the Kavalan was dominated by Basay villagers from Kimaurij, their settlement close to Jilong Castle. As purveyors of food and other vital supplies to the Dutch they took full advantage of their intermediary position. In 1657, Pieter Boons, by then a chief merchant, reported to Batavia that the VOC had been "blindfolded for many years" by the Basay. He had finally found out that the Basay from Kimaurij who visited the Kavalan plain annually in the name of the Company, commonly came back with bountiful supplies of rice, skins and slaves, which they first hid in their village before showing up at the castle with almost empty hands.[26] The Basay also invited Kavalan people to bring rice and skins in their own *proas* to Kimaurij and then told the Dutch chief of Jilong that these visitors came to honour him, so that the latter would feel obliged to feed and entertain them. This so infuriated Boons that he sent his assistant Balbiaen on a fact-finding mission into Kavalan territory.

Balbiaen left by canoe for Kavalan where he was warmly welcomed by the natives who told him that they preferred to trade directly with the Dutch either in their own territory or in Jilong rather than through the Basay who "would give them rags or trash for their deerskins" while the Dutch paid in Spanish silver coins. The villagers of Talabiawan, which Balbiaen described as the central market place of the entire Lan Yang plain, proposed that some Dutchmen should come and live among them to engage in trade. The Kavalan realized they had been fooled for years by the Basay from Kimaurij. To avoid further misunderstandings, they requested that those in the service of the Company should henceforth carry a distinctive sign so that they might recognize true representatives of the VOC. If these conditions were met, the villages were willing to be obedient. It thus became clear to the Dutch that gruesome stories told by the Kimaurij Basay that if any Dutchman appeared among the Kavalan he would be beaten to death might be quite misleading. The outcome of this was that Pieter Boons invited the Kavalan villages to attend the next annual convention of the Northern villages.

A group of Kavalan village elders showed up on that occasion. These headmen or *cabessas* were all presented with a cane mounted with a silver knob as a sign of their dignity. When asked whether their obedience was voluntary, the *cabessas* answered that this was the case although there were admittedly some rascals living in the Lan Yang plain "who enriched themselves by pillaging and roaming around." They also complained about incursions into their land by tribal people living in the mountains situated between Kavalan and Terraboan in the South and kept asking for assistance against these intruders. VOC management postponed a decision on their requests "because we have obtained little information about the area and also have other objections."[27] The nature of the "other objections" is unclear, but may have related to concerns about the impending threat of a Chinese invasion by Zheng Chenggong in the southwest of Taiwan, which would make it unwise to station troops elsewhere. Thus unable to send a detachment of soldiers, the Chief of Jilong Castle, Nicolaes Loenius, sent his assistant Nicolaes van der Meulen and his wife Johanna, who was of Basay descent, to the village of Talabiawan in Ilan to investigate local conditions.

Some time passed before Van der Meulen was able to submit his report. He and his wife both fell ill upon arrival in Talabiawan, and when at long last he found the strength to write he did so in a gloomy mood:

> We regret that in this first letter we are not able to send Your Honour good news. On the contrary I have to write you sad tidings [...] this Kavalan nation is more and more starting to fall back again into its old ways of catching and snaring, even murdering fellow countrymen.

He went on to report that the headman of one village had treacherously cut the throat of another *cabessa* who had earlier fled to another village. The victim had been granted a Company cane, an emblem of VOC power. His murder thus challenged Dutch authority. Van der Meulen complained that, because he was unable to arrest the murderers, the people off Talabiawan had begun to act quite unfriendly towards him and his wife as well.

In his initial reports, Pieter Boons had commented on the beauty of the Kavalan countryside with its well-tended rice paddies. But was Kavalan society a peaceful, prosperous agricultural community surrounded by cruel enemies in the mountains, or were the Kavalan themselves engaged in chronic warfare with each other? Van der Meulen seemed to suggest the latter. Nicolaes Loenius responded by recalling Van der Meulen and his wife. The Company would content itself with Basay go-betweens, who were at least willing to brave the dangers of Kavalan society. The decision to withdraw Van de Meulen and his wife Johanna was welcomed by the governor of Taiwan, Frederic Coyett. He wrote to Loenius:

> We should not risk the lives of even a few people in Kavalan, much less a larger number of people and more expenses. You will tell the Kavalan people that, because they squabble so much among themselves and the profits there for the Honourable Company are still so small, we cannot keep any residents there, let alone incur greater expense founded on dubious expectations. You will, however, exhort them to make mutual peace and to come to us as friends with their merchandise and also participate in the annual *Landdag* in Jilong. In that case Dutchmen may be once more stationed there by the Honourable Company (if the people wish us to), when it sees that greater peace reigns and that more profit is to be gained there.[28]

Governor Coyett had to wait until the winter of 1661 before he received a reply. When Loenius' letter reached him it did so from an astonishing location – the island of Deshima in Japan. Coyett was not the only one to be surprised by Loenius. Hendrick Indijck, the VOC chief at Deshima, describes in his diary of 5 July 1661 how quite unexpectedly two Company vessels from Jilong arrived in Nagasaki with 170 passengers on board: 114 Company servants, thirty women and children and twenty-six male and female slaves.[29] This sudden arrival caused Indijck much trouble: where was he going to lodge all these people until they could finally leave with the northern monsoon in the autumn?

What forced Loenius to take the momentous decision to evacuate all personnel and leave Jilong Castle unattended? He wrote that, after hearing about Zheng Chenggong's April 30, 1661 invasion, he decided in June 1661 to depart before things got worse. Security measures had undoubtedly played a role in taking this far-reaching decision. As Loenius felt that he would not receive any assistance in case of a sudden Chinese assault, he had to evacuate to Japan, and thanks to the prevailing southern monsoon he was able to do so forthwith.

The situation was indeed bleak. When the Basay heard of Zheng Chenggong's landing at Tayouan, they cancelled all collaboration with the Dutch. They incited locals in the Danshui estuary to revolt against the small garrison in the redoubt by the river mouth, who for want of food were then forced to withdraw themselves to Jilong. What has Loenius to say about this sudden change of attitude by the Basay? His letter records the complaints by the Basay, "who had been continually crying out and insisting that they would no longer be slaves of the Honorable Company, meanwhile complaining about the low, stingy payment which was paid for their services."[30]

The wrath of the Basay

The indignant Basay presented Loenius with a detailed list of grievances. Their nine specific complaints illuminate a problematic relationship with the Dutch. Their frustrations spill out on the page. While the Basay doubtless took some pleasure in giving Loenius a kick as they saw the Dutch preparing to depart, their litany clearly expresses an indigenous voice and the view of this particular group of Formosans. First of all the Basay complained about unfulfilled promises of payment for deliveries they had made. They felt unjustly treated because Loenius had not allowed them to bring along their own trade commodities on his recent trip to the allegedly gold-producing village of Terraboang, "their vessels were searched so thoroughly that they could take hardly anything to trade for provisions." They had been ridiculously underpaid – "only some Chinese tobacco" – for their services as ferrymen and transporters for the chief and his staff on his trips to Danshui and back. "Their children were forced to go to school and could not get permission at any time to forage for food" and anyone who went elsewhere without permission was condemned to "bring to the fort some baskets of oyster shells or coral." Whenever they wished to purchase a piece of cloth from a Dutchman: "they had to pay three Spanish reals for it." In these and their other listed grievances, the Basay sought to end what they felt to be long-standing injustices. For his part, Loenius maintained that all these "deceptive and sly pretences" were not that surprising because the Basay were "opposing our policy in the field of trade, because it runs completely contrary to their selfish, false and miserly nature," and he stressed that their "revolt" had not really made him decide to leave, but when stirred by the Basay the people of Danshui and Kavalan had also risen, giving the Dutch no other choice than to leave. Without a steady supply of food the garrison could not survive. Under these circumstance Loenius was powerless. It was as simple as that.

The aftermath

On 1 February 1662, Governor Frederick Coyett surrendered Zeelandia Castle to the Chinese warlord Zheng Chenggong (Koxinga). Yet the sun had not finally set on the period of Dutch rule in Taiwan. When the Company management saw new trade opportunities in the Manchu struggle for the control of the southeastern coastal provinces of China, it decided to join forces with the Qing in fighting the Zheng forces. A large fleet was sent to the Chinese coast under the command of Admiral Balthazar Bort, who decided that it made strategic sense to reoccupy the Jilong fort.[31] On 27 August 1664, he arrived with a fleet of eleven ships and took over the still empty castle without meeting any Chinese or local resistance.[32] The Basay appeared at the castle gate the next day and again offered their services. Lo and behold, after a short time even the Kavalan people sent *proas* loaded with foodstuffs, deerskins and pots to Jilong Castle. Friendships and former trading relationships were thus renewed. When they were asked to come henceforth directly to the castle instead of sailing to the Basay village of Kimaurij, the Kavalan gladly consented. Even Johanna, now known as Mrs. Johanna Verlicht since her remarriage after the death of Nicolaes van der Meulen, returned in the company of assistant Adriaen van Laer to Talabiawan, where the people were delighted to see her again.[33] In the summer of 1667 the last *landdag* was held and all the headmen of the Basay, the Kavalang as well as those of Tarraboan were invited to the fort, where they were merrily regaled with food, drink, pipes and tobacco "according to their custom, as used to be done." Before long, however, the VOC determined that the Jilong outpost served no useful economic function for the Company and a final decision was made to depart permanently from Taiwan. On 6 July 1668, Governor-General Joan Maetsuijcker ordered the abandonment of the fort and its destruction with explosives.[34]

In conclusion

In her study on the colonization process of the peoples living in the vicinity of Zeelandia Castle, Ch'iu Hsin-hui has pointed out how these villages through the years became part of the colonial economy and ended up in the claws of Chinese tax farmers.[35] This is without doubt what happened: because of the

Company's intervention in the indigenous communities far and wide around Zeelandia Castle, the monetization of the local economy, and the reclamation by Chinese immigrants of the indigenous hunting fields, laid the basis for the later Chinese colonization of the island. In that sense her findings corroborate the co-colonization argument made by Tonio Andrade.[36] Indeed it cannot be stressed enough that, in that sense, "Taiwan was made in Holland." When Zheng Chenggong and his kinsfolk took over in 1662 they had at their disposal an infrastructure that enabled them to incorporate the western plain of the island into the Chinese economy and culturesphere. Yet it would take two more centuries, and a Japanese intervention, to annex also the other parts of the island.

This essay seeks to show areas of tension between the servants of the VOC and the native Formosans. How did they react to each other, and how did they cooperate or go about contesting each other? The records show that the indigenous people often stood up for their own causes and whenever possible shifted mutual relations in their favor. Many historians have asserted that the VOC archives are a typical representation of colonial power relations that provide a one-sided view of the Asian world. That shrewd observation would seem to labor an obvious point, because in their reports the Company servants of course described their *faits et gestes* in the Tropics as it suited them. Yet in reality the situation is considerably more complicated as this short essay demonstrates. Whoever looks for indigenous voices plodding "with and against the grain" of the colonial source material, will discover complicated mutual human relationships and the protection of native interests in the Asian world in which Company servants sought to edge their way forward. They will also discover surprising examples of cultural exchange and evidence of how colonial projects were negotiated, received and manipulated at the local level with frequently unforeseen, but often significant consequences.

Notes

1 VOC is the abbreviation of the *Verenigde Oost-Indische Compagnie*, the chartered Dutch East India Company that existed between 1602 and 1799. The VOC archives are preserved today at the *Nationaal Archief*, The Hague.

2 The great exception, of course, was Ts'ao Yung-ho. 曹永和, 台湾早期历史研究, 台北 1979. William Campbell, *Formosa under the Dutch. Described from Contemporary Records with Explanatory Notes and a Bibliography of the Island* (London, 1903).

3 L. Blussé, N. Everts, W. Milde and Ts'ao Ying-ho eds, *De Dagregisters van het Kasteel Zeelandia, Taiwan*. Rijksgeschiedkundige Publicatien, Grote Serie, ('s-Gravenhage, 1986–2000), 4 vols; Chiang Shu-sheng, 江樹生 ed. and trans, *Relandicheng reji* 热兰迪城日记 (Tainan, 2000–11), 4 vols, Cheng Shaogang, De VOC en Formosa 1624–1662 (Leiden, 1995); 程绍刚, Helanren zai Fuermosha 荷兰人在福而摩莎 (Taipei, 2000). Chiang Shu-sheng, 江树生, 荷兰联合东印度公司台湾长官至巴达维亚 总督书信集 *De missiven van de*

VOC-gouverneur in Taiwan aan de Gouverneur-generaal te Batavia (1622–1636), 5 vols (Taichung, 2010–15, National Museum of Taiwan History), 5 vols.

4 Tonio Andrade, *How Taiwan Became Chinese: Dutch, Spanish, and Han Colonization in the Seventeenth Century* (New York, 2007); *Chiu Hsin-hui, The Colonial "Civilising Process" in Dutch Formosa, 1624–1662* (Leiden, 2008). Cheng Wei-chung, *War, Trade and Piracy in the China Seas 1622–1683* (Leiden, 2013). Xing Hang, *Conflict and Commerce in Maritime East Asia: The Zheng Family and the Shaping of the Modern World* (Cambridge, UK, 2016).

5 L. Blussé and N. Everts, *The Formosan Encounter, Notes on Formosan Aboriginal Society* (1623–1668), 4 vols (Taipei: Shung Ye Museum of Aborigines, 1999–2010).

6 These dates may require explanation. Although Zeelandia Castle was surrendered to Zheng Chenggong on February 1, 1662, the Dutch garrison of the fort in Jilong returned in 1664 and remained there until it was finally withdrawn five years later in 1668.

7 Ibid., 14, 21, 17.

8 See for details: Tonio Andrade, "The Mightiest Village: Geopolitics and Diplomacy in the Formosan Plains, 1623–1636," in *Ping pu zu qun yu Taiwan li shi wen hua lun wen ji* 平埔族群與臺灣歷史文化論文集, edited by Pan Inghai (潘英海) and Chan Su-chuan (詹素娟), Taipei, 2001.

9 For a few useful Chinese sources that predate the Dutch arrival see: Laurence G. Thompson, "The Earliest Chinese Eyewitness Accounts of the Formosan Aborigines," *Monumenta Serica*, 23 (1964), 163–204.

10 For a few useful Chinese sources that predate the Dutch arrival see: Laurence G. Thompson, "The Earliest Chinese Eyewitness Accounts of the Formosan Aborigines," *Monumenta Serica*, 23 (1964), 163–204.

11 Ibid., vol. 1, 121.

12 David Henley, "Conflict, Justice and the Stranger King, Indigenous Roots of Colonial Rule in Indonesia and Elsewhere," *Modern Asian Studies*, 38.1 (2004), 85–144.

13 "Dutch Protestant Missionaries as Protagonists of the Territorial Expansion of the VOC on Formosa," in D. Kooiman (ed.), *Conversion, Competition and Conflict* (Amsterdam, 1984), 155–84.

14 Iwao Seiichi, "Litan 李旦, Chief of the Chinese Residents at Hirado, Japan in the Last Days of the Ming Dynasty," *The Memoirs of the Toyo Bunko*, 17 (1958), 27–83.

15 Leonard Blussé, "The Cave of the Black Spirits: Searching for a Vanished People," in David Blundell (ed.), *Austronesian Taiwan, Linguistics, History, Ethnology, and Prehistory* (Berkeley, 2002), 131–50.

16 Leonard Blussé, "The Eclipse of the Inibs: The Dutch Protestant Mission in 17th Century Taiwan and its Persecution of Native Priestesses," in Yeh Chuen-rong (ed.), *History, Culture and Ethnicity, Selected Papers from the International Conference on the Formosan Indigenous Peoples* (Taipei, 2006), 71–88.

17 Jan Huber, "Chinese Settlers Against the Dutch East India Company: The Rebellion Led by Kuo Huai-I on Taiwan in 1652," in E.Vermeer (ed.), *Development and Decline of Fukien Province in the 17th and 18th Centuries* (Leiden, 1990), 265–96.

18 "Missive of the Directors of the Amsterdam Chamber to Governor-general and Council," Amsterdam, 16 April 1655 in *The Formosan Encounter*, IV, 25.

19 *The Formosan Encounter*, II, 60–64. Ch'iu Hsin-hui, *The Colonial "Civilising Process" in Dutch Formosa, 1624–1662* (Leiden, 2008), 73.
20 *The Formosan Encounter*, II, 176.
21 *The Formosan Encounter*, IV, 157.
22 *The Formosan Encounter*, IV, 156.
23 *The Formosan Encounter*, IV, 171.
24 *The Formosan Encounter*, II, 459.
25 *The Formosan Encounter*, II, 475. Letter of 12 October 1644.
26 Missive Merchant Pieter Boons to Governor Frederick Coyett, *Formosan Encounter*, IV, 346–67.
27 Missive Governor-General Joan Maetsuijcker to Governor Frederick Coyett and the Council of Formosa, 26 July 1658. *Formosan Encounter*, IV, 413.
28 Governor Frederick Coyett to Merchant Nicolaes Loenius, 14 April 1661. *Formosan Encounter*, IV, 439.
29 Cynthia Viallé and Leonard Blussé, "The Deshima Dagregisters," *Intercontinenta*, 27, vol. XIII (Leiden, 2010), 16–19.
30 *Formosan Encounter*, IV, 460.
31 John E. Wills, *Pepper, Guns, & Parleys, The Dutch East India Company and China, 1662–1681* (Cambridge, MA, 1974).
32 *Formosan Encounter*, IV, 495.
33 *Formosan Encounter*, IV, 632.
34 John E. Wills, "The Dutch Reoccupation of Chi-lung, 1664–1668," in Leonard Blussé (ed.), *Around and About Formosa, Essays in Honor of Professor Ts'ao Yung-ho* (Taipei, 2003), 273–90.
35 Chiu Hsin-hui, *The Colonial "Civilising Process" in Dutch Formosa, 1624–1662* (Leiden, 2008).
36 Tonio Andrade, *How Taiwan became Chinese. Dutch, Spanish and Han Colonization in the Seventeenth Century* (New York, 2008).

4 Sultan Hasanuddin's rationale for re-expansion

Avenging Tiworo's defeat in the seascape of the spice wars

Jennifer L. Gaynor

Trading systems, interregional cultural exchange, migrations, and diasporic communities have received substantial consideration in studies of Southeast Asia and its surrounding seas. Yet, Southeast Asia's mariners, and the political and social systems they were part of, still seem so opaque. This chapter examines specific connections and interactions along and between coasts, as well as a shift in the relations between maritime-oriented people and particular powers in Sulawesi (Celebes), to contribute to a clearer understanding of how seventeenth-century maritime dynamics in Southeast Asia interfaced with politics and society above the high-water mark.

During the seventeenth century, networks of Southeast Asian maritime-oriented people – "sea people" – were intimately allied with the ruling families of land-based realms. They held positions of rank in those realms, and also led more amphibious polities focused on the littoral. For instance, during the 1660s and 1670s, Sama leaders, or *papuq*, at times held the prominent post of Harbormaster or Chief-of-Port (Mak. *sabannaraq*, Indon./Malay *syahbandar*) in Makassar. Just prior to the attack on Makassar in 1667 by the VOC (Dutch East India Company) and its allies, Arung Palakka, the famous Bugis man from Boné who led those allies, armed and elevated sixty men from Tiworo to comprise half his Guard of Prime Commanders. Tiworo, with its boats and skilled mariners, had previously been a staunch ally of Makassar. Located in the Straits of Tiworo's protected waters and along their perimeter, this fortified non-urban maritime hub provided a haven for fleets sailing under Makassar, and a staging area for conflicts further east. These positions of rank and alliance show that, although Southeast Asia's sea people have often been considered stateless, they took a more direct part in the concerns of states than just provisioning ports, patrons, and rulers with the bounty of the seas and the booty of coastal raiding (see Map 4.1).

Through positions of maritime leadership and the control of key geographic sites in the littoral, such as Tiworo, sea people also played a vital role in opposing European efforts to dominate the spice trade. Based on VOC archives and Sulawesi manuscripts, this new understanding of sea people in regional dynamics adds to the revision of a world history narrative that portrays the spice wars as a conflict between competing European mercantile

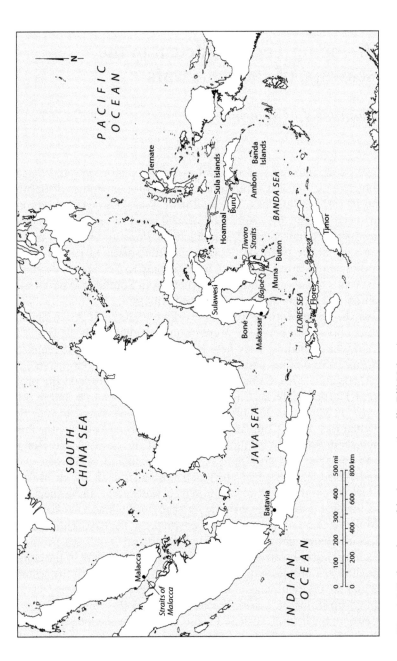

Map 4.1 Indonesian archipelago map (credit: Bill Nelson)

empires. Yet the view of the maritime past presented here does more than alter a Eurocentric narrative. Both here and in my book, *Intertidal History in Island Southeast Asia: Submerged Genealogy and the Legacy of Coastal Capture*, I show how under-utilized European and Southeast Asian sources open a window onto Southeast Asia's maritime past, offering a view that demonstrates the pivotal place of sea people in the dynamics of politics, trade, littoral society, and military cooperation. On the one hand, this helps to integrate the archipelagic past in wider frameworks of Asian maritime history along with the Indian Ocean and the South China Sea. On the other hand, by examining sea people's involvement in archipelagic networks of politics and kinship, this work shows that littoral society was emphatically not just based in cities.[1]

Scholarship on early modern Southeast Asia places less stress on the spice wars as a competition between mercantile empires, and more emphasis on examining how agents of European companies formed alliances with regional polities to obtain spices cheaply, especially cloves and nutmeg, and to subjugate those who opposed these aims. Non-European maritime aspects of the spice wars have received little attention, with the exception of Gerrit Knaap's examination of *hongi* expeditions in the Moluccas, at the far eastern end of what is now Indonesia. He explains how European overlords, first the Portuguese and then the Dutch, incorporated the practice of *hongi* maritime raids, previously carried out by federations of Moluccan chiefdoms, into the colonial arsenal of punitive attacks on spice growers. Knaap has also presented data from Dutch sources on how much support, in manpower and munitions, Moluccan spice growers received from Makassar during the conflicts of the mid-1650s, known as the Great Ambon War.[2]

The present chapter brings within a single frame both the Great Ambon War and the later Makassar War, to show how the Straits of Tiworo formed a fulcrum in the seascape of the spice wars. Although trounced with much luck by VOC forces and their Ternatan allies in 1655, over the next dozen years Tiworo rebuilt. Its resurgence was linked to Makassar's campaign of re-expansion in the eastern archipelago. A threat to Dutch interests, Makassar's re-expansion contributed to the decision by the VOC's Admiral Cornelis Speelman to attack the port of Makassar itself, yet only after subduing Tiworo a second time in 1667.

Makassar's Sultan Hasanuddin justified the expansionist actions of his fleet during the inter-war years with the explanation that he would not have had to maintain his rights to the lands in question if Ternate had not attacked the Makassar territory of "Pancana." Pancana, also known in the sources by the variants "Pantsiano" and "Pangesane," is now known as the island of Muna. However, in this case, the name Pancana was, in fact, a reference to Tiworo. In addition to clarifying this reference to Tiworo, specifically a reference to the 1655 attack on Tiworo conducted by Ternate together with the VOC, the discussion below examines why, as Admiral Speelman called it, "that nasty pirates' nest, Tiworo," mattered so much to Sultan Hasanuddin that his rationale for re-expansion lay in avenging it.[3]

Littoral society

The colonial labeling of sea people as "pirates," an epithet that disavowed them of legitimacy, also located them discursively beyond the bounds of states. Their portrayal as sea nomads or sea gypsies, both in colonial and in scholarly literatures, has similarly situated them as mobile and deterritorialized, supposedly beyond the reach of political authorities. Yet, as touched on above, sources show that during the seventeenth century, maritime-oriented Southeast Asians, such as the Sama (called by others the "Bajo" or "Bajau"), were part of a vibrant, politically interconnected, and socially complex seascape.[4] Their appearance in period sources therefore departs from the usual portrayal of sea people as peripheral. During the early modern period they were not peripheral to states, politics, or war. Rather, what they were peripheral to was simply the land.

Much scholarship, even in maritime history, labors under what the Atlanticist Marcus Rediker has called a *terracentric* bias, that is, a land-based set of assumptions about place.[5] Similarly – with some notable exceptions – much scholarship on maritime Southeast Asia has literally missed the boat.[6] How, then, might one do things differently? My approach, merely one of many possible ways to address this terracentrism, is to depart not from the land, but instead to launch, as people actually did, from the intertidal zone itself. This approach contributes to an expanding body of work on Southeast Asia interested in how maritime-oriented people maintained interconnections, among themselves and with others, at varying scales, to both non-urban littorals and to urban centers.[7] It thus has parallels with some recent work on the region's upland areas, yet is similarly plagued by tensions between enduring romantic idealizations and contrasting facts supported by the sources.[8]

Launching from the littoral brings into focus interactions that unfolded along coastlines, as well as between distant shores. Bennet Bronson's well-known model of upstream-downstream relations in Southeast Asian political systems is useful here (Figure 4.1). While it emphasizes how trade and polity formations were structured spatially along the branches of a river, such political systems were also structured socially by alliances among different segments of descent group lineages. Pierre-Yves Manguin has elegantly shown, through an examination of literary and epigraphic sources, how amorphous coastal polities used terms for riverine geography to position themselves socially and spatially in relation to supposedly subordinate upstream polities. Charles Wheeler and Li Tana have each discussed how parallel watersheds in Vietnam were linked and sometimes unified by coastal routes.[9] What I propose simply builds on this work, extending it further into the maritime realm.

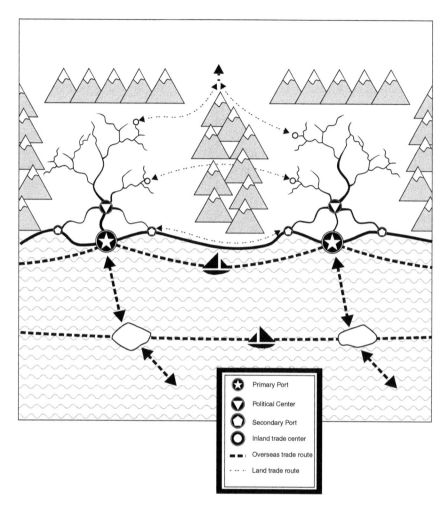

Figure 4.1 Adaptation of Bronson's model to parallel river systems linked by coastal trade

Image Credit: Martin McClellan. Used by permission: American Historical Association. From: Charles Wheeler, "A Maritime Logic to Vietnamese History? Littoral Society in Hoi An's Trading World c. 1550–1830," Conference Proceedings, "Seascapes, Littoral Cultures, and Trans-Oceanic Exchanges," February 12–15, 2003. http://webdoc.sub.gwdg.de/ebook/p/2005/history_cooperative/www.historycooperative.org/proceedings/seascapes/wheeler.html (accessed March 10, 2016)

Because similarly structured relations did not just stop at the downstream port, I suggest transposing this riparian structure to understand the organization of political relations that ran along and between the region's coasts. In other words, take that dendritic form of a river and its branches, and pivot it from its riparian geographic context so that it now reaches out across maritime space to touch other intertidal zones. Transposing this dendritic structure of political and social alliances from a riverine to an intertidal geography provides a model for grasping the connections, and the continuity of relations, across maritime space.

Doing so also equips one analytically to weigh anchor and follow the boats for a view of archipelagic history from the sea. Yet, to really take account of what boats connected, historically, entails refocusing attention on nautical matters in the sources. What the sources show about the complexity of intertidal social interactions calls for recognizing multi-ethnic formations where one might not expect to find them, and refining the picture of how they worked in practice. Such analysis is not without precedent, for instance, the fine examples set by Heather Sutherland, and by James Warren and his student Esther Velthoen, who waded through murky historical waters in order to figure out what some of the region's maritime people actually did.[10]

In the following examination of Tiworo's connections with Makassar and Boné, adversarial polities in seventeenth-century South Sulawesi, I draw on three kinds of sources: Makassar-language sources, especially the published annals and chronicles of Makassar's dual realms, Gowa and Talloq; Bugis-language sources handed down through elite Sama lineages; and the archives of the VOC, the Dutch East India Company. The Makassar sources show that Sama people formed part of Makassar's inner social circle, holding positions of authority under its rulers, while serving, sometimes simultaneously, in Sama positions of leadership. The archival sources offer new evidence that illustrates why Tiworo was called a "nasty pirate's nest," and was twice targeted by the VOC and its allies during the seventeenth century. They also show that Tiworo had been Makassar's close ally, and moreover, suggest that the historically close ties between Sama and Bugis people have their roots in the incorporation of a large group of Tiworo's men into the top ranks of Boné's military. Bugis-language sources, inherited through Sama lineages, offer evidence of the long legacy of those close ties and how they have been recalled in historical memory.

What made Tiworo important enough to be targeted by the VOC and its allies during these two seventeenth-century wars over control of the spice trade: the Great Ambon War and the Makassar War, especially given that it lay so far from the main areas of conflict in each? To answer this question, it may help to put Makassar's alliance with Tiworo in perspective by first understanding Makassar's connections with the maritime-oriented Sama closer to home and how they were vital to its nautical efforts (Map 4.2).

The Papuq was no myth

Prominent Sama people were deeply involved in Makassar's politics and society. As with elsewhere in early modern Sulawesi and in the wider region, intra- and inter-polity ties were commonly formed or reinforced through marriage politics. While Tiworo's significance and how it linked these wars can

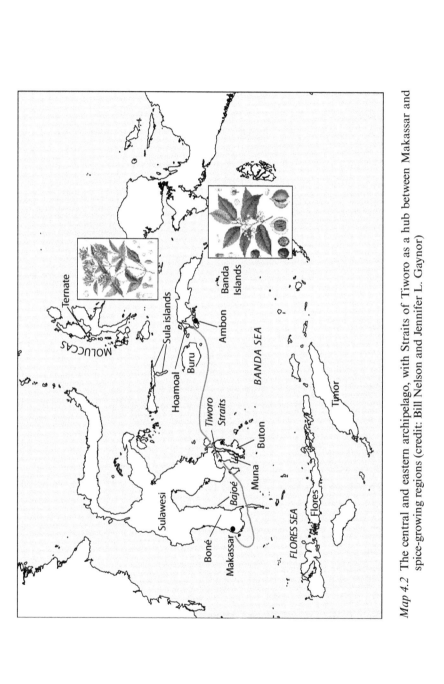

Map 4.2 The central and eastern archipelago, with Straits of Tiworo as a hub between Makassar and spice-growing regions (credit: Bill Nelson and Jennifer L. Gaynor)

be shown without demonstrating familial relations, kin ties probably existed between these allied ruling families, and would add to the other reasons why Sultan Hasanuddin offered his rationale for re-expansion in terms of retaliating for the 1655 assault on Tiworo. In particular, the existence of kin ties between prominent Sama and Makassar lineages in Makassar itself would lead one to expect to find similar relations between Tiworo's top mariners and Makassar's ruling families.

Just how prominent the Sama in Makassar were comes as something of a surprise. Remarkably, the figure of the "Papuq," or I should say, "figures," for we are talking about more than one of them, turns out not to be a chimera of myth and legend, but the stuff of actual history. The term *Papuq*, a Sama-language title for a Sama leader, has appeared rarely and with dubious historicity in the scholarly literature to date. Nevertheless, the *Makassar Annals*, which scholars regard as a fairly reliable source, lists by name three papuq who lived during the late seventeenth and early eighteenth centuries. It is not that these people were entirely unknown, however, it seems their position as Sama leaders was not noticed by contemporaneous observers. Mention of them in the *Annals* indicates that they were in the top echelons of Makassar's political structure. Also considered part of Makassar's inner social circle, the *Annals* noted major events in their lives or those of their children, such as the marriage of a daughter, I Saenaq, to I Daeng Manssaq, and the birth of their child. However, the inclusion of these papuq in the *Makassar Annals* does not necessarily mean that they were chosen as papuq by Makassar's rulers. On the contrary, the *Annals* records that after the death on March 12, 1703, of Papuq Daeng Numalo, I Daeng Makkulle Ahmad was "installed as Papuq by his family" on June 12, 1703.[11] This implies that he did not come from the same kin group as the writer. Hence it appears that these maritime-oriented Sama people at the polity's center had the relative independence to choose their leaders from among their own kin networks, as was often the case with Makassar's tributaries on land.

In addition to Daeng Numalo and Daeng Makkulle Ahmad, the third papuq mentioned in the *Annals* was Daeng Manggappa, born in 1688, and also known as "Mommiq." Like Daeng Makkulle Ahmad, who was installed in 1710 as Makassar's *sabannaraq*, Daeng Manggappa had also served as Makassar's harbormaster. *Sabannaraq* did more than watch the comings and goings at port. The position carried with it some authority to punish transgressors within Makassar itself, and to lead military expeditions.[12] For instance, a previous *sabannaraq* named Daeng Makkulle, presumably the father of Papuq Daeng Makkulle Ahmad (his namesake), was important to Makassar's interwar expansionary campaign under Sultan Hasanuddin.[13] The elder Daeng Makkulle may also have had Sama descent, like his son, or, possibly, the son's Sama lineage came solely through his mother. Dutch sources mention this older Daeng Makkulle returning home in 1666 after a two-month mission to Buton, which followed a major expedition by Makassar's fleet to Banggai and Tobungku on Sulawesi's east coast, as well as to the Sula Islands, to force them to accept Gowa's suzerainty.[14] En route to and from these expeditions, Daeng

Makkulle would almost certainly have passed through Tiworo with the fleet, as Makassar's fleet had done during the Great Ambon War the previous decade, on its way to the eastern archipelago. Similarly, the younger Daeng Makkulle (Papuq Daeng Makkulle Ahmad), while harbormaster, jointly led a military expedition with his son-in-law Daeng Manassaq, to advance against Toring in Flores. Part of a series of such expeditions across the Flores Sea to the south, they show that Makassar's seventeenth-century defeat in the Makassar War did not keep it from launching military campaigns well into the eighteenth century.[15]

The relevance of the above is fourfold. First, it demonstrates the social and political importance of Sama leaders in Makassar. Second, it shows the marriage of the Papuq's daughter to a Makassar son of note. While this resembles patterns of alliance and political structures in the western archipelago, it also suggests that Tiworo's leaders were similarly likely to have kin connections cementing their ties to Makassar, as well. Third, the *Makassar Annals* offer evidence of the military significance of the Papuq's leadership. And fourth, it suggests the importance of Sama followers to these endeavors, for, one has to ask, whom would the Papuq be leading at sea – in other words, who manned the fleets – if not Sama sea people? Corroborating the *Makassar Annals*' evidence suggesting the importance of Sama people to Makassar's fleets, a Dutch report of 1733 remarks that the Sama were the "muscles and sinews" of Makassar.[16]

Tiworo and the Great Ambon War

The Great Ambon War was fought from 1651 to 1656, largely in battles on islands in the vicinity of Ambon. The VOC forces, led by Arnold de Vlaming, were joined by local allies mostly under Ternate's Sultan Mandarsyah, who claimed numerous islands in the region as his dependencies. At the time, Makassar formed the primary transshipment point for goods from the eastern archipelago, including cloves and nutmeg. Makassar, ruled by the dual realms of Gowa and Talloq, was a cosmopolitan port whose diverse merchant communities swelled after 1641, when the Portuguese lost Malacca to the Dutch. Makassar thus had major stakes in the Great Ambon War and it actively supported eastern archipelago clove-growing regions in their struggle against the VOC. Makassar and its supporters provided fighting men and weapons to places such as Asahudi on the Hoamoal peninsula, a sail from Makassar of over six hundred miles (or one thousand kilometers).[17] Scholars usually treat the Makassar War separately, as it came a dozen years after the Great Ambon War and took place in Sulawesi. However, these wars were linked by more than just a shared concern with spices, for, like the route often sailed between Makassar and Maluku, the chain of events that connected these wars ran through Tiworo.

Although the main sites of conflict in the Great Ambon War lay some four hundred miles (or six-hundred fifty kilometers) distant, Tiworo nevertheless supported the interests of its ally Makassar with a number of nautical strengths. First, Tiworo gave Makassar a geographic advantage: it offered a shorter route to the eastern archipelago that, as archival documents show, bypassed rivals such as Buton. Second, Tiworo provided fleets sailing under Makassar a safe haven. Third, it also served as a nautical staging area for trade and engagements further east. Finally, Tiworo's own boats and mariners supported Makassar's endeavors. Dutch sources characterize Tiworo as subject to Makassar, yet also portray their leaders as close friends. This picture fits with political structures common to precolonial Southeast Asia, in which subordinate polities, organized around lineage segments, demonstrated their allegiance within center-weighted political structures.[18]

The assault by Ternate's and the VOC on Tiworo in 1655 had a dramatic outcome, which may in part explain Sultan Hasanuddin's framing his rationale as payback. When the VOC and Ternaten forces attacked, they expected to meet with Makassar's fleet in Tiworo. Indeed, when Ternates' forces advanced five or six miles ahead of the VOC, this motivated de Vlaming, who led the VOC forces, to advise Vice Admiral Roos to take eleven row yachts and three hundred Dutchmen into Tiworo to find and join Mandarsyah, in order to look for the Makassar fleet together. He advised Roos, if it were not too dangerous, to undertake something violent on Tiworo.[19]

However, neither Makassar's fleet, nor most of Tiworo's own fighting men, were present at the time. Three hundred of Tiworo's men had been sent off with their weapons to subdue neighboring regions, while a second contingent, around one hundred and fifty strong, had gone off to hunt buffalo. The Dutch and their allies thus encountered scant resistance. They killed two hundred people at five different places in Tiworo. They also found a vast store of provisions including rice, plus quality merchandize such as clothing and other goods, which lay ready to be shipped, according to the sources, apparently to Asahudi, which was a major site of conflict in the Great Ambon War. VOC forces stole, burned or destroyed the provisions and goods, and they incinerated fifty "beautiful ships," including junks, galleys, and *kora-kora*.[20]

Remarking on their lucky success, Arnold de Vlaming proclaimed, "The name and weapons of the Company will without doubt gain a reputation in these parts, since the oft-mentioned fortress [at Tiworo] was reputed to be very strong and the capital place of Pangesane Island."[21] Here, one may note de Vlaming's singling out the fortress as both well-known to the Dutch, and also the capital place of Pangesane, or what is now called the island of Muna. Among those killed in the attack were Tiworo's king (*raja*), the greater number of his entourage or notables, as well as his sons.[22] De Vlaming remarked that this was a serious blow to Makassar, "to lose their friend, the king, with most of his peers," as he was "a man on whom a lot was riding and in this region was greatly esteemed."[23] In addition, around three hundred women and children were taken alive.[24] Historians might expect they would have been brought to Batavia to be sold as slaves. But this, at least initially, was not their fate.

A familiar feature of early modern warfare in Southeast Asia, the preference for taking captives rather than grabbing land, is something historians often regard as a result of land's abundance and the relative scarcity of labor.

Particularly in the region's cities, manpower, rather than fixed capital, was the principal asset to be protected, and a primary object of warfare was to increase the availability of workers.[25] Yet land, here, was not really part of the equation. Instead, as de Vlaming stated, the captives were given over to the fighters in order to get them off the VOC's hands, and to please and appease their allies so that they would continue with their work. He elaborated that the captives were granted to their allies as an incentive to boost the fighters' willingness to undertake further combat.[26] It is, however, also possible that the VOC's allies had carried out this human expropriation, and in his report de Vlaming was simply putting a "good face" on a fait accompli for the eyes of his superiors.

In either case, captures in the context of colonial conflicts built on long-standing practices of raiding, endemic to the region.[27] As war spoils go, it must be noted that these captives did not all bear equal social significance. Among the three hundred women and children taken alive at Tiworo were the king's wives and daughters.[28] With the bulk of its fighting men away, its villages and remaining boats torched, and its fortress torn down, Tiworo was politically decapitated, and depopulated by slaughter and capture. Within the highly stratified and interwoven society of the region's littorals, these captures would have carried great significance. If Tiworo and Makassar had close kin connections, as seems highly likely, then, in addition to the temporary loss of Tiworo's strategic functions, and the killing of friends and allies, the significance of these captures would have bolstered Sultan Hasanuddin's desire to avenge Tiworo.

Only three days after the attack, Makassar's fleet did arrive in Tiworo. Although the timing of their arrival was unfortunate for Tiworo, the fleet's boats were still able to use Tiworo as a safe haven. The Dutch kept a watch and patrols in nearby waters for months, until Makassar's fleet finally managed to evade the VOC by sailing past them – amazingly – in a very dense fog.[29]

Tiworo and the Makassar War

Between the wars, Makassar's Sultan Hasanuddin undertook a campaign of re-expansion in the eastern archipelago. This campaign threatened both VOC interests and those of Ternate. While the Makassar War was driven primarily by competition for spices, and one can list a number of proximate causes in the lead-up to it (as Leonard Andaya has done),[30] my aim here has been to draw attention to a remark made in 1666, the year before the war, by Sultan Hasanuddin, the Gowa ruler in Makassar. Unpacking this remark and its referents reveals the depth of Tiworo's importance, and that of its maritime-oriented people, to the Sultan and to Makassar's interests.

Sultan Hasanuddin, when discussing his conditions for maintaining the peace, offered a Dutch Commissioner his rationale for Makassar's campaign of re-expansion. He said he *"never would have had to maintain his rights to these lands in question, if Ternate had not attacked the Makassar territory of*

Pancana."[31] "Pancana," like "Pangesane," and "Pantsiano," are variants of the name used at the time for the island of Muna, a part of which was encompassed by Tiworo. Sultan Hasanuddin's remark was, in fact, a reference to Tiworo, the most prominent polity in the vicinity at the time, well-known to the Dutch, not least for its impressive fort. Tiworo's fortress, a sturdy stone structure with bulwarks and walls over ten meters high, was torn down by the VOC after the 1655 attack.[32]

Tiworo's demise in the Great Ambon War presents a striking contrast to the outcome of its defeat in connection with the Makassar War, twelve years later. Although it rebuilt between the wars, now with two fortresses, this second time around, its population was forewarned and had the opportunity to flee. Once again though, the Dutch and their allies were extraordinarily lucky to take Tiworo practically without a fight. Such were the circumstances under which Tiworo fell into the hands of the VOC's main ally in the Makassar War, the Bugis man from Boné who bore the title Arung Palakka.[33]

When the VOC's Captain Lieutenant David Steijger later joined Arung Palakka to take over the watch, curiously, he found Tiworo's new ruler in his fortress in a wooded area on elevated ground six miles from the main settlement. When negotiations with this *raja* failed, he and his followers were pursued to the other fort, and in the skirmish, Arung Palakka was wounded by an arrow and visibly shaken (perhaps because he himself realized he was not, after all, invincible). Tiworo's raja was detained in the fortress, but eventually, after Steijger was called away, the raja was allowed to go for a bath, and on this pretext he escaped, despite being pursued by some one thousand men.[34]

When the combined VOC and allied fleet prepared to depart from its sallying point near Buton for Makassar, the VOC again tore down Tiworo's primary fort, and set fire to Tiworo's main settlement. This time, however, they did not burn Tiworo's boats. Instead, Arung Palakka seized them for himself, explicitly disallowing their appropriation by the Governor General, and he floated them over to where his forces had mustered. Arung Palakka then hand-picked sixty of Tiworo's men, gave each firearms, and made them half of his Guard of Prime Commanders.[35] Such incorporation with rank into the forces of a foe resembles other examples of defeated groups in South Sulawesi conflicts, who sometimes took oaths of loyalty to victorious former enemy leaders.[36]

Interestingly, the advent and rapid expansion of Bajoé, the intertidal settlement named for its Sama people that served as Boné's harbor, dates from shortly after this time. This timing suggests that the figures who left from Tiworo with rank and new allegiances to Boné and the Bugis leader Arung Palakka were indeed Sama people. Boné may have had connections with the Sama before Bajoé's rise. However, Boné's political arrangement with Bajoé rested on a structure of cooperation between Boné's rulers and members of an elite Sama lineage. This fruitful cooperation repeated the earlier successful approach of Makassar. Rare Bugis-language manuscripts memorialize the ties between elite Boné and Sama lineages in some detail. Such manuscripts,

inherited through Sama lineages, attest to the long history of interconnections between the Bugis polity of Boné and Sama people.[37] While often living some distance from Bajoé, these Sama, their descendants, and followers,
nevertheless maintained loyalty to it, just as, earlier, Tiworo had been loyal
to Makassar. Both provide examples of that dendritic structure mentioned
above, reaching along coasts and across waters to connect disparate littorals
in an intertidal history.

Although Tiworo is a rather sleepy backwater now, to the Dutch during the seventeenth century, it was infamous. The role it played as a non-
urban maritime hub led the VOC forces under Arnold de Vlaming and
their Ternatan allies to take it, with no small amount of luck, during the
Great Ambon War. In connection with the war against Makassar, the threat
Tiworo posed was neutralized through flight and demolition, the appropriation of its boats, and the incorporation of many of its men into Boné's
forces. Tiworo's maritime-oriented population, and Sama people more
broadly, were valuable to these polities, with whom they shared interests,
because of their nautical knowledge and skills, as well as their intergroup
connections and networks. The archeologist David Bulbeck has a marvelous
piece about the landscape of the Makassar War on Sulawesi's southwestern
peninsula.[38] This chapter has shown some of the seascape of the spice wars,
the role played in them by sea people, and how these conflicts were linked
through the Tiworo.

Acknowledgment

This chapter was previously published in the Bulletin de l'École française
d'Extrême-Orient and appears here with the kind permission of the BEFEO
and the EFEO's Director.

Notes

1 Jennifer L. Gaynor, *Intertidal History in Island Southeast Asia: Submerged
   Genealogy and the Legacy of Coastal Capture* (Ithaca and London: Cornell
   University Press, 2016).
2 Gerrit Knaap, "Headhunting, Carnage and Armed Peace in Amboina, 1500–1700,"
   Journal of the Economic and Social History of the Orient, 46, 2 (2003): 165–92.
3 Or "vile": "*dat leelijcke roofnest Tiboore*." Cornelis Speelman, "Notitie dienende
   voor eenen corten tijt, en tot naeder last van de Hooge Regeringe op Batavia,
   tot naerrichtinge voor den ondercoopman Jan van Opijnen bij provisie gestelt,
   tot Opperhooft en Commandant int Casteel Rotterdam op Maccassar, en van
   den Capitain Jan France als hooft over de melitie mitsgaders die van den Raede,"
   Dutch National Archives, The Hague, VOC 1276 (1669), 684v.
4 Gaynor, *Intertidal History*.
5 Marcus Rediker, "Toward a People's History of the Sea," in David Killingray,
   Margarette Lincoln, and Nigel Rigby (eds.), *Maritime Empires: British Imperial
   Trade in the Nineteenth Century* (Rochester: Boydell Press, 2004).

6 More than it is possible to cite here has been written about Southeast Asian mariners, regional maritime history, and their interregional connections. For early modern island and peninsular Southeast Asia, see, inter alia, work by Kenneth R. Hall, Pierre-Yves Manguin, Gerrit Knaap and Heather Sutherland. Kenneth R. Hall, *Secondary Cities and Urban Networking in the Indian Ocean Realm, c. 1400–1800* (Plymouth, UK, 2008); Kenneth R. Hall, "Multi-Dimensional Networking: Fifteenth-Century Indian Ocean Maritime Diaspora in Southeast Asian Perspective," *Journal of the Economic and Social History of the Orient*, 49, 4 (2006): 454–81; Pierre-Yves Manguin, "The Southeast Asian Ship: An Historical Approach," *Journal of Southeast Asian Studies*, 11, 2 (1980): 266–76; Manguin, "The Vanishing *Jong*: Insular Southeast Asian Fleets in Trade and War (Fifteenth to Seventeenth Centuries)," in Anthony Reid (ed.), *Southeast Asia in the Early Modern Era: Trade, Power, and Belief* (Ithaca and London, 1993), 197–213; Manguin, "Southeast Asian Shipping in the Indian Ocean During the 1st Millennium AD," in Himanshu Prabha Ray and Jean-François Salles (eds.), *Tradition and archaeology. Early Maritime Contacts in the Indian Ocean* (New Delhi/Lyons, 1996), 181–98; Gerrit Knaap, "Headhunting, Carnage and Armed Peace," 166; Gerrit Knaap and Heather Sutherland, *Monsoon Traders: Ships, Skippers and Commodities in Eighteength-century Makassar* (Leiden, 2004); Heather Sutherland, "Geography as destiny? The Role of Water in Southeast Asian History," in Peter Boomgaard (ed.), *A World of Water: Rain, Rivers and Seas in Southeast Asian Histories*, VKI 240 (Leiden, 2007), 27–70; Heather Sutherland, "On the Edge of Asia: Maritime Trade in East Indonesia, Early Seventeenth to Mid-Twentieth Century," in *Commodities, Ports and Asian Maritime Trade Since 1750*, ed. Anthony Webster, Ulbe Bosma, and Jaime de Melo (New York, 2015), 59–78.

7 Kenneth R. Hall, "Local and International Trade and Traders in the Straits of Melaka Region: 600–1500," *Journal of the Economic and Social History of the Orient* 47, 2 (2004): 252–53; Kenneth R. Hall, "Sojourning Communities, Ports-of-Trade, and Commercial Networking in Southeast Asia's Eastern Regions, 100–1400," in Michael Aung-Thwin and Kenneth R. Hall (eds.), *New Perspectives on the History and Historiography of Southeast Asia* (London, 2011), 56–73; Esther Velthoen, "Pirates in the Periphery: Eastern Sulawesi 1820–1905," in John Kleinen and Manon Osseweijer (eds.), *Pirates, Ports and Coasts in Asia: Historical and Contemporary Perspectives* (Singapore, 2012), 200–21; Leonard Andaya, "Local trade Networks in Maluku in the 16th, 17th and 18th Centuries," *Cakalele*, II, 2 (1991): 71–96; Atsushi Ota, "Pirates or Entrepreneurs? Migration and Trade of Sea People in Southwest Kalimantan, c. 1770–1820," *Indonesia*, 90 (2010): 67–96; Roy F. Ellen, *On the Edge of the Banda Zone: Past and Present in the Social Organization of a Moluccan Trading Network* (Honolulu, 2003).

8 Willem van Schendel, "Geographies of Knowing, Geographies of Ignorance: Jumping Scale in Southeast Asia," *Environment and Planning D: Society and Space*, 20 (2002): 647–68; and James Scott, *The Art of Not Being Governed: An Anarchist History of Upland Southeast Asia* (New Haven, 2009); both are central to the burgeoning field of "Zomia" studies about the upland border areas of mainland Southeast Asia.

9 Bennet Bronson, "Exchange at the Upstream and Downstream Ends: Notes Towards a Functional Model of the Coastal State in Southeast Asia," in Karl

Hutterer (ed.), *Economic Exchange and Social Interaction in Southeast Asia: Perspectives from Prehistory, History, and Ethnography* (Ann Arbor, 1977), 39–54; Pierre-Yves Manguin, "The Amorphous Nature of Coastal Polities in Insular Southeast Asia: Restricted Centers, Extended Peripheries," *Moussons*, 5 (2002): 78–81; Li Tana, "A View from the Sea: Perspectives on the Northern and Central Vietnamese Coast," *Journal of Southeast Asian Studies*, 37, 1 (2006): 83–102; Charles Wheeler, "Re-thinking the Sea in Vietnamese History: The Littoral Integration of Thuan-Quang, Seventeenth–Eighteenth Centuries," *Journal of Southeast Asian Studies*, 37, 1 (2006): 123–53.

10 James Francis Warren, *The Sulu Zone, 1768–1898: The Dynamics of External Trade, Slavery, and Ethnicity in the Transformation of a Southeast Asian Maritime State* (Honolulu, 2007); James Francis Warren, *Iranun and Balangingi: Globalization, Maritime Raiding and the Birth of Ethnicity* (Honolulu, 2002); Esther Joy Velthoen, "Contested Coastlines: Diasporas, Trade and Colonial Expansion in Eastern Sulawesi 1680–1905," (unpublished PhD dissertation, Murdoch University, 2002); Esther Velthoen, "Pirates in the Periphery"; Heather Sutherland, "On the Edge of Asia: Maritime Trade in East Indonesia, Early Seventeenth to Mid-twentieth Century," in Ulbe Bosma and Anthony Webster (eds.), *Commodities, Ports, and Asian Maritime Trade since 1750* (London, 2015), 59–78.

11 William P. Cummings, trans. and ed., *The Makassar Annals* (Leiden, 2010), vol. 7, 176, 233, 236. For a discussion of positions and titles in early modern Makassar, see William P. Cummings, "Introduction," in William P. Cummings (ed. and trans.), *A Chain of Kings: The Makassarese Chronicles of Gowa and Tallok* (Leiden, 2007), 5–6.

12 Cummings, *Makassar Annals*, 156, 196, 203, 233, 268 (note 669: Cummings notes that this was probably but not necessarily the same Daeng Manggappa as the *sabannaraq*), 278, 292, 301 (note 756).

13 "Presumably his father" and "presumably the son and successor" according to Cummings, *Makassar Annals*, 139 (note 358), 176, 196. This first Daeng Makkulle was apparently also called "I Daeng Makkulle I Mappaq," (234).

14 Leonard Andaya, *The Heritage of Arung Palakka: A History of South Sulawesi (Celebes) in the Seventeenth Century* (The Hague, 1981), 60, 65, 126; "Report of Commissioner van Wesenhagen on mission to Makassar and Ternate," VOC 1257, 511. The *sabannaraq* Daeng Makkule also distinguished himself in battle on land:

> Goa's successful campaigns in the interior were a marked contrast to the difficulties it faced against Arung Palakka and the Dutch in the west. The Makassar forces under Syahbandar Daeng Makkulle, joined by a thousand men from Wajo and Lamuru, marched through Soppeng, burning as they went.
>
> (L. Andaya, The Heritage of Arung Palakka, p. 126)

15 Cummings, trans. and ed., *Makassar Annals*, 164 (Note 445), 169, 179, 233, 237, 238, 265, 266, 268.

16 "Makassar to Batavia," May 21, 1733, VOC 2285, 119; Leonard Andaya, "Historical Links Between Aquatic Populations and the Coastal Peoples of the Malay World and Celebes," in Muhammad Abu Bakar, Amarjit Kaur and Abdullah Zakaria Ghazali (eds.), *Historia: Essays in Commemoration of the 25th Anniversary of the Department of History, University of Malaya* (Kuala Lumpur, 1984), 39.

17 Knaap, "Headhunting, Carnage and Armed Peace," 178–81; Livinus Bor, *Amboinse Oorlogen, door Arnold de Vlaming van Oudshoorn als superintendent, over d'Oosterse gewesten oorlogaftig ten eind gebracht* (Delft, 1663), 236–41, 288–98, 301–03.

18 "Originele generale missive," July 12, 1655, VOC 1208 book 4, 538–48, esp. 543r; "Letter from the King of Buton to Arnold de Vlaming and Governor Willem Van der Beecq, Dachregister bij d'Hr. Arnold de Vlamingh van Outshoorn," April 5, 1654, VOC 1205, book 2, 892r–94r; "Letter of January 9, 1655, from Arnold de Vlamingh van Outshoorn aboard the *Erasmus*, delivered express to the Authorities before Tiworo (*Tibore*)," VOC 1211, book 2, 76–77; Bor, *Amboinse Oorlogen*, 273; "Letter of January 17, 1655, to Simon Cos, Provis. President in Ambon, from Arnold de Vlamingh van Outshoorn in the ship *Erasmus* lying at anchor by the east end of the Buton Straits," VOC 1211, book 2, 89.

19 Bor, *Amboinse Oorlogen*, 259; "Letter of January 9, 1655, de Vlamingh aboard the *Erasmus*, to the Authorities before Tiworo (*Tibore*)," VOC 1211, 76–77.

20 Bor, *Amboinse Oorlogen*, 260–62; "De Vlamingh to Simon Cos," VOC 1211, 88–89; "Letter of January 9, 1655, de Vlamingh aboard the *Erasmus*, to the Authorities before Tiworo," VOC 1211, 76–77; "Originele Generale Missieve, 12 July 1655," VOC 1208, 543r; "Letter to Governor Jacob Hustaert and the Council in Malucco, with the Yacht Dromedaris, written on February 2 (1655) from Batoij, signed by Arnold de Vlamingh and Willem Maetsuyker on the chaloup Sumatra, lying at anchor off the coast of Celebes opposite Chassea island," VOC 1211, book 2, 99–100.

21 Bor, *Amboinse Oorlogen*, 260–62; "Letter of January 9, 1655, from Arnold de Vlamingh aboard the *Erasmus*, to the Authorities before Tiworo," 76–77; and "De Vlamingh to Cos," VOC 1211, 88–89.

22 "De Vlamingh and Maetsuyker to Jacob Hustaert," VOC 1211, book 2, 99–100; and "Originele generale missive," July 12, 1655, VOC 1208, 543r.

23 "De Vlamingh to Cos," VOC 1211, 89.

24 Ibid., 89; "De Vlamingh and Maetsuyker to Jacob Hustaert," VOC 1211, 99.

25 Anthony Reid, "The Structure of Cities in Southeast Asia, Fifteenth to Seventeenth Centuries," *Journal of Southeast Asian Studies*, 11, 2 (1980): 243.

26 Bor, *Amboinse Oorlogen*, 236–40; "De Vlamingh and Maetsuyker to Jacob Hustaert," VOC 1211, 99.

27 Laura Lee Junker, *Raiding, Trading and Feasting: The Political Economy of Philippine Chiefdoms* (Honolulu, 1999).

28 "Originele generale missive," December 24, 1655, VOC 1209, book 1, 5v–6r.

29 "Letter of January 9, 1655, from Arnold de Vlamingh aboard the *Erasmus*, to the Authorities before Tiworo"; Bor, *Amboinse Oorlogen*, 273–74.

30 L. Andaya, *The Heritage of Arung Palakka*, 45–72.

31 "Report of Commissioner van Wesenhagen on mission to Makassar and Ternate," July 16, 1666, VOC 1257, 1667, 521; L. Andaya, *The Heritage of Arung Palakka*, 65.

32 "Letter of January 16, 1655, to Marten Doane, Skipper of the Concordia, sent with the Post to Het Haesjen, from Arnold de Vlaming van Outshoorn, in the ship Erasmus at anchor by the (fresh) waterplace in the Buton Straits," VOC 1211 1656 book 2, 79–81; "De Vlamingh to Cos," VOC 1211 1655 book 2, 87–94, especially 88; "De Vlamingh and Maetsuyker to Hustaert and the Council," VOC 1211, 97, 100; Bor, 262 states: "reinforced with seven round towers."

33 "Letter from Admiral Cornelis Speelman to Governor General Joan Maetsuijker and the Council of the Indies," August 18, 1667, VOC 1264, book 3, 44–61, here, 46r.
34 "Speelman to Governor General Maetsuijker and the Council," VOC 1264, 51v–52r.
35 Ibid., 52v–53r, 54v–55r.
36 Stephen C. Druce, *The Lands West of the Lakes: A History of the Ajattapareng Kingdoms of South Sulawesi 1200–1600 CE* (Leiden, 2009), 26–29; Rahila Omar, "The History of Boné A.D. 1775–1795: The Diary of Sultan Ahmad as-Salleh Syamsuddin," (PhD thesis, University of Hull, Centre for South-East Asian Studies, 2003).
37 *LB Lemobajo*, photocopy of manuscript in possession of the author; A. Djamali, copyist, "Geschiedenis van de Badjo's van Zuid Celebes" (History of the Bajos of South Celebes), KITLV, Or 545/262, March 7, 1940 (previously number 260 in the Matthes Foundation catalog).
38 F. David Bulbeck, "The Landscape of the Makassar War," *Canberra Anthropology*, 13, 1 (1990): 78–99.

5 Maritime China in global military history

Some reflections on the Chase model

Tonio Andrade

In 2003, Kenneth Chase published *Firearms: A Global History to 1700*, a compact, well-written book that offered an elegant solution to an age-old question: why did Europeans "perfect" firearms when it was the Chinese who invented them?[1] Rejecting standard explanations (e.g. Europeans had superior technology or experienced higher levels of warfare), Chase focused instead on military context, arguing that China failed to perfect firearms because its primary foes were mounted nomads: early firearms were so slow to load and inaccurate that they couldn't be used effectively on horseback, whereas infantry forces armed with guns had trouble defeating nomads because the logistics were too difficult. Therefore, states that faced nomadic threats tended to focus on cavalry warfare, and their cavalry units ended up being armed much like the nomads themselves, that is, with traditional weapons, most importantly bows. Thus, Chase concludes, the Chinese had less incentive to improve their firearms than did western Europeans, whose wars tended to involve infantry forces.

Although the Chase model was initially challenged by some experts in Chinese military history, its influence has continued to increase.[2] It's a primary support of Phil Hoffman's widely-read explanation of why Europeans "conquered the world," as outlined in his book of that name and in articles.[3] It underlies key arguments in the much-read works of historian Ian Morris, who similarly uses it to explain how China fell behind militarily.[4] It also appears, unquestioned, in many other major surveys and syntheses, such as those by Max Boot, Azar Gat, Timothy May, Peter Golden, Jack Levy, and William R. Thompson.[5]

This chapter offers a reassessment of the Chase thesis. First, it asks whether Chinese warmakers did in fact find guns less useful against nomads than against infantry armies. In general, the answer is no, but there are some intriguing exceptions, and it seems possible that nomadic military challenges may have pushed the development of guns in different directions than did more standard types of infantry challenges.

Second, and more importantly, this chapter shifts the focus from China's northern borders to its maritime regions. As Jack Wills has long argued, maritime China played a significant and often underrated role in China's history.[6]

This is especially true of China's military history. The Chase argument – like so much historiography concerning military matters in pre-modern China – focuses on China's northern borders. There's a logic to this northern focus, of course. For most of the imperial period – from the Han Dynasty through the mid-eighteenth century – the greatest threats to the Chinese court came from the mounted warriors of the Central and Northern Asian steppes.[7] Yet, as historians Kenneth Swope, Stephen Morillo, and others have pointed out, we must not forget that Chinese warfare was not limited to campaigns against mounted nomads.[8]

In fact, the maritime realms of southern China acted as a key locus of military innovation, a sort of crucible within which ideas from without and adaptations from within contended, leading to new structures, techniques, and technologies, which then spread throughout China. Vietnamese guns, Portuguese breech-loading artillery, Western-style muskets, large Western muzzle-loading cannons, and huge "red-barbarian" cannons, took root in southern China and then spread northward, as did techniques and tactics pertaining to their use.

Thanks to these maritime influences, military innovation was so rapid and pervasive during the mid-Ming and early Qing periods that we might challenge the very question Chase purports to solve: whether Chinese did in fact fail to "perfect" firearms. Certainly, China led the world in firearms usage from the thirteenth century (when guns were invented) through the mid-fifteenth century. During these two centuries, the armies of China deployed firearms in the field far more effectively than did Europeans.[9] But even through much of the early modern period (1500–1750), Chinese adaptations and innovations put China and its neighbors at the forefront of a Eurasian-wide process of firearm innovation. Most of this innovation began in China's southern maritime regions, which thus played a key role in China's military history.

Guns against nomads

According to Chase, "the people who wanted to fight nomads found firearms of little help."[10] To make his point, he surveys a wide variety of cases throughout Eurasia, and he makes compelling observations. Yet if we look carefully at the case of China, we must reassess his answer. It seems that throughout the Ming and early Qing periods, Chinese warmakers in fact felt that guns were very effective – indeed invaluable – against mounted nomads, and they therefore put great effort into developing, producing, and deploying them.

Consider, for example, the great expeditions of the Yongle Emperor. He understood warfare against mounted nomads as few others did. Indeed, he had developed an expertise in the subject long before he was called Yongle. As the imperial Prince of Yan, he was trained in the north, accompanying generals on campaigns against the Mongols, most significantly in a famous expedition of 1381, when he proved his mettle on the battlefield.[11] In subsequent years, he conducted raids and expeditions against nomads, and he also incorporated mounted Mongols into his own forces. When he fought against his nephew to usurp the Ming throne, his most trusted and effective troops included a corps of Mongol riders, who on one occasion rescued him when he was nearly captured, his standard troops having been thrown into confusion by his nephew's gunners.[12]

Given his understanding of northern warfare, it is telling that when, after assuming the throne, he launched massive expeditions against the Mongols in the early 1400s, he made sure that firearms were a key armament for his troops. And sources show that firearms played significant roles in his victories.

He led his first such campaign in the spring of 1410, and although Western-language discussions of it tend not to mention firearms – including Kenneth Chase's own short treatment – Chinese sources make clear that gun units played a role.[13] On July 13, 1410, for example, Yongle was pursuing his arch-enemy, Mongol leader Arughtai (阿鲁台), in the area near the Great Khingan mountains, and his general Liu Sheng "used firearms, serving as the advance guard, and badly defeated Arughtai."[14] The *Ming Veritable Records* has a few more details:

> The emperor chased the enemy to Huiqujin and ordered the Anyuan Marquis Liu Sheng to take the magical-device guns and serve as the vanguard. The guns fired and their sound thundered forth for ten li (three or so miles), and each arrow penetrated two men, and also struck the horses, and all immediately died. The enemy, frightened, spurred their horses and departed. Our troops advanced bravely and defeated them, beheading their famous generals and hundreds of men.[15]

The *Veritable Records'* rather terse accounts of other battles in this expedition don't mention firearms per se, but there's no reason to believe guns weren't deployed effectively in those battles as well. Moreover, the fact that they were used in this particular battle, when Yongle was moving fast to catch Arughtai, suggests that they didn't slow the Ming forces down as much as Chase's model would suggest. We must remember that early Ming guns, especially those employed by individual soldiers (as opposed to those used on ships or forts), were quite light, usually less than 3 kg in weight.[16]

Yongle's second expedition against the Mongols offers even clearer evidence. It, too, was a massive expedition, which left Beijing in the spring of 1414 with as many as half a million men.[17] After a long trek, Yongle's troops encountered the enemy: four great Mongol leaders occupying four hills and commanding around thirty thousand mounted troops, each of which had three or four extra horses. Yongle put on his armor and the Ming troops arrayed themselves on the plain. There were skirmishes, but no encounters of consequence. Then, at dusk, Yongle himself led a vanguard of crack troops toward them, followed closely by firearm units. The Ming troops arrayed themselves and the enemy came down the hills to meet him. The Ming guns began firing, under the command of Liu Sheng, and several hundred Mongols were killed. They were thrown into disarray, and Yongle himself led forth his elite cavalry corps, known as the iron horsemen, forcing the enemy to abandon horses and withdraw into the hills.

There were more attacks, but the enemy could not be budged from their positions, until, at dusk, Yongle took several hundred crack troops forward, followed by gunners. The enemy found the emperor and this small force a target too tempting to resist and came out to fight. An account by civil official Jin Youzi (金幼孜), who accompanied the expedition, describes what happened next:

> Before they even got a chance to strike, the guns fired in secret [火銃竊發], and the crack troops then moved forward and attacked with great force, and each could stand against a hundred. The enemy was badly defeated, and the number of men and horses killed and hurt was uncountable, and they all screamed out in pain and left…. Henceforth that place was called "Barbarian Slaughtering Hold."[18]

The *Ming Veritable Records* adds the intriguing detail that the guns were "fired in continuous succession" [連發神機銃炮].[19] Early guns were slow to load and fire, so to keep up a continuous barrage took careful coordination, achievable only through dedicated drilling. This, thus, appears to be an early use of some form of countermarch technique, which historians of early modern Europe have hailed as a pathbreaking innovation of the late 1500s. Other early Ming sources similarly contain references to such techniques, and this isn't surprising, because the technique was used with crossbows for centuries before being applied to guns in the early Ming period.[20]

After this victory, in which Mongol leaders were killed and several thousand heads were captured, Yongle pursued the remaining enemy, and guns continued to show their value. On one occasion, when Mongol forces occupied some highlands and small lakes, the Ming troops

> again used guns (火銃) to first pound those occupying the two ponds, and these enemy, knowing they could not resist, withdrew. The remaining bandits, those who were on the peaks of the gorge, feared the guns would come again and also withdrew and left.[21]

Chase doesn't make much of the use of guns in these expeditions, noting merely that guns frightened the Mongols.[22] Yet these passages clearly suggest that the guns were useful for more than frightening the enemy: they were devastating weapons in their own right.

Guns were also brought on Yongle's subsequent Mongolian expeditions, which occurred in the 1420s. During these campaigns, Yongle's attention to training his gunners was even more pronounced. On the third expedition

(1422), for example, he instructed his generals on the precise way to drill for the integration of gunners and conventional troops:

> The emperor ordered that all the generals train their troops outside each encampment by arraying the gunnery units [*shen ji chong*] in the front and the cavalry in the back, ordering the officers to practice and train in the free time. He admonished them as follows: "A formation that is dense is solid, while an advance force is sparse, and when they arrive at the gates of war and it's time to fight, then first use the guns to destroy their advance guard and then use cavalry to rush their solidity. In this way there is nothing to fear."[23]

Yet the troops had little chance to put their practice into action, because this expedition, and the following two, saw little actual fighting. The enormous army – hundreds of thousands of troops, 235,000 porters and workers, 340,000 donkeys, and 117,000 carts – failed to find its prey.[24] The following two expeditions, which occurred in 1423 and 1424, were similarly fruitless. The main event of the last expedition – the 1424 one – was the death of Yongle, who had grown increasingly despondent. He died in Mongolia (at Chahar), not on the battlefield but to disease. His body was placed in a sealed tin coffin and carried back to Beijing, where a massive funeral was held, with more than thirty palace women killing themselves to accompany him in death.[25]

One might object that these failures to find the Mongols actually lend support to the Chase model, and indeed, as Chase argues, the trickiest part of attacking the nomads was to actually find and engage the enemy. Thus, there is truth to the proposition that the effectiveness of the weapons themselves was less important than the effectiveness of scouting and logistics. Still, guns certainly played a role when the enemy was engaged, and it is the case that Yongle and his successors themselves believed in the effectiveness of guns against mounted nomads. Since it was hard to find mounted nomads, no matter what kinds of weapons you had, you might as well use guns, which were, we must remember, quite light, not terribly difficult to bring on expeditions. Indeed the Ming cavalry itself, although armed like the nomads, lacked the adversary's range, to say nothing of the nomads' ability to melt into the steppes and live off the land. The nomads controlled huge herds, with each warrior having access to several horses, which he could take turns riding to lessen the animals' fatigue. When food was scarce he could even open up a horse's vein and drink its blood. There was no surefire way to catch nomads, no matter what weapons one had available.

Thus, Yongle and his commanders found guns useful to take on expeditions against mounted nomads, but there is also another important point: Chinese warmakers were not just interested in using guns against nomads offensively. They also – and perhaps more importantly – used them defensively.

Many sources attest to the significance of guns when defending against mounted nomads, but one of the most intriguing episodes was sparked by a foolish decision by Yongle's great grandson, Zhu Qizhen, who ruled as the Zhengtong Emperor. He decided to revive the practice of grand Mongolian expeditions, with disastrous consequences. In 1449, he led a massive expedition northward. It was defeated by a much smaller Mongol force, and he was captured, a stunning humiliation to the Ming court.[26] The Mongols offered to deliver the emperor in exchange for a ransom, but the Ming court refused, at which the Mongols marched on Beijing. Fortunately, the capital had good leadership. Guns were set up at Beijing's nine gates and other vital points. Ming troops came out of the city and attacked the Mongols, luring them into a gun ambush. Ming sources suggest that the result was large-scale carnage: ten thousand or more Mongols were killed by bullets.[27] The Mongol leader withdrew. Chase discusses these 1449 events but devotes no attention to the defense of Beijing, focusing merely on the foolish offensive expedition of Zhengtong. The records make clear, however, that guns were enormously effective in defending the capital and probably contributed significantly to the Ming victory.

In fact, throughout the next centuries, Ming officials believed that gun defenses were vital to defending the northern borders against the Mongols, and they invested considerable time and treasure to acquire and build those guns.

For example, in the second half of the 1400s, many Chinese officials noted that "Great General Cannons" were vital to the northern defenses, not just on walls but also in carts. According to Ming scholar He Rubin 何汝宾,

> In Tianshun 6 (1463), 1200 military carts were made, and each carried large bronze guns. In Chenghua 1 (1465), they made 300 great general [guns] and five hundred gun-carrying carts. All of this was a good use of the technology of China to control the enemy, a superior strategy.[28]

(Note that these Great General Cannons were not the massive behemoths of the late Ming period – they were much smaller.)

Similarly, the *Veritable Records* of the Hongzhi reign notes, in a passage from Hongzhi 13 (1501), that "Great general guns are placed in carriages, and one waits until the enemy masses charge forth and then one measuredly attacks them."[29] He Rubin also noted that other types of guns were useful against nomads, including the three-barrel gun, which, if the bullets themselves didn't do the trick, could in last resort always be wielded as a cudgel:

> The three-barrel gun (*san yan chong*) is one staff with three guns, and each gun can fit two or three hundred pellets. Just wait for the enemy to get within thirty-four paces, and then aim and open fire, with one piece shooting three times, so that its sound doesn't cease, and there won't be any [enemy] who hasn't been hit. Those enemy horse that come charging forth can be dealt staggering blows by holding the gun like a cudgel.[30]

Thus, it seems clear that guns were considered effective at defending against nomads in the early Ming period, but there is another way that Chase's argument must be reassessed, by turning our attention from China's northern borders to its maritime south.

Southern warfare

Yongle himself recognized the significance of southern warfare, because he was not just focused on the Mongols but also dispatched large campaigns against Vietnam – or, more accurately, the Dai Viet state – whose armies were decidedly not of the mounted nomad type.[31]

Chase discounts the influence of the Vietnam campaigns, arguing that guns proved ineffective in Vietnamese jungles and against the guerilla tactics of the Vietnamese.[32] Yet, as Sun Laichen and others have argued, the Vietnamese Wars actually involved many large infantry battles and sieges, in which firearms played key roles. Indeed, Sun has argued that the constant warfare that the Dai Viet state conducted against its Southeast Asian neighbors stimulated Dai Viet gunpowder warfare technology, and he shows that when the Ming encountered Vietnamese weapons, they were impressed and began adopting Vietnamese innovations, even as the Dai Viet state adopted and adapted Ming gunpowder weaponry.[33] Ming generals also captured Vietnamese firearms experts and sent them back to northern China, where they helped build guns and institutions that were used on the northern borders. Some went on to fight in Yongle's Mongolian campaigns.[34]

This pattern – innovations from southern warfare being brought to bear in the north – continued throughout the Ming Dynasty. Even if Chase is right that fighting against the Mongols and other mounted nomads did not stimulate firearms innovation as much as fighting against infantry forces (and it's not clear that he is), we must nonetheless remember how much warfare Chinese regimes carried out in southern areas. The Vietnamese Wars were one example, but there were many others.

For instance, in 1521 and 1522, Ming forces fought against the Portuguese near Guangzhou. Jack Wills examined the events surrounding this odd episode.[35] It was not a major conflict from the perspective of Beijing, but what seems clear is that it inaugurated a period of intense innovation and experimentation in firearms technologies and techniques in China. Indeed, one can see the process of stimulation and adaptation occurring during the Sino-Portuguese conflict itself. The war was, in fact, two separate conflicts, one in 1521 and one in 1522. It seems, from the sources, that in the first conflict the Ming forces were outgunned by the Portuguese, whereas the following year it was the other way around: Ming forces outgunned the Portuguese.[36]

This suggests that adaptation was swift and that the military gap was narrow. Indeed, the technological difference between Portuguese guns and traditional Ming guns was slight. Aside from the fact that the Portuguese guns were breech-loaders (something that Chinese observers found quite ingenious), the most significant difference between them and then-current Ming guns was barrel length. Starting in the second half of the 1400s Europeans began making guns that were much longer than previously, and the process stabilized into a new and very long-lasting form around 1480. This new design, which some historians have labeled the "classic gun," achieved greater power at lower weight, because it allowed the gunpowder reaction to accelerate the projectile for a longer time before ejecting it from the barrel.[37]

But what is intriguing is that Chinese guns were already trending in this direction, toward a longer barrel relative to muzzle bore.[38] That development seems to have slowed or even stopped in China around 1450 or so, which was precisely the time when it accelerated in western Europe. Why? It's intriguing that the process stopped occurring in China at precisely the time that the threat of mounted nomads began to recede in northern China. The year 1450 marks the end of a period of Mongol resurgence, and the Mongol threat would not re-emerge in an existential fashion until the mid-1500s. This suggests that in fact warfare – whether against Mongols or not – was indeed stimulating innovation in gun design in China. Although China saw massive levels of warfare from the 1350s through 1450, those levels tapered off from 1450 until around 1550, even as western Europeans fought even more vehemently and on a larger scale than they had done before.[39] Perhaps Chase is wrong to dismiss the frequency of warfare as a factor.

Still, we must be careful making comparisons between Europe and China. Ideally, one would compare the speed of gun developments in each area, by plotting the ratio of muzzle length to bore width per year in China and western Europe. Unfortunately, however, we lack good data from Europe. Whereas we have dozens of extant guns with firm dating from China in the 1300s and early 1400s, we have very few from Europe, where the practice of stamping dates on guns was not so prevalent. In the absence of good data from Europe, all we know is that the lengthening of barrels in China was evident in the late 1300s through 1450 or so, and that in Europe the process appears to have sped up after 1450, when it seems to have slowed in China. In any case, it seems that the development of the "classic gun" might well have occurred indigenously in China as well if overall rates of warfare hadn't decreased, because gun designs were trending in that direction.

Equally intriguingly, the Chinese immediately began adopting these long Portuguese guns, and they were most excited about using them, not against the Portuguese or other southern threats but against mounted warriors in northern China. Wang Hong, the commander of the Ming forces against the Portuguese, argued that Portuguese guns would prove vital to use to defend China's north. As he wrote in a famous memorial of 1529 (Jiajing 9), Portuguese guns should be deployed along the Great Wall:

> Today on the strategic borders the fortifications and walls are not fully secured, and when the enemies come there is ravaging and devastation.

The towers (墩台) have been constructed merely as lookout towers, but the walls and fortifications (城堡) lack any capacity to defend at long range, and so frequently there are troubles. It would be suitable to use the Frankish guns I have submitted. The small ones weigh just twenty pounds [*jin*] or less, and in terms of range they can reach six hundred paces. They can be deployed on the lookout platforms (墩台), with each placement (墩) being equipped with one, with three men to protect it. The large ones can be seventy pounds [*jin*] or more, and they have a range up to five or six li. They should be deployed on the forts (城堡), with each fort being equipped with three, with ten men to protect them. Thus, every five li there will be one lookout tower (墩), and every ten li one fort (堡), and the small and large can back each other up, and the near and far as well. The enemy generals have nothing to counter this sort of thing, such that [if my plan is adopted] one can just sit and wait for them, achieving victory without attacking.[40]

Wang Hong's idea was thus to use guns in defense, not offense, and his plan was adopted. As the official *Ming History* notes, "this is the point at which [our] guns began to include Frankish guns."[41]

Many other officials besides Wang Hong championed guns for northern defenses. Weng Wanda (翁 萬 達, 1498–1552), who was in charge of border defenses in the north during the period 1544–49, when the Mongols were resurgent, felt that only with firearms could one fight against the swiftly moving Mongols.[42] He wrote a special memorial, "On The Placement and Construction of Guns" (置造火器疏), that described gun designs he had developed, and that were in essence modifications of Portuguese guns and Western matchlock designs. It seems that these guns and others played a significant role in warfare against Mongols.[43]

There were many other innovations and adaptations involving the Frankish gun, which quickly became nativized to China, but there were also other types of innovations during the 1500s that came out of China's maritime experience and that, like the Frankish gun, were also transferred to northern China for use against mounted warriors.

One example is the musket, which was adopted in China at around the same time it was adopted in Japan, and with similar results.[44] Sun Laichen's chapter in this volume compellingly explores the process of musket adoption in China's maritime provinces, particularly Zhejiang, which began as a response to the depredations of the Wo pirates, whose Japanese-influenced fighting styles and exposure to Western weapons made them particularly deadly. Chinese military leaders – most notably the famous general Qi Jiguang – responded by incorporating muskets into their military organization. As Qi Jiguang wrote, the Wo pirates were a challenging foe, and he found himself unable to defeat them at first. But, as he wrote, "Having suffered setbacks and been thus forced to consider things, [I] used defeat to strive for victory and replaced [our] bows-and-arrows with the tactic of proficiently firing muskets (*niao chong*)."[45] Muskets, combined artfully with troops bearing standard weapons, and trained and drilled assiduously, became a core part of his armies, which succeeded in defeating the Wo invaders. What is particularly intriguing from the perspective of global military history is that Qi Jiguang employed muskets in countermarch formations well before the most standardly accepted date of the technique's adoption in Europe (c. 1600) or Japan (c. 1575).[46]

Qi Jiguang, like Wang Hong, also brought his experiences fighting in the maritime regions to northern China, where he was posted in the late 1560s and 1570s. His second major military manual, the *Lianbing shiji*, was composed during and in reference to his tenure in the north, and it notes that muskets were quite useful against northern enemies.[47]

Yet it is highly intriguing that there are also strong hints in Qi Jiguang's writings that the musket was perhaps not ideally suited to battles with nomads. He frequently complained that northern troops were too stubborn to adopt the musket: "In the north," he wrote,

> soldiers are stupid and impatient, to the point that they cannot see the strength of the musket, and they insist on holding tight to their fast lances (快鎗). Despite the fact that when comparing and vying on the practice field the musket can hit the bullseye ten times better than the fast-lance and five times better than the bow and arrow, they refuse to be convinced.[48]

Qi Jiguang attributed their stubbornness to a lack of proper training: you can't expect muskets to work effectively on the battlefield if soldiers aren't trained properly to use them, and this training must be both individual and collective.[49]

Yet, perhaps these stubborn northerners were onto something. The musket was slow to fire. In contrast, the fast lance was, as its name implies, fast. It was a long-handled short-barreled weapon, which sometimes had more than one barrel for multiple shots. It may have been less accurate than the musket, but it was probably faster to load, and it was likely far more useful at close range, such as when horsemen were bearing down on one.

Corroborating this notion is evidence suggesting that when other Chinese military leaders adapted Western guns for use on the northern frontier they made them shorter, decreasing accuracy but increasing speed and spread, making them useful for short range stopping power. For instance, Weng Wanda developed a gun known as the "vanguard gun" (先鋒炮), which was, as he himself described it, "copied from the Frankish guns but with modifications" (仿佛郎機而損益之也).[50] It was similar to Frankish guns in that it was a breech-loader with multiple removable chambers for quick loading; it was similar to muskets in that it had a matchlock mechanism; but it was much shorter than either of these Western types. This allowed it to be used on horseback against nomads, and it appears to have been successful.[51]

Although muskets were certainly used in northern warfare, it does seem that they didn't take root there as rapidly as they did in the south. Qi Jiguang himself felt that they were far more useful in the south than in the north. "In the south, the fields are muddy and the bogs treacherous. Infantry must be light and agile, and heavy weapons are difficult to transport. So [in this region] muskets (*niao chong* 鳥銃) are the best."[52] He Rubin had a similar opinion: "the musket is suitable for the south but not for the north; the three-eye gun [a variant of the fast lance] is suitable for the north but not for the south."[53]

Muskets did come to play an important role in northern warfare during the Japanese Invasion of Korea, 1592–98, but that is because they were suitable against the Japanese troops, whose fighting style was much more similar to the southern styles of Qi Jiguang than to the fighting style of Chinese generals schooled in warfare against the mounted nomads. Indeed, as Kenneth Swope has shown, when northern Chinese armies faced musket-bearing Japanese troops, they faltered, and they therefore deliberately adopted the tactics and weaponry of southern Chinese troops, including muskets. Ming general Li Rusong (李如松), who fought against the Japanese, wrote,

> I am a general who hails from the north and I have much experience in the fighting tactics used by the nomads, but here they are of no use. Now that I've come here [to Korea], I am using the tactics of battling the Japanese discussed in General Qi [Jiguang's] *Jixiao xinshu*, and I am able to attain total victory.[54]

Korean warmakers were also impressed with the southern troops of the Ming. When they revamped their military structures after the Japanese Invasion, they focused on the methods of Qi Jiguang, issuing new editions of his work with Korean commentaries. Subsequently, Korean musketeers employing countermarch techniques were among the best in East Asia – perhaps among the best in the entire world, because they certainly proved capable of defeating Russian musketeers.[55]

Historian Wu Zhao has argued that the infantry revolution that occurred in southern China during the 1540s and 1550s, when Qi Jiguang and others focused on drilling with small units and arquebuses, did not permeate effectively to the north. The two cultures, he argues, remained separate, and this explains China's difficulties during the Imjin War. He acknowledges that southern generals such as Qi Jiguang himself were sent northwards, but he argues that they couldn't change northern military traditions because northern military leaders "conservatively believed that large-calibre guns, for the attack of fortified positions, were superior, and they didn't apply the guns of southern battlefields, such as the musket ..., to northern battlefields."[56] He believes that it would have been better for the northerners to adopt the musket, implying that their conservatism was the major impediment.

But it seems quite likely that in fact larger-caliber, faster guns were more suited to fighting nomads. Weng Wanda explicitly redesigned long, thin guns to make them shorter, higher in caliber, and faster to fire. Similarly, as we've noted, northern troops, in the words of Qi Jiguang, stubbornly "insisted on holding tight to their fast lances (快鎗)."[57] This suggests that there is something to Chase's idea that the nomadic menace exerted a different sort of selective pressure on gun development than did more standard infantry threats. That doesn't mean that the nomadic menace prevented innovation in gun usage – it just pointed that innovation in different directions: toward large caliber firearms on the battlefield; and toward quick-firing guns on walled defenses.

Another example of southern-to-northern diffusion is the Red-Barbarian-Cannon, about which I and others have written at length elsewhere.[58] These were not the first large muzzle-loading guns to be adopted in China – the much less-known *fagong* was adopted in southern China in the 1550s or so.[59] But the red-haired-barbarian guns, which were first seen aboard the vessels of the light-haired Dutch and British (whence the name) proved much more influential. It was immediately clear how useful they would be, and they were adopted and adapted – at tremendous expense and effort – not just by southern Chinese but also in the north. Indeed, as Kenneth Swope and others have recently argued, they revolutionized Chinese siegecraft and defense, since they were capable of blowing breaches in China's massively thick walls, whereas previous cannons that had been brought to East Asia appear to have been relatively ineffectual against Chinese walls.[60] These powerful guns spread beyond China itself, taken up by the powerful Manchu state in the 1620s and 1630s, and they became a core part of the Manchu arsenal, helping it to defeat the Ming Dynasty and establish the Qing Dynasty as rulers over "All under Heaven."

Qing armies subsequently used variants of red-barbarian cannons in northern warfare, deploying them against the Russian artillery fortress of Albazin, in the Amur River region, and also – in smaller versions – in the massive campaigns of the Kangxi and Qianlong Emperors against the nomads. As Peter Perdue has shown in his magisterial work, logistics and statecraft were key underpinnings of the great Manchu conquests of Xinjiang, but cannons were also significant.[61] Certainly, Kangxi himself felt that they were invaluable.

Indeed, it seems that Kangxi became convinced of the necessity to invest in cannons by his experience in the War of the Three Feudatories, another southern war that I believe played a huge stimulative role in Chinese warfare and in the evolution of firearms. When I and some Emory students constructed a database of the frequency of the use of the term "cannon" and "gun" in the *Ming* and *Qing Veritable Records*, we found that one of the most significant periods of the occurrence of those terms fell during the Three Feudatories War period.[62] This indicates that there was considerably more discussion of guns and cannons then than at any other time in the Qing Dynasty until the Opium War. This was a surprise, and it suggests that the

Three Feudatories War was far more important in Chinese military history than has probably been appreciated. Indeed, we know that Wu Sangui created many cannons to use in the war, and that Kangxi did as well. The Three Feudatories War was, of course, a southern war, and the fact that it was so formative is further evidence that we must take the southern military context seriously.

Conclusions

Chase's *Firearms* is a great book. It introduced many readers to the field of Chinese military history and has stimulated productive debate. Yet I hope that this chapter may help point the way to a more nuanced understanding of the development of Chinese firearms, supporting the work of other scholars critical of the Chase model, such as Kai Filipiak, Stephen Morillo, and Kenneth Swope.[63] Chase's overall argument – that the Chinese failed to "perfect" the gun because they faced nomads rather than standard infantry – needs to be modified. For one thing, the Chase model focuses overly much on offensive war. It was of course difficult to use guns to attack mounted nomads in the field, but that's because it was difficult to catch mounted nomads in the field at all. As Chase notes so compellingly, they simply dissolved into the steppe, living off the land. It didn't matter so much whether one had cavalry or infantry, or how one's troops were armed. The armed forces of agriculturally-based states like China – whether infantry or cavalry – couldn't compete with nomads on their own turf until those states developed effective and far-reaching logistical networks.

But that didn't mean that guns were not considered worth investing in, and this was particularly the case when it came to defense. Guns were considered vital protection against nomadic incursions, as was made so clear in 1449, when guns played a key role in the defense of Beijing against the Mongol incursion. Throughout the following centuries, guns were integral to northern defenses. Ming officials themselves frequently said as much, and they invested heavily in gun research and production, filling the northern frontiers with gun placements.

To be sure, in some cases, guns were indeed used offensively against nomads, as in Yongle's early Mongolian expeditions, and, even more spectacularly, in the Kangxi, Yongzheng, and Qianlong emperors' protracted wars of the eighteenth century. Those campaigns relied closely on cannons and to a lesser extent, muskets, and they eventually succeeded in quelling the nomadic menace once and for all. Yet we must remember that the key to these victories was less technological (the Mongols, too, had guns) than logistical. There was no shortcut to defeating the nomads. It was done one supply depot at a time, and the eventual Qing victory over the nomads, which occurred during the eighteenth century, was a logistical operation of stunning reach and sophistication. Even so, guns did play a role, and they were the object of considerable investment.

Most important of all, we must always keep in mind that warfare in China was varied and diverse. The northern frontiers were certainly more important than other frontiers, at least for the perceived safety of the realm. The founder of the Ming Dynasty, the Hongwu Emperor, famously said that whereas most military threats to China were "no more than mosquitos and scorpions," the northern peoples were a constant "danger to our heart and stomach."[64] Yet as he himself realized, warfare in southern China was also important. From the Vietnam Wars of Yongle in the early fifteenth century, through the Portuguese wars of the 1520s, through the wars against the "Wo" pirates in the 1550s, through the wars against the Dutch in the 1600s, and through the War of the Three Feudatories, military innovations were forged in southern regions and spread thereafter to the rest of the realm.

Yet we shouldn't reject the Chase thesis altogether. It does seem to be true that the nomadic menace pointed gun evolution in a different direction: toward shorter, faster-firing, less accurate guns, at least in field warfare. The fact that the Chinese court was located in northern China may indeed have led to some kind of neglect of southern innovations, although at times that neglect was pointedly re-examined, as in the Japanese invasion of Korea, when northern troops proved so much less useful against the Japanese than did southern troops.

One final point. If Chase's answer must be challenged, aren't we still left with a puzzle? Why did Europeans "perfect" guns whereas Chinese didn't? Perhaps this puzzle is a chimera. As I've described above, and as I – and many others have – shown elsewhere, Ming and early Qing warmakers innovated furiously and effectively with guns throughout the period from 1550 or so through the early 1700s. We must, then, explain not a general failure to "perfect," but a short period of falling behind: during the second half of the 1400s, European guns evolved rapidly even as developments slowed or stopped in China. This period of Chinese military stagnation, such as it was, was over by the 1510s or so, when Chinese warmakers began to adopt newer Western designs with alacrity.[65]

So why did China fall behind for this short period? And why did it begin innovating again so rapidly during the mid-1500s? This puzzle is made especially acute if we recognize that developmental trends were quite similar up to around 1450, at least in terms of the shape of guns, which were getting longer relative to muzzle bore on both sides of Eurasia.[66] The answer probably lies in an explanation that Chase too hastily rejects: the frequency of warfare. From the mid-1300s to 1450, there was a lot of warfare in China, of all types. From 1450 to 1550 there was considerably less of it. From 1550 through 1683 there was, once again, an enormous amount of warfare in China. In contrast, Europe saw fairly constant (and quite high) levels of warfare throughout the period 1450–1700.[67]

The nomadic threat probably did play some role in China's differing patterns of military innovation, but China's military history was much more complex than is commonly recognized, and the maritime South is a key part of the story.

Notes

1 Kenneth Chase, *Firearms: A Global History to 1700* (Cambridge, 2003).
2 See especially Kenneth Swope, "Review of Kenneth Chase, *Firearms*," *Journal of the Economic and Social History of the Orient*, 47(2) (2004): 284–86; and Stephen Morillo, "Review of Chase, *Firearms*, and Lynn, *Battle*," *Journal of World History*, 15 (2004): 525–30. Swope's and Morillo's critiques are compelling. Certain other critiques are less so, such as Harald Kleinschmidt, "Review of Kenneth Chase, *Firearms*," *Journal of Military History*, 68(1) (2004): 242–43; cf. "Chase's Response to Kleinschmidt in Kenneth Chase, Letter to the Editor," *Journal of Military History*, 69(1) (2005): 311–12.
3 Philip T. Hoffman, *Why Did Europe Conquer the World?* (Princeton, NJ, 2015); Philip T. Hoffman, "Why Was It Europeans Who Conquered the World?" *Journal of Economic History*, 72(3) (2012): 601–33.
4 Ian Morris, *The Measure of Civilization: How Social Development Decides the Fate of Nations* (Princeton, NJ, 2013), 216–17; Ian Morris, *War! What is it Good For? Conflict and the Progress of Civilization from Primates to Robots* (New York, 2014), 176–77.
5 Max Boot, *War Made New: Technology, Warfare, and the Course of History, 1500 to Today* (New York, 2006); Azar Gat, *War in Human Civilization* (Oxford, 2006), 459–560; Azar Gat, "What Constituted the Military Revolution of the Early Modern Period?" in Roger Chickering and Stig Förster (eds.), *War in an Age of Revolution, 1775–1815* (Cambridge, 2010), 21–48, see esp. 24–25, 38–39; Jonathan Daly, *The Rise of Western Power: A Comparative History of Western Civilization* (London, 2014); Peter Golden, *Central Asia in World History* (Oxford, 2011), 104; Timothy May, *The Mongol Conquests in World History* (London, 2012), 150; Jack S. Levy and William R. Thompson, *The Arc of War: Origins, Escalation, and Transformation* (Chicago, 2011), 183.
6 See especially John E. Wills, Jr., "Maritime China from Wang Chih to Shih Lang: Themes in Peripheral History," in John E. Wills, Jr. and Jonathan Spence (eds.), *From Ming to Ch'ing: Conquest, Region, and Continuity in Seventeenth-Century China* (New Haven, 1979), 203–38.
7 As Frederick Mote once noted,

> Against external threats, only the northern frontier seemed to the Chinese to pose problems of state significance quite regularly, decade by decade. The boundaries on the other three sides marked "soft" frontiers on which conflicts between Chinese and non-Chinese normally were manageable at the level of local militia and police activity. Even when border problems on those frontiers demanded campaigns by the central armies (as Annam had in 1406, and as the southwest frontier had, to an extravagant and strategically unjustifiable degree in the decade prior to 1449), they never, or only very rarely, portended threats to the center; they did not topple dynasties, nor were invasions of the Chinese heartland ever in the offing.

Frederick W. Mote, "The T'u-Mu Incident of 1449," in Edward L. Dreyer, Frank Algerton Kierman and John King Fairbank (eds.), *Chinese Ways in Warfare* (Cambridge, MA, 1974), 243–72, 244.
8 Kenneth Swope, "Review of Kenneth Chase, Firearms," *Journal of the Economic and Social History of the Orient*, 47(2) (2004): 284–86; and Stephen Morillo,

"Review of Chase, Firearms, and Lynn, Battle," *Journal of World History*, 15 (2004): 525–30. Indeed, the Chinese military experience might be effectively compared to that of other large empires in the pre-modern period, such as the Byzantine Empire and the Ottomans. Like these empires, Chinese empires were consistently confronted by a multiplicity of military challenges by land and sea that often needed to be managed simultaneously. See, for instance, David Graff, *The Eurasian Way of War: Military Practice in Seventh Century China and Byzantium* (London, 2016); and Kenneth M. Swope, "Manifesting Awe: Grand Strategy and Imperial Leadership in the Ming Dynasty, *The Journal of Military History*, 79(3) (July 2015): 597–634.

9 See Tonio Andrade, *The Gunpowder Age: China, Military Innovation, and the Rise of the West in World History* (Princeton, 2016).

10 Chase, *Firearms*, 27.

11 Shih-shan Henry Tsai, *Perpetual Happiness: The Ming Emperor Yongle* (Seattle, 2001), 28.

12 Gu Yingtai 谷應泰, "Yan wang qi bing" 燕王起兵, *Ming shi jishi benmo* 明史紀事本末, Juan 16. There are different interpretations of this battle. The *Ming shi lu*, for example, treats Yongle's defeat in the battle as a mistake caused by the disobedience of his soldiers, who did not listen to his careful instructions, and it also emphasizes his own role in saving himself from encirclement, rather than crediting the "barbarian cavalry" who, it seemed, really did save his skin, as well as crediting him with saving a soldier who had lost his horse, sweeping the man under his arm and galloping to freedom. *Ming shilu, Taizong Shilu*, juan 6. www.jjwxc.net/onebook.php?novelid=377293&chapterid=10 retrieved November 26, 2012. My interpretation of this battle also differs a bit from that of David B. Chan, *The Usurpation of the Prince of Yen, 1398–1402* (San Francisco, 1976), 72ff.

13 Chase, *Firearms*, 44. Tsai, *Perpetual Happiness*, 168–70. Tsai suggests that guns were not used until the second expedition, writing that in it Yongle "made use of prototype cannons and also blunderbusses," (171); W. Franke, "Yonglo's Mongolei-Feldzüge," *Sinologische Arbeiten*, 3 (1945): 375–428, 379–81.

14 *Ming shi*, juan 154, Liezhuan 42 列 传 第 四十 二, Liu Sheng 柳 升.

15 *Ming shilu, Taizong shilu* 太 宗 文 皇 帝 實 錄, Yongle 8, Month 6, dingwei day (July 13, 1410), juan 105.

16 See Andrade, *Gunpowder Age*, 76–102.

17 Tsai, *Perpetual Happiness*, 170.

18 Jin Youzi 金幼孜, "Bei zhen hou lu" 北征後錄, one juan, www.guoxue123.com/other/gcdg/gcdg/021.htm, retrieved October 29, 2012.

19 Ming shilu, Taizong shilu 太 宗 文 皇 帝 實 錄, juan 152.

20 See Tonio Andrade, "Late Medieval Divergences: Comparative Perspectives on Early Gunpowder Warfare in Europe and China," *Journal of Medieval Military History*, 13 (2015): 247–76; and Tonio Andrade, "The Arquebus Volley Technique in China, c. 1560: Evidence from the Writings of Qi Jiguang," *Journal of Chinese Military History*, 4(4) (2015): 115–41.

21 Jin Youzi, "Bei zhen hou lu."

22 Chase, *Firearms*, 44–45.

23 *Ming shilu, Taizong shilu* 太 宗 文 皇 帝 實 錄, juan 262, Yongle 21, Month 8, bingyin day (September 22, 1423). Sinophone historians have interpreted this passage as indicating the use of volley fire. Wang Zhaochun, for example, writes,

The meaning of this is that when fighting, the shen ji qiangs and pao troops line up in front of the entire formation, and between them there must be a certain amount of space, so that they can load bullets and powder, and employ shooting by turns and in concert, to destroy the enemy advance guard. Once the enemy has been thrown into chaos, the rear densely arrayed cavalry troops together come forth in great vigor, striking forth with energy to topple mountains and turn over oceans.

Wang Zhaochun 王兆春, *Zhongguo huoqi shi* 中國火器史 (Beijing, 1991), 110. There's no doubt that early Ming troops deployed volley fire, but this passage doesn't seem to make a clear case for it.

24 Tsai, *Perpetual Happiness*, 173.
25 Tsai, *Perpetual Happiness*, 176–77.
26 The best English-language account of this episode is still Frederick W. Mote, "The T'u-Mu Incident of 1449," in Edward L. Dreyer, Frank Algerton Kierman and John King Fairbank (eds.), *Chinese Ways in Warfare* (Cambridge, MA, 1974), 243–72.
27 Wang Zhaochun, *Zhong guo huo qi shi*, 111.
28 He Rubin 何汝賓, *Bing lu* 兵 錄, juan 12, cited in Li Yue 李悦, "Ming dai huoqi de puxi" 明 代 火 器 的 譜 系, MA Thesis, Dongbei shifan daxue, 2012 (Department of History), 31.
29 *Ming Xiaozong shi lu* 明 孝 宗 實 錄, hongzhi 13, 7th month, cited in Li Yue, "Ming dai huo qi," 31.
30 He Rubin, *Bing lu*, juan 12, cited in Li Yue, "Ming dai huo qi," 16.
31 It's important to note that these were not solely maritime expeditions – they also involved huge numbers of ground troops, who marched by land. But what is clear is that the campaigns against Vietnam had a significant effect on early Ming military history, not to mention the history of Vietnam, as the Dai Viet state subsequently used Ming-derived firearms to defeat and annex its longtime rival, Champa.
32 Chase, *Firearms*, 48–49.
33 See the brilliant article Sun Laichen, "Chinese Gunpowder Technology and Dai Viet, ca 1390–1497," in Nhung Tuyet Tran and Anthony Reid (eds.), *Viet Nam: Borderless Histories* (Madison, 2006), 72–120.
34 Sun Laichen, "Chinese Military Technology and Dai Viet: c. 1390–1497," Asia Research Institute Working Paper Series No. 11, September 2003, 14–15.
35 John E. Wills, Jr., "Relations with Maritime Europeans," in Denis Twitchett and Frederick W. Mote (eds.), *The Cambridge History of China Volume 8: The Ming Dynasty, 1368–1644, Part 2* (Cambridge, 1998), 333–75. See also John E. Wills, Jr. (ed.), *China and Maritime Europe: 1500–1800: Trade, Settlement, Diplomacy, and Missions* (Cambridge, 2011), esp. 24–77; and Tonio Andrade, "Cannibals with Cannons: The Sino-Portuguese Clashes of 1521–1522 and the Early Chinese Adoption of Western Guns," *Journal of Early Modern History*, 19 (2015): 1–25.
36 See Andrade, "Cannibals."
37 Kay (formerly Robert) Smith, "All Manner of Peeces: Artillery in the Late Medieval Period," *Royal Armouries Yearbook*, 7 (2002): 130–38, 137; Bert S. Hall, *Weapons and Warfare in Renaissance Europe: Gunpowder, Technology, and Tactics* (Baltimore, 1997), 92; Kelly DeVries and Kay (Robert) D. Smith, *Medieval*

Military Technology, 2nd Edition (Toronto, 2012), 154; Kelly DeVries and Kay (Robert) Smith, *The Artillery of the Dukes of Burgundy, 1363–1477* (Woodbridge, UK, 2005), 42.

38 See Andrade, "Late Medieval Divergences."

39 For more on the argument that levels of warfare influenced military innovation in China, see Andrade, *Gunpowder Age*, esp. 1–28 and 312–16.

40 *Ming History*, juan 235, *Foreign Countries Part 6* (外 國 六) section on "Fo lang ji."

41 *Ming History*, juan 235, *Foreign Countries Part 6* (外 國 六) section on "Fo lang ji."

42 Feng Zhenyu 馮 震 宇, "Lun Folangji zai Mingdai de tuhua," 論 佛 郎 機 在 明 代 的 本 土 化, *Ziran bian zhengfa tongxun* 論 佛 郎 機 在 明 代 的 本 土 化, 34(3) (2012): 57–62, 59.

43 Weng Wanda 翁 萬 達, "Zhizao huoqi shu," 置 造 火 器 疏, Weng Wanda ji 翁 萬 達 集 (Shanghai, 1992), 378–79, cited in Feng Zhenyu, "Lun Folangji," 59.

44 Here I use the generic term "musket," when perhaps a more precise term would be "arquebus." Muskets tended to be heavier than arquebuses, with larger bores, but following previous scholars, I will here use "musket" as a general term for long-barreled matchlock firearms from the sixteenth and seventeenth centuries.

45 Qi Jiguang 戚繼光, *Lianbing shiji* 練兵實紀, edited and annotated by Qiu Xintian 邱心田 (Beijing, 2001), 242 ("Zaji, juan 2" 雜集卷二, "Chu lian tonglun" 儲練通論).

46 Andrade, "The Arquebus Volley Technique in China, c. 1560."

47 Qi Jiguang, *Lianbing shiji.*

48 Qi Jiguang 戚繼光, *Jixiao xinshu: shisi juanben* 紀效新書:十四卷本, edited and annotated by Fan Zhongyi 范中義 (Beijing, 2001), 57.

49 Qi Jiguang, *Jixiao xinshu*, 135–36.

50 翁 萬 達, "Zhizao huoqi shu," 置 造 火 器 疏, Weng Wanda ji 翁 萬 達 集, cited in Feng Zhenyu, "Lun Folangji," 59.

51 Feng Zhenyu, "Lun Folangji," 59.

52 Qi Jiguang, *Jixiao xinshu*, 49.

53 He Rubin 何汝賓, *Bing lu* 兵錄 (1606), juan 12, cited in Li, "Ming dai," 16. He Rubin believed that the reasons had to do with the intense northern winds, which had a tendency to blow the powder out of the musket's flashpan, as well as with the greater speed of the fast lance, which was less accurate than the musket but much easier to load, and thus more effective against mounted adversaries.

54 Li Rusong, cited in Kenneth Swope, *A Dragon's Head and a Serpent's Tail: Ming China and the First Great East Asian War, 1592–1598* (Norman, 2009), 163.

55 On these reforms, see Tonio Andrade, Hyeok Hweon Kang, and Kirsten Cooper, "A Korean Military Revolution? Parallel Military Innovations in East Asia and Europe," *Journal of World History*, 25(1) (2014): 47–80; on the victories over the Russians, see Hyeok Hweon Kang, "Big Heads and Buddhist Demons: The Korean Musketry Revolution and the Northern Expeditions of 1654 and 1658," *Journal of Chinese Military History*, 2(2) (2013): 127–89.

56 Wu Zhao 吳超, "16 zhi 17 shiji Riben huoqi zai Dongya quyu de liubu yu yingxiang kaoshu," 16至17世紀日本火器在東亞區域的流布與影響考述, *Dongfang luntan* 東方論壇, no. 2 (2013): 12–16, 15.

57 Qi Jiguang, *Jixiao xinshu*, 57.

58 Huang Yi-Long 黃一農, "Hongyidapao yu Ming Qing zhanzheng–yi huopao cezhu jishu zhi yanbian wei li," 紅夷大砲與明清戰爭——以火砲測準技術之演變為例, *Qinghua xuebao* 清華學報 (Taiwan), 26(1) (1996): 31–70; Huang Yi-Long 黃一農, "Ming Qing dute fuhe jinshupao de xingshuai" 明清獨特複合金屬砲的興衰, *Qinghua xuebao* 清華學報, 41(1) (2011): 73–136; Huang Yi-Long 黃一農, "Ming Qing zhi ji hongyidapao zai dongnan yanhai de liubu ji qi yingxiang," 明清之際紅夷大砲在東南沿海的流布及其影響, *Zhongyang yanjiuyuan lishi yuyan yanjiusuo jikan* 中央研究院歷史語言研究所集刊, 81(4) (2010): 769–832; Tonio Andrade, *Lost Colony* (Princeton, NJ, 2011), 244–45.

59 Zheng Cheng 鄭誠, "Fagong kao: 16 shiji chuan Hua de Oushi qianzhuang huopao ji qi yanbian," 發熕考 – 16 世紀傳華的歐式前裝火炮及其演變," *Ziran kexueshi yanjiu* 自然科學史研究, 32(4) (2013): 504–22.

60 See especially Shi Kang 石康 (Kenneth Swope), "Ming-Qing zhanzheng zhong da pao de shiyong," 明清战争中大炮的使用, *Qingshi yanjiu* 清史研究, no. 3 (2011), 143–49.

61 Peter Perdue, *China Marches West: The Qing Conquest of Central Eurasia* (Cambridge, MA, 2005).

62 See Andrade, *Gunpowder Age*, 312–15.

63 See Kai Filipiak, "Technological Advance in the War against the Mongols," in Kaushik Roy and Peter Lorge (eds.), *Chinese and Indian Warfare: From the Classical Age to 1870* (London, 2015), 121–33.

64 Cited in Frederic Wakeman, Jr., *The Great Enterprise: The Manchu Reconstruction of Imperial Order in Seventeenth-Century China*, vol. 1 (Berkeley, 1985), 24.

65 See Andrade, *Gunpowder Age*, 75–123.

66 See Andrade, *Late Medieval*.

67 See Andrade, *Gunpowder Age*, esp. 310–11.

6 The military implication of Zhu Wan's coastal campaigns in southeastern China

Focusing on the matchlock gun (1548–66)

Sun Laichen[1]

"The Introduction of these sophisticated [matchlock] arms in the Orient by the Portuguese modified significantly the History of Asia…"[2]

– Rainer Daehnhardt, 1994

"Ever since the Japanese pirates rose up on the sea, besides [their] sword formation, [their] most dreadful weapons were firearms. [They] had ravaged [the coast regions] for many years, and dead bodies piled up. The Wu and Yue [Jiangsu and Zhejiang] people gradually learned their [Japanese] techniques, came up with ways of breaking their sword formation, and also copied their [matchlock] firearms to fight against the pirates, thus the pirates were defeated and never came back again."[3]

– Wang Tonggui, 1598

Introduction

The smuggling trade and piracy on the southeastern coast of Ming China during the 1520s and 1550s, and the suppression of them by Zhu Wan 朱紈 in 1548–49, are well documented. In 1547, Zhu Wan was appointed governor of Zhejiang with additional responsibilities for the coastal area of Fujian to deal with the piracy problem. Over the next two years he mobilized troops under his command in two provinces and successfully and summarily defeated the smugglers and pirates. But Zhu Wan met an unexpected tragic end by committing suicide in 1550 due to charges laid against him for having executed captives without permission from the Ming court.[4]

This episode in late Ming history has attracted much attention and as a result many studies have been produced.[5] Most of these, however, approach the piracy issue of the 1520s to 1550s and especially the crackdown of it by Zhu Wan from political, economic, and social perspectives, with few approaching it from a military perspective, especially when it comes to technology. For example, scholars have discussed the consequences of Zhu Wan's actions, including the occupation of Macao by the Portuguese, the subsequent disturbances, and especially raids by pirates on China's coastal regions, and the formation of the Eastern Asian trading network.[6] To be sure, there are a few discussions of the transfer of military technology as a result of Zhu Wan's campaigns, but these are to different degrees brief, general, or narrowly focused.[7] Most of these are either in Japanese or Chinese, hence a comprehensive and deep study in English is much needed.

For the sake of space and depth, I will focus on the spread of the matchlock gun to China during the period of 1548–66. The issue sounds very familiar, and the topic seems to have received much attention already. But as Tonio Andrade has pointed out, "[m]any questions remain unanswered."[8] For example, so far the existing studies, as represented by Joseph Needham and Wang Zhaochun, have discussed the spread of the matchlock from Japan, but have not dealt with its military implications for its role in the war against the pirates in particular and in the late Ming wars in general.[9] Hence, basically, they have dealt with the "transmission" issue but still left many questions unanswered. Above all, they have not broached the "application" and "implication" issues.

Therefore, my first goal is to go further to discuss some of the issues surrounding the spread of the matchlock gun to China (careful reading of Zhu Wan's reports *Piyu zaji* 甓餘雜集 and other sources will shed valuable light on this matter). My second goal is to show the important role the matchlock gun played in military actions against the pirates in southeastern China up to 1566.[10] The matchlock gun was given several Chinese names, such as "niaozui chong" (bird-beak gun) and "niaochong/niaoqiang 鳥鎗" (bird gun), and several explanations on the origin of them have been offered. As one of the important issues surrounding the transmission of the matchlock gun to China, it has not received sufficient attention. Hence, my third goal is to provide a lengthy discussion on this and hope to shed more light on it. In this section, I will challenge Qi Jiguang's 戚繼光 long-established and influential view that the "bird gun" was so named because it was used for shooting birds. My overall argument is that the military technology in general and the matchlock gun in particular, acquired by the Chinese, played a significant role in late Ming China.

Issues surrounding the early spread of matchlocks into China

Five years prior to Zhu Wan's crackdown on the smugglers, an interesting skirmish had already taken place. In 1543 (Jiajing 22), Ming forces were sent to fight Hu Sheng 胡勝 and Xu Dong 許棟, the leaders of the multinational smugglers, on the Shuangyu Island (off Ningbo city, on today's Liuheng 六橫 Island). But due to the fierce firepower of the cannons and firearms (大小鉛子火銃) the smugglers possessed, Ming troops suffered a huge defeat and humiliation: many were killed. Chin concludes,

> The victory the multinational smugglers achieved in their clashes with the Ming coastal forces paved the way for smugglers to create a sizable

community at Shuangyu. From that time onwards, they not only established trading settlements on islands off the Zhejiang coast, but gradually expanded their activities to markets in southern Fujian, eastern Guangdong, and even to the city of Nanjing.[11]

Three years later, in 1546, the smugglers even kidnapped several low-ranking officers and demanded goods and monetary compensation from the local government in Zhejiang.[12]

Where did Hu Sheng and Xu Dong obtain their weapons? Some years previously, Xu Dong and his followers (including his biological brothers) sailed to the Portuguese colony of Melaka and purchased merchandize and weapons including big and small guns and swords (大小火銃槍刀).[13] These big and small guns no doubt included matchlocks and other European-style guns (see below). Zhu Wan's account highlights the power of these weapons in Hu and Xu's defeat of the Ming troops. It was probably through this type of encounter that the Ming forces obtained a small number of matchlocks. For example, in the first clash between the Ming forces and the smugglers in the fourth month of 1548, Ming soldier Li Guangshou 李光守 used a matchlock gun to kill one enemy and was later on rewarded.[14]

The turn of the Ming troops arrived when in 1548–49 Zhu Wan launched his military campaigns from Zhejiang to Fujian against the multinational smugglers including Chinese, Japanese, Siamese, Malay, Africans, and particularly Portuguese. It was an easy and quick victory for the Ming side. In these encounters, Zhu Wan's troops captured a large number of weapons, especially huge muzzle-loading cannons ("falcon" in Portuguese, or *fagong* 發貢/發鑛/發熕 cannon as has been identified by Zheng Cheng), Frankish breech-loading cannons, matchlock muskets, swords, etc.[15] The Ming military also captured many ships, among them, the Southeast Asian style ship *prahu* (*balahu* 叭喇唬).[16] The falcon cannon, matchlock guns, and the *prahu* ship were basically new to China, and all of these weapons went on to play a key role in China's military, being deployed, for example, against the Japanese when they invaded Korea in the 1590s. Indeed, they would remain in use until the end of the Qing Dynasty in the early twentieth century. The most important of these was the matchlock musket, the topic of this chapter.

It has been widely acknowledged that it was during Zhu Wan's campaigns that the Chinese acquired matchlock guns. But technically this was not true. Indeed, data from Zhu Wan's own reports can help us determine how European-style matchlock guns spread to China in earlier years.

Chinese scholars, most notably Wang Zhaochun, have tended to argue that matchlock guns reached China by way of Japan.[17] Joseph Needham, however, although recognizing the weight of this view, suggested an alternative, a Turkish or Ottoman route:

Perhaps the most likely conclusion is that there were two introductions of the matchlock to China, first from Turkey by way of the Muslim of

Sinkiang (Xinjiang), forming a tradition known only to restricted circles in the north and northwest; and secondly, in the south and south-east, a little later, either from the Japanese pirates or directly from the Portuguese merchant-adventurers.[18]

Needham's source is the *Shenqi pu* by Zhao Shizhen, a work on Turkish guns (called *Lumi chong* 嚕蜜銃 in Chinese, meaning musket of Rum, which referred to Byzantium, later the Ottoman capital) and was completed in 1598. The basis is a historical episode told by Zhao Shizhen's grandfather to him around 1568, during the early years of the incursions of the *Wonu* (Japanese pirates). It is translated by Needham as below (with my slight modifications):

My grandfather once spoke to me as follows: "I heard that during previous reigns the Turfan princedom [Tulufan] annexed its neighbor Hami. The Middle Kingdom then appointed someone as Commander of an Expeditionary Force [*jinglue dachen*], who enlisted tens of thousands of soldiers, and went to the aid [of Hami] from different directions. But because the Turfan troops borrowed efficacious firearms from Rum [*Lumi*] our soldiers could not rescue [Hami], which ultimately fell into their hands. Now Rum is near the Water [Greater?] Western Ocean region [i.e. Europe] by sea. Could it be that this weapon was transmitted from there to the Western Ocean people, who in turn brought it to the Japanese?"[19]

Three other Chinese texts contain passages similar to the above, though they fail to acknowledge the role of the Turkish guns. The first two put the event in 1473, the ninth year of the Chenghua Emperor; while the third one by Gu Yingtai put it seven years earlier.[20] Based on the story recorded by Zhao Shizhen, Needham speculated that Turkish guns could have spread to China prior to 1530, as the Ottomans sent envoys to China in both 1524 and 1526, and also in 1543–44. Those envoys would have had guards, who might have carried guns.

Zhu Wan's reports, however, contain three pieces of information that are salient. The first one is a memorial he wrote during the second month of 1549, which discusses the battle at Zoumaxi in Fujian. He commented upon the capture by his troops of a large number of Portuguese cannons and other weapons:

And Frankish cannons surpass those of both the barbarians and the Chinese. [This is shown that] in the past [Turfan] took Hami, captured its king and his seal. For the time being the important officials simply could not come up with a policy of attacking [the aggressor].[21]

Here Zhu Wan implied that the reason for the lack of a good policy was because Turfan possessed powerful weapons like Frankish cannons. Shortly after, in the same report, Zhu Wan provided very important information. He stated:

> Your servant once inquired concerning the arrest of the bandits Tang Hongchen and others; they all said that the Portuguese ships sailed from the outer sea in the northwest, and it took them four-odd months to arrive in the Min (Fujian) Sea. In the early years, [the Portuguese] were only making troubles in Guangdong. Due to the scheme of the vice naval commander Wang Hong, which killed all of them, [the Portuguese] dared not to enter Guangdong anymore. Hence they only come to Fujian, etc. Thus, this view and the story of the seizing of the Hami king's seal as told by Ke Qiao can reinforce each other![22]

This passage requires some unpacking. The first thing to note is that the Tang Hongchen that Zhu Wan references here was a soldier from Guangdong who appears several times in Zhu Wan's reports. He was one of the first Chinese to learn the geographical location of Portugal, and he also learned how much time was needed to sail from Europe to China. Tang Hongchen's information was quite significant because at that time most educated Chinese didn't know where Portugal was, a situation that didn't change markedly until the spread of world geography by missionaries such as Matteo Ricci in the late sixteenth century. Most Ming accounts are unclear about the geographical location of Portugal (*Folangji*), such as the *Ming shi* (Liezhuan 213, Waiguo 6), which states that "Folangji is near Malaka (Melaka)." Zhu Wan's passage also mentions the name Ke Qiao: he was the vice naval commander in Fujian, the highest-ranking official there.[23] It is in fact noteworthy that Ke Qiao knew the Turfan-Hami campaign well. Indeed, Zhu Wan himself mentions the Turfan-Hami conflict in one of his poems.[24]

It appears that Zhu Wan integrated Ke Qiao's story on the Turfan-Hami war with Tang Hongchen's knowledge and concluded that these two could support each other. In other words, Zhu Wan implicitly suggested Frankish cannons/guns could have spread to Turfan, which employed them in its conquest of Hami. This was indeed a precursor of Needham's speculation over four hundred years later! It also suggests that the Hami incident was well-known in Ming China. Though conclusive evidence for this speculation that Turkish matchlock guns spread first to China is still needed, the circumstantial evidence contained in Zhu Wan's reports is important. It also attests to the ongoing importance of overland routes to China as crucial to the dissemination of technologies and ideas, something that is often obscured amid the emphasis upon seaborne interactions in the post-Mongol world.

It is in this context that we should read and understand this Chinese account. In 1562, Zheng Ruozeng stated that, prior to the capture of Japanese muskets in 1548 (Jiajing 27), bird-[beak] guns had already been in China: "The transmission of the bird guns from the Western Barbarians (*xifan*) to China had been a long time ago, but manufacturers had not been able to perfect it."[25] Whether this refers to the Turkish matchlocks cannot be ascertained, but it at least indicates the date of the earliest spread of matchlock guns to China.[26] Nonetheless, Zheng Ruozeng may have meant something else. As discussed above already, Chinese merchant-smuggler-pirate groups had already obtained matchlocks in Southeast Asia, especially Melaka.[27]

The early use of the matchlock gun by Ming troops (1553–59)

The years from 1550 (when Zhu Wan committed suicide) to 1558 were a time during which Ming China acclimatized to the captured gunpowder technologies and ships. During this period, falcon cannons and Japanese-style matchlock guns were used by the Ming side, but only sporadically, and it seems that the pirates did not employ them very much either.

Yet evidence from the *Ming shilu* (Ming Veritable Records) suggests the Ming military started to employ the newly captured or manufactured weapons quite quickly. As early as 1553, several Nanjing officials made many suggestions regarding the coastal defense. Among them censor (御史) Zhao Chen 趙宸 suggested building warships, *lianzhu* cannons, and bird-beak guns ("wuzui huochong 烏嘴火銃," "wu" should be "niao 鳥") for use against the pirates. The Jiajing emperor adopted many of the suggestions.[28] This suggests that matchlock guns could have been manufactured at the provincial level already, four years after Zhu Wan's campaigns. In the next year (1554), according to Hu Zongxian's report to the Ming court, during a battle in Jiashan (嘉善), Zhejiang Province, a Ming officer was shot by a matchlock (bird) gun wielded by pirates, leading to the rout of a Ming force six hundred strong.[29] In 1555, Ming soldiers fired [matchlock] guns (*huochong* 火銃) at the pirates from the city wall of Nanjing.[30] During fighting along the Fujian coast in 1558 many pirates were gunned down by Ming forces using [matchlock] guns (*Zhejiang*).[31]

An eyewitness account by Cai Jiude of Haiyan, Zhengjiang Province provides us with valuable information. In 1553, different groups of pirates arrived by sea to pillage Haiyan. In the fifth month, for instance, there arrived thirty-seven ships and over 1000 pirates. Chou stresses at the very beginning that the pirates only carried spears, swords, bows and arrows, but not firearms. In contrast, the Ming forces, led by commander Tang Kekuang 湯克寬, did have guns. On the twenty-fifth day of the fifth month, they used matchlocks to kill several pirates, and cannons were also fired. The following year (1554), on the fourth day of the fifth month, firearms (probably falcon cannons) fired from Lu Tang's warship destroyed a pirate ship and killed several pirates. On the seventeenth day, Ming *fagong* cannons breached another pirate ship, and 340 pirates died. This made Chou Jiude happy and proud, and he comments that Ming troops could defeat the pirates easily because they had gunpowder weapons. Ten days later, the Ming soldiers took a stronghold by shooting gunpowder tubes (*huoyao tong* 火藥筒) and arrows. On the eighth day of the tenth month, gunpowder weapons (probably *fagong* cannons) destroyed another pirate ship, killing over eighty and capturing thirteen alive.

On the twenty-third day of the third month of 1555, the continuous roaring of cannons (*huopao* 火炮) at Ganpu (澉浦) town in Haiyan county scared the pirates, and they turned to another direction. On the twenty-fifth day of the fifth month, Ming warships fired cannons which scared the pirates again. On the thirteenth day of the ninth month, the vanguards of the Ming forces killed three pirates with swords and several dozen with matchlock(?) guns. On the sixth day of the fourth month of 1556, Ming matchlocks killed more than ten pirates, but more pirates stood up from their hiding places and killed more than a hundred Ming soldiers.

But it seems as though the pirates began arming themselves with firearms, too. On the twentieth day of the fourth month, a group of Ming northern soldiers were killed by enemy matchlocks. Yet it seems that the Ming held the edge. Five days later, for example, the pirates brought a bronze general cannon (*tong jiangjun* 銅將軍), but the Ming troops fired Frankish cannon, and the pirates retreated. On the twenty-ninth day of the seventh month, cannons on Ming warships roared among the islands, and the pirates under the chief Xu Hai retreated. On the twenty-fourth and twenty-fifth days of the eighth month, the two sides exchanged fierce fire from their warships, using *fagong* cannons. Eventually Xu Hai was defeated. The Ming side held a big celebration.[32]

Evidence suggests that cannons and firearms were employed in increasing numbers as time went on. In 1556–57, Ming troops under Lu Tang (盧鏜) employed the "bird[-beak] gun" to destroy enemy ships and kill many pirates in Cixi near (north of) Ningbo, Zhejing and Miaowan Huai'an in Jiangsu province.[33] In 1558–59, Ming troops under Tang Shunzhi (唐順之) and Lu Tang fought several fierce battles with pirates under Wang Zhi in the Miaowan (modern Funing) and Sansha (on Chongming island) region, Jiangsu Province. They concluded that "only gunpowder weapons can strike ships and break walls," hence the Ming troops carried with them Frankish cannons, son-mother cannons (*zimu pao* 子母砲), matchlock guns, falcon cannons, and Chinese-style flamethrowers, rockets, and general cannons (将軍砲).[34] Tang Shunzhi's memorials mention 500 matchlock gunners for one battle and 340 for another; they were always the first to charge and played a significant role in the victory. Many pirates were hit by lead bullets (*qiandan* 鉛彈 or *qianwan* 鉛丸). At the climax of fighting, "cannons and matchlocks fired at the same time, the sound shook the open country; walls collapsed and ships were destroyed, and the corpses of the pirates who were hit by lead bullets piled up inside the walls." At the end of one battle, Tang Shunzhi commented: "In this battle, without gunpowder weapons [we] could not have held the Laoying fortress." In another battle, gunpowder weapons – including matchlocks – routed the pirates:

> Our soldiers chased [the pirates], and the pirate battalions were all aggressive and arrogant. Lu Tang's battalion fired falcon and Frankish cannons and felled seven pirates. The various battalions [of the Ming] also fired matchlock guns at the enemies who thus retreated.[35]

This was a decisive battle and a real gunpowder war, and the beginning of a heightened level of employing cannons and firearms, especially on the Ming side. It is in this context that the Arsenal Bureau of the Ming in Beijing manufactured the first 10,000 matchlocks in 1558.[36] This is both symbolically and practically significant. By 1559, Ming diplomatic ships (*fengchuan* 封船) were heavily armed with cannons and firearms, etc., including as many as twenty Frankish cannons and 100 matchlocks.[37] Matchlocks were by now increasingly employed in China.

The official and unofficial historical accounts reinforce each other, and we can see from the above that the Ming troops had already benefited from the gunpowder technologies they acquired in 1548–49. An even more intensive use of them was carried out by the great generals Qi Jiguang and Yu Dayou.

The Qi Jiguang and Yu Dayou years (1560–66)

This section is divided into two parts, the first is on the origin of Chinese matchlock gun and some technical issues of the matchlock gun. The second is about the effectiveness of the matchlock gun in actual fighting under Qi Jiguang and Yu Dayou. Though I can finally solve some problems, my goal is to further the existing research.

The Japanese origin and technical aspects of the matchlock gun

The year 1560 saw a significant milestone in sixteenth-century Ming gunpowder technology, because that was the year that Qi Jiguang's and Yu Dayou's (俞大猷) military treatises were first published. We now focus on the matchlock gun. In 1560, 1571–77, and 1584, Qi Jiguang published three military treatises, *Jixiao xinshu* (18 chapter edition), *Lianbing shiji* (練兵實紀), and *Jixiao xinshu* (14 chapter edition). In all three of them, Qi introduced and discussed the matchlock gun.

Unequivocally but tersely, Qi expressed the opinion that the matchlock gun came to China from the Japanese. Perhaps he didn't find the issue terribly important, because he did not even mention the origin of the matchlock in his first manual, which was, as we have noted, published in 1560. It was in his 1571–77 treatise *Lianbing shiji* that he broached this issue for the first time: "China originally did not have this gun; it was obtained from the Japanese (woyi)."[38] In his 1584 revised edition of the *Jixiao xinshu*, he repeated this sentence but also added a piece of indirect information, which is an illustration of a horn-shaped container of priming gunpowder. He explained that the Japanese used horn instead of bamboo tubes for this purpose, but it was not as convenient as the latter.[39] The Japanese origin of the powder horn reinforces the Japanese origin of the matchlock gun.[40] There is certainly more evidence in this regard. For example, Guizhou provincial governor Guo Zizhang (郭子章) stated clearly in 1602 that during the Jiajing reign (1522–66) China obtained the Frankish cannon and the "bird-beak gun," the former came from Portugal (Folang) while the latter from Japan (Wo). Guo was also one of the two major commanders of the campaign against the rebellion of Yang Yinglong in Guizhou in 1600. He ordered the manufacture of weapons including the "bird-beak gun" and highly praised them:

> Nowadays one cannot talk about victory-winning weapons without talking about firearms [火器], [but these weapons] by and large are derived from Frankish cannon and bird-beak guns, just innovations based on these two… [That we could] break [Yang Yinglong's] fortress and annihilate the enemy was primarily due to the effective weapons.[41]

Zheng Ruozeng's discussion and diagrams of the matchlock gun were basically derived from Qi Jiguang. Zheng's only new information is that Zhu Wan captured, on Shuangyu Island, a "barbarian chief who was skillful in making guns [番酋善铳者]," from whom the Chinese acquired the knowledge of matchlock guns, such that the soldiers Ma Xian 馬憲 and Li Huai 李槐 were ordered to make guns and gunpowder respectively, and were able to construct even better guns than the Western Barbarians themselves (*xifan* 西番).[42] The term *fanqiu* (番酋) has caused much confusion and misunderstanding among scholars, because it has been interpreted as European, and specifically Portuguese.[43] Hora has proposed that "*fanqiu*" should be understood as "*wonu*" (倭奴) and specifically Shinshiro (新四郎).[44] I agree with Hora's speculation, especially the first part, and would like to go further. Through careful reading of Zheng Ruozeng's text, we found out that the word *fan*, although it typically refers to Europeans (or Southeast Asians), included the Japanese as well when used in a broader sense.[45] For instance, in Zheng's *Chouhai tubian*, on two occasions the word could mean Japanese or Japanese.[46] In any case, there seems good reason to revisit the idea that Zheng Ruozeng's work necessarily supports the hypothesis of Japanese transmission.

Now, let us turn to the quality and effectiveness of the matchlock gun. Qi Jiguang consistently held the matchlock gun in high regard and was an ardent promoter of it. In all three military manuals, Qi spoke highly of and introduced it in an extremely detailed way. Among its many excellent features, accuracy was the foremost. On different occasions in the three books, he explained that the reason it was called the "bird gun" was because it could shoot birds in the forest, with an ability to hit targets eight or nine times out of ten. It could shoot through not only a willow leaf from a hundred paces away, but also through the hole of a copper coin.[47] This accuracy resulted from the way the gun could be fired steadily with two hands, along with the sights on the barrel. The matchlock gun was also extremely powerful, thanks to its long and straight barrel and gunpowder formula. Qi emphatically discussed the length of the gun barrel on many occasions, explaining that in order for lead bullets to travel far and with force, the barrel should be long and its inside should be smooth and straight. Similarly, the lead bullets must fit the muzzle perfectly to prevent "gas [*huoqi* 火氣]" from leaking. A long barrel made the bullet go straight, and this was why it could hit the target and pierce through heavy armor.[48]

Interestingly, however, Qi failed to specify the length of the barrel. Song Yingxing, the versatile scholar of seventeenth-century China, did tell us that a bird gun should be about three *chi* long. Within thirty paces, the bird gun could smash the feather and flesh of a bird, and beyond fifty paces a bird would be smashed to pieces, but at 100 paces the gun would exhaust its force. Song Yingxing was probably the only one who made a distinction in 1637 between a *niaochong* and a *niaoqiang*, which provides us with an even better understanding of the correlation between the barrel and the shooting distance. He wrote that a *niaochong* was about three *chi* in length and had a range of one hundred paces, while a *niaoqiang*, which was made just like a *niaochong*, but possessing a barrel twice as long and using double the amount of gunpowder, could shoot beyond two hundred paces.[49] Before him, the term *niaoqiang* was already used, but very rarely.[50]

Thanks to the influence of the matchlock and other Western guns during this period, longer barrel lengths also began appearing on more traditional Chinese guns. When discussing other weapons Qi Jiguang also emphasized the length of the barrel. For example, the long neck or barrel (*xiangchang* 項長) and the matching of lead cannon balls and its muzzle of the *sai gong chong* (賽貢銃) (a type of cannon more powerful than the falcon cannon) made the cannon a powerful weapon. As for the Frankish cannon, the ingenious part was its long barrel, which could be made in various configurations: a barrel of seven *chi* would be the best, one of five *chi* would be fine, and one of three *chi* was the minimum. Shorter than three *chi* would be useless. In 1584, Qi even divided the Frankish cannon into five types based on the length of its barrel, that is, from nine to one *chi*. Due to its short belly (barrel), big muzzle, and short neck (gunpowder chamber), the barrel of the bowl-sized cannon (*wankou chong* 碗口銃) must be over three *chi* for it to be useful. Regarding the quick-firing gun (*kuai qiang* 快槍), the barrel used to be too short, and now it must be two *chi* long, the longer the better.[51] After the matchlock gun spread to Korea, the Koreans also learned about the effect of the longer barrel, as one scholar commented: "hence a gun with a long barrel is especially powerful."[52]

The third aspect is the corning of its gunpowder. According to Qi Jiguang, the formula for making gunpowder was 40 *liang* of saltpeter, five *liang* and six *qian* of sulfur, and seven *liang* and two *qian* of charcoal (Needham states the percentage is 75.7 percent saltpeter, 10.6 percent sulfur, and 13.7 percent carbon or charcoal). The "secret method" was to granulate the mixed and half-dried powder like beans ("Eventually it is broken up into pieces each as big as a small pea").[53] According to Zheng Cheng, even if corned gunpowder had existed before the late Ming, it was not popular. He points out that the fact that Qi Jiguang stressed his "secret method" suggests that it was something new, and the corned gunpowder spread from southeast China to the northern frontier by the 1590s.[54]

The increased length of European-style firearms and cannons was also discussed by others after Qi Jiguang (such as Zhao Shizhen 趙 士 楨),[55] and has been noted briefly by modern scholars,[56] and the Chinese may have known the corning process of gunpowder by the 1200s to the 1370s,[57] or at least relearned from the Portuguese in the 1520s and after. Chinese texts states that Portuguese gunpowder was different from the Chinese formulas (implying here the former being "corned gunpowder"), and several recipes are also available in late Ming texts.[58] Also, the advantages of the Frankish (Folangji) cannons, such as the longer barrel, were indicated in Gu Yingxiang's 顧應祥 and Weng Wanda's 翁萬達 descriptions and comments in the 1520s and 1540s respectively, especially the latter clearly pointed out that "the long barrel can concentrate gasses, making the firing speedy."[59]

Our point of discussing these is that it was through Qi Jiguang's emphasized introduction that the Chinese relearned the significance of long barrels and of the gunpowder corning process. He was not the first to discuss these things, but his treatment was the most systematic, and his works were highly influential. They reinforced, renewed, and certainly popularized these techniques. Qi was however the first to discuss and illustrate the matchlock gun in detail in Chinese history, and his descriptions, illustrations, and discussions were followed, often in verbatim, by almost every military writer who touched upon the topic after him, including Mao Yuanyi, He Rubin, and other well-known military writers.

There is another reason that scholars have suggested that the Chinese adopted the matchlock via Japan: the features of the guns themselves. For one thing, the Chinese guns had a "breech-screw plug," an innovation that solved the problem of inefficiency due to the leaking of gas from the breech. According to Wang Zhaochun, the Japanese invented this feature. Since Chinese matchlocks had such a screw plug, he concluded that a Japanese origin was likely.[60] Yet a closer examination of the guns themselves suggests that in fact European guns of the period already had "breech-screw plugs."

Qi Jiguang was the first to introduce this breech-screw plug in China, which appears in his 1560 treatise *Jixiao xinshu* (18 chapter edition). He illustrated the threaded breech (female screw) and the breech-screw plug (male screw), and explained it thus:

> In the breech [of the bird gun] there is a screw [{*luo*} *sizhuan* {螺} 丝轉], this is because this gun has a long barrel; after firing its insides often get wet, and it must be cleaned once in two to three days. Hence use a piece of cloth to wrap around the ramrod and dip into water to clean the barrel. If lead bullets are stuck inside the barrel or the touchhole is obstructed, then unscrew the breech-screw plug to fix it. It is extremely convenient.[61]

Joseph Needham calls this a "breech-screw" and speculates that it might well have been a direct imitation of Portuguese guns, because neither Japanese nor Chinese had a tradition of employing screws.[62] Wang Zhaochun, on the other hand, has contended that it was a Japanese invention, without further investigation. The breech plug has received much attention, especially among Japanese scholars, but nobody has discussed its origin.[63]

It turns out, however, that Wang was wrong and Needham was right: it was a European invention. Through research on existing artifacts of the early matchlock guns throughout the world, Rainer Daehnhardt has concluded that Japanese matchlock weapons were directly derived from the matchlock gun introduced by the Portuguese, with only slight modifications in decoration and other secondary details. More interestingly, Daehnhardt notes that such guns were already being used – and even manufactured – elsewhere in Asia before their introduction to maritime East Asia. He quotes Alfonso de Albuquerque's letter to Portuguese king Manuel I, saying that the gunsmiths in Goa "make guns as well as the Bohemians and equipped with screwed [*sic*] in breech plugs." According to Daehnhardt, "it was to the method of closing the breech with a thread and a screw," a Bohemian style different from the Islamic-Indo matchlock guns which had a welded breech plug. Moreover, it had a snap or quick ignition mechanism, as opposed to other European, Islamic-Indian slow ignition mechanisms. According to Daehnhardt, it was the fusion of the Bohemian-Goan style that gave rise to the Indo-Portuguese type of matchlock guns that were brought to Ceylon, Java, and Japan by the Portuguese.[64] Historical sources do show that the Japanese did consult with a Portuguese blacksmith to solve the breech-sealing issue. According to the *Teppoki* (the "Record of the Musket"), the Japanese on Tanegashima copied the gun from the Portuguese in 1543, hence

> [t]he form of the new weapon was much like [the foreign original], but the workers could not figure out how to close the bottom end [of the barrel] ... The next year ... there was among the traders one blacksmith ... Tokitaka ... ordered Lord Kinbee Kiyosada to learn how to close the end of the barrel that fitted into the stock. Finally, after some days and months he could manage to roll it to a close and had it completed.[65]

In addition, archeological evidence also shows that the Portuguese matchlock guns (*nanbanzutsu* 南蛮筒) that spread to Japan did indeed have this feature.[66]

The intensified use of matchlock guns under Qi Jiguang and Yu Dayou

Though there are still many lacunae in our understanding of the matchlock gun in China, one's impression is that the Japanese matchlock gun impressed the Chinese who started to adopt it immediately after their encounter with it. Yet Qi Jiguang's systematic descriptions of the matchlock gun were a milestone in Chinese people's understanding of it, becoming the fountainhead of subsequent Chinese discussion of the bird gun. Thus it is not surprising that the Chinese showered their praises on the gun.

Such praise is plentiful in the writings not just of Qi Jiguang but also generals such as Tang Shunzhi, Yu Dayou, and others. Tang Shunzhi, for example, wrote, "the bird-beak gun is today's effective weapon," and "in terms of soldiers' weapons, the foremost is the Big Frankish cannon; the second is the bird-beak gun; and the third is the bow and arrow."[67] Qi Jiguang, for his part, wrote, "bird guns can shoot far with extreme accuracy;" "Bird guns are originally effective weapons, the number one among all the weapons against the northern barbarians;" "On horseback and for foot soldiers the bird gun is the most effective weapon;" and "In southern China ... the bird gun is number one, and the rocket is number two."[68]

Apparently, the matchlock guns played a crucial role in field battle formations.[69] One of the most difficult problems when employing matchlocks was handling the fuses, which stayed lighted while reloading, a process that required the pouring of gunpowder. A spark could cause an explosion, which would not just harm the soldier and his neighbors, but also cause chaos among the formations. Qi Jiguang devised a way to tackle this problem: organize soldiers into groups of five. One held the gun, one ignited it, two loaded the gunpowder, and one passed it over. But he also pointed out that this method could only be used when defending a city, not in the field battles.[70] He required that the matchlock gunners must carry all the necessary accompanying equipment.[71] Gunners should only fire when the enemies were within, not beyond, 100 paces.[72]

In South China, when coastal battles occurred, warships were always important. In Qi Jiguang's training manual, matchlock guns were deployed on different sizes of warships: ten were used on the largest warships (*fuchuan* 福船, 64 soldiers on board); sixty-four were used on the second-largest warships (*haicang chuan* 海滄船, 51 soldiers on board); and four were used on the third-largest warships (*chongjiao chuan* 艟舟喬船 or big *cangshan chuan* 蒼山船, 37 on board). Even small patrol boats called *wangchuan* or *wangsuo chuan* were deployed with two or three matchlock gunners aboard. Gunners could fire at enemies near the shallow areas, and Qi Jiguang described the results as "very spectacular." If hard pressed by the enemies, gunners could abandon the patrol boats and flee, since the cost of this type of boat was merely one *liang* of silver.[73] Gunners were tested and low performers would be punished.[74] In his 1584 edition of the *Jixiao xinshu* (also known as the 14-chapter version), Qi Jiguang increased the total numbers of soldiers and matchlock gunners on warships: twenty matchlock gunners were placed on the #1 (largest, 100 soldiers on board) and #2 (81 on board) warships, twelve gunners on #3 (70 on board), ten gunners on #4 (58 on board), eight gunners on #5 (41 on board), six guns (at least four gunners) on #6 (29 on board), six guns (at least four lancers who also operated guns) on #7 and #8 (about twenty-four on board) warships. The #7 and #8 warships included prahu (*balahu*), eight-oared (*bajiang* 八槳) boats, fishing boats and scouting boats, which were all small sized.[75]

Qi Jiguang's manuals were meant for training troops, and it is of course an open question whether they reflected actual practice. How can we determine the actual role of matchlocks in battle? Fortunately, a highly reliable book, compiled by one of Qi Jiguang's sons, offers valuable information about this issue.[76] In the wars involving Qi Jiguang in Zhejiang and Fujian in the 1550s and 1560s, we learn that the pirates did have matchlock guns and occasionally Qi's troops were defeated; but overall the matchlocks (and cannons) on the Ming side played a big role in their victories, because our source frequently describes how Ming matchlock guns killed the pirates.[77] Another equally reliable source, Zheng Ruozeng's *Chouhai tubian*, records that in 1558, Ming soldiers employed bird guns to kill many pirates.[78]

Among the numerous battles between the Ming and the piratic troops, the Taizhou Battle in Zhejiang in 1561 stands out as one of the most important battles involving extensive use of firearms and as a stunning victory for Qi Jiguang. Also important is that both Qi Jiguang's son, Qi Zhuoguo, and Zheng Ruozeng record this battle in detail and substantiate each other, proving the reliability of the Chinese accounts. The accounts point to the extensive employment of firearms, such as "[Qi Jiguang's soldiers] fired bird guns at them [the pirates], killing over one hundred;" "first [Qi Jiguang's soldiers], using bird-beak guns, exchanged fire with the pirates .... The pirates were routed and wounded, [and] well ... over sixty pirates died;" and "[the Ming soldiers] used bird-beak guns to fire at the pirates, [and] countless died." Both accounts stress that Qi Jiguang's troops followed his strategy and technique (including the famous Yuanyang – or mandarin duck – battle formation 鴛 鴦 陣) closely. Qi Zhuoguo records: "My father fired the signal gun, the vanguards laid out bird guns to repel the enemies, then the rest advanced in groups. ... One shot broke his [the pirate chief's] lance." This is clearly in line with Qi Jiguang's technique: When the enemies were within one hundred paces, bird gunners fired first.[79] This may have been an instance of Qi Jiguang's other technique: volley firing. According to Zheng Ruozeng, Qi's soldiers "laid out their [bird] guns in layers, which killed over ten enemies.[80] The phrase "liechong fenfan" (列銃分番) sounds very much like Qi Jiguang's discussion of volley firing.[81] All in all, fierce fighting between the two sides and the overwhelming firepower of especially Qi Jiguang's troops, are clearly shown in these accounts, and one can even argue the firearms and cannons possessed by the Ming forces contributed significantly to the Ming victory.

In the defense of the coastal cities, such as Suzhou in the 1550s and early 1560s, new style gunpowder weapons were used, including bronze falcon, Frankish breech-loaders, matchlock guns, lead-and-tin guns (*qianxi chong* 鉛錫銃),[82] and *xuanfeng* cannon 旋 風 炮, in addition to more traditional Chinese-style gunpowder weapons (such as fire balls, rockets, flamethrowers). For example, one Frankish breech-loader was put at each strategic point inside and outside the city, and fifty soldiers equipped with effective matchlock guns were stationed at each city gate, while one hundred brave soldiers armed with matchlock guns were placed on one side of the city wall.[83] Qi Jiguang also discussed the role of matchlock guns in city wall defense and even invented a sturdy shield to block lead bullets from enemy fire.[84] According to Qi, each gunner on the city wall should be given one *jin* of gunpowder, fifty-three bamboo tubes of ignition gunpowder, fifty-three lead bullets, and one match of three-*zhang* long. When enemies were far away, soldiers should fire Frankish cannons; when they were approaching, then fire matchlock guns.[85]

Unsurprisingly, accounts of battles also show that the pirates possessed firearms themselves, and that sometimes their firepower overwhelmed the Ming troops. For example, in 1556, troops under the command of Zong Li (宗禮) and Huo Guandao (霍貫道) from northern China were defeated by pirates armed with matchlocks, and the two commanders were killed.[86] In 1558, followers of the Chinese smuggler Wang Zhi, based in Zhejiang and Fujian, possessed many firearms, which killed many Ming soldiers. On one occasion, in Fujian, they fired cannons at the city wall of Min'an (閩安) and it fell.[87] In 1563, at Xianyou, Fujian, the pirate gunners laid in ambush and were extremely fierce, and several people on the Ming side were wounded.[88] Two years later, Chinese pirate Wu Ping's followers deployed firearms against Qi Jiguang's troops, killing Ming soldiers.[89] Yu Dayou was another Ming military commander battling the pirates on the southeastern coast of China. He was Qi Jiguang's colleague, and the two of them fought battles together in Zhejiang and Fujian. Like Qi, Yu was an authority on gunpowder weapons and published his writing on military matters in 1565. He claimed authoritatively: "Having been in the military for several dozen years, I know so well about gunpowder, guns, and cannons."[90]

Yu placed a great emphasis on gunpowder weapons, especially cannons and firearms in both naval and land warfare. He has been well known for his words: "Those with guns beat those without guns; bigger guns defeat smaller guns."[91] For this reason he emphasized the crucial role that Frankish cannons could play in naval warfare.[92] This does not mean that Yu Dayou didn't favor the matchlock gun. As a matter of fact, he consistently spoke highly of it and equipped his troops with it. He stated: "The bird-beak gun is a powerful weapon in the military."[93] In the first month of 1568, Yu requested permission to build, in Fujian, forty large ships and fifty white ships (*baichao* 白艚), with 4720 soldiers and sailors on board. Each large ship would be equipped with ten Frankish cannons and twenty bird-beak guns, while each white ship would be equipped with six Frankish cannons and ten bird-beak guns. Altogether 1300 bird-beak guns were to be manufactured in Fujian or Guangdong.[94] In the seventh month of the same year, Yu requested permission to build thirty large ships (one hundred soldiers on each ship) and fifty *dongzai* (冬仔) ships (about forty soldiers on each ship); twenty bird-beak guns would be placed on each large ship, while sixteen or fourteen on each dongzai ship.[95]

Both Qi Jiguang, Yu Dayou, and others all held that even the smallest patrol boats such as eight-oared, suo boats (suochuan 梭船) and fishing boats should have one, two, or three bird-beak gunners, because this would make them more effective in battle. Zheng Ruozeng pointed out that a fishing boat carrying three people (one oar-rower, one sail holder, and one matchlock gunner) captured many enemies in recent years because its smallness avoided detection by enemy ships.[96] In the successful suppressing of the 1564 mutiny of a naval force in Chaozhou, Guangdong, Yu Dayou's troops relied on sophisticated bird-beak guns and powerful [Frankish] cannons.[97]

From the above discussion, we can see that matchlocks were employed at a much more extensive level during the years of 1560–66 and they played a decisive role in defeating the pirates.

What is in a name? The etymology of the bird(-beak) gun

Here I would like to discuss the Chinese terminology of the matchlock gun in order to clarify the meaning of the Chinese terms. Among the Chinese terms for matchlock gun, two terms are most common: "niaozui chong" and "niaochong." Explanations about the origins of these two terms have been divergent.

Qi Jiguang in the late sixteenth century was the first to discuss the etymology. His view was that the name "bird gun" ("niaochong") came from the fact that the gun could shoot birds and was used as a fowling piece, and this explanation was accepted by many in China and echoed in Korea.[98] Even today, in the Chinese mind, the terms "*niaochong*" and "*niaoqiang*" are associated with their function as fowling pieces. But over three hundred years later, W.F. Mayars speculated that the term "bird mouth" (bird-beak, or *niaozui*) may have referred to the bell-shaped muzzle of the early type of blunderbuss, while Tenney Davis and J.R. Ware opined that "bird mouth" referred to the shape of the lock (particularly a flintlock).[99] Joseph Needham, comparing these two views, sided with Davis and Ware. Though he did not deny the possibility that Qi Jiguang was right, he noted that "[t]he term bird-beak must have been derived, one would think, from the pecking action of the cock that held the match, paralleling the term 'snaphance' which developed in the West." Needham also pointed out another possibility: the short stocks of matchlock guns in China looked like the shape of bird-beaks.[100] These various views can be divided into two categories: Qi Jiguang's speculation was about the function, while the others focused on the physical attributes of the matchlock gun, whether muzzle, lock, or stock. Modern (mostly Chinese) scholars either follow Qi Jiguang's "bird-shooting" view or Needham's "pecking action" explanation, or the stock shape view.[101] Only one Chinese scholar clearly notes that the term "niaochong" was due to the fact that the muzzle was just the same size as a bird beak, and it was also called "bird-beak gun," changing to "niaoqiang" only during the Qing Dynasty.[102] This last view is similar to Mayars' speculation.

I would like to bring up the Japanese scholar Naganuma Kenkai's speculation to further the discussion. Naganuma, through a careful reading of Chinese and Japanese texts, proposed two points. First, he argued that "niaochong" was an abbreviation of "niaozuichong," or, in other words, the latter was the original name. Second, he suggested that "bird-beak gun" was so named because the shape of the muzzle appeared similar to a bird-beak.

Regarding the first point, the Japanese text Naganuma cited is the *Shogen jikō* (書言自考) which was prefaced in 1698. Based on reading the Chinese treatise *Wubei zhi*, the author of the *Shogen jikō* concluded that the formal name of "niaochong" was "niaozuichong."[103] Checking the original text of the *Wubei zhi*, indeed, one finds that Mao Yuanyi uses "niaozuichong" in his major headings but "niaochong" (or simply "chong") in his more detailed discussions.[104] But Mao was not the first one to do this, before him Zheng Ruozeng was already doing the same thing, as were others.

Naganuma's points are important, and at least his first point is a solid proposition and supported by further evidence. The earliest Chinese mentions of "niaochong" and "niaozuichong" occur in Zhu Wan's reports. In them "niaochong" appears at least three times, while "niaozuichong" one time.[105] Moreover, the same text also mentions "lead-bullet gun" 鉛子銃 (*qianzi chong*) at least twice which should refer to the European-style lead-bullet matchlock gun as well (compared with the Chinese-style guns which mostly did not shoot lead bullets).[106] These three terms should point to one fact: when this new type of firearm spread to China, it was called different names, while the "niaozuichong" is probably earlier than "niaochong." Moreover, a Chinese man named Zheng Shungong (either from Zhejiang or Guangdong), who visited Japan as an envoy during 1556–57, stated that the Japanese acquired guns (*shouchong* 手銃) from the *Folangji* (the Portuguese here), and Japanese hunters employed guns (such as *shouchong*) for hunting; China, he noted, also acquired this type of gun and changed its name to "niaozui."[107] Zheng Shungong's words are very weighty and even authoritative (perhaps more than Qi Jiguang in this regard) because he was from an area (either Guangdong or Zhejiang) where the matchlock gun spread first in China and he understood both the Chinese and Japanese situation well.

That the term "niaozuichong" was used earlier can also be inferred from the fact that Ming military writers who composed original texts (meaning they did not copy others) during the late sixteenth century, employed both "niaozuichong" and "niaochong," sometimes juxtaposing the two terms (clearly suggesting the interchangeability of the two). The trend was that "niaochong" was used much more frequently, whereas "niaozuichong" was used less frequently and soon disappeared altogether. For example, in Tang Shunzhi's *Wubian*, "niaozuichong" is employed three times and "niaochong" four times.[108] The term "niaochong" appears forty-three times in the *Jixiao xinshu* (18 chapter edition) of 1560, while "niaozui chong" only three times (in chapter 18 the two terms are juxtaposed); but in the *Lianbing shiji* of 1571–77, "niaozuichong" doesn't appear at all and "niaochong" is used throughout the treatise (81 times).[109] In *Chouhai tubian*, "niaozuichong" is used at least eight times (including "niaozui" one time), while "niaochong" twenty-six times. Tan Lun in his work uses "niaozuichong" seven times but "niaochong" thirty-three times.[110] In the local gazetteers of Zhejiang Province and Dinghai, compiled in 1561 and 1563 respectively, it seems that "niaozui chong" is used more times than "niaochong."[111] In

Yu Dayou's *Zhengqitang ji*, as discussed above, he uses more frequently "niaozui chong" than "niaochong." In the veritable record of the Shizong (for an entry for 1553, "niaozui huochong" (mistakenly written as *wuzui huochong* 烏嘴火銃) appears once, while in the account for the Shenzong reign (*Shenzong shilu*), "niaozuichong" is twice used ("niaochong" thirteen times), while once in the veritable record of Xizong.[112] These accounts suggest that the term "niaozui chong" appeared early but was, relatively gradually, replaced by "niao chong."

In other texts, either "bird-beak gun (*niaozuichong*)" or simply "bird-beak (niaozui)" was used. In a local stele erected in Miaowan, Huai'an in Jiangsu to commemorate a battle against the pirates in 1557, "bird-beak gun" is used (and appears only once).[113] In the same year, Gansu governor Chen Fei (陳棐) recommended twenty bird-beak guns to be manufactured for the northern frontier (the small number indicates this was a trial).[114] Ye Quan in his work *Xianbo bian* (written around the late 1560s), cited already, only uses "niaozui chong" twice, never uses the short form "niaochong." "Niaozui" without "chong" was also occasionally used by a few Chinese generals and military writers during the late Ming, such as Song Yingchang, Zheng Dayu, and others.[115] Despite that the Chosŏn (Korea) *Veritable Records* consistently use the term "niaochong" from the late sixteenth century on, in an entry for 1739, they also employ the term "niaozui chong" (bird-beak gun).[116]

All the above should suggest that the original Chinese name for the matchlock gun from Japan was "niaozuichong" or "bird-beak gun," and then was shortened to "niaochong" or "bird gun." From the Qing Dynasty onward, "niaoqiang" almost completely replaced "niaochong."[117] This thread of reasoning logically leads to Naganuma's second proposition: The name "niaozuichong" was derived from the "bird-beak" shape of the gun's muzzle. What is Naganuma's evidence? It is a sentence from the *Wubei zhi*, which discusses the process of making the gun, including "*qian chongzui chang muchuang ercun* [前銃嘴長木牀二寸]," meaning the front muzzle of the gun is two *cun* longer than the front stock.[118] Though Naganuma has cited more sources to prove his point that "niaozui" was from the muzzle of the gun, the evidence still looks slim at best.[119] Calling the gun or cannon muzzle "*zui* [嘴]" has been rare in Chinese texts, and much more often the Chinese word "kou [口]" is used, both in pre-modern and modern times.[120]

However, there are parallel sources to support Naganuma's proposition. Consider, for example, the case of the "bird-beak ship [鳥嘴船]." The rationale for the naming of this type of ship and the evolution of its names are extremely similar to the case of the matchlock gun in China: initially the ship was named for its bird-beak-shaped prow, but later the name was shortened to "bird ship" (*niaochuan*).

Regarding the history of this bird(-beak) ship there is little research so far,[121] but we do know that it started as a civilian cargo ship in Fujian (perhaps from the late Ming) and was adopted by the people of Zhejiang.[122] The term "niaozui chuan" first appears in Zheng Ruozeng's *Chouhai tubian* (juan 9) of 1562 in the context of Zhejiang,[123] and then in Mao Yuanyi's *Wubei zhi* (composed in 1621) which not only has an illustration of this ship but also offers a reason for it to be called "bird-beak ship." Mao Yuanyi explains that the bird-beak boat was from Wenzhou, Taizhou, Songmen and Haimen, and other places in Zhejiang, and it was thus called because "the prow of the ship looks like a bird beak [船首形如鳥嘴];" also, "with wind, sails are used, but without wind, sculls [櫓] are used, which are 4–5 *chi* long."[124] Indeed, in Mao Yuanyi's illustration, the prow looks very much like a bird beak and the whole ship looks much like a bird. Song Yingchang, who was in command of the Ming troops in Korea, mentioned bird-beak ships in one of his reports in the 1590s.[125] Ming scholar Song Yingxing summarized that Chinese ships were named after shape (animals), capacity, or building material (types of wood), while modern Chinese have concluded that Chinese traditional ships were shaped after water birds (as opposed to their European counterparts, after fish).[126]

Probably from the early seventeenth century on, "niaozui chuan" was shortened to "niaochuan." In 1602, Fan Lai began his description (and illustration) of warships in Zhejiang with "niaochuan" (which is unusual, indicating its specialness) which had a long body, three sculls (oars?) on each side and two rear sculls; it was better than other ships and could compete with Sha ships and prahu ships. This type of ship was deployed at different maritime garrisons in Zhejiang.[127] Four years later, He Rubin's *Bing lu* (composed in 1606, modified edition in 1630) presented an illustration of a "bird ship" and a more detailed but slightly different explanation regarding its name: "It has a small head (prow), big belly, long and straight body; at the rear there are two sculls; sails are employed with wind, while sculls are operated without wind; it turns effortlessly with long sails and nimble oars, just like a bird is flying. Though it has a big body, it runs as fast as the *sha* ship and *prahu*."[128] Compared to Mao Yuanyi's brief note above, the other two descriptions have more detail; while Fan Lai does not explain the name "niaochuan," He Rubin's emphasis is on the whole ship as a bird. He Rubin does not use the term "bird-beak" directly, but his term "small head (prow)" implies that. Though He Rubin's illustration is somewhat different from its counterpart by Fan Lai and Mao Yuanyi, the three sources seem to be referring to the same type of ship. Modern Chinese scholars also concur that "niaochuan" was named due to its bird-beak shape.[129] Therefore, from the early seventeenth century on, the name "bird ship" began to become popular, completely replacing the original "bird-beak ship." The "bird ship" continued into the Qing Dynasty, functioning as a major warship and cargo ship.

Thus we can see a striking parallel of the evolution of both the "bird-beak gun" to "bird gun" and the "bird-beak ship" to "bird ship."

More examples will help illustrate this point better. The shape of bird beak was applied to more Chinese things, such as "fengzui dao" (風嘴刀) (phoenix-beak sword), "yazui hao" (鴨嘴蒿 [or gao 篙?]) (duck-beak barge pole), and "yazui gun" (鴨嘴棍)(duck-beak stick).[130] Other Chinese ships and weapons were also named after their shapes, such as "haihu (海鶻船)" (sea falcon ship), "wugong ship (蜈蚣船)" ([European-style] centipede ship), "bie-wei chong (鱉尾銃)" (turtle-tailed cannon – another name for Frankish cannon in Fujian), "goulian qiang (鈎鐮鎗)" (sickle-shaped lance), "chuiqiang (槌鎗)" (drum-stick-shaped lance), "maisui qiang 麥穗鎗" (wheat-ear-shaped lance), "Taining bi (太寧筆鎗)" (Taining-brush-shaped lance), "suantou (蒜頭鎗)" (garlic-head-shaped lance), and "yatou qiang (鴉頭鎗)" (crow-head-shaped lance). Only a very few were named for their functions such as "zhanma dao(斬馬刀)" (horse-cutting sword), and "juma qiang(拒馬鎗)" (horse-blocking lance).[131] Zhao Shizhen, however, mistakenly thought the Japanese (*Wo*) named their matchlocks after birds, and hence he was inspired to call one type of his modified Frankish cannon "yingyang pao(鷹揚砲)" (soaring eagle cannon).[132]

Thinking outside of the Chinese box, one wonders if the "bird gun" in China had any foreign connection. For example, the different European words for matchlock (and also flintlock) gun, the English "musket," French "mousquet," and Spanish "mosquete," were all derived from the Italian word "moschetto" or "mosquetto," which could mean a type of hawk (originally "mosca," meaning "fly"). It should have nothing to do with the Chinese naming, as it was the Portuguese who spread the matchlock gun to Asia, and the Portuguese (and Spanish) word was "espingarda" which was from the Old French and German meaning "spring" or "jump."[133] Thus we can rule out the European linguistic connection.

The above lengthy discussion supports Naganuma's first point, that is, the Chinese named the matchlock gun first "bird-beak gun," and then it was shortened to "bird gun." The change from "bird-beak ship" to "bird ship" is an excellent example to shed light on our issue. Thus the influential Qi Jiguang's view that the "bird gun" was called thus due to its function as fowling pieces does not hold water and should be challenged, and so the age-old association of "niaochong/niaoqiang" and bird hunting in the Chinese mind should be put to rest.[134] All in all, the Chinese overwhelmingly tended to name things based on their shapes rather than their functions. However, exactly which part of the matchlock gun looked like a bird beak – the muzzle, lock (cock's pecking action), or stock – is still not clear, because no concrete evidence is available. Therefore, Needham's speculation about the "cock's pecking action" cannot be confirmed either.

Concluding remarks

Regarding the diminution of the rampant piracy on China's southeast coast after 1557, the late John Wills in his pioneering piece on maritime Asia adduced several explanations, including socio-economic factors such as the lifting of the maritime ban in 1567, the implementation of the single-whip taxation system, which alleviated peasants' situation, and the effective organization of Qi Jiguang's and Yu Dayou's armies fighting against the pirates.[135] This chapter has discussed a technological element of the latter military aspect, that is, the spread and utilization of the matchlock gun by the Ming troops under Qi Jiguang, Yu Dayou, and others, and what role this gun played in the suppression of the piracy.

It is more than clear that matchlock guns imported from Japan as a result of Zhu Wan's campaigns played a crucial role in this process. As the first quote at the very beginning of this chapter argues, matchlocks arrived in Asia and affected Asian history in profound ways. The role of the Japanese matchlock in Japan and in the Japanese invasion of Korea during 1592–98 has been much better studied, but its place in Chinese history is just now beginning to be appreciated.

As the second quote at the beginning of this chapter informs us, it was the Chinese who employed the weapons they had so quickly learned about from the Japanese to defeat the pirates. The Ming pirate wars of the mid-1500s served as a crucible for military innovation, and matchlock guns played a key role in the Ming victory. Without the proactive adoption of the foreign matchlock gun and other weapons, especially gunpowder ones, the Ming victory would have been unthinkable.

John Wills, in his famous 1993 article about maritime Asia, stressed the deep and protracted history of interactions between Asians and the Europeans in the early modern era.[136] This chapter reinforces Wills' approach. On the one hand, European overseas expansion was indeed important in causing changes in different parts of the world; on the other hand, non-European peoples were also playing a crucial role through their encounters with Europeans.

This was especially true during the era I call the "Century of warfare in Eastern Eurasia" (c. 1550–1683), during which Southeast and East Asians adopted and adapted many European military technologies and hired European (and Asian) mercenaries. The pace of learning and the scale of innovation were unprecedented, and the adoption and spread of the matchlock gun was just one of many exciting cases of military interaction. In these stories, the Europeans were important actors, but the Asians dominated the stage. My approach to early modern Asian military history during the "century of warfare" is to stress the interaction between the Asians and the Europeans, rendering more credence to the latter than other scholars, but also emphasizing the critical role of the Asians.[137] Zhu Wan, Qi Jiguang, Yu Dayou, and the many pirates (both Chinese and Japanese), who appear in this chapter, are just a few stars in the galaxy of Asian actors.

This chapter has focused on the matchlock gun on China's southeast coast during the years of 1548–66, but the matchlock actually had a much farther-reaching influence. Spreading from the southeastern coastal areas, the matchlock gun influenced warfare throughout China, becoming an indispensable weapon in naval and land warfare across the imperium throughout the late Ming and Qing periods. A complete history of the matchlock gun in early modern China could fill many volumes, but here I offer just a few examples to help us understand its spread and influence. It has long been known that the late Ming scholar-cum-official Zhao Shizhen invented more powerful and efficient matchlocks, but we should be clear that it was the Japanese invasion of Korea that acted as the major driving force, and the Japanese-style matchlock served as one of the models for Zhao's innovation. Zhao compared Japanese, Western (*Xiyang*), and Turkish (*Rum*) styles of matchlock and concluded that in fact the Japanese version was the worst.[138] He may be correct (as new technologies always replace the old ones), but the stimulating role of the Japanese-style matchlock nonetheless should be recognized. For example, in his memorial to the Ming court, Zhao stated that in the process of his making better matchlocks, he consulted (around 1592) the subordinates of Hu Zongxian and especially Qi Jiguang, listing by name six officers who had once fought under Qi Jiguang.[139] In addition, Zhao also studied Qi Jiguang's other firearms and cannons, such as the crouching tiger cannon (*hucun pao*) and the 100-bullet-gun (*baizi chong*).[140]

Finally, the last point I would like to touch upon is the increasing weight and significance of southeast China (or maritime China) to the rest of China. Though Wills, in his "Maritime China" piece, more than once emphasized the marginality of maritime China in the whole story of China, this special part of China was about to play an increasingly significant part of Chinese history. From a (military) technological perspective, maritime China was a source or channel of advanced weapons, particularly gunpowder ones. Just as one Chinese author stated in 1602, "all gunpowder weapons were from the southeast (coast)."[141]

Almost all of the advanced weapons came to interior China through the southeast coast, including the Frankish cannon, our matchlock gun, and the *prahu* ship. The late Ming and early Qing witnessed the first technological wave from Europe and the Middle East, and the nineteenth and early twentieth centuries witnessed a second great wave from the West (including Japan). During these waves, maritime China acted as a technological frontier, a window, a place where new things, ideas, and personnel were embraced for the first time.

During the late twentieth and early twenty-first centuries, a third wave from the West has been washing on China's southeastern shores, but this time it is happening on China's terms, due to the open door policy adopted by the PRC since 1978. China's developmental, national security, and economic need to "tread blue water" have made maritime China more crucial than ever: Matters such as Taiwan, the Diaoyu Island, the South China Sea, and the building of submarines all enlarge and expand the significance of maritime China. From the sixteenth to the twenty-first century, many things have changed for maritime China, with aircraft carriers replacing matchlock guns, but a constant and enduring theme has been military technology.

Notes

1 I would like to offer my heartfelt thanks to Xu Jingsong for purchasing books by and on Qi Jiguang; to Liu Xiufeng and Ye Shaofei for providing important sources; to Zheng Cheng and Chang Xiuming for sending their papers or dissertation; to Yang Liye for obtaining one article; and to Tonio Andrade and Kenneth Swope for their careful reading of the drafts and making constructive suggestions. For the sake of brevity, I will shorten the links of some websites where some Chinese texts are available. If Jack Wills were still alive, he would have certainly read this chapter and offered many comments. Without him, the world is indeed different. To him I dedicate this chapter.

2 Rainer Daehnhardt, trans. by Ronnie Percival, *Espingarda Feiticeira=The Bewitched Gun: The Introduction of the Firearm in the Far East by the Portuguese* (Lisbon, 1994), 64.

3 Zhao Shizhen, edited by Shimizu Shōtoku (清水正德), *Shenqi pu* (Japanese reprint, 1808,), juan 1: 4a–b, Wang Tonggui's (王同轨) preface to Shenqi pu. The original Chinese text is: 自倭奴起海上, 刀陣之外, 最毒火器, 蹂躪歲久, 屍成京觀, 吳越人漸習其技, 破刀陣皆有法, 而又仿效其火器以擊賊, 賊始敗衄去不來. Korean scholar Yu Hyŏngwŏn (유형원 柳馨遠, 1622–1673) echoes this in his Bangyesurock (반계수록 磻溪隧錄) (Seoul, 1958), 21: 42B–43A:

> [I]n recent times in China they did not have muskets [either], they first learned about them from the Wakō pirates in Che-chiang Province. Ch'i Chi-kuang trained their troops in their use for several years until they became one of the skills of the Chinese, who subsequently used them to defeat the Japanese.

The translation is by James B. Palais, Confucian Statecraft and Korean Institutions: Yu Hyŏngwŏn and the Late Chosŏn Dynasty (Seattle, 1996), 519.

4 See *Ming shi*, juan 205, "Zhu Wan"; and L. Carrington Goodrich and Chaoying Fang (eds.), *Dictionary of Ming Biography, 1368–1644*, vol. 1 (New York, 1976), 372–75 for Zhu Wan's biography.

5 Shen Dengmiao (沈登苗), "Mingdai Wokou yanjiu Zhongwen lunzhu tilu wubaizhong ji bianzhu ganyan 明代倭寇研究中文論著題錄 500 種及編著感言" (www.annian.net/show.aspx?id=12856&cid=18, accessed on November 19, 2016) has listed 500 works in Chinese on pirates during the Ming, and also mentioned that there were still 200 in Japanese, 100 in English and other languages. Many of these studies are on the 1520s to the 1550s period, and quite a few (Shen says impressionistically "half") are about Qi Jiguang (1528–88), the famous general who fought against the so-called pirates in the 1550s and 1560s. In fact, another volume on Qi has just appeared in English. See Y.H. Sim (ed.), *Qi Jiguang and the Maritime Defence of China* (Singapore, 2017).

6 For example, Liao Dake (廖大珂), "Zhu Wan shijian yu Dongya haishang maoyi tixi de xingcheng 朱紈事件與東亞海上貿易體系的形成," *Wen shi zhe*, 2 (2009): 87–100; James K. Chin, "Merchants, Smugglers, and Pirates: Multinational Clandestine Trade on the South China Coast, 1520–50," in Robert J. Antony (ed.), *Elusive Pirates, Pervasive Smugglers: Violence and Clandestine Trade in the Greater China Seas* (Hong Kong, 2010), 43–58; Xu Xiaowang 徐曉望, Lun Mingdai Putaoya ren zai Zhangzhou de maoyi ji Dongnanya lishi de guaidian 論明代葡萄牙人在漳州的貿易及東南亞歷史的拐點," in idem; *Minshang yanjiu*

閩 商 研 究 (Beijing, 2014), 107–22. Wills, "Maritime China from Wang Chih to Shih Lang: themes in peripheral history," in Spence and Wills (eds.), *From Ming to Ch'ing.*

7 Joseph Needham, *Science and Civilisation in China, Volume 5, Chemistry and Chemical Technology, Part 7, Military Technology: The Gunpowder Epic* (Cambridge, 1987), 429–40; Hora Tomio (洞富雄), *Teppō: Denrai to sono eikyō* 鉄砲: 伝来とその影響 (1st ed., 1991; reprint, Kyōto, 2001), 270–82.

8 See Tonio Andrade, *The Gunpowder Age: China, Military Innovation, and the Rise of the West in World History* (Princeton, NJ, 2016), 172. Also see chapter 9, pp. 124–31 on Sino-Portuguese skirmishes in the 1520s; chapter 10, pp. 135–43 on Frankish cannon.

9 Needham, *Science and Civilisation in China*, 429–40; Wang Zhaochun, *Zhongguo huoqi shi* (Beijing, 1991), 134–42.

10 Indeed, the history of the matchlock gun in China beyond 1566 and up to the Qing time deserves much more attention, and there are at least two recent doctoral dissertations: Zhang Jian 张建, "Huoqi yu Qingchao neilu Yazhou bianjiang zhi xingcheng 火器与清朝内陆亚洲边疆之形成" (Ph.D. dissertation, Nankai University, 2012); Chang Xiuming 常修銘, "Shiliu shiqi shiji Dongya haiyu huoqi jiaoliu shi yanjiu 16–17 世紀東亞海域火器交流史研究" (Ph.D. dissertation, National Qinghua University, Taibei, 2016) which have made progress in this regard.

11 James K. Chin, "Merchants, Smugglers, and Pirates: Multinational Clandestine Trade on the South China Coast, 1520–50," in Robert J. Antony (ed.), *Elusive Pirates, Pervasive Smugglers: Violence and Clandestine Trade in the Greater China Seas* (Hong Kong, 2010), 47.

12 Zhu Wan, *Piyu zaji*, in the Sikuquanshu cunmu congshu jibu 78 四庫全書存目叢書, 集部 78, (Ji'nan, 1997), juan 4: 8a–b.

13 Ibid., juan 4: 7.

14 Zhu Wan, *Piyu zaji*, juan 2: 48; juan 8: 50.

15 Japanese sword fighting started to impact China in a significant way as a result of Qi Jiguang's fighting with the pirates, and this is another aspect of the military implication of the wars in southeast China. For details, see Ma Mingda, Shuojian conggao (Beijing, 2007), 247–53. This is also available at www.weixinnu.com/tag/article/1922311764.

16 Zhu Wan, *Piyu zaji*, juan 2–6, 9; Nakajima Gakusho, "16 shiji 40 niandai de Shuangyu zousi maoyi yu Oushi huoqi 16 世紀 40 年代的雙嶼走私貿易與歐式火器," in Guo Wanping 郭万平 and Zhang Jie 张捷 (eds.), Zhoushan Putuo yu Dongya haihyu wenhua jiaoliu 舟山普陀与东亚海域文化交流 (Hangzhou, 2009), 35–40; idem, Nakajima Gakusho, "Ichi go shi rei-nendai no higashiajia kaiiki to Seiō-shiki kaki – Chōsen, sōsho, Satsuma, "一五四〇年代の東アジア海域と西欧式火器—朝鮮, 双嶼, 薩摩," in Nakajima Gakusho (ed.), Nanban, kōmō, tōjin – Ichi roku ichi nana seiki no higashiajia kaiiki 南蛮, 紅毛, 唐人—一六 一七世紀の東アジア海域 (Kyoto, 2013), 105–14, especially 134, 138 (Tables 1 and 2); Zheng Cheng, "Fagong kao – 16 shiji chuan Hua de Oushi qianzhuang huopao jiqi yanbian 發熕考 — 16 世紀傳華的歐式前裝火炮及其演變," Ziran kexueshi yanjiu 自然科學史研究, 32, 4 (2013): 504–22. Regarding the details of the spread and use of the Southeast Asian type of boat prahu in Ming-Qing China, see my forthcoming study "The Prahu in Ming-Qing Times: Another Example of Southeast Asian Influence on China."

17 Wang Zhaochun, 134–37.
18 Needham, Science, vol. 5, pt. 7, 33, 432, 440–44, 569 (quote on page 444). Also see Yano Jinichi (矢野仁一), "Shina ni okeru kinsei kaki no denrai ni tsuite 支那に於ける近世火器の伝来に就いて," *Shirin*史林, 2, 3–4 (1917), included in idem, Kindai Shina no seiji bunka 近代支那の政治及文化 (Tokyo: Idea Shoin, 1926), 357 and Hora, Teppō, 282–84. Yano was the first to notice this. Both Wada Hironori (see below) and Wang Zhaochun discussed the spread of Rum (Turkish) guns to China, but only focused on the Zhao Shizhen's contribution in the late sixteenth century. Wada's "Mindai no tekkpo denrai to Osuman teikoku: Jingi fu to saiiki tochi jinbutsu ryaku 明代の鐵砲傳來とオスマン帝國: 神器譜と西域土地人物略史學,"31, 1–4 (1958): 692–719. Wada, like Wang Zhaochun, also ignored the possible early dissemination of Turkish guns to China. Other Japanese scholars seem to have commented on this issue, see Sasaki Minoru (佐々木 稔), *Hinawajū no denrai to gijutsu* 火縄銃の伝来と技術 (Tokyo, 2003), 64. Also see Ma Jianchun (马建春), "Ming Jiajing Wanli chao Lumi chong de chuanru zhizao ji shiyong 明嘉靖万历朝噜嘧铳的传入制造及使用," *Huizu yanjiu* 回族研究, 4 (2007): 70–76.
19 Zhao Shizhen, juan 2: 2a–b; Needham, 441. "Shui Xiyang (水西洋)" should be Da Xiyang (大西洋) which referred to Europe or Portugal since the late Ming. Se Xie Fang, Chen Jiarong, Lu Junling, *Gudai Nanhai dimng huishi* 古代南海地名匯釋 (Beijing, 1986), 140–41.
20 Xu Jin (許 進), *Pingfan shimo* 平番始末, www.readers365.com/biji/mydoc400.htm; Ma Wensheng (馬文升), *Xingfu Hami guowang ji* 興復哈密國王記 http://ctext.org/; Gu Yingtai (谷應泰), *Mingshi jishi benmo* 明史紀事本末, http://ctext.org/). These three, especially the first two, are very similar in their describing of the events.
21 Zhu Wan, juan 5: 44.
22 Ibid., juan 5: 58.
23 For more details on Ke Qiao, see Xu Xiaowang, "Lun Mingdai," 116–19.
24 Zhu Wan, Juan 10: 5.
25 *Chouhai tubian*, juan 13, pt. 2: 909. Gu Yanwu (顧炎武), *Tianxia junguo libing shu* (天下郡國利病書), juan 7: 31b, also stressed that "bird guns came from the west."
26 Wang Zhaochun (Zhongguo, 137) understood this as the matchlocks the Chinese captured from the Portuguese in the 1521 fighting at Xicaowan in Xinhui, Guangdong, but offers no evidence to support this. It has been well-known that the Ming only obtained Frankish breech-loader cannons from the Portuguese. For a detailed study on this Frankish cannon in China, see Zhou Weiqiang, *Folangji chong zai Zhongguo* (佛郎機銃在中國) (Beijing, 2013).
27 Chase, 144.
28 *Ming shilu – Shizong* [Jiajing 32] juan 401, 8th month, *renyin*. All citations from the *Ming shilu* are available on http://ctext.org/.
29 *Ming shilu – Shizong* [Jiajing 34] juan 419, 2nd month, *xinsi*.
30 *Ming shilu – Shizong* [Jiajing 34] juan 424, 7th month, *bingchen*.
31 *Ming shilu – Shizong* [Jiajing 37] juan 459, 5th month, *jiaxu*.
32 Cai Jiude (采九德) *Wobian shilue* (倭變事略), http://wenxian.fanren8.com/06/15/85.htm; Ye Quan (叶权), *Xianbo bian* (賢博編), the entry of "Zong jiangjun (宗將軍)," http://wenxian.fanren8.com/05/06/241/1.htm.
33 Aying, Aying quanji 阿英全集, vol. 4 (Hefei, 2003), 242; "Shi Fu zhuan, Jia Yong deng fu (史符傳賈勇等附)" (www.jhwsw.com/rwcq/ShowArticle.asp?ArticleID=8873); Chang Xiuming, 27, 30.

34 For "son-mother cannon" see Qi Jiguang (戚繼光), *Jixiao xinshu* (紀效新書), 18 chapter ed. (Beijing, 2001), 254–55.

35 Tang Shunzhi, *Xinkan Jingchuan xiansheng waiji* (新刊荆川先生外集), juan 2: 20–30b; juan 3:21-1b-10b, 30b (www.kanripo.org/); Zheng Ruozeng (鄭若), *Chouhai tubian* (籌海圖編), annotated by Li Zhizhong (李致忠) (Beijing, 2007), 1031. See also *Ming shilu – Shizong* [Jiajing 38] juan 472, 5th month, *jiawu*; Zhou Weiqiang, Folangji, 105–06.

36 Wang Zhaochun (139) cites *Da Ming huidian-huiqi*.

37 Xiao Chongye (蕭 崇 業), *Shi Liuqiu lu* (使 琉 球 錄), vol. 1, "zaozhou (造舟)," www.guoxue123.com/biji/ming/slql/027.htm.

38 Qi Jiguang *Lianbing shiji* (Beijing, 2001), 317.

39 Qi Jiguang *Jixiao xinshu*, 14 chapter ed. (Beijing, 2001), 55–56. See also Mao Yuanyi (茅元義), *Wubei zhi* (武備誌) (Block print, 1621), juan 134: 26b.

40 Nan Bingwen(南炳文), "Zhongguo gudai de niaoqiang yu riben 中國古代的鳥槍與日本," *Shixue jikan* (史學集刊), 2 (1992): 63 has already noticed this horn-shaped flask/container but he cites *Bing lu* and *Wubei zhi* which copied from Qi Jiguang.

41 Wen Bian (溫編), comp., edited by Zheng Cheng, "Liqi jie利器解" (unpublished manuscript, 2015), "Guo Zizhang xu," 32.

42 *Chouhai tubian*, 909–10.

43 Wang Zhaochun, 136.

44 Hora, 275. Chang Xiuming (25–31), utilizing newly discovered sources, points to the important role played by Lu Tang's son Lu Xiang 盧相 who was sent to Beijing to teach on newly obtained matchlocks.

45 For example, both the *Ming shi* and the *Ming shilu* contains this broader use of this word (and its variation Fan 番), especially the term "*sifang fanguo* 四 方 蕃 國," meaning foreign countries in all the four directions. See Wang Xiangrong, edited by *Ming shi Riben zhuan jianzheng* (Chengdu, 1987), 49, 87, 95–96, 109.

46 On page 625 (also see 1029–30), the "foreign monk Deyang (Tokuyo) (番僧德阳)" refers to the Japanese monk-cum-envoy; on page 928, the scope of "Fan" obviously includes Japan. The *Ming shilu* calls the Japanese monk "[Wo]seng Deyang [倭]僧德阳." See Wang Xiangrong, 129–30. Here apparently "Wo" and "Fan" are interchangeable. Chang Xiuming (29, 31) has also reached this conclusion (Fan=Wo) independently.

47 *Lianbing shiji*, 100, 238, 317–18; *Jixiao xinshu* (14 chapter ed.), 56–57, 136. That Andrade speculates that Chinese matchlocks may have been rifled guns is a bit far-fetched, see his "The Arquebus Volley Technique in China, c. 1560: Evidence from the Writings of Qi Jiguang," *Journal of Chinese Military History*, 4.2 (2015): 122, n.24.

48 *Jixiao xinshu* (18 chap. ed.), 249; *Lianbing shiji*, 238–39, 317–18; *Jixiao xinshu*, (14 chapter ed.), 57. Andrade, "Arquebus Volley," 128–30, has refuted the view that has downplayed the role of the Chinese matchlock gun.

49 Song Yingxing (宋應星), *Tiangong kaiwu* (天工開物) (Changsha, 2004), 350.

50 Zheng Ruozeng, *Chouhai tubian*, juan 12 & 13; Qi Jiguang, *Lianbing shiji*, juan 1; *Yansui zhenzhi* (延绥镇志)(compiled in the Wanli reign), quoted in Zheng Cheng, "Liqi jie yu Shenqi pu – 1600 nian qianhou de liangzhong huoqi zhuzuo《利器 解》與《神器譜》- - - 1600 年 前 後 的 兩 種 火 器 著 作) (unpublished manuscript, 2015), 6.

51 *Jixiao xinshu* (18 chap. ed.), 253, 256; *Lianbing shiji*, 239, 313, 319; *Jixiao xinshu* (14 chap. ed.), 276–77, 316.

52 Yi Ik李瀷 (이익, 1681–1763), Sŏngho sŏnsaeng sasol (星湖先生僿說 gwan 5, "manmulmun 萬物門: hwachong火銃." The original is: "故銃長則勢尤猛" (http://db.itkc.or.kr).

53 *Jixiao xinshu* (18 chap. ed.], 250; *Lianbing shiji*, 318; Jixiao xinshu (14 chap. ed.], 58; Needham, 358–59. Corning was first described around the early fifteenth century in Europe. For discussion on corning process of gunpowder early modern Europe, see M. I. Brown, *Firearms in Colonial America: The Impact on History and Technology, 1492–1792* (Washington, D.C., 1981), 20–21; Bert Hall, *Weapons and Warfare in Renaissance Europe: Gunpowder, Technology, and Tactics* (Baltimore, 2001), 69–74. According to Brown, corned powder could reduce hygroscopicity and the tendency of the ingredients to solidify, eliminate gravity separation, improve combustion, and enhance the explosive force. Brown also explains the meaning of "corned" as the small kernels of gunpowder were similar in size to the cereal grains such as barley, rye, and wheat which have been collectively called "corn" in Europe, not as the conventional understanding it as the size of corn kernels. It is wrong for Hall to say that corning was introduced into China by the Jesuits. Hall maintains that the reason for corning was not because of the problem of the separation in transit process of the three ingredients making gunpowder, but rather the problem of atmospheric moisture absorption, as early European gunpowder may have contained lime saltpeter or calcium nitrate, $Ca(NO_3)_2$, which is mostly hygroscopic of the three ingredients. The corned powder was stronger from a ballistic perspective and had a longer life.

54 Zheng Cheng has gleaned late Ming records on gunpowder corning process in China.

55 *Shenqi pu*, juan 2: 1b, 5b ("The longer, the better"); juan 4: 5b and juan 5: 7b, where Zhao Shizhen emphatically points out that the shooting distance increased due to the long barrel.

56 Wang Zhaochun, 138, 145; Yin Xiaodong (尹 曉 冬), "Mingdai Folangji yu niaochong de zhizao jishu," *Ming Qing haifang yanjiu luncong* (明清海防研究論叢) 3 (2009): 56–57 (51–71); Andrade, *The Gunpowder Age*, 107–10. Early Ming Chinese-style guns were only about 40–44 centimeters long, with caliber ranging from 2 to 2.2 centimeters (Wang, 87–88), thus the ratios of (barrel?) length to caliber was about 20:1. The ratios of European-style matchlocks were about 50:1 to 70:1, far bigger than the early Ming ones. The lengthened barrel, Wang reasons, allowed the fuller burning of gunpowder inside the barrel, producing more powerful push, increasing the velocity of the bullets, resulting in a flat trajectory.

57 Wang Zhaochun, *Zhongguo huoqi shi*, 201; Andrade, *The Gunpowder Age*, 110; Shi Jungui 石 俊 貴) and Li Hong (李 鴻), "Neimenggu chutu de Mingchao chunian tieke dilei jishi," 內 蒙 古 出 土 的 明 朝 初 年 鐵 殼 地 雷 紀 實, Qing bingqi 輕 兵 器 4 (2002): 36.

58 Huang Xun (黃訓), *Huang Ming mingchen jinji lu* (皇明名臣進士錄) (1551 edition), Wang Hong's memorial and Gu Yingxiang's reflection, quoted in Zhou Weiqiang, *Folangji*, 22, 51; Chase, 144. Zheng Cheng (14) quotes a source from the 1561 edition of *Guangdong tongzhi* saying that a Yunnan official learned from the Portuguese (Folangji) about gunpowder making techniques. This passage also appears in Guo Fei (郭棐), annotated by Huang Guosheng (黃 國 聲) and Deng Guizhong (鄧 貴 忠), *Yue da ji* (粵 大 記) (gazetteer of Guangdong) (compiled during 1582 and 1598; reprint, Guangzhou, 1998), 793–94. Zhao Shizhen in *Shenqi pu* (juan 4: 21a–21b) also mentions this process.

59 Quoted in Zhou Weiqiang, *Folangji*, 21–22, 82, and the abridged version of Gu Yingxiang's account is translated in Needham, 373, 376. Also see Wang Zhaochun's comments on 118.

60 Wang Zhaochun, 136–37.

61 See 250, 252 (quote on this page). Also see *Jixiao xinshu* 14 chap. ed., 51. Zhao Shizhen in his *Shenqi pu*, juan 2: 5b, 7b; juan 4: 7a–b, 14a, 25b emloys terms such as "luosi di (fangtou) (螺蛳底方头)" and "luosi xuan (螺蛳旋)."

62 Needham, 436–37 and 437, n.b.

63 For example, Sawada Hira (澤田平), *Nihon no kojū* (日本の古銃) (Sakai, 1995), 10–11; Sasaki, *Hinawajū*, 102–30, 151–55.

64 Daehnhardt, *Espingarda Feiticeira*, 20–21, 38–43 (quote on page 39), 49–55, 65, 66–67 (diagram of the "Evolution of Ignition Mechanisms through Luso-Oriental Contact"). Also see Sasaki, *Hinawajū*, chapter 3 and Nakajima Gakusho, "Ichi go shi rei-nendai no higashiajia kaiiki to Seiō-shiki kaki – Chōsen, sōsho, Satsuma, 一五四〇年代の東アジア海域と西欧式火器—朝鮮, 双嶼, 薩摩," in Nakajima Gakusho (ed.), *Nanban, kōmō, tōjin – Ichi roku ichi nana seiki no higashiajia kaiiki* (南蛮, 紅毛, 唐人—一六 一七世紀の東アジア海域) (Kyoto, 2013), 105–14. Related and similar to this breech-screw plug is the bullet worm used in Europe from around the early fifteenth century for removing lead balls and gunpowder residue from the gun barrel and touch hole. Brown (13) has described it this way:

> Shaped like a corkscrew in its early form, the worm was merely screwed into the soft lead ball and it was then easily extracted, while the sharp prongs readily removed the powder charge even if it had solidified after remaining in the bore for a prolonged period. The worm was a common accessory throughout the muzzle-loading era. In their earliest form scowers and worms were forged integral with the iron rod, though by c. 1425 they were provided with a threaded tang which screwed into a metal sleeve at the end of the wooden ramrod.

Brown has provided illustrations of four Danish and German bullet worms of the sixteenth and seventeenth centuries on this page, the screws shown here reminds one of the breech-screw on Japanese matchlock guns.

65 Olof G. Lidin, *Tanegashima: The Arrival of Europe in Japan* (Copenhagen, 2002), 40, 186–87 (original text in classical Chinese).

66 Sasaki, *Hinawajū*, 116, 119. Brown (26, 246, 200, 204–05), however, states that shortly after the introduction of the matchlock guns, the improved breech-sealing method or what he terms "threaded breech plug" was made, and two of them are dated c. 1425 and c. 1440. It could be removed easily and made reboring and clearing up the barrel much easier. Brown discusses this matter in the whole European context and does not restrict to one specific country or region (say Bohemia). Though the difference between Daehnhardt and Brown still needs to be reconciled, it is clear that the Japanese breech-screw technique was derived from the European tradition.

67 Tang Shunzhi, *Jiangnan jinglue*, juan 1, "lianbing;" idem, *Wubian*, juan 2: 52b.

68 *Lianbing shiji*, 18, 100, 237, 239, 318; *Jixiao xinshu* (14 chap. ed.], 40, 57.

69 *Lianbing shiji*, 51, 132–33, 155.

70 *Jixiao xinshu* (18 chap. ed.), 52.

71 Ibid., 53, 93.

72 Ibid., 65, 117.

73 Ibid.

74 Ibid., 98, 337–38.

75 *Jixian xinshu* [18 chap. ed.], chapter 12.

76 As for the reliability of Qi Zhuoguo's book, see Le Ke and Hao Jiaosu, "Foreword" to Qi Zhuoguo (戚祚國), *Qi Shaobao nianpu qibian* (戚少保年譜耆編) (Beijing, 2003), 1–9.

77 Qi Zhuoguo, 66, 126, 152, 154, 165 (pirates' matchlocks); 24–25, 27, 28, 58–63, 90, 98, 124, 129, 141, 150, 155–56, 171 (Qi's troops' matchlocks). This is also reflected in a late Ming novel on Qi Jiguang's fighting against the pirates, entitled Qi *Nantang Jiaoping Wokou zhizhuan* 戚南塘剿平倭寇志傳 (http://nuoha. com/book/10306/00001.html), in which matchlock guns were effectively employed by Qi's troops to defeat their enemies.

78 *Chouhai tubian*, 271–72.

79 Qi Jiguang, *Jixiao xinshu*, (18 chap. ed., 117–18.

80 All the citations and quotations in this passage are from Qi Zhuoguo, 56–66 and *Chouhai tubian*, 630–34. See also Fan Zhongyi, *Qi Jiguang zhuan* (Beijing, 2003), 130–46.

81 Qi, *Jixiao xinshu*, (18 chap. ed.), 26; Qi Jiguang, *Qi Shaobao zouyi* (Beijing, 2001), 163; *Lianbing shiji*, 244; *Jixiao xinshu* (14 chap. ed.), 136, 167. For an excellent study in this regard, see Andrade, "Arquebus Volley," 115–41.

82 This was a small type of Frankish cannon/gun, according to Zheng Ruozeng, *Chouhai tubian*, 902.

83 *Chouhai tubian*, juan 12, pt. 1: 795, 798, 800, 810, 820–21. Traditional Chinese gunpowder weapons including *dachong* (大銃), *xiaochong* (小銃), *qihuo* (起火), *wankouchong* (碗口銃), and the *shouchong* (手銃)were relegated to less important occasions such as sentry soldiers. See Zheng Ruozeng, *Chouhai tutian*, juan 12, pt. 2: 827.

84 *Jixiao xinshu* (18 chap. ed.), juan 15: 239, 240, 243–44.

85 *Jixiao xinshu* (18 chap. ed.), 239–40, 243–44, 306–07.

86 Cai Jiude, *Wobian jilue*, 20th day of the 4th month, Jiajing 35; Ye Quan, Xianbo bian "Zong jiangjun." Also see Mao Kun, in Wu Dengqi (吳曾祺), comp., *Jiu Xiaoshuo* (舊小說) (Shanghai, 1935), "Wuji: Jin, Yuan, and Ming," 76, which attests to the extensive use of gunpowder weapons and attributes the defeat of Zong and Huo to the lack of gunpowder.

87 *Chouhai tubian*, 271, 625.

88 Qi Zhuoguo, 126.

89 Ibid., 154, 165.

90 Yu Dayou, annotated and punctuated by Liao Yuanquan and Zhang Jichang, *Zhengqitang ji* (正氣堂集) (Fuzhou, 2007), 559.

91 Ibid., 559 (also see 864).

92 Ibid., 173.

93 Ibid., 235.

94 Ibid., 797–98.

95 Ibid., 815–26.

96 Ibid., 237; *Chouhai tubian*, 872–73, 884.

97 *Zhengqitang ji*, 383.

98 Qi Jiguang's sources are cited above already. See *Chosŏn wangjo sillok* (朝鮮王朝實錄), Seonjo 29 (1596), gwan 71, 1st month, 30th day. The original is: "倭銃能中飛鳥, 故曰鳥銃" (http://hanji.sinica.edu.tw/).

99   W. F. Mayars, "On the Introduction and Use of Gunpowder and Firearms among the Chinese," *Journal of the North China Branch of the Royal Asiatic Society*, New Series, 6 (1869–70): 98; Tenney L. Davis and J. R. Ware, "Early Chinese Military Pyrotechnics," *Journal of Chemical Education*, 24 (1947): 536.

100   Needham, *Science*, 432.

101   For example, Wang Zhaochun, *Zhongguo gudai bingqi* (中 國 古 代 兵 器) (Beijing, 1996), 28; idem, *Shijie huoqi shi* (世界火器史) (Beijing, 1960); Chang Xiuming, 16 (the shape of the gun stock was like a glede tail).

102   Xin Zilin (信自力), *Bingqi zhenfa: Lidai junshi yu bingqi zhenfa* (兵 器 陣 法: 歷 代 軍 事 與 兵 器 陣 法) (Beijing, 2014).

103   Naganuma Kenkai (長沼賢海), *Teppo no tenrai (hosetsu)* 鐵砲の傳來 (補説), 24, 4 (1914): 347–48; "Teppo no tenrai (oto)" (鉄砲の傳來 (應答), *Rekishi chiri* (歷史地理) 25, 1 (1915): 56–57.

104   *Wubei zhi*, juan 124: 1a–9a.

105   Juan 2: 46, 55; Juan 5: 41, 55 (middle- and small-sized *niaochong*).

106   Juan 3: 41, 49.

107   Zheng Shungong, *Riben yijian* (日本一鑑) (Shanghai, 1939), "Qionghe huahai 窮河話海," juan 3, "yulie 漁獵," 9b.

108   See https://zh.wikisource.org/. For one time, "niaochongzui" should be a mistake for "niaozuichong."

109   Both *Jixiao xinshu* (18 chap. ed.) and *Lianbing shiji* are at http://ctext.org/.

110   Tan Lun's work *Tan Xianggong zouyi* is available at http://ctext.org/.

111   Quoted in Chang Xiuming, 30.

112   *Ming shilu*, Shenzong, juan 8, Longqing 6, 12th month; Shenzong, juan 569, Wanli 46, the leap 4th month; Xizong, juan 36, Tianqi 3, 3rd month (http://ctext.org/).

113   *Aying quanji*, 242; "Shi Fu zhuan," 27.

114   Chang Xiuming, 61.

115   Song Yingchang (宋应昌), *Jinglue fuguo yaobian* (經略復國要編), juan 2, military orders of Wanli 20, 9th month, 28th and 10th month, 14th month; Jingguo xionglue, "Wubei kao," juan 6: 10b; *Huang Ming jingshi wenbian*, juan 304, Liu Tao (劉 燾), "Liu Daichuan bianfang yi 劉 帶 川 邊 防 議" (http://ctext.org/); Guo Zaoqing (郭造卿), "Suzhen luoyao yi 薊鎮火藥議," in Gu Yanwu, *Tianxia junguo libingshu*, juan 48: 23b (www.kanripo.org).

116   *Chosŏn wangjo sillok*, gwan 48, Injo 15, 2nd month, 10th day.

117   See "niaoqiang" and "niaochong" on www.kan ripo.org/.

118   *Wubei zhi*, juan 124: 6a.

119   Such as "tiezui huoyao, mushen tiezui 鐵嘴火藥, 木身鐵嘴," which is ultimately from the Song work *Wujing zongyao* by Zeng Gonglian (http://ctext.org/).

120   Some modern Chinese (mostly literal) works, including Xiao Hong, *Xiao Hong xiaoshuo jingpin* (蕭 紅 小 說 精 品) (reprint, 2017); Liu Baiyu, Liu Baiyu wenji (劉 白 羽 文 集), juan 3: 401 (1995); Zuopin (作 品), 7–12 (2006): 45; Zuopin yu zhengming (作 品 與 爭 鳴), 1–6 (2010): 74, employ terms such as "chongzui," "qiangzui," and "paozui," but "chongkou," "qiangkou," and "paokou" have been much more frequently used. For example, late Ming military treatises including *Jixiao xinshu* (18 chap. ed.) and *Lianbing shiji*, and the *Shenqi pu* (juan 2: 6a, juan 4: 26a; juan 5: 10b, 19b, 28b–29a), use "chongkong," but never "chongzui."

121 See however Tang Zhiba (唐志拔) and Zheng Ming (郑明), illustrated by Gui Zhiren (桂志仁), "Zhongguo gudai chuantong haichuan sizhong zhuming chuanxing xilie (中國古代傳統海船四種著名船型系列)," in Xiandai jianchuan 現代艦船 (2010): 56; Zhang Yan and Liu Hanze, "Zhongguo dugai sizhong zhuming haichuan qianxi (中国古代四种著名海船浅析)," Sheji 設計 (2015): 41–42; Bai Chenguang (白晨光), "Zhongguo 17 shiji de fengfan zhan-liejian – Mingchao niaochuan 中國 17 世紀的風帆戰列艦 – 明朝鳥船," https://kknews.cc/zh-my/history/kyb3gq.html.

122 Fan Lai (範淶), *Liangzhe haifang leikao xubian* (兩浙海防類考續編) (block print, 1602), juan 10: 1b.

123 In juan 3 of *Chouhai tubian*, in the context of Guangdong, there are terms like "niaocao 鳥艚" and "niaochuan 鳥船," but I suspect there is a misprinting here, as "niao鳥" should have been "wu烏" due to the similarity of the two words. Tang Shunzhi 唐順之's *Jingchuan ji* 荊川集 juan 8: 41a mentions correctly "wuchuan 烏船."

   Both Zhu Wan's *Piyu zaji* (juan 5: 44) and *Chouhai tubian* (juan 12: 24b; juan 13: 23a and 27b) mentions "wuwei chuan 烏尾船" in Guangdong. This is indeed very confusing, as one Chinese text says that the "wuwei ship" in Guangdong was just "niao or bird ship" (Guangdong wuwei ji niaochuan ye 廣東烏尾即鳥船也). See *Shandong tongzhi* 山東通志, juan 20, "Haijiang zhi 海疆志," 33: 34a (www.kanripo.org).

124 *Wubei zhi*, juan 117: 14a–b, with an illustration of a "bird-beak boat" (*niaozui-chuan*). However, *Wubei zhi*, juan 116: 18b, does mention "niaochuan (bird ship)" as #5 of the Fu ship series; along with #6 the "kuaichuan (fast boat)," it was used for scouting or fetching heads (of dead enemy soldiers). On juan 116: 20b, Mao Yuanyi both illustrates and explains that a "kailang ship" was also called "niao-chuan (bird ship)." Qi Jiguang in the 18th chapter of the *Jixiao xinshu* already mentions this "kailang ship," which had a pointed head, thus called "kailang" meaning "piercing the wave." Qi also says that "its shape is like (a bird) is flying." Probably for this reason it was also called "bird ship."

125 *Huang Ming jingshi wenbian*, juan 362, "Song Dufu zoushu (宋督撫奏疏): Haifang shanhou shiyi shu (海防善後事宜疏)" (http://ctext.org/).

126 *Tiangong kaiwu*, chapter 9, "zhou 舟"; Tang Zhiba and Zheng Ming, 54.

127 Fan Lai, *Liangzhe haifang*, juan 2: 36b–39a; juan 10: 1a–b.

128 *Bing lu* (block print, 1630, Waseda University), juan 10 (non-paginated). "zhan-chuan shuo." He Rubin has a very detailed discussion of this "bird ship."

129 Tang Zhiba and Zheng Ming, "Zhongguo gudai," 56; Zhang Yan and Liu Hanze, "Zhongguo gudai," 41.

130 *Wubei zhi*, juan 103: 20b; Zheng Dayu, *Jingguo xionglue*, "Wubei kao," juan 5: 16a; Qi Jiguang, *Lianbing shiji*; Lu Xixing et al. comp. *Zhongguo gudai qiwu dacidian* (中國古代器物大詞典) (Shijiazhuang, 1997); Liu Yuemei (刘月), *Zhongguo jingju yixiang* (中國京劇衣箱) (Shanghai, 2002), 206.

131 Zeng Gongliang 曾公亮, *Wujing zongyao* 武經總要, *qianji* 前集, juan 11, #20 (http://ctext.org/); *Wubei zhi*, juan 116: 13b–14a; juan 117: 12b–13a; Jingguo xionglue, "Wubei kao," juan 5: 7b, 10a–12b; juan 6: 9b. The word 鵲 is also pronounced gu.

132 *Shenqi pu*, juan 2: 20a, 24a (倭既以鳥名銃). It was not that the Japanese named their guns "bird gun," rather it was that the Chinese term "niaochong" spread

to Japan and appeared in a Japanese account for 1572 (元亀3). See Naganuma Kenkai, 348. This Chinese term never took roots in Japan.

133 Walter W. Skeat and Walter William Skeat, *The Concise Dictionary of English Etymology* (Oxford), 294; Daehnhardt, 42; Chang Xiuming, 17–18; Edward A. Roberts, *A Comprehensive Etymological Dictionary of the Spanish Language with Families of Words Based on Indo-European Roots*, vol. 1 (A–G) (Xlibris Corporation, 2014), 661.

134 Some evidence does tend to reinforce Qi Jiguang's view: First, the matchlock gun which was brought from Southeast Asia to Japan was a type of fowling piece, and Zhao Shizhen (*Shenqi pu*, juan 4: 10a) already clearly pointed out that "bird guns" in Southeast Asia ("hainan") were initially employed to shoot birds, so their stocks were shorter. See also Need Romanized name (中島楽章), "Porutogaru-jin no nippon hatsu raikō to higashiajia kaiiki kōeki ポルトガル人の日本初来航と東アジア海域交易," *Shien* 史淵, 142 (2005): 53–54. Second, during the early years of matchlock gun in Japan, as Udagawa Takehisa has shown, was used extensively for hunting (Zheng Shungong's account cited above also reinforces this point). See Udagawa, "An Encyclopedia of Guns: The Significance of Anzai Minoru's Collection of Secret Books on the Art of Gunnery in the Museum Collection," www.rekihaku.ac.jp/e-rekihaku/126/rekishi.html, accessed in 2008 (no longer available). Nonetheless, it is very difficult to reconcile the following: Though matchlocks were used for hunting in Southeast Asia and Japan, they were also employed as personnel weapons, and this is clearly shown in the so-called pirates attacking the Chinese coast. More importantly, as discussed above, we can be sure that the Chinese named the matchlock gun first "bird-beak gun," which was based on the shape of the gun (or a part of it), not the function.

135 "John E. Wills, Jr, "Maritime China from Wang Chih to Shih Lang," in John King Fairbank and John E. Wills (eds.), *From Ming to Ch'ing: Conquest, Region, and Continuity in Seventeenth-Century China*" (New Haven, CT, 1979), 211.

136 John E. Wills, "Maritime Asia, 1500–1800: The Interactive Emergence of European Domination," *American Historical Review*, 98, 1 (1993): 83–105.

137 Sun Laichen, "The Century of Warfare in Eastern Eurasia, c.1550–1683: Repositioning Asian Military Technology in the 'Great Divergence' Debate" (unpublished manuscript, 2014).

138 *Shenqi pu*, juan 2: 6b–7a. Chang Xiuming (chapter 2) tries to argue that the Qing matchlock or niaoqiang was a different version of this.

139 *Shenqi pu*, juan 1: 4a–5a, 8a.

140 *Shenqi pu*, juan 2: 1b–2a.

141 Wen Bian, "Liqi jie," "Wu Zhengzhi xu 吳正志序," 32 (引火諸具皆產東南). The Rum (Lumi) gun also came to China from the overland route.

7 The seventeenth-century Guangdong pirates and their transnational impact

Xing Hang

The late Professor John E. Wills, Jr. was undoubtedly one of the preeminent scholars of maritime East Asia. His pioneering works have revealed much about the integrated nature of the region, from the development of overarching structures and institutions to the roles played by individual actors, such as merchants, pirates, sealords, and migrants.[1] Professor Wills never conceived of maritime East Asia as a closed system or one purely built upon trade. Accordingly, he has examined its role in globalization and cultural contacts with the West.[2] He has also paid careful attention to the overbearing presence of the Chinese state, from its imperial institutions and Confucian value system to its policies on maritime trade, which have had the longest, deepest, and most sustained impact on the region.[3]

This examination of piracy in coastal Guangdong during the seventeenth century draws upon some of these enlightening approaches. Indeed, it was an eventful and turbulent period even for the usually volatile littoral of the province. The transition from the ethnic Han Ming Dynasty (1368–1662) to the Manchu Qing (1636–1911), along with a worldwide economic crisis, precipitated a wave of piracy from Chaozhou in the east to the Leizhou Peninsula. Initially, disorganized pirate groups arose in reaction to the massive dislocation caused by warfare and a brutal Qing removal of residents on the coastline. Some sought protection from the newly established Qing or Ming loyalist remnants, while others rendered allegiance to Vietnam or even charted an independent course of action.

Starting from the 1660s, most of them became incorporated as regular military divisions under the unified leadership of the Ming loyalist Zheng mercantile organization based in Taiwan. They further initiated a wave of overseas Chinese migration to Southeast Asia. In the sparsely populated frontier of the Mekong River Delta, in southern Vietnam and Cambodia, they established settler colonies that initially rendered allegiance to Taiwan but later became largely autonomous political entities after the Zheng surrender to the Qing in 1683. The politicization of these groups contributed to a strong sense of ethnic exclusivity among Cantonese immigrants that would work against complete integration into their new host societies.

The trajectory of piracy in Guangdong simultaneously reflected and strengthened an existing set of transnational maritime networks connecting southern China with Southeast Asia. The global trading configuration, which, since the sixteenth century, had centered upon the exchange of Chinese luxury goods for silver from Japan and Manila, gradually gave way to one dominated by Indian textiles and natural resource flows to densely populated economic cores. Southeast Asia grew in strategic importance because of its maritime passageways to the subcontinent and its abundant natural resources and sparse population. Guangdong's proximity to these new product sources and markets allowed it to replace Fujian as China's most important gateway for overseas trade during the late seventeenth century, a process culminating in the Guangzhou System of the 1750s.

Dynastic transition and economic crisis

Guangdong was no stranger to piracy, having experienced local upsurges of maritime predation since at least the fourth century CE.[4] After 1548, however, as the Ming court tightened its prohibition on foreign trade and travel, bands of armed multinational smugglers (*wokou*) consisting of Chinese, Japanese, and some Europeans and Southeast Asians gravitated southward, farther away from the imperial center. Plundering ships and raiding villages only formed one aspect of their operations.[5] In fact, many of these groups ran sophisticated commercial enterprises that sought to seize the opportunities afforded by the rise of an intra-East Asian trading structure involving the exchange of Chinese silk and other luxury goods for silver from Japan and, after 1571, the Spanish Philippines. The surplus, in turn, bought into the spices and other tropical products of Southeast Asia. The tremendous volume and profitability of the exchange made it impossible for the Ming to continue its rigorous implementation of the maritime ban.[6]

Over the 1550s, the Guangdong authorities tacitly permitted the Portuguese to establish an outpost at Macao, a move that gradually received recognition from the court in Beijing.[7] In 1567, the court itself gave up on its ban and authorized a licensed trade with Southeast Asia. These avenues, while still limited, eventually brought most commercial activities back into legitimate channels. At the same time, the unification of Japan, which reached its final stage with the Tokugawa *bakufu* (1603–1868), along with Ming offensives against the main pirate leaders, a product of the court's earlier mobilization of naval fleets and coastal defenses in reaction to the Japanese invasion of Korea, successfully restored order to the Guangdong coast.[8]

The seventeenth century, however, in contrast to the economic growth and expansion of before, ushered in a period of severe depression for East Asia. Some historians perceive of this downturn as a common worldwide phenomenon known as the seventeenth-century crisis, although much about it remains a subject of controversy, including its causes, timeframe, severity, and universal applicability. Nonetheless, Geoffrey Parker, William Atwell, and others agree that the resource base and food supply in many parts of East Asia simultaneously contracted, resulting in a decline in handicraft production and consumption. In the worst cases, massive deaths amid famine and pestilence ensued. Since the amount of available resources could not support as many state entities or elites, economic woes often triggered political crises in the form of rebellions, coups, and military invasions. On the flip side, the malaise presented opportunities for ambitious state-builders and monopolists to overturn the existing order, eliminate their competitors, and build more uniform, consolidated enterprises.[9]

The crisis exacerbated the worldwide decline of Spain as a power, which, in turn, contributed to a drastic decrease in the supply of silver from Manila.[10] The Tokugawa *bakufu*, beset by a major famine and rebellion, promulgated five edicts between 1633 and 1639 that expelled the Spanish and the Portuguese, and forbade subjects from leaving or returning to Japan on pain of death. Known as the Maritime Prohibitions (*kaikin*), they had the effect of further curtailing the circulation of silver.[11] An intense competition broke out to dominate the decreased trade flows in maritime East Asia. When the dust settled around 1640, Chinese piratical remnants and segments of the Ming military in Fujian and eastern Guangdong had come under the domination of the Zheng family. This primarily mercantile organization successfully controlled the foreign trade in its area of control. At the same time, the Dutch East India Company (VOC), with its powerful ships and weapons, secured an outpost in Taiwan, allowing it to readily access both product sources in China and the Japanese market. The favorable position of the two monopolies received a further boost in 1640, when the Tokugawa *bakufu* restricted all private trade to the port of Nagasaki, and in the hands of Chinese merchants and the VOC.[12]

The reduced flow of silver, and its monopolization in the hands of two major quasi-governmental enterprises, exacerbated the economic difficulties faced by the Ming. A steep drop in the agrarian surplus of grain-producing areas had led to widespread famine, from the desolate northwestern backwater and resource-deficient southeastern coast to even the most prosperous urban centers of the Yangzi River Delta. Now, the court lacked the revenues to effectively relieve famine and transfer grain to the places most needed.[13] Peasant uprisings soon broke out and spread across the empire. In the summer of 1644, Beijing fell to a rebel group under Li Zicheng (1606 to c. 1645), and the last Ming emperor committed suicide. Taking advantage of the disorder, the Ming general Wu Sangui (1612–78) led the Manchus into the capital and drove out the rebels.[14] While North China fell to the Manchus by the end of the year, staunch resistance from Ming loyalists slowed down their advance to the south and would continue for the next four decades.

Economic crisis, along with the turbulent dynastic transition, hit Guangdong hard. As Robert Antony has shown, floods, droughts, food shortages, and famines afflicted the province almost every year between 1645 and 1662. The population decreased from nine million in 1640 to two million in

1661.[15] During this period, Guangdong became a zone of political contestation for four distinct political players. On the Ming loyalist side, the gentry leader Su Guansheng (d. 1647) upheld Zhu Yuyue (1646–47) as the Shaowu Emperor (r. 1646–47) in Guangzhou in 1646. A year later, another pretender, Zhu Youlang (1623–62), proclaimed the reign name of Yongli (r. 1646–62) in Zhaoqing, in the western part of the province.[16] After 1648, this court acquired the support of Li Dingguo (1621–62) and Sun Kewang (1608–60), former rebel commanders against the Ming. The Chaozhou area came under the domination of the Zheng mercantile organization, based in neighboring Fujian.

By the late 1640s, the Qing had entered the scene. Its troops seized Guangzhou and exterminated the Shaowu court, and drove Yongli and his entourage farther to the west. In 1649, it appointed Shang Kexi (1604–76) and Geng Jimao (d. 1671), two trusted Han bannermen, as semi-autonomous feudatory leaders of the province. They controlled their own military forces separate from the rest of the Qing military hierarchy, and shared broad administrative privileges in their jurisdiction. Until 1655, however, the Qing victory remained incomplete. In his effort to join forces with the Zheng in eastern Guangdong, a rendezvous that came close to actualization, Li Dingguo's troops continued to launch successful counterattacks extending Ming loyalist power into the Pearl River Delta.[17]

The incessant warfare and constantly shifting areas of jurisdiction spawned an even greater range of independent local political actors, among them piratical groups that infested the coastline of Guangdong. A great number of them rallied behind the Ming cause, as it was the nearest and most organized resistance movement. The biggest group consisted of pirates from the Leizhou Peninsula, broadly speaking, the area around the Gulf of Tonkin that also extends into present-day eastern Guangxi and serves as a gateway to Vietnam and the rest of Southeast Asia. By the middle of the 1650s, they had come under the leadership of Deng Yao (d. 1660) and his lieutenant, Yang Yandi (d. 1688). They opened a base at Longmen, near the prefectural seat of Qinzhou. Outside this garrison town, a multiplicity of forested, mountainous islands fan out into the Gulf of Tonkin, cutting up the open sea into narrow, winding passageways. Known as the Seventy-two Passages, this area provided a perfect hideout for outlaws. Farther out into the Gulf of Tonkin, the island of Hainan similarly served as a den for a variety of pirates and defeated Ming loyalist troops.[18]

Toward the east, Xu Long operated around the Pearl River Delta. His associate, Su Li, was based near Lufeng and Haifeng. Initially, the two men attempted to establish independent dynasties, but they later submitted to the Qing, which granted them broad autonomy so long as they helped it clear the coastal areas of its rivals. They were fierce competitors with the Zheng over territory and access to overseas trade in eastern Guangdong.[19]

Another round of dislocation and fragmentation would result from a draconian decision by the Qing court in 1662 to remove to the interior the residents of the entire Chinese coastline, from Guangdong all the way to Liaodong in the north. The aim was to prevent them from supplying trading goods and provisions to the Zheng organization. In tandem with the decision, the court established a feudatory position in Fujian for Geng Jimao, leaving Shang Kexi solely in charge of Guangdong. The policy, combined with military offensives, successfully forced the Zheng to seek a new base of operations by seizing VOC-held Taiwan in 1662, and, two years later, completely withdraw from the mainland coast. Around the same time, in 1664, Qing forces exterminated Su Li, who had tried to defy the evacuation order, and pressured Xu Long to withdraw into the interior.[20] However, as Dahpon Ho shows so vividly, enforcement of the removal brought about severe suffering and dislocation to coastal residents, who depended upon the sea for fish, salt, and other essential necessities. The feudatory lords also became powerful regional satraps through the massive wealth accumulated through smuggling, protection rackets, and the rapacious extortion of evacuees.[21]

Those who refused to comply with the policy congregated in the islands and littoral zones outside of the evacuated boundaries. Many of them belonged to a subethnic caste group known as the Dan, whose entire existence revolved around the sea; they lived and worked onboard their boats. Because of their distinct cultural and social characteristics, they had long endured discrimination from their counterparts on land and from the continental imperial dynasties.[22] Now they and other coastal residents took up arms to defend their way of life. A dizzying array of piratical groups proliferated along the entire length of the evacuated Guangdong littoral in the wake of the ban. Besides smuggling salt and fish, and trading goods from abroad, they plundered passing ships and raided villages in the interior.

A young man named Qiu Hui (d. 1683) commanded a squadron of boatpeople in the area around present-day Shantou. Nicknamed "Stinky Red Meat" (*Chou hongrou*), he and his men raided villages and towns for women and children, whom they would traffic to Taiwan, a rough and tumble frontier of its own with a surplus of single men. Qiu also controlled the fishing and salt industries along the eastern Guangdong coastline. His underlings sold illicit licenses for access to the evacuated zone at the Guangji bridge, outside the Chaozhou prefectural gate, and under the noses of the Qing authorities.[23] To the west of Qiu's sphere of influence, in the Pearl River Delta, another group of Dan congregated under the leadership of Zhou Yu and Li Rong in 1663. It took over a year for Shang Kexi's feudatory troops to suppress this insurrection right on the doorstep of the provincial capital.[24]

Hazy, overlapping jurisdictions presented additional challenges. The Portuguese trading port of Macao, on account of its special status, was barely spared the evacuation around it despite its location outside of the removal boundary. Naturally, the city became a place of refuge for lawless elements.[25] Piratical groups also congregated on Nan'ao and other islands along the border between Guangdong and Fujian, taking advantage of its proximity to the Zheng on Taiwan.[26] Relentless attacks from Manchu bannermen and feudatory forces successfully dislodged Deng Yao from his Longmen base in 1660, and he was caught and executed. His subordinates, including Yang Yandi (also known as Yang Er), his brother Yang San, and Xian Biao and his family, fled across the border into Tonkin, where they came under the protection of an enigmatic Vietnamese district official named Phan Phú Quốc. When the Qing demanded their extradition in 1666, Phan not only refused, but fired his cannon from the defensive walls of his town against the troops sent by the court to arrest them. As a result, Yang and his associates continued to ravage the Gulf of Tonkin unchecked, and seized several outposts on the island of Hainan.[27]

The Zheng consolidation

From the middle of the 1660s, the Zheng organization on Taiwan took an active interest toward the Guangdong coast. This focus resulted from fundamental economic changes on a worldwide scale. Amid a severe economic depression compounded by the draconian Qing removal policy, China gradually lost its role as a preeminent exporter of silk and other fine luxury items. Meanwhile, in Japan, the largest market for Chinese goods, the silver mines that supplied the bullion to fund the purchases, gradually became depleted. The Tokugawa *bakufu* enacted measures to reduce imports and encourage domestic handicraft production.[28] At the same time, the Indian subcontinent emerged as a leading producer of textiles and other manufactures for the world market.[29] Southeast Asia acquired particular importance in this new configuration as a strategic gateway to the Indian Ocean zone. It was also a region fertile in natural resources, such as copper, tin, and rice, that could supply the needs of the Asian cores, where population was already pressing upon ecological limits in certain areas.[30]

Within this overall context, Zheng Jing (1642–81), the leader of the organization, increasingly found himself unable to sustain his core operations in the trade of Chinese silk for Japanese silver. Unlike his predecessors, who focused upon acquiring access to bases off the coast of Zhejiang and in the Yangzi River Delta, Zheng set his sights upon Guangdong, which, like Taiwan, provided convenient access to the sea lanes of Southeast Asia. After 1665, he seized upon the chaotic vacuum left by the Qing evacuation, which amounted to a voluntary inward retreat of official power, to consolidate his hold over the littoral. He did so by cultivating relations with the main pirate leaders, most of whom already enjoyed close smuggling relations with his organization. In 1669, Zheng Jing formally incorporated the partisans of Qiu Hui as regular divisions within his military organization. The island of Dahao, off Shantou, was opened up as a legitimate port for overseas trade and put under the rationalized administration and laws of Taiwan.[31]

At Macao, Zheng Jing engaged in complex negotiations with the Portuguese authorities of the enclave, as well as the governor of Spanish Manila, an important trading partner of both. At the same time, Zheng obtained the connivance of Shang Kexi, who had his own retinue of mercantile agents engaged in smuggling on his account. From the early 1670s, Macao became a neutral zone for this strange mix of interests to meet and conduct business. The Portuguese authorities sheltered a sizable community of Zheng partisans in the city, sharing jurisdiction over them with Ke Gui, a naval commander dispatched from Taiwan to patrol the waters around the Pearl River Delta. One Korean source noted with surprise that a Zheng junk from Macao, which washed onto the shores of Cheju Island during a storm while on its way to Nagasaki in 1670, contained a crew with some donning Ming-style long hair and robes, and others with shaved heads in Manchu and Japanese costumes.[32]

The multiplicity of fashions onboard the ship, on the one hand, constitutes an outward manifestation of the stark nature and exclusivity of ethnic boundary lines in maritime East Asia during the seventeenth century. These differences, in turn, are played out in ideological conflicts, such as the Ming resistance to Manchu rule and the Tokugawa *bakufu*'s refusal to acknowledge China's centrality.[33] At the same time, however, the ability to cross boundaries, while highly risky, presented opportunities for profit too lucrative to pass up.[34] Thus, many, from official down to commoner, formed elaborate networks that thrived upon exploiting the intersections and margins of legality as defined by each cultural sphere.

In 1666, relentless Qing diplomatic pressure on Tonkin forced the ruler to expel Yang Yandi, Xian Biao, and their band of Leizhou pirates. As a result, they fled to Taiwan and joined Zheng Jing as an official division of his military force. They now became utilized as an instrument of his wider ambition of forging a maritime kingdom that could encompass his entire sphere of economic influence in the China Seas. Among the weak spots in the region that Zheng identified as ideal beachheads for expansion was the Mekong Delta, a fertile frontier zone that belonged to Cambodia, but proved increasingly difficult for it to effectively control. Fierce succession struggles raged at the Cambodian court in Oudong between rival claimants throughout this period. Siam and the Nguyễn lords of Đàng Trong (Cochinchina), in central and southern Vietnam, fought a proxy war with each other by supporting particular pretenders, who would offer the two outside powers territory in exchange for their "assistance."[35] The Dutch East India Company took advantage of the perennial political crisis to establish a permanent trading post near Oudong and obtain a monopsony on deer hides, the kingdom's preeminent export.[36]

In 1666, Zheng Jing dispatched Xian Biao to the Mekong Delta to acquire a new base for resource extraction and carve out a sphere of influence for himself at the court in Oudong. With a fleet of eight to nine junks, Xian and his crew of fifty-six men arrived in this liminal water world and proceeded to engage in the interception and plunder of passing ships. The following year, in February 1667, they arrived at Oudong, and received the warm welcome of King Paramaraja VIII. Over the course of a year, several thousand more Zheng partisans from Fujian and Guangdong arrived in Cambodia, apparently to establish a colony. It may be safe to assert that this settlement was located around the area of present-day Saigon, where they did much of their predation. Xian and prominent members of his crew were made *shahbandar*, or headmen of the newcomers.[37] The dispatch of Xian Biao introduced a fresh political element that severely shook up the entire balance of power. For the warring Cambodian elites, he and his men became seen as a potentially powerful new ally, able to counterbalance the Siamese and Đàng Trong.

Xian Biao rapidly gained influence at the court of Paramaraja by supporting it against the Vietnamese immigrants, who had established colonies in parts of the delta.[38] These settlers received the protection of the king's influential son and contender for the throne, Prince Ramadhipati, who, in turn, was sponsored by the Nguyễn lords. With the tacit encouragement of Paramaraja VIII, Xi and his agents engineered a systematic massacre of over one thousand Vietnamese in the spring of 1667. Although they subsequently promised not to kill anymore, the king suspended the payment of tribute to Đàng Trong and terminated all trade. In exchange for this act of merit, the Chinese *shahbandars* were confirmed in their territorial acquisition, allowed to maintain a private army and navy, and given a free hand in the country.[39]

They next took aim at the exclusive privileges enjoyed by the Dutch East India Company in Cambodia. According to Dutch sources, Xian, whom they call Piauwja (Biaoye), demanded a payment of several thousand taels, ostensibly as restitution for a previous debt owed to him by a Chinese merchant now living in Batavia. A haggling over the precise amount ensued. Then, on the fateful night of July 9, 1667, Xian along with several hundred followers, robbed and burned down the Dutch trading lodge. They killed the head agent, Pieter Ketting, and several of his native servants. They also plundered the ship, *Schelvisch*, docked at the harbor, and took away massive quantities of silver and silk. Ketting's assistants fled and hid in the jungles of the Mekong for weeks, before boarding the *Schelvisch* and fleeing for Nagasaki. A study of the subsequent written exchanges between the VOC authorities at Batavia and Oudong reveal that under heavy Dutch pressure, the Cambodian court detained Xian and six other co-conspirators and ordered their execution.[40] Yet, later Chinese gazetteers continued to mention him as a main instigator of raids along the Guangdong coast during the 1670s.[41] It is possible that the king spared the lives of the six men and sent them away, while bluffing to the Dutch.

At any rate, the move did nothing to hinder the continued growth of Leizhou influence. The VOC never recovered from the devastation and, in 1670, shut down the factory because of dismal sales. A year later, King Paramaraja VIII was assassinated by his nephew, ushering in another round of chaos. Over the decade, the Leizhou Zheng forces remained an influential presence in Cambodian politics. They supported a claimant to the throne against a rival backed by Đàng Trong, and the two sides fought several major, albeit inconclusive, naval battles.[42]

Meanwhile, back in China, the Guangdong feudatory lord, Shang Kexi, and his son Zhixin (d. 1681) and Geng Jingzhong (d. 1680), son of Geng

Jimao and the new feudatory lord of Fujian, joined forces with Wu Sangui, by then feudatory lord of southwestern China, in a massive rebellion against the Qing court. Zheng Jing took advantage of this opportunity to ally with the insurgents and move his base to the Fujian coast. He put off his goal of a maritime kingdom and devoted his entire attention to affairs in China. Shang Zhixin further ceded to him the control over all Guangdong prefectures east of Dongguan, as well as large parts of the littoral.[43]

Zheng's successful campaign allowed Yang Yandi and Chen Shangchuan to set sail from Taiwan in 1677 with a thousand men and eighty ships, and regain their Longmen stronghold. Over the following year, they helped him secure a base of operations around the Gulf of Tonkin and Hainan Island. Control over this littoral, in conjunction with Xian Biao's Mekong colony, allowed the Leizhou divisions to patrol the South China Sea and offer safe passage for Zheng commercial ships. They were also able to conduct a profitable exchange of products between Guangdong, Taiwan, and Southeast Asia.[44] Longmen enjoyed a brief period of prosperity as a bustling trading hub, as evidenced by the multitude of remains of porcelain and other luxury products from those years unearthed in the area.[45]

From partisans to exiles

By 1681, the Qing had managed to eliminate the feudatories and expel Zheng Jing from the mainland coast. The Zheng withdrawal to Taiwan the same year left open a power vacuum that precipitated a renewed outbreak of smuggling and piratical activity on the Guangdong coastline. The Pearl River Delta became a multinational zone for illicit trade, a meeting point for Chinese (both the long-haired Ming partisans and shaved Qing subjects), Southeast Asian, English, Dutch, and Iberian ships.[46] Also operating in this area was Zheng Jing's main commander, Liu Guoxuan, who refused to go along with his leader to Taiwan. Instead, he attacked Macao and nearby ports in attempts to seize a new base of operations on the mainland.[47] Likewise, Qiu Hui, who was previously assisting Zheng in Fujian, returned to Dahao. However, a massive Qing naval offensive in 1681 and 1682 quickly dislodged Liu and Qiu once again. Both men fled back to Taiwan.[48] The following year, the bulk of the Zheng navy was decimated in an epic battle in the Taiwan Strait near the Penghu Islands. Qiu sank with his ship to the bottom of the sea. Liu Guoxuan, along with other Zheng commanders and generals, surrendered Taiwan to the Qing in September 1683.[49]

The Qing offensive on the Guangdong coast also struck a severe blow to the Leizhou contingent under Yang Yandi, Chen Shangchuan, and Xian Biao. After a disastrous engagement near Hainan in April 1681, they were forced to flee their Longmen base.[50] The primary records give conflicting narratives about what happened next. Although they do not reveal much about Xian Biao's fate, they agree that Yang Yandi, Chen Shangchuan, and the other Leizhou commanders ultimately ended up in the Mekong Delta. However, according to the Veritable Records of the Nguyễn court, Yang and Chen, along with fifty war junks and more than 3000 troops, first docked at the port of Đà Nẵng. Yang and Chen presented themselves before the Nguyễn lord as "exiled subjects of the Ming, who out of a righteous choice, refuse to serve the Qing. We are willing to submit to you and become your ministers." The lord responded that he had no use for their troops, but authorized them to settle farther south at Đông Phố, near present-day Saigon, where they could rely upon the vast and fertile land to sustain themselves. He further commanded the ruler of Cambodia in an edict to treat these men as "his own subjects."[51]

Interestingly enough, the Veritable Records date the year of their appearance at Đà Nẵng as 1679, which does not seem to match the time-line of events presented in other sources. The 1683 report of a Chinese junk from Cambodia at Nagasaki, for instance, mentions Yang and Chen setting foot on Cambodia sometime in 1682 with "3,000 men and seventy war junks," a figure quite close to the official Vietnamese source.[52] Moreover, the Veritable Records give the impression that the Leizhou commanders had never been to the Mekong Delta before. However, evidence points not just to a high degree of familiarity with the area, but also their continued involvement for over a decade. As it turns out, the Veritable Records, compiled during the nineteenth century, when the Nguyễn had unified Vietnam, were recalling and conflating events that occurred two hundred years earlier. As Brian Zottoli further asserts, the work itself was a product of censorship and reinterpretation of historical events for the glorification of the ruling dynasty and Confucian ideological correctness.[53]

In spite of the embellishments, it is possible, based upon a careful reading of the Veritable Records in conjunction with several other documents, to piece together a rough sketch of what happened to the Leizhou commanders. Almost certainly, their departure occurred after their defeat at the hands of Qing forces in 1681, when Yang and Chen realized that the Zheng were on their last legs and could no longer offer them any protection. Faced with a bleak choice between their Longmen base and overseas interests, they decided to leave China permanently and recenter their activities upon their Mekong colony. It appears that Yang and Chen first set foot in the Saigon area before their visit to Đà Nẵng.

The motivation for their arrival at the central Vietnamese port and their subsequent correspondence with the Nguyễn appeared to have resulted more from deliberate calculation than desperate circumstances. Without the maritime power of the Zheng around to provide backing, they could no longer function as an independent actor and, therefore, had to find a new patron. Naturally, a fierce competition soon broke out between the two other stakeholders in Cambodian politics – Siam and Đàng Trong – over this valuable source of arms, ships, and manpower. The Siamese king specially sent an envoy to Yang Yandi to persuade him to submit, arguing that the ruler once enjoyed a deep friendship with Taiwan.[54] In the end, the Leizhou commanders chose the Nguyễn, who granted them the continued right to their colony

in the Saigon area. In exchange, they offered their submission and backed the
Đàng Trong choice for the Cambodian king.[55]

Leizhou forces, working together with Nguyễn troops, soon expanded their
territorial holdings to include three or four present-day provinces in the delta.
During this time, an enigmatic figure known as Mao Jiu (Mạc Cửu, 1655–1735)
appeared on the scene. He, too, hailed from Leizhou, arriving in Cambodia in
1680 to serve as an official for the court, perhaps a sign of Xian Biao's residual
influence. Although his exact connection to the main Leizhou commanders
remains unclear, he and Chen Shangchuan enjoyed a close relationship, since
Mao betrothed his daughter to Chen's son.[56] Mao would acquire a power base
at Hà Tiên, on the present-day Vietnam–Cambodia border and, by the end
of the seventeenth century, expand his area of control to include a large part
of the littoral along the Gulf of Thailand, as well as Phú Quốc Island. The
settlements founded by Chen Shangchuan, Yang Yandi, and Mao Jiu continued to thrive as autonomous political entities under their successors until
well into the eighteenth century. Their administrations retained Ming-style
institutions and cultural characteristics in their realms. They thus played a
huge role in the formation of the Minh Hương (Ming loyalist descent) communities, which remained prominent in the political life of Vietnam into the
twentieth century.[57]

Concluding remarks

Seventeenth-century piracy along the Guangdong coast arose as a result of an
economic crisis that contributed to the collapse of the Ming and the ascend-
ancy of the Manchu Qing. The Qing court's draconian evacuation policy, in
effect from 1662 to 1683, intensified the maritime predation during the initial
stages of implementation. However, the prolonged state of crisis also opened
up unprecedented opportunities. As the China–Japan–Manila axis gradually
gave way to a wider system of exchange centered upon Indian textiles and
Southeast Asian natural resources and minerals, coastal Guangdong grew in
importance on account of its proximity to the new product sources and markets. Taking advantage of the power vacuum left behind by the Qing removal,
the Zheng mercantile organization, based in Taiwan, consolidated its hold
over the area, and incorporated the major piratical bands as formal military
divisions. These groups now became the instruments of Zheng Jing's efforts
to forge a maritime kingdom that sought to encompass his already formid-
able zone of economic influence. Even after the demise of the organization,
the Leizhou pirates, in particular, continued to play an active role through
their colonization efforts in the Mekong Delta and involvement in the complex geopolitical scramble over Cambodia.

The story of the Guangdong pirates epitomizes, on a broader level, the
gradual triumph of ports within their province, especially in the Pearl River
Delta area, over those of neighboring Fujian as China's preeminent hubs for
overseas trade. The 1684 Qing legalization of private trade and travel abroad

further solidified Guangdong's position.[58] Even though the court had reversed its tolerant stance and enacted a more restrictive commercial regime by the middle of the eighteenth century, it still chose Guangzhou to serve as the sole major window to the rest of the world. Enticed by the lucrative product sources and, later, access to the vast demand from European markets, Chinese flooded into Southeast Asia. Merchants and immigrants from Guangdong, especially Chaozhou, Hakka, and Leizhou, were crucial participants in what Leonard Blussé has aptly called the "Chinese century." Their junks traversed the sea lanes of the South China Sea and docked at its ports, procuring rice, medicinal ingredients, and seafood, while their settlers went into the remote hinterlands to dig up minerals, such as gold and tin.[59] The crucial economic role played by them and other Chinese groups in the burgeoning modern global economy during the eighteenth century has been well-studied.

However, the Guangdong settlers in Southeast Asia were unique in their simultaneous politicization. As Anthony Reid has pointed out with great insight, affiliation with the Zheng organization marked "a kind of legitimation, for the first time, of a separate Chinese identity outside China."[60] This strongly held exclusivism emanated from the symbolic and cultural connections to the continental power centers that had long characterized and conditioned internal cohesion and integration in the China Seas. Moreover, the influence was not merely imposed from the outside by continental powerholders. The Leizhou colonies of Chen Shangchuan, Yang Yandi, and Mao Jiu actively utilized and adapted these symbols in forging autonomous, sea-based entities that lasted for sixty years to a century. They, in turn, would presage the rise of quasi-Republican polities founded by Chaozhou and Hakka gold miners on the island of Borneo, which flourished from the late eighteenth century until the 1880s.[61] The story of the Guangdong pirates thus forces a reconsideration of the commonly accepted notion of overseas Chinese as a stateless people just waiting for outsiders, such as the Europeans and native Southeast Asian kingdoms, to control and exploit them.[62] In fact, politically autonomous maritime Chinese states always posed a viable contingency in the region.[63]

Notes

1 For one classic example of his ability to interplay broad structural changes with individual characters, see John E. Wills, Jr., "Maritime China from Wang Chih to Shih Lang: Themes in peripheral history," in Jonathan D. Spence and John E. Wills Jr. (eds.), *From Ming to Ch'ing: Conquest, Region, and Continuity in Seventeenth-Century China* (New Haven, 1979), 201–38.

2 Refer, for instance, to John E. Wills, Jr., *China and Maritime Europe, 1500–1800: Trade, Settlement, Diplomacy, and Missions* (Cambridge, 2010).

3 The best and most recent articles that emphasize this approach to maritime East Asian history are John E. Wills, Jr., "The South China Sea is not a Mediterranean," in Tang Xiyong (ed.), *Zhongguo haiyang fazhan shi lunwenji* (Taipei, 2008), vol. X,

21–22; and "A Very Long Early Modern? Asia and Its Oceans, 1000–1850," *Pacific Historical Review*, 83.2 (2014): 189–203.

4 Zheng Guangnan and Shanghai China Maritime Museum, *Xinbian Zhongguo haidao shi* (Beijing, 2014), 40–41.

5 Robert J. Antony, *Like Froth Floating on the Sea: The World of Pirates and Seafarers in Late Imperial China* (Berkeley, CA, 2003), 25–27. See also Y. H. Teddy Sim, *The Maritime Defence of China: Ming General Qi Jiguang and Beyond* (Singapore, 2017).

6 By the end of the sixteenth century, Japan was producing up to a third of the world's silver, most of it ending up in China. See Naohiro Asao and Bernard Susser (trans.), "The Sixteenth-century Unification," in John Whitney Hall (ed.), *The Cambridge History of Japan* (Cambridge, 1991), vol. IV: Early Modern Japan, 60–61. Another scholar has estimated that a whopping 50,000 to 90,000 kg of silver entered China from Manila in a good year. See William Atwell, "Ming China and the Emerging World Economy, c. 1470–1650," in Denis Twitchett and Frederick W. Mote (eds.), *The Cambridge History of China* (Cambridge, 1998), vol. VIII. 2: *The Ming Dynasty, 1368–1644*, 389–92.

7 For a concise narrative of how the Portuguese secured Macao and their relations with the Ming in general, refer to John E. Wills, Jr., "Maritime Europe," in Wills (ed.), *China and Maritime Europe*, 25–40.

8 Kenneth Swope, *A Dragon's Head and a Serpent's Tail: Ming China and the First Great East Asian War, 1592–1598* (Norman, 2009), 13–40; and Chao Zhongchen, *Ming dai haijin yu haiwai maoyi* (Beijing, 2005), 289–90.

9 For an introductory overview of the seventeenth-century crisis, refer to Geoffrey Parker and Lesley M. Smith, "Introduction," in Parker and Smith (eds.), *The General Crisis of the Seventeenth Century*, second edition (London, 1997), 7–17, 19–22. See also Parker, *Global Crisis: War, Climate and Catastrophe in the Seventeenth Century* (New Haven, CT, 2013), 1–114.

10 William S. Atwell, "A Seventeenth-century 'General Crisis' in East Asia?" *Modern Asian Studies*, 24.4 (1990): 669–70; and "Emerging World Economy," 408–09; and Parker, *War, Climate and Catastrophe*, 254–90, 445–83.

11 Ronald Toby, *State and Diplomacy in Early Modern Japan: Asia in the Development of the Tokugawa* Bakufu (Stanford, 1991), 11–13. As a result of the maritime ban, total silver exports from Japan declined from an average annual high of four to five million taels (150,000 to 187,500 kg) in the early seventeenth century to under 1,500,000 taels (56,250 kg) in 1642. See Richard von Glahn, *An Economic History of China: From Antiquity to the Nineteenth Century* (Cambridge, UK, 2016), 295–347.

12 Toby, *State and Diplomacy*, 11–13.

13 William S. Atwell, "General Crisis," 666.

14 Kenneth Swope, *The Military Collapse of China's Ming Dynasty, 1618–44* (London, 2014), 91–207, contains a precise narrative of the Ming fall. For more on the Qing conquest and consolidation, see Frederic Wakeman, *The Great Enterprise: The Manchu Reconstruction of Imperial Order in Seventeenth-century China*, 2 vols (Berkeley, CA, 1985), vol. I, 818–21.

15 Antony, *Like Froth*, 30; Antony, "'Righteous Yang': Pirate, Rebel, and Hero on the Sino-Vietnamese Water Frontier, 1644–1684," *Cross-Currents: East Asian History and Culture Review* 11 (2014): 9.

16 Lynn Struve, *Southern Ming: 1644–1662* (New Haven, 1984), 101–03.

17 Liu Fengyun, *Qing dai Sanfan yanjiu* (Beijing, 1994), 107–12.

18 Antony, "Righteous Yang," 12–13 and tour of the Seventy-two Passages, organized by the Guangxi University for Nationalities, Qinzhou and Fangchenggang, Guangxi, March 2015.

19 Yang Ying, *Congzheng shilu*, Taiwan wenxian congkan, 32 (Taipei, 1958), 4; Cheng Wei-chung (Zheng Weizhong), *War, Trade and Piracy in the China Seas, 1622–1683* (Leiden, 2013), 167.

20 Ibid., p. 215.

21 Dahpon David Ho, "Sealords Live in Vain: Fujian and the Making of a Maritime Frontier in Seventeenth-century China," PhD dissertation, University of California-San Diego (2011), in particular, 200–97.

22 A classic study of the Dan is Chen Xujing, *Danmin de yanjiu* (Shanghai, 1946).

23 Zhou Shuoxun (ed.), *Chaozhou fuzhi* (Zhulan Bookshop, 1893), 62–63.

24 Zheng Guangnan and China Maritime Museum, *Xinbian haidao shi*, 244–45.

25 John E. Wills, Jr., *Embassies and Illusions: Dutch and Portuguese Envoys to K'anghsi, 1666–1687* (Cambridge, MA, 1984), 86–92.

26 Zheng shi shiliao sanbian, Taiwan wenxian congkan, 175 (1963), 62–63; 66–73; 74–87.

27 Niu Junkai and Li Qingxin, "Chinese 'Political Pirates' in the Seventeenth-Century Gulf of Tongking," in Nola Cooke, Li Tana and James A. Anderson (eds.), *The Tongking Gulf Through History* (Philadelphia, 2011), 139.

28 Nakamura Tadashi, *Kinsei Nagasaki bōekishi no kenkyū* (Tokyo, 1988), 282–83.

29 Om Prakash, *The Dutch East India Company and the Economy of Bengal* (Princeton, NJ, 1985), 126.

30 Richard von Glahn, *Fountain of Fortune: Money and Monetary Policy in China, 1000–1700* (Berkeley, CA, 1996), 214.

31 Jiang Risheng, *Taiwan waiji*, Taiwan wenxian congkan, 60 (1960), 239.

32 Wu Han (ed.), *Chaoxian Li chao shilu zhong de Zhongguo shiliao*, 12 vols (Beijing, 1980), vol. IX, 3968.

33 Toby, *State and Diplomacy*, 53–109 and Swope, *Dragon's Head*, 191.

34 Take, for instance, the example of the Chinese double-agent farmer Sait, vividly portrayed in Tonio Andrade, "A Chinese Farmer, Two African Boys, and a Warlord: Toward a Global Microhistory," *Journal of World History*, 21.4 (2010): 573–91.

35 For more on the complex intrigues at the Cambodian court, and the role of Siam and Đàng Trong during this period, refer to the PhD dissertation by Brian Zottoli, "Reconceptualizing Southern Vietnamese History from the 15th to 18th Centuries: Competition along the Coasts from Guangdong to Cambodia," University of Michigan (2011), 282–92.

36 Cheng (Zheng), *War, Trade and Piracy*, 218–19.

37 Ibid., 220–21.

38 Zottoli, "Reconceptualizing Southern Vietnamese History," 283–84.

39 For more on this episode, see Mak Phoeun and Po Dharma, "La deuxième intervention militaire vietnamienne au Cambodge (1673–1679)," *Bulletin de l'Ecole française d'Extrême-Orient*, 77 (1988): 233–35.

40 W. J. M. Buch, "La Compagnie des Indes néerlandaises et l'Indochine," Bulletin de l'Ecole française d'Extrême-Orient 37 (1937): 233–37; Jacobus Anne van der Chijs (ed.), *Dagh-register gehouden int Casteel Batavia vant passerende daer ter plaetse als over geheel Nederlandts-India* (The Hague, 1897), 1668–1669, 5.

41 Lin Taiwen and Li Gaokui, *Guangdong Wuchuan xianzhi* (1825), juan 10, 29.
42 Mak Phoeun, *Histoire du Cambodge: de la fin du XVIe siecle au début du XVIIIe* (Paris: 1995).
43 Jiang Risheng, Taiwan waiji, 304.
44 Antony, "'Righteous Yang,'" 20; Zheng Guangnan and China Maritime Museum, *Xinbian haidao shi*, 239.
45 Tour of Leizhou pirates' former base at Longmen and interview of the Qinzhou Museum staff, fieldwork in Qinzhou and Fangchenggang, Guangxi, March 2015.
46 Zheng Weizhong (Cheng Wei-chung), "Shi Lang 'Taiwan guihuan Helan' miyi," *Taiwan wenxian*, 61.3 (2010): 43.
47 VOC 1362: 1011–1054v, Fuzhou to Batavia, 3 and 9 March 1681, at 1011–1015v, citation found in the unfinished manuscript of John E. Wills, Jr, who generously made it available for perusal and consultation.
48 Zheng Guangnan and China Maritime Museum, *Xinbian haidao shi*, 238.
49 Jiang Risheng, *Taiwan waiji*, 406–23.
50 Cheng (Zheng), *War, Trade and Piracy*, 245.
51 Xu Wentang and Xie Qiyi, Da Nan shilu *Qing-Yue guanxi shiliao huibian* (Taipei, 2000), 3.
52 Hayashi Shunsai and Ura Ren'ichi (ed.), *Ka'i hentai* (Tokyo, 1958–59), vol. 1, 367.
53 Zottoli, "Reconceptualizing Southern Vietnamese History," 16, 290.
54 Hayashi Shunsai, *Ka'i hentai*, vol. 1, 398.
55 Phouen, *Histoire*, 370.
56 Li Qingxin, *Binhai zhi di: Nanhai maoyi yu Zhong wai guanxishi yanjiu* (Beijing, 2010), 341.
57 Ibid., 343.
58 Zheng (Cheng), "Shi Lang," contains a detailed survey of this competition at its height, during the early 1680s, just before the Qing lifted its maritime prohibitions.
59 Leonard Blussé, "The Chinese Century: The Eighteenth Century in the China Sea Region," *Archipel*, 58 (1999): 107–29.
60 Anthony Reid, *Southeast Asia in the Age of Commerce: 1450–1680* (New Haven, CT, 1993), vol. 2, 314.
61 The most complete study to date on the Borneo republics is Yuan Bingling, *Chinese Democracies: A Study of the Kongsis of West Borneo (1776–1884)* (Leiden, 1999).
62 As Wang Gungwu argues, "it was astonishing how many disparate groups of Chinese, compatriots as well as competitors, managed to devise ways to serve foreign rulers, powerful mercantile companies as well as themselves, even while European powers consolidated control over new colonial states." See his excellent foreward to Eric Tagliacozzo and Chang Wen-chin (eds.), *Chinese Circulations: Capital, Commodities, and Networks in Southeast Asia* (Durham, NC, 2011), xiii.
63 John E. Wills, Jr., "South China Sea," 21–22.

8 A ship full of Chinese passengers

Princess Amelia's voyage from London to China in 1816–17

Paul A. Van Dyke

Introduction

Research of individuals and their connections to global issues has been at the heart of John E. Wills, Jr.'s (aka Jack's) studies for decades. When I sat in his classes many years ago, I was amazed at how one person's experience could represent an entire world of seemingly endless interactive connections and exchanges. Instead of studying history through generic and unfriendly terms such as imperialism, colonization, and diasporas, one could do the same thing by looking at a real person with a real name, a real family, and a real face. Like many of Jack's students, I became hooked on the individual and the common man approach to global history.

This chapter is about the common Chinese seamen who began to circumnavigate the globe en masse in the 1780s aboard ships of all nations. More specifically, it is about 380 of those seamen, who returned to Asia from London in 1816–17 as passengers aboard the English East India Company (EIC) ship *Princess Amelia*. But like Wills' ever evolving and ever expanding biographies of historical characters, the story is actually about more than the experiences of those 380 men. Their example represents a much broader arena of global phenomena that affected the entire world. Their story is about new sea routes being explored in Asia in the mid to late eighteenth century; about European ships encroaching upon the traditional trade of the Chinese junks in Southeast Asia; about the decline of the large European trading monopolies and their inability to compete with the rising power and influence of private enterprises; about the success of the Canton trade and the enormous attraction it had to aspiring businessmen of all nationalities and ranks; about the versatility of the Chinese people to adapt to a multitude of environments and establish themselves in major seaports throughout the world; and finally, it is about ancient diseases and Europeans dying aboard the ships that went to Asia and the need to replace them with indigenous seamen in order to keep international commerce moving forward.

Because the expansion of Chinese seamen throughout the world has been little known or understood, I begin the story of the Chinese sailors in the late eighteenth century with the establishment of new sea routes to

China and the European encroachment on the traditional Chinese junk trade in Southeast Asia. That discussion will be followed by a number of examples of East India companies hiring Chinese seamen in China from the 1780s onward. In passing, I will discuss historical events that led to the 380 seamen seeking employment aboard British ships. And finally, I end the story with reasons why the men returned to Asia as passengers rather than as crew. Their numbers had risen to the point that they were threatening the livelihoods of indigenous seamen in the United Kingdom (UK). Their story is truly one with global dimensions and perfect for a Wills'-style approach to historical research.

Chinese seamen aboard country ships

Chinese seamen were active in global commerce centuries before 1780. They were navigating Asian waters for hundreds of years aboard Chinese junks; and they were much involved with Portuguese and Spanish vessels that were based in Manila and Macao. We also know that many Chinese seamen were being employed aboard the country ships that sailed between India and China.[1] All of this was going on many decades before the 1780s. I present a couple of examples.

In 1751, a Swedish naturalist wrote the following:

> An *Englishman*, whose men were run away during his stay in *China*, could with difficulty get so many *Chinese* sailors as were necessary to navigate his ship to the *East Indies*; though he assured them he would send them back by the first opportunity.[2]

On October 17, 1776, the EIC officers in Canton mentioned that they had been informed "by a Chinese seaman belonging to one of the country ships" that one of their ships would be measured soon. There were many country ships at Whampoa in 1776 and others probably had Chinese seamen aboard them as well. In 1786, the private mariner John Pope mentioned that they had Chinese aboard their ship.[3] These are just a few examples out of many that show Chinese seamen being regularly employed by country ships that sailed between India and China.

This chapter, however, is not about these earlier seamen, but rather about a later phenomenon that emerged in the 1780s, which led to Chinese seeking employment aboard other foreign vessels, including British, Dutch, Danish, French, American, and others. Most of these seamen were hired in China, before the ships departed. Even though the European ships were continually in need of seamen to replace men who died, it was not until the 1780s that they were successful in hiring Chinese to fill those positions.[4] In order to understand the reasons for this change in Chinese attitudes, we need to look at the new sea routes that were established, which impacted the junk trade to Southeast Asia.

New sea routes to China and the decline of the Chinese junk trade

Beginning around the 1780s, Chinese seamen began to seek employment aboard other Western ships, and their numbers increased rapidly thereafter. By 1800, there was hardly a seaport in the world that did not have Chinese seamen present. The 380 Chinese passengers aboard the *Princess Amelia* discussed below were part of this latter phase in global migration and labor.

The story begins in the mid-eighteenth century with the establishment of new sea routes to China. Before the 1750s, the Sino-European trade was very much regulated by the monsoons. Most of the ships sailed to China via the Malacca or Sunda Straits, and then proceeded in a northeasterly direction past the southern coast of Cambodia and South Vietnam, Hainan Island and then to Macao. They arrived there with the southwest monsoon from July to September and departed with the northeast monsoon from November to February.

In the early eighteenth century, some French ships sailed to China across the Pacific, via South America. Spanish ships, of course, had been sailing the Pacific regularly, between the Americas and the Philippines, but they did not usually go directly to China, as the French were doing. When vessels approached China from the east they could arrive any time of the year. In 1713, for example, the French ship *Grande Reine d'Espagne* arrived at Whampoa from Peru on March 31. Owing to contrary winds, an arrival from the west in the spring time was impossible. These trans-Pacific French voyages, however, ceased in 1714 and then most French ships approached China from the west thereafter.[5]

In the 1740s, French captains began experimenting with a new route that took them along the west coast of Palawan and the Philippines and then to Macao and Whampoa (黃埔, the anchorage downriver from Canton). This route is shown in Map 8.1 and was used by ships that arrived late in the monsoon season. Captain Alain Dordelin of the French ship *Jason* was one of the early pioneers of this passage.[6] In September 1740 he encountered contrary winds near Hainan Island, making it impossible to proceed eastward. Rather than layover there until the change in the monsoon, he decided to alter the route toward Palawan, which enabled them to bypass the contrary winds.

When the *Jason* arrived at Whampoa in mid-October, Europeans at Canton were quick to note their success in using this new route, which led other captains to follow their example.[7] Map 8.1 shows the track of the Private English ship *Louisa*, which took this route in 1774 and arrived at Whampoa in mid-October. As captains became more familiar with this new passage, they discovered that in some years they could actually arrive in China as late as December, via this route, which saved many months of having to layover at Malacca or Hainan Island. As more captains made use of this sea lane, they began stopping in ports along the way, looking for products they could sell in China.

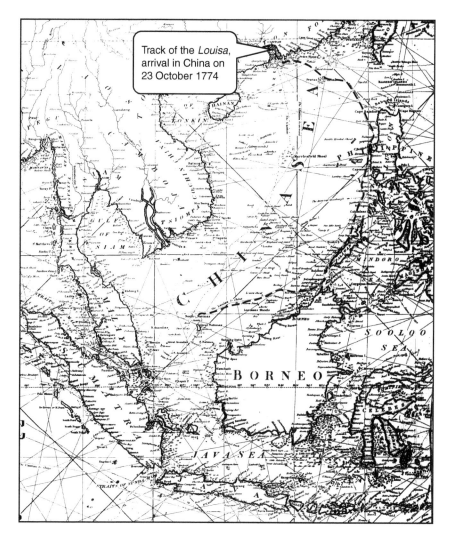

Track of the *Louisa*, arrival in China on 23 October 1774

Map 8.1 Map showing the track of Private English ship *Louisa* from Malaysia to China in 1774. The *Louisa*'s track shows the route ships took when sailing to China late in the monsoon season (October to December).

Title unknown. Bound volume of charts prepared by J.W. Norie and Co. Early Nineteenth Century. Australian National Library: PMB Film No. 214, Doc. 149

In the 1750s, British captains also began experimenting with routes that took them through the Spice Islands and east of the Philippines. Map 8.2 shows the course that the EIC ship *Warren Hastings* took in 1787–88. This route took much longer than the passages through the South China Sea but enabled ships to bypass the monsoon winds and arrive in China at any time of the year.

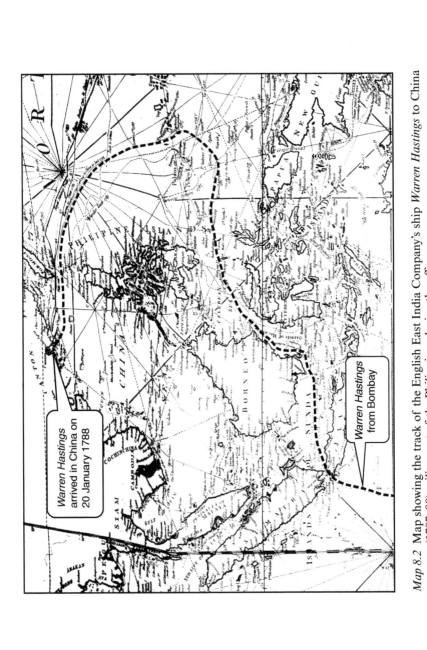

Map 8.2 Map showing the track of the English East India Company's ship *Warren Hastings* to China (1787–88) sailing east of the Philippines during the off-season.

Laurie, Robert and James Whittle. *The Complete East-India Pilot, Oriental Navigator.* 2 vols. London: Printed for the East India Company by Robert Laurie and James Whittle, 1799. vol. 1, chart 37, map entitled "The Indian and Pacific Oceans"

Within a few years all of the Europeans involved in the China trade began using these new sea routes.[8] As they sailed through the many islands in the region, they stopped at ports looking for fresh provisions, and of course, products that they could sell at Canton. Before long, captains were purchasing items in Southeast Asia such as beetle nut, pepper, cloves, nutmeg, various kinds of wood, herbs, plants, birds' feathers, edible birds' nests, sago, shells, dried fish, sea plants, sea creatures, roots, oils, dyes, and other products. All of these items were part of the traditional trade of the Chinese junks.[9] As more European ships made use of these new routes, they began to undermine the traditional Chinese junk trade.[10] After 1784, American ships also began sailing to China via the Pacific and some of them stopped in Australia and ports in Southeast Asia looking for products they could vend in China.

It is important to understand that for the junks, the trade with Southeast Asia was their staple. The profit margins on the products that they handled needed to be maintained in order to make the voyages viable. For the foreign ships, however, these Southeast Asian products were simply backhauls that helped to reduce the costs of the voyage. Their staple products were the exports that they purchased in China such as tea, silk, and porcelain. Thus, foreigners could undercut the asking prices of the Chinese shippers, which affected the profitability of junk voyages.[11]

The market for Asian seamen in China

Throughout the eighteenth century, European ships that traded at Canton were in continual need of seamen to replace the men who died en route. Before leaving China, captains did whatever they could to entice other seamen to join their ships so they could be ensured that they had a sufficient crew for a safe passage home. Up until the 1780s, Chinese had not been willing to join those crews, perhaps because they did not want to be stuck in a foreign port with no way home. Or perhaps they could make more money serving on the Chinese junks.[12]

In the 1780s, we begin to see one European ship after another taking in Chinese sailors in China before embarking on their return passages home. As I have argued in another study, one factor that brought about this change in attitude among Chinese seamen was a parallel decline in the junk trade to Southeast Asia. Displaced sailors had to find employment somewhere and now they found that working aboard European ships was a viable option.[13] At the same time, there were also changes taking place in the foreign trade at Canton, with a huge increase in the number of private traders arriving and a decline in the East India companies trading there.[14]

Most of the large companies' vessels required crews of upwards of 100 to 150 seamen, with a conservative average being about 120 men. It was very common to lose 10, 20 or even 30 or 40 men on the way to China. Some men became ill and had to be left at a previous port in order to recover. Other men died en route and were buried at sea. Desertion was always a problem for all ships sailing to China. When the Company's crews were depleted to less than a hundred seamen per ship, they needed to be replenished with new men.[15]

While the ships were lying at Whampoa for three or four months, unloading and loading their cargos they did not need so many seamen. With the increasing numbers of private ships trading in Canton and carrying cargo to Europe, the East India companies – especially the British – began to seek ways to cut costs. One way was to keep a skeleton crew while at anchor at Whampoa, and then hire new men just prior to leaving China. Seamen might also be hired for just one leg of the journey such as from China to India. In India, these temporary men could be discharged and more European seamen engaged for the return passage to Europe. When there were not enough European seamen available, Asian seamen were used to fill the ranks.

The advantage to hiring Asian seamen at Macao (who were usually Lascars or Chinese, but might also include Malays, Filipinos, and others) was that they could be employed for just one leg of the voyage. Lascars and Chinese were also engaged at other ports such as at St Helena, Cape Hope, various Indian ports, Malacca, etc., and then discharged when the ships arrived at Macao. This was an effective way to ensure that there was sufficient crew for the safety of the voyage and a way to cut the costs during the time the ship lay at anchor at Whampoa. This was necessary in order to become more competitive with the increasing numbers of private traders involved in the China trade, whose tons per man ratios were often much more efficient.[16]

Chinese, of course, did not need means of supporting themselves once they were landed in China, because they could stay with their families. Lascars also had ghaut serangs stationed in Macao who cared for them and found new employment.[17] At Whampoa, however, there were no such services available, because foreigners were not allowed to stay in that port and were required to leave with the ships. Nonetheless, by 1800, the discharging of Lascars at Whampoa was indeed becoming a problem. The men had no place to go for food or shelter, and of course, Chinese authorities did not want sailors wandering about causing trouble. Consequently, the EIC issued orders that captains who discharged seamen at Whampoa would be charged for their maintenance until the men found new employment.[18] And it should be pointed out that it was not only the EIC that had this problem, but included all of the nationalities trading in China. In 1833, for example, we find the following notice in the *Chinese Courier*.

NOTICE

WHEREAS some of the *Colonial* Dutch vessels having sailed from hence during this season and left several Javanese and Malay sailors behind without the means of subsistence, from which much trouble has arisen, such persons daily coming for support, notice is hereby given to the Commanders of the *Colonial* Dutch vessels in Java, that in future all such sailors left behind or discharged for what reason soever, will be provided for during their stay in China or returned to the place from whence shipped, on account and at the expence of the Ship from which they are so left behind or discharged.

M. J. SENN VAN BASEL
In charge of the affairs of the Neth. Consulate in China.
Macao, 7th August, 1833. [Chinese Courier, 1833.09.14]

When we take all of these factors into consideration, we begin to see why there was an increase in Chinese seamen aboard Western ships in the 1780s and after. Ships picked up Asian seamen on the way to China, dropped them off at Macao, went upriver with a skeleton crew, unloaded and loaded their cargo, went back downriver to the lower delta, picked up Chinese and/or Lascar seamen near Macao to fill out the crews, and then began their return passage home. Chinese who had lost their employment on the junks were now more than willing to serve aboard foreign ships. And they were willing to engage for just one leg of the passage or go all the way to Europe. There were not enough available European seamen in China to fill this void. Once the ships arrived at India, Cape Hope or ports such as St Helena, captains could find more European seamen. The Chinese sailors were then discharged at those ports, where they stayed until another ship arrived heading east.

Chinese sometimes found themselves left at a port where there were few opportunities to hire on another ship to return home. In December 1824, for example, the EIC ship *Canning* stopped at Singapore on its way to Whampoa. The captain agreed to take in ten Chinese seamen who worked "their passage to China."[19] They were not hired as part of the crew or given a wage, but received a free ride in exchange for their labor during the passage. They were landed at Lintin Island on January 20, which shows that there were indeed ways to return home even when there were no opportunities to hire on another ship.

Chinese seamen aboard British East India Company ships

Table 8.1 shows a list of 380 Chinese men who boarded the EIC ship *Princess Amelia* in the UK in 1816. They arrived in Britain on nineteen different EIC ships. These men are representative of the dearth of marine labor at the time to fill the needs of ships sailing to Asia. It was better to pay the additional costs of sustaining the Chinese in the UK and their return passages than to risk the safety of the voyage with an insufficient crew.

Prior to about 1805, these seamen were just dropped off in the UK and then they found employment on other ships. At that time, captains were still allowed to hire displaced Asian seamen on outbound voyages as part of the crew. In February 1782, for example, the *Antelope Packet* left the UK with twelve Chinese seamen aboard. When the ship arrived at Macao in June

Table 8.1 List of 380 Chinese passengers received on board the *Princess Amelia* at Gravesend on July 11, 1816 and the ships in which they arrived in the UK

No.	Ships upon which arrived in the UK	Chinese	Year the ship was in China
1	*Alnwick Castle*	30	1815
2	*Atlas*	23	1815
3	*Bridgewater*	19	1815
4	*Ceres*	29	1815
5	*Charles Grant*	18	1815
6	*Cuffnells*	5	1815
7	*David Scott*	18	1815
8	*General Harris*	14	1815
9	*Hope*	26	1815
10	*Inglis*	18	1815
11	*Lowther Castle*	22	1815
12	*Marquis Camden*	11	1815
13	*Princess Amelia*	36	1815
14	*Royal George*	15	1815
15	*Vansittart*	27	1815
16	*Walmer Castle*	20	1815
17	*Warley*	17	1815
18	*Warren Hastings*	31	1815
19	*Wexford*	1	1814
	Received at Gravesend 1816.07.11	380	
	Died at Sea	1	
	Subtotal	379	
	Left the ship at Bally on 1816.11.30	154	
	Subtotal	225	
	Left the ship at Lintin on 1817.02.02	225	
	Balance	0	

Source: BL: IOR L/MAR/B/36-O *Princess Amelia* 1817
Note: I have grouped the entries from ship *Camden* with those of *Marquis Camden*. There was no EIC ship that simply went by the name *Camden*, at that time. Besides the *Marquis Camden*, there were also the *Earl Camden* and *Lord Camden*. These latter vessels, however, were not active in 1816. See Farrington, *Catalogue*.

1783, Captain Henry Wilson reported the following to the EIC committee in Canton.

> 1783, Jun 9: Captain Henry Wilson having represented to us, that he had been obliged to employ the Chinese on Board the *Antelope* all the voyage, as the few hands in the vessel had rendered that measure absolutely necessary, and accordingly recommended them to us, we therefore agreed to give each man a gratuity of 20 dollars (12 men 240 dollars) also to allow two dollars to each, for being at short allowance two months (24 dollars). We hope the Hon'ble Court will approve of

this disbursement as we think the men were well entitled to it from Captain Wilson's account of their extreme good behavior, and the length, and hardship of the voyage. One man having behaved very ill, did not receive the gratuity. To the petty officers as seamen (27) were also paid each two dollars for two months short allowance amounting to 54 dollars.[20]

The *Antelope Packet* was a small vessel used to deliver mail so it only had a crew of thirty-nine men. The Chinese made up about one-third of the crew. Not all of the captains were as generous toward Chinese seamen as Wilson. As the following example from the EIC committee in Canton shows, sometimes captains tried to deprive the men of their wages.

> 1785, Aug 10: We received an application from thirty two Chinese seamen, stating that they came from England in the *Locko*, and had been discharged here [China] by Captain Baird, who refused to give them any wages, that they were poor and had no money to support their families, and therefore requested the Company would make them a small present in consideration of having served on board their ships. For that reason and to encourage the Chinese Seamen to enter on board our ships, when they may be wanted, we agreed to advance them 4 dollars p[er] man, and to place the amount to charges extraordinary.[21]

If the EIC had not reimbursed the Chinese seamen for their services, word would have spread very quickly. It would likely have resulted in Chinese refusing to go aboard EIC ships or requesting full payment in advance before boarding them. The latter situation could be very risky for the captain, because the seamen might desert and leave the ship with all their wages (see example below).

When Captain Baird and the *Locko* returned to China in 1787, they again needed more men to fill out the crew. Before leaving China, he stopped at Macao and took on board 19 Chinese seamen.[22] Had the EIC committee not paid the sailors mentioned in the example above, Captain Baird might have had difficulty procuring these men – given his past reputation.

If Chinese died at sea, then the EIC paid their relatives or friends aboard ship the wages that were owed to the deceased, which were then forwarded to their families in China. On October 27, 1784, for example, the following entry appears in the EIC Canton Diary:

> 1784, Oct 27: Payment23
>
> To the respective Families or Friends of the following persons who died on board the *Essex*, as p[er] order of the Hon'ble Court of Directors.

```
£ St. 33,15,6 ............................................... Tales 101.775
Vizt.        Awang          £ 7,13,6
             ATum            7,15,_
             AChow           8,10,6
             AChoie          9,19,6
    £ 33,18,6
```

When engaging Chinese seamen in China, it was often necessary to give them an advance on their wages upfront. As the following entry shows, Chinese compradors (provision purveyors) were the usual mediators who found the Chinese seamen for the captains, and then made arrangements to have them secretly transported to the ship.

> 1785, Mar 3: Mr. Pigou reported that Captain Gore while in Macao Roads had drawn on him for 200 dollars in favor of his compradore who had advanced that sum to some Chinese seamen that had engaged to go with Captain Gore. It being a particular circumstance, the Council agreed to pay the money to debit the owners for the *Nassau* for the same upon our books.[24]

From 1781 to 1800, 51 out of the 361 EIC voyages that were made to China had Chinese seamen aboard. That is about 14 percent of the total or one out of every seven or eight ships. There are references to 921 Chinese seamen being involved in those fifty-one voyages, which averages to eighteen men each.[25] Many of these seamen were obviously the same people from one year to the next. In some years, only two or three EIC ships hired Chinese in China and might engage a total of about fifty men. In other years, such as 1797, nine EIC ships engaged a total of 182 Chinese in China before departing for Europe.[26] Thus, the 921 men who were hired from 1781 to 1800 probably represent only a couple hundred seamen. The percentage of EIC ships taking in Chinese continued to grow into the early nineteenth century.

We might ask where the Chinese slept aboard the ship. The answer is they were given hammocks, just like the rest of the crew. In 1806, the EIC ship *Bombay Castle* engaged 36 Chinese seamen on February 27, 1806, just before leaving China.[27] In preparation for taking them in, the captain, on February 25, purchased "4 Bolts Manilla Canvas for Chinamen's Hammocks."[28]

As the numbers of Asian seamen aboard British ships increased, new problems began to emerge in the UK in managing them. They were not only taking jobs away from indigenous seamen, but also creating social problems within the UK when they remained there for long periods of time. The EIC responded to these problems with the following outcome:

Memo reflecting Lascars & Chinese &c.

5 March 1812

Lascars or Chinese brought home on Country ships not in the Company's service, are maintained in England, and returned to their native country at the expense of the Owners. The license, allowing the ship to come to Europe, provides that if the Owners neglect, or refuse to maintain and return such natives, the Company may take charge of them, and charge the expense to the Owners. But, notwithstanding this precaution, it frequently happens that Lascars desert in London, or from the ships at the out-ports, & being found wandering about, are brought to the East India House and from the difficulty of understanding their language, the name of the ship in which they came to England is seldom ascertained; the charge, therefore of maintaining and returning such men falls upon the Company, the annual expense of which is about £500.[29]

Because of the additional expense of maintaining the seamen – after the voyages were completed – the EIC required that captains receive permission from the select committee at Canton before engaging Chinese aboard company ships. But as the example of the *Princess Amelia* shows, the supercargos of the select committee usually complied with captains' requests for more men. They often redistributed seamen aboard EIC ships at Whampoa so that each of them had an equal crew. If there were not enough men to go around, then the committee might ask their comprador to find some Chinese sailors to fill out the crews.

It was against China's laws for Chinese to seek employment aboard foreign ships or to go abroad on them so most of these transactions were done in secret in a remote location in the lower Pearl River Delta and Macao.[30] After 1780, it was fairly easy to arrange with the Chinese compradors for any number of Chinese men desired. And there were many locations where the men could board the ships undetected (see Map 8.3). When they returned to China, they usually disembarked in the lower delta before the ships went upriver to Whampoa, so that they would not be discovered by Chinese officials.

The repatriating of Asian seamen as passengers actually began much earlier than 1812. The practice in earlier years, however, was inconsistent. In 1783–84, for example, the EIC ship *Foulis* repatriated ten Lascars and ten Chinese as passengers.[31] In 1789, the EIC ship *Nottingham* repatriated 12 Chinese as passengers, who boarded the ship in London on February 2, and were landed at Macao on September 17.[32]

The next EIC repatriation was the *Contractor*, which received 20 Chinese passengers at Gravesend on March 25, 1798. Nine of the men ran from the ship before they reached China. The remaining 11 men were landed at Macao on December 1. Included with the Chinese were fifty Lascar passengers who

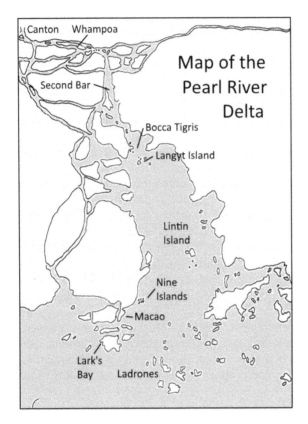

Canton Whampoa

Second Bar

Bocca Tigris

Langyt Island

Map of the
Pearl River
Delta

Lintin
Island

Nine
Islands

—Macao

Lark's
Bay Ladrones

Map 8.3 Map of the Pearl River Delta by the author

were returned to India and 17 "Manila Men" passengers who were landed in the Strait of Alas, near Bally.[33] From this year forward, repatriations of Chinese seamen began in earnest. Almost every year thereafter upwards of a hundred men or more were sent back to China as passengers. As the figures in Table 8.1 show, those numbers continued to grow over time. By the mid-1810s, there were well over three hundred Chinese seamen being repatriated each year. This means that EIC ships were now employing about 600 different Chinese men, which are about three times as many as were employed before 1800.

I have only analyzed the crews of the ships that went to China. Overseas Chinese seamen who lived in Southeast Asia were undoubtedly being hired by American and European ships as well, but they are not the concern of this chapter. Moreover, if the ships did not go to China then I have no way of tracking those men. But I have consulted hundreds of journals of vessels that went to China, which reveal this new phenomenon emerging in the 1780s of Chinese being hired before leaving, and then landed again near Macao on their return. There are very few examples of this happening before 1780, but many after that year.

Eighteen of the nineteen ships that carried the 380 Chinese seamen to the UK in 1816 had been to China in 1815. One of the ships, *Wexford*, was in China in 1814, but it did not arrive in the UK until the summer of 1815. Most of the Chinese seaman would have boarded the ships in China, as the example of the *Princess Amelia* reveals.

The *Princess Amelia* made voyages to China in 1809, 1811, 1813, 1815 and 1816. The ship journals, pay books and ledgers show that the ship employed Chinese sailors in each of those years, and also carried passengers back to China. In 1809, the *Princess Amelia* picked up 25 Chinese seamen on March 5, 1810 before leaving Macao. Two of the men died en route and the rest of them were apparently landed in the UK (the records provide no specific place or date of disembarkation). On December 4, 1810, the ship took on board 31 Chinese passengers, fifteen of whom had arrived in the UK on the *Princess Amelia* and the rest on seven other EIC ships. One of the men died at sea, and the remaining seamen were landed in China on December 28, 1811. At some point before the ship left Macao on March 4, 1812, the captain engaged another 35 Chinese who served as part of the crew on the return passage to the UK.[34]

On November 28, 1812, by order from the EIC directors, sixty-four Chinese passengers boarded the *Princess Amelia* at Gravesend to be returned to China. When the ship arrived at Penang in late July 1813, 22 of the Chinese passengers deserted. The remaining 42 men disembarked in the lower Pearl River Delta on October 21. The ship then went upriver to Whampoa and unloaded and loaded its cargo. On February 17, 1814, the ship was again downriver at Lintin Island where it took in thirty-six Chinese sailors for the return passage. The men were landed in Long Reach on August 20. On September 22, the thirty-six men were paid their wages for the voyage.[35]

The *Princess Amelia* carried fifteen Chinese passengers from the UK to China in 1815. The ship's logbook does not say when the men left the ship but it would probably have been sometime between September 7 and 9, when they were in the lower delta. The *Princess Amelia* passed the entrance of the river, Bocca Tigris, on September 10. Chinese were not supposed to be aboard foreign ships when entering China so they would probably have disembarked before then (see below and Map 8.3).

On December 6, 1815, the *Princess Amelia* was fully loaded and began its descent downriver past Bocca Tigris. On December 8, while anchored at the Ladrone Islands outside of Macao, the ship secretly took on board 36 Chinese seamen. These men were landed at Blackwall on May 14, 1816. They were paid wages for the five months and six days they served aboard the ship. On June 15, 1816, the thirty-six Chinese seamen boarded the *Princess Amelia* again, but this time as passengers. Their sustenance during the time they were in port at Greenwich was charged to the ship. They were part of the 380

Chinese passengers shown in Table 8.1. The remaining 344 men boarded on July 11. The wages of the thirty-six seamen are listed in the ship's pay ledgers for 1815 and 1816, and the first names (without surnames) of all 380 men are shown in the ship's journal.[36]

Because the *Princess Amelia* was sailing out of season, it took the route south of Java, north through the Strait of Alas near Bally, and then east of the Philippines to Macao. The ship stopped at Bally for provisions and to send greetings to the local ruler. On November 30, 1816, while at Bally, 154 of the Chinese passengers disembarked. The ship's journal does not give a reason for them leaving, but as the example above suggests, the Strait of Alas was where sailors from Manila were discharged. Because the ship was heading eastward from there, Bally was probably the best place for them to get off and find passage aboard a junk or Portuguese ship back to the Philippines. Otherwise they would have had to go all the way to Macao and then find a ship to take them back to Manila, which would have extended their travel by several weeks.

One Chinese passenger aboard the *Princess Amelia* died en route and the remaining 225 men were landed at Lintin Island on February 2, 1817. The ship went upriver, unloaded and loaded, and left Whampoa in early March. There is no mention of the ship taking in more Chinese seamen before it left Macao on March 11, 1817.[37]

The *Princess Amelia* is only one example out of nineteen ships shown in Table 8.1. Many of the other vessels followed a similar pattern of picking up Chinese seaman in the lower delta on the homeward passage, and taking in Chinese passengers in the UK on the outbound voyage.

There are examples of Chinese passengers going the other way as well. On January 21, 1802, the EIC ship *Boddam* picked up 16 sailors near Lintin Island to help work the ship on the return passage home. The next day when the ship was near the Grand Ladrone Islands south of Macao two Chinese passengers, Antonius Thun and Stephanus Sie, came aboard. The Chinese sailors and the two passengers were landed at Gravesend in June. Chinese servants of English officers often boarded EIC ships in China as passengers, and their employer paid the fares. But in Thun and Sie's cases, there is no mention of them being servants. As far as we know, they were just traveling on their own and going to the UK for whatever reasons.[38]

In other cases, the Chinese passengers who boarded EIC ships in China appear to have been colonists. On January 17, 1812, for example, the ship *Cuffnells* picked up 12 Chinese passengers near Lintin Island and landed them at St Helena on June 7, 1812. The passenger list in the ship's journal shows the following entry: "Passengers from China to St Helena. Twelve Chinese Mechanics."[39] The journal provides no explanation as to what was meant by "mechanic." Watch and clock repairmen were called mechanics at this time, but that was not likely to have been the case with these twelve men.[40] They must have been skilled in working some type of machinery. The reference also makes no mention as to who paid for the men's passage, but other examples below will show that they were probably colonists who were recruited by the EIC. If this assumption is correct, then they would have been transported to St Helena at the expense of the Company.

As far as I know, the twelve men would not have got off the ship at St Helena in order to be hired by other ships. The policy that required Chinese sailors in the UK to be transported free of charge back to China appears to have been applied to St Helena as well. On July 1, 1807, for example, the EIC ship *Alfred* took on board 20 Chinese passengers at St Helena and landed them at Macao on February 9, 1808. They were entered as "Chinese Charter party passengers," which means the EIC paid for their passage. These men were brought to St Helena by the EIC ship *Ganges*, probably as seamen.[41] They were very lucky to have landed at St Helena because the *Ganges* was lost at sea on May 29, 1807 near St Vincent Island in the Caribbean.[42]

There are other examples of Chinese boarding in China and landing at St Helena. The *Albion* took in ten Chinese seamen in March 1809 just before leaving China and landed them at St Helena on May 25.[43] On March 18, 1811, the EIC ship *Alnwick Castle* picked up 22 Chinese passengers in the lower Pearl River Delta and landed them at St Helena on July 13. At the same time, fourteen additional Chinese seamen came aboard and were entered as part of the crew. On the 1812 voyage to China, the *Alnwick Castle* hired fourteen Chinese seamen again just before leaving China. They were also entered as part of the crew.[44]

On March 19, 1811, while anchored at the Second Bar (downriver from Whampoa, see Map 8.3), the EIC ship *Canton* took on board 23 Chinese passengers. One man died en route and the remaining 22 men were landed at St Helena on July 13. In addition to these men, the ship also took in thirty-six Chinese seamen on March 28, in the lower delta, just before leaving China. These latter men were entered as part of the crew and landed in the UK.[45]

On April 1, 1815, the following entry appears in the EIC's Canton Diary: "Chinese embarked for the Island of St Helena 500 [Dollars]."[46] On October 14, 1816, another entry reads: "Advanced to the Chinese Laborers of the Island of St Helena Do[llars]. 5,100."[47] These men were obviously recruited in Canton and given advanced payment to encourage them to go to St Helena as settlers and workers.

As most of the examples show, Chinese usually did not leave or board foreign ships above Bocca Tigris. This was the case because every ship had to be inspected when it arrived and took in two Chinese tidewaiters at Bocca Tigris who stayed with the ship until it returned again to that station on the outward passage.[48] If the Chinese seamen were discovered by these customs officers, then they would be arrested and fined because it was illegal for them to leave or arrive on foreign ships. Obviously, the captain of the ship *Canton* above did not expect any problem. Perhaps he bribed the tidewaiters to allow the Chinese to board, or perhaps he somehow disguised the men as foreign seamen, or entered them as Chinese workers and shipwrights who were commonly employed to repair foreign ships before their departure from China.[49]

Whatever the case may have been, the captain of the ship *Canton* seemed to have little difficulty getting the men aboard while at anchor above Bocca Tigris, which, like the smuggling of opium, shows the gaps in the customs administration.

By the early 1800s, it had become so commonplace for Chinese to be coming and going on foreign ships that tidewaiters and guard posts at Bocca Tigris were ineffectual at stopping them. As a result, customs officers made the licensed Chinese compradors and pilots (who guided ships up and down river) responsible for reporting Chinese whom they noticed aboard the ships. If Chinese were found aboard foreign ships, the Hong merchant who secured the vessel was also penalized.

In January 1805, for example, the EIC ship *Walmer Castle*, took on board 25 Chinese seamen at the Second Bar, before departing downriver. The men were apparently hired to fill out the crew and ensure a safe passage home. However, either the proper bribes had not been given to the customs officers, or perhaps the Hoppo or Governor General heard about the men being aboard and ordered them to be removed from the ship. Whatever the case may have been, the men were arrested and the security merchant Puiqua (another name for Houqua, Wu Bingjian 伍秉鑑) was charged and fined for neglecting to prevent this from happening. The EIC officers in Canton responded by ordering their captains to only discharge and take in Chinese sailors when the ships were in the lower delta (south of Bocca Tigris) so that they could avoid problems with the customs officers.[50]

EIC ships continued to hire Chinese sailors to ensure that they had a sufficient crew for the safety of the voyage, so, as one might expect, the threat of getting caught was a problem in later years as well. In 1819, for example, the EIC committee in Canton issued the following order to the captains of their ships.

> 1819, Aug 27: The Mandarins have threatened to extort a sum of money from a pilot should Chinese subjects be found on board the ship to which he had been appointed and not regularly reported by him to the Officer commanding the fort at the Bocca Tygris. We recommend therefore your dismissing from your ship at Lintin all Chinese whom you may have brought from England or elsewhere who if discovered are liable to severe punishment should they be found in your Vessel in the river, a heavy mulct [fine] will probably be imposed on your Comprador and Pilot – and some embarrassment may occur in loading or unloading your ship, for all of which after this notice we shall hold you and your owners responsible.[51]

Most EIC captains were aware of this situation and had been complying with this order all along – discharging and/or engaging Chinese seamen only when the ships were below Bocca Tigris. On January 9, 1817, for example, the EIC ship *Windham* received 20 Chinese passengers in the lower delta. They were provided with "20 Hammocks & two suits of clothes for each man."

The twenty men were landed at St Helena on March 20 "on account of the Hon'ble Company."[52]

Other EIC captains were not as willing to abide by this policy. After sitting at Whampoa for three, four or five months, officers and crew members were anxious to get underway as quickly as possible. In their eyes, the Qing law that forbade Chinese from working on foreign ships was simply out of touch with reality. Hundreds of Cantonese sailors were now being employed by foreign captains every year, and there was little that the Qing government could do about it. Consequently, in order to avoid delaying voyages another day by making a stop in the lower delta, EIC captains continued to sneak Chinese sailors aboard at the Second Bar, despite their orders to the contrary. Almost every year after 1805, there are examples in the EIC ship journals of Chinese sailors and passengers boarding and/or being discharged above Bocca Tigris.[53]

What still needs to be shown is that most of these activities began in the 1780s. In addition to the examples above, I will provide other evidence here to support this idea. I've read through every one of the 760 EIC Canton-bound ship journals that have survived from the years 1700 to 1800. I found only one journal before 1780 that mentions Chinese seamen. It was the *Stringer* in 1711. The ship was in much need of men so before leaving China the captain stopped at Macao on December 11. He managed to hire five Chinese seamen from the Portuguese. They were given two months' wages in advance. The captain had actually engaged six Chinese but one of them changed his mind and left the ship before it set out to sea.[54] Many foreign ships were in desperate need of seamen, and captains did everything they could to replenish their crews including giving rewards to sailors who left other ships. Before the 1780s, however, Chinese seamen were, for the most part, unwilling to fill those positions, regardless of which European company wanted them.[55] As I have shown in another study, the evidence suggests that the men could probably earn higher wages working for the Chinese junks. But when that trade began to decline in the late eighteenth and early nineteenth century, they were displaced and were then more willing to seek employment aboard foreign ships.[56]

Chinese seamen aboard Danish Asiatic Company ships

The Danish Asiatic Company (DAC) also began hiring Chinese seamen in the early 1780s. Because the DAC records are some of the best documents we have that show how these men were hired and what happened to them after they arrived in Europe, and because there are only a few examples, I will reproduce all of them below. These entries give us a better understanding of these itinerant seamen, who wandered the globe entirely on their own.

I have read through the 116 ship journals that have survived from the 131 DAC voyages to China from 1734 to 1833. The first mention of Chinese being employed is on February 14, 1783. On that day, the Danish officers in Canton sent a letter to Captain Petersen of the ship *Princess Charlotte Amelia*, mentioning that they had made arrangements for thirty-five Chinese seamen to go aboard his ship when it reached Lintin Island. On February 22, at 10 pm, the ship came to anchor near the Nine Islands (see Map 8.3). The captain fired two eight-pound cannons, and shortly thereafter three sampans proceeded out from shore with forty-seven Chinese seamen aboard. The captain entered all of the men as part of the crew, and paid them six months' wages in advance. The ship arrived at Copenhagen on November 8, 1783.[57]

As we will see from an example below, it was not wise to pay seamen so much money up front. If they jumped ship before the six months were up, then the captain lost those wages that were not fulfilled. However, sometimes a large advance was the only way to entice the men to join the crew.

I looked through all of the DAC ship account books (*skibsprotocoler*) to see what happened to the forty-seven Chinese seamen after they arrived in Copenhagen. We would expect to find them boarding other ships bound to China, which proved to be the case. On April 17, 1784, the DAC ship *Mars* took in twenty-four Chinese seamen at Copenhagen. The ship arrived at Macao on July 30, 1785. The next day, twenty-three Chinese were paid their wages and discharged. One man left the ship at Malacca. The ship did not take in any Chinese when it left China a few months later.[58]

After returning to Copenhagen in November 1783, the *Princess Charlotte Amelia* was quickly fitted-out for another voyage to China. On April 19, 1784, the vessel took in twenty-one of the Chinese seamen it had brought from China in the previous year. The ship arrived at Macao in late July 1785, and the men were paid 15 months' wages (April 1784 to July 1785) and discharged.[59]

These two examples account for forty-five of the forty-seven Chinese seamen who arrived in 1783. I have not found an explanation as to what happened to the other two men. The forty-five men were apparently in Copenhagen for five months before departing in mid-April 1784. This would have been wintertime in Denmark and they would have needed food, clothing and a warm place to sleep. An example below shows that their food and lodging was paid for by the DAC while they were in port.

When the *Princess Charlotte Amelia* was about ready to leave China, Danish officers decided they wanted to take their Chinese cook Attey with them. He had probably cooked for them in the factory at Canton, and now they wanted to keep him in their employ. An entry dated December 31, 1785 shows Attey going aboard the ship. He was allotted 6 piastres per month as his wage.[60] It is unclear whether the wages were paid by the DAC or privately by the Danish officers. I did not find other entries for Attey in the DAC records so it is still unclear what became of him after he arrived in Copenhagen.

The next entry that I have found for Chinese seamen being employed by the DAC does not appear until 1797. On January 12 of that year, the DAC ship *Princess Charlotte Amelia* engaged seven European and fourteen Chinese seamen at Macao, just before leaving China. The European seamen were given three months' wages in advance and the Chinese were given five months' in advance. Two muster roles in the ship's *protocoler*, dated October 2, 1797 and February 21, 1798, show the fourteen Chinese seamen as part of the crew. The April 10, 1798 muster role, however, shows only eight Chinese seamen. At some point six men seemed to have left the ship. The remaining 8 men apparently went with the ship to Copenhagen, which arrived in May.[61]

In early June of 1798, the ship *King of Denmark* was at Copenhagen making her final preparations for a voyage to China. Chinese sailors were apparently helping in these preparations, because on June 18, there is an entry stating that one of the Chinese seamen died aboard the ship.[62] We find out later in the ship's *protocoler* that when the ship left Copenhagen in late June, there were seventeen Chinese sailors aboard. Eight men were probably transferred from the *Princess Charlotte Amelia*; it is unclear where the other nine men came from. There were several private Danish ships in China in 1797 and they may have engaged some Chinese sailors. The captain of the *King of Denmark* picked up two additional Chinese sailors at Batavia, on his way to China. On February 11, 1799, a total of nineteen Chinese were paid and discharged at Langyt Island, just south of Bocca Tigris (see Map 8.3). The seventeen men from Copenhagen were given seven months' wages and the two men from Batavia were given one month's wage.[63]

When the *King of Denmark* was ready to leave China on April 21, 1799, she took in nineteen Chinese seamen near Lintin Island. It is unclear whether these were the same men who were discharged in February. They were given three months' wages in advance. Two of the men died before reaching Anjer, in Sumatra, so only seventeen Chinese completed the trip to Copenhagen. They arrived on May 1, 1800.[64] These examples show that giving advances to Chinese was only necessary in China. On the return passage, no advance was needed, probably because the men were anxious to return home.

It was a very timely arrival for these Chinese seamen, because in early May 1800 the ship *Denmark* was in Copenhagen preparing for its upcoming voyage to China. The seventeen Chinese who arrived on May 1 were apparently transferred to the *Denmark*. Entries in the ship's *protocoler* dated May 8 and 10 show that they took in provisions for the Chinese crew of peas, rice, pork and other items.[65] This entry suggests that the men may have been given different rations from the European seamen. However, another entry below states that the Chinese employed by the DAC were to receive the same rations as European seamen, so the provisions above may have been just supplemental to the same items that were already aboard the ship for the European crew. The seventeen men boarded the ship in Copenhagen on May 13 and were paid and discharged seven months later on December 12 at Macao.[66]

On December 5, 1798, 14 Chinese seamen boarded the DAC ship *Cron Prinsen* in Copenhagen. Seven of these men were hired temporarily to help with the final preparations before sailing. On December 31, the ship took in provisions for the Chinese. All fourteen of the men appear to have returned to China as passengers. When they reached Macao on September 29, 1799, the men were discharged and given a douceur (tip) of three months' wages for their good services. According to the *skibsprotocoler*, they were passengers. If they had been hired for the voyage to China, then they would have received full wages for 8½ months.

Besides mainland Chinese, on December 8, 1798 this ship also took in two Malaysians and one Chinese sailor from Java while it was still at anchor in Copenhagen. These three men were paid and discharged at Batavia. After reaching China, the Danes made a contract with their Chinese comprador Akau to hire fourteen more Chinese sailors for the return passage home. Akau mentioned that these men were some of the same sailors whom the DAC had hired in 1782 and had gone to Copenhagen on the *Princess Charlotte Amelia*. On January 11, 1800, when the ship was still at Whampoa, ten Chinese seamen went aboard. It is unclear what happened to the other four men.[67]

This time the Danes made a formal contract with the men before they left Canton, which they recorded in the ship's *protocoler*. I have translated and paraphrased the four points of the contract below.

Contract

We have found it necessary to engage 10 Chinese for the ship *Cron Prinsen*, on the following terms and conditions.

The Chinese who are engaged as weighers (*wejers*) will receive 6 piastres per month for wages, on both the passage from China to Copenhagen and the return to China, and those who are engaged in unskilled deck labor will receive 5 piastres per month.

Their costs and lodging [room and board in Copenhagen] will be borne by the Honorable Company until an opportunity arises when they can go aboard again. In the meantime, those who work for the Company in unloading, etc., will receive the same daily wage as other seamen.

Their rations on board will be the same as European seamen.

Until the ship is unloaded, they are to remain on board and their monthly salary will continue until this is completed.

Cron Prinsen de 17 Jan: 1800. Aggersborg [supercargo], J Holm [captain][68]

This contract guaranteed that the Chinese sailors would be returned to China, and that they would be provided room and board while waiting for another ship in Copenhagen. They received the same pay and treatment as other sailors, including the same rations as European seamen. The *Cron Prinsen* arrived at Copenhagen in April 1801.[69]

On December 4, 1801, six of the ten Chinese referred to in the contract above boarded the *King of Denmark* at Copenhagen. On December 7, another man joined them. These sailors had apparently been waiting in Copenhagen for more than seven months. They were paid and discharged at Macao on October 26, 1802.[70]

As can be seen, we do not have an exact account of every Chinese who worked for the DAC. A few of them seemed to have remained in Copenhagen for extended periods of time. On November 23, 1802, for example, an entry in the *Princess Louise Augusta* ship's *protocoler* states that "the Chinese Afoa came aboard, whom we had engaged as a sailor on August 22."[71] The only previous arrival of Chinese in Copenhagen that I could find in the DAC records was *Cron Prinsen* in April 1801. If Afoa had arrived on that ship, then it is unclear what he was doing for the 18 months prior to joining the *Princess Louise Augusta*. Perhaps he worked for the DAC in Copenhagen, or maybe he was employed by a private ship for which we have no records.

The final examples I have from the DAC records are from 1804–05. On February 2, 1804, 13 Chinese boarded the ship *Cron Prinsen* in Copenhagen. They were paid and discharged at Macao on December 15, 1804.[72] These men had probably also gone to Copenhagen on a private ship. The final DAC reference is Chinese passenger Assing, who boarded the ship *Norge* in Copenhagen on April 28, 1804 and was landed at Macao on February 5, 1805.[73] In 1806, the DAC ceased sending ships to China so the references to Chinese seamen also ended.

Chinese seamen aboard Dutch East India Company ships

In the 1780s and after, other foreign records begin to show Chinese sailors aboard their ships. In 1781 and 1783, the Dutch East India Company (VOC) engaged Chinese seamen for the ships *Diamant* and *Breslaw*, respectively. The Chinese comprador at Canton, Tan Assouw, made the arrangements for the men to go aboard the ships.[74] In 1785, the Dutch engaged six Chinese seamen who sailed to the Netherlands and back again to China. They were permitted to board another VOC ship leaving China and made the voyage to the Netherlands and back again the next year.[75] The VOC undoubtedly cared for the men while they were in Holland. On January 20, 1786, Captain Kappelhoff of the VOC ship *Pollux* engaged eight Chinese sailors at Macao, just before he left China.[76]

In a report dated December 13, 1792, the Dutch in Canton mentioned that some Chinese passengers from Batavia had arrived safely in China from one of the Dutch ships. It is unclear whether these men were seamen being returned to China or whether they were indeed passengers who paid their own fare. Chinese passengers were sometimes allowed aboard the VOC ships traveling between Macao and Batavia.[77]

The Dutch were able to procure thirty-four Chinese seamen at Macao in 1792 to replenish the crew of the ship *Rozenburg*. They were known to be trustworthy men who had previously worked on Portuguese ships and had sailed to Europe so the Dutch gave them one Spanish dollar as a gratuity and four months' wages in advance.[78] In 1794, however, the Dutch were not so fortunate. They engaged 50 Chinese at Macao in that year to serve as sailors aboard their ships. The men were paid six months' wages in advance, but then they absconded with their money in hand. In this case, the men insisted on receiving the money upfront as a precondition to going aboard the ship.[79]

What the British, Danish and Dutch entries above tell us is that all three of those companies began hiring Chinese sailors in the 1780s for their long-haul voyages. These companies were in need of sailors before 1780 as well but no Chinese could be procured at that time. It was not until the early 1780s that they could find Chinese willing to go aboard, and even then, they had to pay them several months in advance before they agreed to join the ships. Once these Chinese engagements began, they continued on both return passages (China to Europe) and outward passages (Europe to China). Some seamen disembarked before reaching China and others joined the ships in ports such as in India, Penang, Malacca or Batavia.

Chinese seamen aboard French ships

I have not found any entries showing ships based in the French port of Lorient employing Chinese seamen on voyages to and from Europe. Most of those ships' musters and many of the journals have survived but there are no Chinese listed among the crews.[80]

There were Chinese servants and missionaries that sometimes went to Europe aboard French ships, but I have few examples of sailors doing this. The two Chinese Louis Ko and Etienne Yang, for example, were in France in the early 1760s and had adopted French names. They returned to China as passengers aboard the ship *Duc de Choiseul*, which left Lorient in February 1765 and landed the men at Whampoa on July 26.[81]

There are later references that show the French ships engaging Chinese seamen in Asia. In May and June of 1787, the French ship *La Reine* took in eight Chinese sailors at Pondicherry and seven Chinese seamen at Madras. The men were paid their wages and discharged at Macao on October 3.[82] The ship then went upriver to Whampoa, unloaded and loaded its cargo and sailed back to France. Two French frigates that were in the lower delta in 1787 also took in six Chinese seamen each, to replenish their crews, before they set out for Manila.[83]

Chinese seamen aboard American ships

There are many examples of Americans hiring Chinese sailors, but I will only give a few of them here. In late 1790, the scow *Gustavous* was anchored in Lark's Bay near Macao (see Map 8.3). The American mariner John Bartlett joined the ship before it departed for the Northwest Coast of America. He commented in his journal that there were four Chinese sailors aboard, named Angee, Highee, Chinkqui and Arch ching.[84]

In February 1801, the Dutch made arrangements with their comprador Ajouw to have twenty-one Chinese sailors picked up in the outer islands of the lower delta. They were to go aboard one of the American ships, which had apparently freighted some cargo for the Dutch. The ship was bound for the United States.[85]

On March 27, 1807, the ship *Arthur* from Providence engaged two Chinese sailors Ahap (亚春) and Ayong (亚杨) at Macao and paid them three months' wages in advance (at $8 per month). Captain Solomon Townsend hired the men through John Budwell, who was the owner of the Macao Tavern.[86] The advance was paid directly to Budwell so he seems to have been the middleman in this transaction, for which he would have probably received a commission.

Even in this arrangement, however, a written contract was made with the owners of the ship *Arthur*, which Ahap, Ayong and the rest of the crew signed showing their consent to the terms. The documents clearly state each man's monthly wage and rank aboard the ship. We can only speculate as to whether Ahap and Ayong actually understood the terms, because they were written in English.

The *Arthur* arrived at Providence in September and the crew was paid the remainder of their wages for the voyage. A new contract was then made for another voyage to China, which Ahap, Ayong and the rest of the crew signed. By this time, the two men would have certainly been aware of what was expected of them. They were paid and discharged at Macao on June 27, 1808.[87]

In 1822–23, the American ship *Washington* listed seven Chinese seamen in the ship's muster as a regular part of the crew: Jon, Ahou, Asam, Ashing, Amuy John, Accow and Kingyou. The ship only had thirty seamen aboard so the Chinese made up almost one-fourth of the crew. Accow served as the ship's steward and Kingyou as the ship's cook.[88] And a final example is the ship *New Jersey* from Philadelphia which engaged three Chinese seamen in early 1828 before leaving China. They were each given one month's wage in advance.[89] There are many more American references but these should be sufficient to show that Chinese were a regular part of many of those crews as well.

Taking all of these references together, we can see that by the 1780s, Chinese were boarding any ship that would agree to their terms. Many Chinese were getting on and off ships at ports in India, Malaysia, St Helena, Europe, the Americas, and numerous other places throughout the world. Local Chinese living in those ports may have helped them find accommodation and employment. Obviously, there are many unanswered questions that still need to be researched, such as which nationals offered the best terms, and which destinations Chinese preferred and why? And we might also ask if there was any connection between the rise in piracy in the South China Sea in the late eighteenth century and the parallel change in the attitudes of Chinese seamen to join the crews of foreign ships. Hopefully, more data will emerge in the future to help clarify some of these issues.

Conclusion

What do the 380 Chinese passengers aboard the *Princess Amelia* and the other scattered references above tell us about what was happening in the maritime world in the late eighteenth and early nineteenth century? For some reason, Chinese attitudes toward seeking employment aboard foreign ships began to change in and around the 1780s. There were always Chinese going abroad in foreign ships such as those of the Portuguese, Spanish and private traders from India. But we have few examples of them engaging on board the East India Company's ships in China before the 1780s. I think this reluctance may have had something do to with the new sea routes to China that were established at this time and the encroachment of foreign ships into the traditional Southeast Asian markets of the Chinese junks.

As more foreign ships began purchasing Southeast Asian products and carrying them to China, the Chinese junks lost their comparative advantages which caused a decline in their numbers. As more Chinese seamen were displaced, they needed to find other employment, which is undoubtedly one of the reasons why they start showing up on the East India Company's musters. At the same time, private trade in China was expanding, which created more competition for the companies. There were not enough European seamen in Asia to go around. Lascars had long been used aboard European ships sailing to China. Beginning in the 1780s, captains were successful at engaging Chinese seamen as well.

Hiring Asian sailors for just one leg of a voyage rather than for the entire trip also helped to make the Company ships more competitive with the private traders. They could avoid the costs of keeping a full crew while anchored at Whampoa for three or four months. These factors were probably interrelated. On the downside, however, if the Chinese were employed all the way to Europe, then the ship that brought them had to support those men until they found new work and/or had to pay for their passage back to China. Thus, it is questionable whether the hiring of temporary Asian sailors actually made the Company ships more competitive with the private ships. But those men were considered to be necessary for the safe sailing of the vessels so the additional costs of their maintenance and return to China were probably minimal compared to the threat of losing a ship and cargo at sea.

The 380 Chinese passengers who were repatriated aboard the *Princess Amelia* in 1816–17 represent much more than simply a passage to China. They were the product of all these global trends and transitions that were reshaping and redefining how international trade operated. We are only now beginning to understand the effects these seamen may have had on the ports they visited. In some cases, such as in the UK, they were seen as threats to the livelihoods of the indigenous seamen. As a result, in the early nineteenth century, the EIC forbade captains from engaging Asian seamen on outbound voyages.

Finally, we have also learned several things about the Chinese seamen themselves. Once they began boarding the Company's ships, they were extremely flexible as to where they were landed. They could go to India, Africa, St Helena, Europe, the Americas, or wherever the captains wanted them to go. Upon arriving in those places, they somehow coped, even though many of them probably had no idea what to expect when they got there and probably had very limited language skills.

It is hard to imagine what it must have been like for the first Chinese to visit St Helena, London, Amsterdam, Copenhagen, or New York. In some cases, the men were hired just for one leg, so they did not know how they would survive at their destination, or how to find a new job. In other cases, they were guaranteed a return trip to China.

While in the port of destination, there was often an interval of several months before other ships departed for Asia so the seamen had to cope with these delays. We have seen how some employers supplied them with clothing, a place to live and food to eat. In other cases, such as New England destinations, they just went there, and figured all these matters out after they arrived. Over and over again we find Chinese sailors venturing into unknown places with little hesitation. They were truly pioneers who filled the gaps in the maritime world's labor supply.

What would have happened if Chinese seamen had remained unwilling to go aboard those ships after 1780? Lascars, Malays, Manila men and others would have undoubtedly helped to fill in the gaps. But few other Asian sailors could stand up to the reputation of the Chinese. After 1800, knowing that they would likely be shipped back to China as passengers, without pay, and would have to stay in the UK for several months in the interim, they nevertheless continued to board EIC ships. They received sustenance the entire time, but lost upwards of a year's wages. In contrast, if they had boarded a Danish, Dutch or American ship, they might have received wages both ways, to the West and from the West back to China. While many of these men were driven by economic need, there were undoubtedly a number of them who were going just for the sake of adventure. Whatever their motives may have been, their dedication and flexibility made them an important labor source in the advancement of international commerce.

Notes

1 The term "country ship" applies to privately owned vessels that sailed between intra-Asian ports. The country ships that went to China were usually from India, and were often commanded by British or French captains. But they might be commissioned by indigenous Indian traders such as Muslims, Armenians or Parsees.
2 John Reinhold Forster, trans. A Voyage to China and the East Indies, by Peter Osbeck. Together with a Voyage to Suratte, by Olof Torren, and An Account of Chinese Husbandry, by Captain Charles Gustavus Eckeberg. Translated from the 1765 German ed., 2 vols (London, 1771), 1: 272.
3 Anne Bulley, *Free Mariner: John Adolphus Pope in the East Indies 1786–1821* (London, 1992), 78.

4   There were of course Chinese going to Europe aboard Western ships much earlier than the 1780s. But most of those persons were either Christian converts going for edification, servants of European officers, or just travelers. For one example of a Chinese traveler by the name of Whang-At-Ting, who was 22 years old, from Canton and in London in 1775, see *The Bee or Literary Weekly Intelligencer*, vol. 11, issue dated 1792.09.12, article entitled "Hints Respecting the Chinese Language," dated 1775.02.18, 50–52. There are exceptions, but most of the Chinese seamen do not begin to show up working on British, Dutch, Danish or French ships until the 1780s.

5   Susan E. Schopp, "The French in the Pearl River Delta: A Topical Case Study of Sino-European Exchanges in the Canton Trade, 1698–1840," (Ph.D. diss., Department of History, University of Macau, 2015).

6   Schopp, "The French in the Pearl River Delta," 84.

7   The British and Dutch in Canton noted that the *Jason* managed to arrive in China by using this new route. British Library (BL): India Office Records (IOR) G/12/86, 1740.10.02, p. 40; and the National Archives, The Hague (NAH): VOC 8718, *dagregister*, 1740.10.13, 223.

8   For a list of 200 foreign ships that used these new routes to China before 1800, see Paul A. Van Dyke, "New Sea Routes to Canton in the 18th Century and the Decline of China's Control over Trade," in *Studies of Maritime History* 海洋史研究, ed. Li Qingxin 李庆新. vol. 1 (Beijing: 2010), 57–108.

9   For a list of eighty some commodities that the Chinese junks purchased in Southeast Asia in the eighteenth century and imported to China, see Paul A. Van Dyke, *Merchants of Canton and Macao: Politics and Strategies in Eighteenth Century Chinese Trade*, vol. 1 (Hong Kong, 2011), appendix 4J.

10 For several maps showing these new sea routes, see Van Dyke, "New Sea Routes to Canton," 57–108.

11 There are many references in the foreign archives to ships experimenting in the late eighteenth and early nineteenth century with products that they picked up in Southeast Asia and sold in Canton. I am assembling a more complete list of all foreign ships trading at Canton, which will take a few years to compile. This new list will make it easier to document which ships were visiting Southeast Asian ports, which can then be matched with the import cargos of those vessels that are available in the British and Dutch archives. For examples of these Southeast Asian products being brought to China aboard foreign ships, see the many cargo lists in BL: IOR G/12/1–291 series and NAH: Canton and VOC collections.

12 Paul A. Van Dyke, "Operational Efficiencies and the Decline of the Chinese Junk Trade in the Eighteenth and Nineteenth Centuries: The Connection," in *Shipping Efficiency and Economic Growth 1350–1800*, ed. Richard Unger (Leiden, 2010), 223–46.

13 Van Dyke, "Operational Efficiencies," 223–46.

14 For a brief summary of the increase in private traders in the late eighteenth century, a parallel decline in companies trading at Canton, and some of the effects that those changes had on the landscape, see Paul A. Van Dyke and Maria Kar-wing Mok, *Images of the Canton Factories 1760–1822* (Hong Kong, 2015), chapter 6, "Rise of the Private Traders 1790–1799."

15 Van Dyke, "Operational Efficiencies," 223–46.

16 The tons per man ratio of a typical EIC ship of 1200 tons, for example, was about
    9:1. The tons per man ratio of an American vessel of 500 tons, on the other hand,
    was about 16:1. Van Dyke, "Operational Efficiencies," 237.
17 Carl T. Smith and Paul A. Van Dyke, "Muslims in the Pearl River Delta, 1700 to
    1930," *Review of Culture*, International Edition, No. 10 (April 2004), 6–15.
18 BL: IOR G/12/131, p. 11, paragraphs 28–29.
19 BL: IOR L/MAR/B/23D.
20 BL: IOR G/12/77, 1783.06.09, 43.
21 BL: IOR G/12/79, 1785.08.10, 33–34.
22 BL: IOR L/MAR/B/457E, 1788.02.25.
23 BL: IOR G/12/80, 1784.10.27, 43, see also G/12/79, 1784.10.27, 84, which shows
    the following entry: "To the Friends of four Chinese who died on board the Essex
    on their passage to England Tas [Taels] 101.775."
24 BL: IOR G/12/79, 1785.03.03, 9.
25 BL: IOR L/MAR/B/46E, 172G, 356G, 438-O, 441A, 443A, 41A-B, 86B, 308H,
    390-I, 455A, 490D, 507G, 458G, 563A, 332A, 346A, 457E, 107B, 203A, 205A,
    149B, 170A, 179B, 181A, 215J, 287L, 288D, 351D, 410H, 91F, 182C, 205B, 398B,
    107D, 351E, 8G, 86-I, 149C, 150-O, 168B, 178B, 179C, 181B, 182D, 212A, 215K,
    267C, 288E, 341D, 349E. For the number of EIC ships in China, see Anthony
    Farrington, *Catalogue of East India Company Ships' Journals and Logs 1600–1834*
    (London, 1999).
26 BL: IOR L/MAR/B/410H, 351D, 288D, 287L, 149B, 170A, 179B, 181A and 215J.
27 Greenwich, National Maritime Museum (NMM): HMN 45 *Bombay Castle*
    Expense Book 1806, 36.
28 NMM: HMN 45 *Bombay Castle* Expense Book 1806, 34.
29 BL: IOR L/MAR/C/902 Papers on Lascars 1793–1818, ff. 38r–v.
30 For an example of a Chinese seaman who got caught by a Chinese official serving
    as a carpenter aboard an American ship in 1833, see Phillips Library, Peabody
    Essex Museum (PEM): MH-219 B4 F1 5th Voyage 1833–34 Tilden's typewritten
    manuscript p. 856. Tilden suspected that he would be "bamboo'd and banished" as
    punishment for quitting "china in a foreign vessel." See also Bulley, *Free Mariner*,
    78. On October 30, 1786, the seaman Pope recorded the following while at Macao:

    We had a few Chinamen on board who we were forced to discharge at Macao.
    … The reason why you must discharge any Chinamen you may have on board
    is this – that all emigration is forbid under severe penalties. A Chinese there-
    fore found returning from foreign parts would be liable to lose his head and
    therefore is forced to get ashore in a clandestine manner.

31 BL: IOR L/MAR/B/455A, see list of passengers in the front.
32 BL: IOR L/MAR/B/287H, 1789.02.02 and 1789.09.17.
33 BL: IOR L/MAR/B/319H, 1798.12.01, see also passenger list in front.
34 BL: IOR L/MAR/B/36K-L.
35 BL: IOR L/MAR/B/36JJ (2) and 36M.
36 BL: IOR L/MAR/B/36KK (1–2) and 36N.
37 BL: IOR L/MAR/B/36-O.
38 BL: IOR L/MAR/B/351F, see the passenger and crew list in the front, and entries
    dated 1802.01.21–2. The passenger list in the front also shows that fifteen Chinese
    passengers boarded the *Boddam* at Gravesend on January 13, 1801. Five men died

en route, seven men ran at Penang, and the remaining three were landed at Macao on September 24, 1801.

39 The names of the twelve Chinese passenger/mechanics were Amu, Amung, Assam, Assu, Aye, Assah, Apat, Shap Lok, Shap Sat, Shap Yat, Shap Yu and Shap Sam. BL: IOR L/MAR/B/178F, see passenger list at the end of the journal.

40 Felix Laurent, for example, was a clock repairman in Canton in 1791 and he was referred to by the Dutch as a "mechanicus." NAH: VOC 4446, report dated 1791.12.19, paragraph No. 102. In March 1798, another clock repairman by the name of James Lindley was in Canton and the British also referred to him as a "mechanic." BL: IOR G/12/122, 20 and 126, 70. The Dutch also referred to Lindley as a "Mechanicus" in 1798. NAH: Canton 97, 1798.08.30.

41 BL: IOR L/MAR/B/140L, see crew and passenger list in the back.

42 BL: IOR L/MAR/B/86M.

43 BL: IOR L/MAR/B/81J, see passenger list in front.

44 BL: IOR L/MAR/B/189E and 189F, see crew lists in the front.

45 BL: IOR L/MAR/B/288-I, see crew and passenger lists in the front.

46 BL: IOR G/12/192, 1815.04.01, 108.

47 BL: IOR G/12/204, 1816.10.14, 44.

48 Paul A. Van Dyke, *The Canton Trade: Life and Enterprise on the China Coast, 1700–1845* (Hong Kong, Reprint, 2007), 21–23.

49 Van Dyke, *The Canton Trade*, 62.

50 BL: IOR G/12/148, 1805.01.01–02, 47–53.

51 BL: IOR G/12/216, 1819.08.27, 96.

52 BL: IOR L/MAR/B/230-I. The quotation "20 Hammocks & two suits of clothes for each man" is under the entry dated 1817.01.09 and "on account of the Hon'ble Company" is under the entry dated 1817.03.20.

53 For a few examples of Chinese seamen boarding or being discharged above Bocca Tigris after 1805, see BL: IOR L/MAR/B/230F, 189C, 149F, 201C, 288-I, 215Q, 48G, and 39A.

54 BL: IOR L/MAR/B/688B-C, 1711.12.22.

55 For more examples of Chinese aboard EIC ships in a Chinese article, see Yu Po-ching (游博清), "shijiu shiji qianqi zai lundun he sheng he lei na dao shenghuo de huaren" (十九世紀前期在倫敦和聖赫勒那島生活的華人) ("Chinese in the early nineteenth century in London and life at St Helena"), in *lüyou wenxue yu dijing shuxie*. ed. Wang Yiqi (Kaohsiung, 2013), 1–28.

56 Van Dyke, "Operational Efficiencies," 223–46.

57 Rigsarkivet (National Archives), Copenhagen (RAC): Ask 948, 1783.02.14, pp. 100r–v, 1783.02.22, pp. 104r–v, and Ask 1073. See also RAC: Ask 236, letters dated 1783.01.11 and 1783.02.17.

58 RAC: Ask 957, 1784.04.17, pp. 2r–v, 1785.07.30–1, 56v. The payment of their wages appears on 1785.08.24, 59v.

59 RAC: Ask 959, 1784.04.19, p. 1v, *Capitainens Extra Expencer*, 96r and Ask 1199, 1785.07.29, 66v.

60 RAC: Ask 959, 1785.12.31, 93r.

61 RAC: Ask 972, 1797.01.12, 186v, 188v, and Ask 973, 1797.08.17, 360r, 1797.10.02, pp. 269r–v, 1797.11.18, 78r, 1797.02.21, 300r–v, 1798.04.08, 305r–v, 320v.

62 RAC: Ask 976, 1798.06.19, 6r, and Ask 1096, 1798.06.18–19,. 3r.

63 RAC: Ask 976, 1799.02.11, 88v–89v. The transliterated names of the seventeen seamen are shown on these pages, and it is interesting to note, that unlike many

other entries of Chinese seaman, none of these men have the prefix "A" attached to their name. See also RAC: Ask 976, 1799.04.21, 150r, *Udgifter*, 151r–152r, 1799.06.29–07.05, 160v–162r, 164v, and *Omkostnings Regning*, 183v–184r, 197r, *Aparte Udgifter*, 219r, and 231r.

64 RAC: Ask 976, 1799.04.21, 150r, *Udgifter*, 151r–152r, 1799.06.29–07.05, 160v–162r, 164v, and *Omkostnings Regning*, 183v–184r, 197r, *Aparte Udgifter*, 219r, and 231r.

65 RAC: Ask 979, 1800.05.08–10, 8v–9r.

66 RAC: Ask 979, 1800.05.13, 10–11, 1800.12.12–13, 112–14, 1801.03.06, 224.

67 RAC: Ask 977, 1v, 2r, 6r, 10v, 55r, 93r–v, 98v, 160r–161r, Ask 1097, 2v, 68r, Ask 1213 36r–37r, Ask 1214, 1799.09.29, 12r–v, 1799.10.11–2, 17v–18v, 1800.01.11, 59v.

68 RAC: Ask 977, 1800.01.17, 161v–162r.

69 RAC: Ask 978.

70 RAC: Ask 982, 1801.12.04, 1801.12.04–07, 10–11, 1802.10.26, 251, Ask 1216, 1802.10.26, 117.

71 RAC: Ask 984b, 1802.11.23, 5, 1803.09.24, 199, Ask 1105, 1802.11.23, 3.

72 RAC: Ask 986a, 1804.02.02, 3, 1804.12.15, 243, "Extra Udgifter," 103, 1805.03.11, 392 and Ask 1221, 1804.12.15, 107.

73 RAC: Ask 987a, 1805.02.05, 245.

74 NAH: VOC 4423, *dagregister*, 1781.04.22, VOC 4447, *grootboek*, f. 9.

75 Christiaan J. A. Jörg, *Porcelain and the Dutch China Trade* (The Hague, 1982), 334, n.11.

76 NAH: Canton 91, 1786.01.20, 158.

77 Another example involves six Chinese passengers who apparently arrived in China from Batavia aboard the VOC ship *Vrijburg* in 1756. NAH: Canton 120, doc. beginning with *Verders Dient … dated* 1756.08.12.

78 NAH: VOC 4447, report dated 1792.12.13, par. 52 and 54, doc. entitled *Nadere Onkost Rekening*, dated 1793.01.05, *dagregister*, 1792.12.01–2, 120–21, resolution dated 1792.12.13, and letter dated 1793.03.12.

79 Jörg, *Porcelain and the Dutch China Trade*, 334, n.11; NAH: Canton 195, doc. No. 53 and 819–23.

80 See Lorient, Service Historique de la Défense (SHD): 2P 1–19 *Armements au long cours*, 1721–1790 and 2P 20–53 *Désarmements au long cours*, 1719–1788. There are no Chinese mentioned in these records. Some of the French journals have survived and can be found in the Archives Nationales, in Paris (ANP): 4JJ 129–41 *Voyages en Chine. Journaux de bord*, 1698–1788.

81 SHD: 2P 40, Armement for *Duc de Choiseul*, entry entitled "Passagera Pour Chine." See also an article by Jean-Paul Morel, "Bertin, Turgot et deux Chinois," which is available online at www.pierre-poivre.fr/Bertin-Turgot-Chinois.pdf [accessed February 23, 2017].

82 SHD: 2P 53 Désarmements au long cours.

83 Julius S. Gassner, trans. *Voyages and Adventures of La Pérouse* (Honolulu, 1969), 58.

84 PEM: Log of Ship *Massachusetts*.

85 NAH: Canton 264, 1801.02.20 and Asip Nasional Republick Indonesia (ANRI): *Realia*, under subject "Chinesen," "Aan W. V. Hutchings Capitein van het Americaansch schip *Massachusetts*, gepermitteerd 21 Chineesche zeevarende te engageeren voor de terug reize na America, mits vrij transport na herwaards te rug verleenende, 10 Maart 1801." www.sejarah-nusantara.anri.go.id/realia-browse/?selected=43524&page=581 [accessed October 3, 2013]. The Dutch called

this ship the *Massachusetts*, but I have no record of that vessel being in China at this time so it was perhaps one of the other American ships.

86 Van Dyke, *The Canton Trade*, 38–39.

87 Brown University, John Carter Brown Library (JCB): Brown Papers B.497 F.4 Ship *Arthur*, "Account Current" and "Account of Charges for Factory" (under "Disbursements at Macao"), and B.497 F.1 and B.497 F.10 printed contracts beginning with "It is agreed, between the owner."

88 JCB: Brown Papers B.671 F.12 Ship *Washington*, Seamen's Accounts.

89 Philadelphia, Independence Seaport Museum (ISM): Whitall Papers "Account of Money paid the Crew of Ship New Jersey at Canton."

9 Hierarchy and anarchy in early modern East Asia

The tribute system as an international system

David C. Kang

Introduction: International systems in world history

Are many contemporary international theories, mostly derived implicitly or explicitly from the European, Westphalian experience of identical units – nation-states – interacting under anarchy, both universal and inevitable? The world is wider, and older, than many of the ideas embedded in most contemporary international relations theory assume it is. Did that older world act the same way across time and space as does the contemporary, European-derived order? Or, do different international systems have different fundamental organizing principles, which produce distinct patterns of cooperation and conflict?

Recent years have seen increasing discussion about whether, and in what ways, international relations ("IR") scholarship may be derived too closely and inductively from the example of the recent past.[1] In this Westphalian system, anarchy leads to a Hobessian world of incessant war of all against all, equality is not only most stable, but is also inevitable and normatively sought, and those equal and identical units – nation-states – lead to a balance of power system. Perhaps the most clear proponent of this approach was Kenneth Waltz, who argued, "hegemony leads to balance … through all of the centuries we can contemplate."[2] Yet, as Phillips and Sharman point out, "IR is neither European area studies nor contemporary history, but rather a social science. Its practitioners frequently generate claims that are said to be transferable across different historical and geographical domains."[3] To that end, scholars have begun to explore the possibility that the European historical experience, the contemporary Westphalian international system that arose from that experience, and the theories of international relations that are inductively derived from this contemporary experience, might be neither universal nor inevitable. In short, scholars have begun to take seriously the possibility that other international systems may have existed, and may exist again.

However, even this debate has been conducted mostly with reference to the contemporary Westphalian system.[4] Research about fundamental principles of international systems such as hierarchy and anarchy tends to be focused on the Western experience.[5] For example, David Lake's scholarship about hierarchy is focused exclusively on the contemporary international system, although he makes purportedly much more general claims about international systems, while a forthcoming book about hierarchy contains eleven chapters, all of which are focused on the contemporary, Western-derived system.[6] But this "presentist" and Eurocentric focus brings with it its own problems of selection bias. The best way to study the contemporary system is to compare it to another international system. Yet this sort of comparison requires a very long historical perspective, or to seek for international systems that truly antedate the gradual triumph of the Westphalian order.

There is, however, a burgeoning scholarly literature that directly addresses these debates, studies a different empirical international system, and spans the fields of both history and international relations.[7] By far the most researched non-Western international system is the "tributary system" of historical East Asia. A growing body of scholarship on pre-modern East Asia, built on rich empirical research, provides new perspectives on the inevitability and universality of the contemporary Westphalian system. John Wills' enormous contributions to the study of East Asian history have primarily been appreciated by historians. But this new research program is seeing his influence and value to add to debates within the field of international relations, as well.

This chapter argues that different international systems with different organizing principles have existed and may exist again; and that the East Asian international system experienced measurably different patterns of war, trade, and alliances. This East Asian system, often referred to as the "tributary system" of international relations, is a key example that demonstrates that hierarchy, not anarchy, defined large swaths of historical East Asian international relations and perhaps even world history. Indeed, the scholarship on this point is in such agreement that it might even be called a general consensus.

Within this overarching point, this chapter will make three main arguments: First, the tributary system had different rules, norms, and institutions than did Westphalia or pre-Westphalia in Europe. Although it may seem self-evident, these ordered interactions among the units but had a different organizing principle: hierarchy instead of anarchy. Second, different international systems are only interesting if they produce different empirical patterns. The East Asian tributary system of international relations produced measurable and distinct patterns of war; patterns that were distinct from those at the time who did not participate in the system, and distinct from the contemporary patterns of conflict and cooperation that we find among the Westphalian nation-state system. Finally, the arrival of the West in the nineteenth century changed the East Asian tributary system in fundamental ways. The tributary system of international relations is gone forever, and although historical memory informs the perceptions and goals of contemporary East Asian countries, the tributary system will not return in the contemporary era.

The tributary system as an international system

Stephen Krasner notes that "every international system or society has a set of rules or norms that define actors and appropriate behavior," which Christian Reus-Smit calls the "elementary rules of practice that states formulate to solve the coordination and collaboration problems associated with coexistence under anarchy."[8] In short, an international system is a set of institutions and norms that survive over time and that are widely used to organize relations between political units that are not simply a reflection of the values or ideas of the units. As Kenneth Waltz pointed out, a systemic perspective reveals that interactions are not simply the sum of unit preferences: "Just as peacemakers may fail to make peace, so troublemakers may fail to make trouble. From attributes one cannot predict outcomes if outcomes depend on the situations of the actors as well as on their attributes."[9]

We tend to think that international systems are only comprised of nation-states interacting under anarchy, and as Buzan and Little point out, "the image of the international system as an interstate system is now so deeply ingrained that the two concepts are treated as synonymous."[10] Yet by the definitions above, the East Asian "tribute system" from 1368 to 1841 was clearly an international system, as it comprised an enduring, stable, and hierarchic system with China clearly the hegemon, in which cultural achievement was as important as economic or military prowess. Built on a mix of legitimate authority and material power, the China-derived tribute system provided a normative social order that also contained credible commitments by China not to exploit secondary states that accepted its authority.

This order was explicit and formally unequal, but informally equal: secondary states did not believe nor did they call themselves equal to China, yet they had substantial latitude in their actual behavior. China stood at the top of the hierarchy, and there was no intellectual challenge to the rules of the game until the nineteenth century and the arrival of the Western powers. Korean, Vietnamese, and even Japanese elites consciously copied Chinese institutional and discursive practices in part to craft stable relations with China, not to challenge it.

The core of the tribute system was a set of institutions and norms that regulated diplomatic and political contact, cultural and economic relations, and in particular explicitly stated a relationship between two political units. In contrast to the modern Westphalian ideal of equality among nation-states, the tribute system emphasized the "asymmetry and interdependence of the superior/inferior relationship," and inequality was the basis for all relations between two units.[11] The tribute system was formalized in two key institutions: recognition by the superior state, known as "investiture," and the sending of embassy envoys to the superior state. Investiture involved explicit acceptance of subordinate tributary status and was a diplomatic protocol by which a state recognized the legitimate sovereignty of another political unit, and the status of the king in that tributary state as the legitimate ruler.[12]

Tribute embassies served a number of purposes – they stabilized the political and diplomatic relationship between the two sides, provided information about important events and news, formalized rules for trade, and allowed intellectual and cultural exchange among scholars. Missions themselves, composed of scholar-officials, interpreters, physicians, alternates, messengers, and assistants, could comprise hundreds of people.

Two common criticisms about scholarship on historical East Asia are that the system was not called the tribute system at the time, and that the tribute system itself was not an all-encompassing complete set of norms and institutions that were used everywhere by everyone. Yet these criticisms are really calls for more research about the system and for greater delineation of the ways the system operated. What the actors themselves called their behavior can be completely different from how an outside observer characterizes it. After all, the "Westphalian" system of international relations wasn't called that until the 1970s, even though the system ostensibly came into existence in the 1600s; the "balance of power" system in historical Europe was not called that until American scholars coined the term in the post-WWII era. What matters is not what the people at the time called it, but whether there was, in fact, an identifiable set of ideas, institutions, norms, and practices that endured over time and across space. By that definition it is clear there was a system, the institutions of tribute relations were the central element of that system, and that constituent units used those practices even when not dealing with the Chinese hegemon itself.[13]

Some scholars, such as Joshua Van Lieu, point out that tribute was merely one form of interstate relations in the Ming/Qing period, and that relations with Russia and other units did not follow the tribute model.[14] However, there are always exceptions to the overall institutional and normative form – no international system has ever been complete and total. The key question is whether there were systematic or consistent enough patterns to call them a system. In examining the Westphalian system, Stephen Krasner's scholarship on Westphalia points out the basic non-existence of a totalizing Westphalian system, despite the fact that those ideas and institutions affect, funnel, and channel virtually all international behavior today. Krasner notes that,

> There are no universal structures that can authoritatively resolve conflicts. Principles and rules can be logically contradictory .... Westphalian and international legal sovereignty, the major concerns of this study, are examples of organized hypocrisy. They are both defined by widely understood rules. Yet, these rules have been compromised.[15]

No system is universal and total, and there are always challenges and exceptions. The key point, though, is that these challenges came against the institutions – challenges can only exist in opposition to a system. John Wills' own scholarship articulates this view and shares a sensitivity to the nuances of how and when a system operates. While pointing out that the tribute system was not a total or comprehensive system, Wills also recognizes the existence and influence of the tribute system in certain instances. He writes,

> it is crucial to my critique of the tribute system as a master concept that important parts of Qing foreign relations had little or no relation to the institution of the tribute embassy. But the relations with Siam and with Annam were very much within the tribute system ... relations with Siam were managed with far better information about the foreign polity and far more realistic policy making than in most cases.[16]

Indeed, one reason there may be too much emphasis on a totalizing tributary system is that almost all scholarship on the tribute system has focused on its most complete manifestation, which occurred unsurprisingly more recently as opposed to the distant past. And, because the purpose of this first wave of scholarship has been to contrast the tribute system with the European Westphalian system, much more nuanced emphasis may not yet have been emphasized in favor of drawing and emphasizing the contrast in the general principles from both systems. In this way, Wills and other sophisticated historians are beyond where the IR literature is, and IR has only just begun to catch up.

Indeed, IR scholarship is beginning to engage in just such an exercise of looking beyond the past few centuries to explore different ways in which the tribute system, and hierarchy, existed in historical East Asia. For example, Jiyoung Lee of American University has written about the domestic politics of historical Korea and Japan in their relations of China and significantly moving forward the discussion with novel empirical information and a focus on how domestic elites used relations with China as a key element in legitimating themselves. She writes that a view of an all-powerful Chinese empire:

> misses the remarkably varied responses of East Asian actors to Chinese hegemonic order and fails to recognize that these responses shaped the Asian hegemonic system itself in important ways .... Crafty political leaders of less powerful actors engaged in symbolic politics, manipulating external recognition from the hegemon in ways that enhanced their positions against domestic rivals. More broadly, a study of Chinese hegemony in early modern East Asia suggests that top leaders at the intersection of domestic and international politics often make foreign policy choices with their own domestic legitimacy in mind.[17]

Feng Zhang has recently written about Chinese hegemony in the early Ming era, and writes that, "The East Asian order during the early Ming era (1368–1644) was not a complete hierarchy of Chinese authority over its neighbors. Its degree varied with different foreign relationships."[18] These are all important ways in which scholars and scholarship is moving towards a more "international" study of international systems while at the same time adding nuance and specificity to more general arguments.

And make no mistake, early modern East Asia was clearly an international system. Ideas that originated in China spread across the region and ordered relations and had recognizable influence on other political units. Units interacted with each other using the principles and institutions of the tribute system even if China was not involved. Not all states acted the same way at all times, but certainly the tribute system was the institution that all reacted to, either by joining it or rejecting it. As John Wills notes,

> Chinese hopes that their "civilizing influence" might spread to foreign peoples … bore fruit among peoples of the most varied cultural and geographic backgrounds … these included Korea; Japan and the Ryukyu islands, and the area that became modern Vietnam … the real story of the 600s was a great flow of Japanese students of Buddhism and of Chinese traditions and political practices to China.[19]

China, Vietnam, Korea, and Japan aspired to be territorially-organized, centralized bureaucratic political systems.

However, although this was clearly a system of constituent units, those units existed in hierarchy, not equality. Even similar units were not identical and were not viewed as equal. Even among the nascent, Sinicized, states, it is clear that these units did not view each other as equals or as identical. For example, China was able to create long-lasting and stable borders with political units that it, literally, recognized: these were the units that borrowed many China-derived ideas and practices. For example, both Korea and Vietnam demarcated a clear border with China by the eleventh century. Womack notes:

> To say China was "among equals" would be missing a key element of the regional situation. Even to Toyotomi Hideyoshi, Japan's second "great unifier," the (unachieved) ultimate glory would have been to rule China. China was at the center of a set of regional relationships that it could not force, but were not transposable.[20]

The tribute system of international relations served a purpose for the political regimes in these Sinicized East Asian countries; it was a resilient system and endured a remarkably long time. Bandwagoning and regional diplomatic order, rather than constant balance of power politics involving displays of resolve and commitment, appears to have been a consistently successful strategy.

Less war among tributary system participants

Finding different international systems is only important or interesting if the empirical patterns among constituent units differ, as well. Perhaps the key question involves war: did East Asia experience distinct patterns of warfare? In previous work, I identified two broad patterns during the early modern period of East Asia, which I define as 1368–1841:

> China's relations with the Central Asian peoples on its northern and western frontiers were characterized by war and instability, whereas relations with the Sinicized states on its eastern and southern borders were characterized by peace and stability. Unipolarity – Chinese military and economic predominance – cannot account for both of these simultaneous outcomes.[21]

Explicitly acknowledging *both* patterns is important, because as Peter Perdue notes, "crucial events of the fifteenth century [should be treated] as a single process, while most historians discuss them separately."[22]

This is a key point of contention among scholars who study this era. For example, Peter Perdue writes,

> it is surprising to see today's commentators reviving many of the same illusions about China. David Kang, for example, who thinks that tribute relations exerted benevolent pressures, makes truly ludicrous claims about warfare in Asia.[23]

Victoria Hui argues, "There were as many wars in an East Asia allegedly dominated by the tribute system as in a Europe unable to implement the Westphalian peace," while Morris Rossabi cites the Qing expansion along its western frontier as evidence that "belies" the peacefulness on its eastern borders.[24] Indeed, some scholars, such as Perdue, Hui, and William Callahan all make literally the identical claim that a key Chinese-language source, 中国历代战争年表 (*"Chronology of Wars throughout Chinese Dynasties"*), documents 3,756 wars throughout Chinese history.[25] However, these scholars simply counted the number of entries without coding them by type and many entries had nothing to do with war. Thus Perdue, Hui, and Callahan greatly overestimate the number of wars in Chinese history.

There was, in fact, less war among those units that participated in the tributary system than between those that did not. In *East Asia Before the West*, I devoted an entire chapter defining, providing scope and boundary conditions, and measuring war, border skirmishes, and pirate raids in early modern East Asia.[26] Furthermore, I used exactly the same Chinese-language source that Hui, Perdue, and Callahan cite, the *Chronology of Wars throughout Chinese Dynasties*. However, I coded the entries by type, rather than simply assuming each entry was a war, and the result was a database of over 800 entries of both internal and external violence. This is a much more explicit measurement of all types of domestic and external violence China experienced during the early modern period. This more granular and specific analysis confirms the essential peacefulness of the tributary system, especially as compared to those non-participants.

Indeed, the scholarly task is to explain both patterns of war and patterns of peace within a discrete time period, not to explain just one pattern or attempt to draw conclusions about the entire sweep of history.[27] For example, it is not clear how Hui measured war and whether she has bounded her claim either over time or across space. Some of the confusion can be sorted out by being aware of biased selection of cases: If one is interested in war, it is natural to look where there is fighting. But that leads to selecting on the dependent variable – an overweighting of war – and a biased explanation for the overall patterns of *both* conflict and stability. Just as important as explaining why there was war in some areas is to explain why there was peace in others.

In fact, the theoretical lens of hierarchy can explain both war and peace. We would expect that political units that mutually negotiate their respective positions in a hierarchy will be able to craft stable relations, and that those units that do not sort out their relative standings would experience more conflict. Indeed, Central Asian polities and East Asian states both operated within a unipolar system, but whereas the states accepted Chinese authority, the semi-nomadic polities did not. Generated by a common Confucian worldview, Sinic states possessed a shared sense of legitimacy that presupposes that relations operate within an accepted hierarchy, and the institutions of the tribute system played a stabilizing role in their relations. The tribute system – and hierarchical relations in general – is effective only when both sides believe in the legitimacy of its norms and institutions and work within that worldview.[28] Thus, it is not surprising that Central Asian polities that rejected Confucianism and Sinic notions of cultural achievement were unable to arrive at stable relations with China.

Recent scholarship on China-nomad relations continues to refine and further delineate the ways in which hierarchy manifested itself and influenced relations among political units at the time, sometimes even among units that chose not to participate in the explicit tributary system. Kwan argues,

> China and the nomads formed an international society for much of their history, one based not on a common Confucian heritage or China's immutable centrality, but on the principle of an adaptable hierarchy based on common diplomatic norms and practices that allowed its members to affirm and contest their status within this hierarchy,

while Mackay argues, "China's treatment of the steppe constituted a deliberate identity-securing strategy" in order to further reaffirm its own centrality.[29]

Furthermore, Hui, Perdue, and Callahan are Sinologists, and write only about China. But East Asia was comprised of much more than simply China, and a truly regional view would ideally incorporate perspectives in addition to a view from the Chinese perspective. With the goal of making research of the

Table 9.1 Years in which conflicts occurred in Korea or China, 1368–1841

	Border skirmish	*Interstate war*	*Pirate/wakō raid*
China	166	28	43
Korea	25	16	19
Total	**168**	**28**	**43**

Source: Based on Kang, Fu, and Shaw, "Measuring War in Early Modern East Asia"

study of East Asian historical foreign relations more genuinely international, along with Ronan Tse-min Fu and Meredith Shaw, we are building upon the initial research from *East Asia Before the West* and are continuing to explore this central question of how to measure war and other violence in early modern East Asia. We have produced an extensive dataset of over 1100 entries that measures war and other violence in early modern East Asia from 1368 to 1841 that relies principally on both Chinese and Korean language sources.[30]

This dataset improves on the Chinese dataset but is also truly comparative, as we introduce a key Korean language source, the 한민족 전쟁통사 (*Chronology of Wars of the Korean People*).[31] This new research empirically corroborates earlier characterizations of relations between Sinic East Asian polities as being unusually peaceful and stable, which is attributable to the participants' shared subscription to a common and accepted hierarchy framed by a Confucian worldview. More broadly, we provide direct empirical evidence supporting the view that international hierarchies derive their stability from cultural consensus rather than simply asymmetries in material power. Asia was comprised of much more than simply China, and bringing in scholarship from other areas of early modern East Asia reflects a trend of moving past national studies to research the region more holistically.

Our findings are summarized in Table 9.1,[32] which counts the number of years in which a particular type of conflict occurred, rather than simply counting events (Table 9.1). Measured this way, between 1368 and 1841 – a 473-year period – there were 43 years in which China experienced a pirate raid, 166 years in which it experienced a border skirmish, but only 28 years in which China experienced a war. Similarly, Korea experienced pirate raids in 19 years, border skirmishes in 25 years, and wars in 16 years. Perhaps most notable is the stability of the countries: early modern Korea and China faced far more instances of border skirmishes and raiding along borders than they did instances of actual war.

We are moving this research forward in other ways, as well, by beginning to code a key mid-nineteenth-century Vietnamese language source (欽定越史通鑑綱目 "Complete Annals of the Dai-Viet," last published in 1861). The introduction of this Vietnamese source not only forms the basis of a unique dataset that is unprecedented in its granular attention to internal and external violence in early modern East Asia, it also widens scholarship about East Asian war beyond the typical focus on China, Korea, and Japan.[33] The Annals were written before the arrival of the West in Vietnam, and thus provide a fascinating perspective on how Vietnamese at the time viewed themselves and their foreign relations.[34] Initial findings are consistent with our earlier arguments: the Dai Viet were much more concerned with internal stability than with China, and indeed reveal almost no military attention to their relations with China, which were conducted extensively through the tribute system institutions and principles. Rather, the concern of various Vietnamese leaders was on quelling chronic domestic instability and in relations with the Champa to their south and west.

There are other eras, and other regions to study. Although historians have been exploring war and many of these issues in depth for some time, IR scholars are only beginning to do careful empirical work measuring broad patterns of behavior in East Asian history. East Asia has changed as much as any other part of the world: some traits have historical roots, others do not, and all are constantly evolving, depending on the circumstance, situation, institutional constraints, political and economic exigencies, and a host of other factors. We should avoid making sweeping claims that present either an unbroken chronological continuity or an encompassing geographic component.

In sum, careful delineation of scope and boundary conditions, of geographic and temporal domains, and clear definitions of war and other violence results in a clear pattern: peace among tributary system participants, war between those who do not engage in the tributary system. There was a tributary system, and it produced clear empirical pattern of behavior.

Systems change: the arrival of Westphalia and "modernity"

Questions of different systems and different eras come sharply into contrast in much of the nineteenth and twentieth centuries. Perhaps the key questions here are how did East Asia change, and in what ways? No matter what happened in the past, the tribute system of international relations is gone and will never return. All states now unquestioningly use the institutions and norms of the Westphalian system – nation-states are the only legitimate political unit in world politics, they all use Western-derived symbols such as flags and national anthems, and they use a particular set of diplomatic rituals in their relations with each other. There does not exist any viable alternative set of institutional arrangements in the contemporary world. As Muthiah Alagappa wrote, "[A]mong the countries in the world, it is the Asian states that most clearly approximate the Westphalian state .... The aspiration of the Asian political elite is to build strong, sovereign nation-states."[35]

However, how East Asian countries learned these Westphalian ideas and practices is often overlooked by IR scholars. But the transition to "modernity" was neither smooth nor obvious.[36] Seo-hyun Park addresses these issues by exploring changing conceptions of sovereignty; she argues that Japan and Korea derived a different mix of definitions based on different roles within the tribute system and different domestic political exigencies.[37] Arguing that in both the tribute system and the Westphalian system, Korea and Japan pursued similar goals of autonomy and mitigating vulnerability against more powerful countries. Korea's ruling regime "derived much of its authority and legitimacy from its close ties to Chinese (or universal) civilization," and thus Korea was more hesitant to abandon the traditional manner of international relations in responding to the arrival of the West, while Japan had historically been more insulated from the China-centered order, and was more open to considering new modes of relations.

Thus, between 1882 and 1895, the Korean court faced more external and domestic political barriers in embracing economic, diplomatic, and political reforms that could potentially have allowed it to modernize in ways that would have sustained or extended its independence as a nation. Korean domestic debates between the traditional ruling regime and reformers were never fully reconciled, resulting in a hesitation in Korean foreign policy that ultimately left it without any means to respond to Western and eventually Japanese imperialism. In contrast, the Japanese had much earlier on engaged in civil war and regime change that overthrew the existing order by 1868, and "Western political concepts such as privilege, right, and sovereignty were carefully studied and reconstructed during this time to connote the power of the state."[38] In contrast to Korea, Japan embarked on a rapid series of diplomatic and domestic modernization reforms in areas that ranged from the military, education, and domestic political structures.

Shogo Suzuki finds that Japan's incorporation into "international society" was hardly smooth or eager. Suzuki writes,

> the Meiji Japanese leadership continued to look upon the great powers – the very states that had forced the unequal treaties upon them – with the utmost suspicion and regarded them as the biggest threat to the survival of the Japanese state.[39]

However, today China has in many ways become the most enthusiastic supporter of Westphalian customs; China defines the territorial sovereign integrity deeply. Allen Carlson argues that the predominant approach in Chinese normative thinking about the world order

> is premised upon an acceptance of sovereignty as the bedrock of the international system, tempered by a realistic acceptance of enduring US hegemony, and a degree of flexibility on questions of multilateral intervention and the diminution of states' sovereign rights.[40]

Yet despite the fact that all East Asian states now unquestioningly accept these Westphalian ideas, there is still considerable political debate about the impact and role of the historical tribute system on contemporary East Asia affairs. This arises, in part, as because Buzan and Waever point out, "[T]he Asian subsystem is dressed in Westphalian clothes, but is not performing according to a Westphalian script."[41] For decades, scholars have expected East Asian countries to begin to behave like European countries – most notably, this has meant an expectation that regional states would begin to engage in competitive balance of power politics. Yet for decades, this has not happened. East Asia is not conforming to any Western expectations, whether they are realist or liberal.[42]

If there is a core theoretical expectation that arose out of the competitive European state system, it is that that states balance against power. And, transposed to contemporary East Asia, balance of power realists have been predicting since the early 1990s – over a quarter-century – that China's massive rise would lead to counterbalancing by its neighbors.[43] But this has not yet happened in any meaningful manner.[44] If it has not happened yet, it is hard to imagine that it will happen in the future as China grows even more powerful and the gap is even wider between China and its neighbors. Japan became the second richest country in the world and the 2nd largest economy in the world in the 1980s, trailing only the United States, and with an economy twice the size of unified Germany. Since the 1980s, scholars have breathlessly anticipated a return to a "normal" Japan, where it created military and diplomatic power commensurate with its economic power. That has not yet happened, either, and even current Japanese Prime Minister Abe Shinzo has not been able to meaningfully change that dynamic.[45]

Liberals have had their Western expectations confounded, as well. Both Japan and Korea are stable democracies with thriving capitalist economies. Both Japan and Korea are deeply intertwined with their trade and investment relations, and both share institutionalized military alliances with the United States. Yet Japan and Korea have surprisingly frosty relations, and both seem more annoyed at each other than they do perhaps with China, the potential regional hegemon.[46]

For example, there have been continual predictions that Seoul would (or should) fear a rapidly growing, geographically, and demographically massive authoritarian and Communist China that sits on its border.[47] There have also been calls for greater Korea–Japan security cooperation, and indeed perhaps even an alliance. After all, not only does China already have the military capability to threaten the peninsula, but the power disparity between China and South Korea is widening. Yet South Korea has rapidly become China's largest trade partner, it focuses its military more on contingencies with North Korea than on China, and its diplomatic relations are more tense with Japan than they are with China. This has led to claims that Seoul may be misguidedly accommodating Beijing or that it is "tilting" toward China and has entered its orbit or sphere of influence.[48] Partly, South Korea's willingness to have good relations with China arises from South Korean attempts to affect the foreign policy of North Korea's closest supporter. After all, North Korea has been South Korea's main external threat since 1945. Yet this pragmatism does not change the reality that South Korea has drawn closer to China over the past two decades, not farther away.

In contrast, relations with Japan have not been smooth. South Korea has had endemic friction with Japan, even though Japan shares with South Korea the traits of a capitalist market economy, a democratic political regime, and an alliance with the United States. Indeed, there are voices in South Korea that appear to be more worried about Japanese (re-)militarization than fearful of Chinese armaments.[49] This has led to a flourishing academic discourse about why the two cannot seemingly get along, and an accordant theoretical adjustment to explain why we may not be seeing balancing in the traditional sense of military one-upmanship, but more of a *"soft*-balancing" variant. Similar notions of "hedging" have also become a popular mode to explain South Korea's behavior.[50]

Perhaps the best evidence of this non-conformity with expectations of state behavior comes from opinion polls over thirty years. Japanese newspaper *Asahi Shimbun* and Korean newspaper *Dong-A Ilbo* have conducted joint public opinion surveys in both countries since the 1980s, which provide telling insights on how sentiments between the two publics have shifted over time (Figures 9.1 and 9.2). Most notably, the data reveal that there has been a consistent South Korean dislike for Japan. In 1984, 38.9 percent of Koreans "disliked" Japan, while an historical high of 22 percent "liked Japan." Those numbers have stayed roughly the same: like for Japan fell to a low of 5.4 percent in 1990, even lower than 2015's 6 percent. Dislike for Japan peaked in 1995 at 69 percent, and in 2015 was 50 percent. As for Japan, the predominant

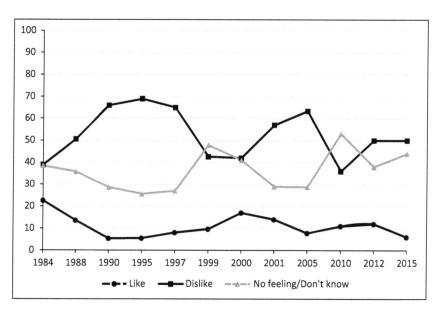

Figure 9.1 Survey results of South Korean sentiments toward Japan, 1984–2015
Source: Dong-A Ilbo & Asahi Shimbun Joint Surveys (1984–2015)

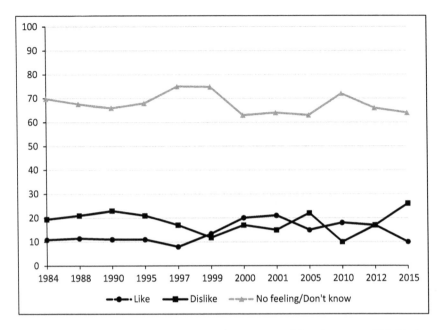

Figure 9.2 Survey results of Japanese sentiments toward South Korea, 1984–2015
Source: Dong-A Ilbo & Asahi Shimbun Joint Surveys (1984–2015)

feeling is one of apathy or uncertainty, with a large percentage since the 1980s responding as having no particular feelings toward South Korea one way or the other. Japanese "like" for Korea peaked in 2001 at 21 percent, but by 2015 was only 10 percent; "don't' know" peaked in 1997 at 75 percent, and in 2015 was 64 percent. In short, neither country particularly likes the other.

That East Asian countries' behavior often poses problems for contemporary theories has led numerous scholars to ask whether part of the reason lies in these countries' past histories.[51] Perhaps history and historical memory play a greater role in formulating national identities, grand strategies, and foreign policy priorities than is generally believed using contemporary IR theories that emphasize relatively quick national responses to changes in the distribution of material capabilities or other economic incentives.

Yet the deep policy and scholarly interest in the historical tribute system arises for other reasons, as well. Unfortunately, research on historical East Asia and the tributary system could be used to support one particular political or ideological position about East Asian security that arises in contemporary debates.[52] For example, Sankaran Krishna argues that *East Asia Before the West* is both Eurocentric at its core, and also,

> runs the danger of powerfully legitimating the soft power of China as emerging hegemon … History looks very different from the perspective

of a contemporary Uyghur or Tibetan ... From their perspective, the current violence against them is the latest in an effort to pulverize their territory.[53]

Indeed, East Asian history is deeply contested and manipulated by contemporary elites and states, and indeed common citizens in every country in East Asia for political ends.

Yet the question of politicized history is also much wider than simply one's position on the PRC – all countries in the region to a greater or lesser degree are deeply engaged in writing and rewriting narratives about their history. The Abe administration in Japan has just removed the Murayama Statement from the website of the Prime Minister in all languages as of 2014; removed from the Foreign Ministry website the appeal for the Asia Women's Fund; initiated a Government Study group to examine the Kono Statement – the result is that doubt embedded into the discourse, the denials are now on official record; initiated an LDP Study Group to examine how Japan is portrayed, especially its history abroad – which recommends aggressive measures to counter what the current government considers "lies"; and in August 2015 initiated an LDP Study Group to examine the Tokyo War Crimes Tribunal and its results.

The solution to politicized research is not to become even more political, but rather to become even more scholarly. How do we define and measure states, wars, and their relations? How do we define a region and a time period? What are the scope and boundary conditions? What is the causal logic that explains the observed patterns? Approaching scholarship in this manner allows for actual cumulation of research to occur; one can debate whether or not the historical political units were "states," and if so what were the consequences for our understanding of the time and our more general theories.

Conclusion

The careful research on East Asian historical international relations has only just begun. Scholarship on truly "international" relations across time and space is blossoming. Phillips and Sharman have written extensively on different international systems in South Asia.[54] Yuen Foong Khong argues that there is a contemporary American tributary system.[55] Brantly Womack argues that asymmetry – his word for hierarchy – has characterized China–Vietnam relations historically and today.[56] These are all important ways in which scholars and scholarship is moving toward a more "international" study of international systems.

This chapter has identified numerous areas for further research that can extend, refine, and move forward the debate about historical East Asian international relations. Two areas in particular stand out. The first is empirical: to become much more directly engaged with the granular variation that existed across time and space in the political units and their behavior and interactions with each other in pre-modern East Asia. Given the importance of the region, we still have a surprisingly superficial view of the way that "international" relations worked at the time and the ways in which international and domestic politics, economics, and society interacted and functioned. Scholars need to be more confidently able to address questions about the nature of the politics at the time, and the ways in which people at the time may have viewed themselves and their relationships.

The second is theoretical: research should be more sensitive to the complex question of whether and in what ways we can import concepts and ideas from the Western experience back into historical East Asia. How do hierarchy, hegemony, diffusion, emulation operate in historical East Asia? How do those concepts operate today? Does either the contemporary or historical existence of these types of ideas challenge contemporary social science biases and expectations? Do they confirm the universality of the dominant theories of contemporary social science? How would we know? What kind of evidence would allow us to adjudicate between competing claims? Good scholarship should ask whether what happened in East Asia is sui generis, or whether it is part of a global pattern of state-building, violence, and identity formation.

Notes

1 Amitav Acharya and Barry Buzan, "Why Is There No Non-Western International Relations Theory? An Introduction," *International Relations of the Asia-Pacific*, 7, no. 3 (2007): 287–312; Daniel J. Levine and Alexander D. Barder, "The Closing of the American Mind: 'American School' International Relations and the State of Grand Theory," *European Journal of International Relations*, 20, no. 4 (2014): 863–88; Catherine Weaver, "Reflections on the American School: An IPE of our Making," *Review of International Political Economy*, 16, no. 1 (2009): 1–5; Ole Waever, "The Sociology of a Not So International Discipline: American and European Developments in International Relations," *International Organization*, 52, no. 4 (1998): 687–727.

2 Kenneth N. Waltz, "The Emerging Structure of International Politics," *International Security*, 18, no. 2 (1993): 44–79; Kenneth N. Waltz, *Theory of International Politics* (Reading, MA, 1979).

3 Andrew Phillips and J.C. Sharman, "Explaining Durable Diversity in International Systems: State, Company, and Empire in the Indian Ocean," *International Studies Quarterly*, 59, no. 3 (2015) 436–48, 437.

4 Edward Keene, "The Standard of 'Civilization,' the Expansion Thesis and the 19th-century International Social Space," *Millennium: Journal of International Studies*, 42, no. 2 (2014): 651–73; Helen Milner, "The Assumption of Anarchy in International Relations Theory: A Critique," *Review of International Studies*, 17, no. 1 (1991): 67–85.

5 Ayşe Zarakol, *Hierarchies in World Politics* (Cambridge, forthcoming).

6 David Lake, *Hierarchy in International Relations* (Ithaca, 2009); David Lake, "Legitimating Power: The Domestic Politics of U.S. International Hierarchy," *International Security*, 38, no. 2 (2013): 74–111.

7 John E. Wills, Jr., *Embassies and Illusions: Dutch and Portuguese Envoys to K'anghsi, 1666–1687* (Cambridge, MA, 1984); Jonathan Spence and John E. Wills, Jr.,

From Ming to Ch'ing: Conquest, Region, and Continuity in Seventeenth-Century China (New Haven, 1979); Kenneth Swope, *A Dragon's Head and a Serpent's Tail: Ming China and the First Great East Asian War, 1592–1598* (Norman, 2009); Alastair Iain Johnston, *Cultural Realism: Strategic Culture and Grand Strategy in Chinese History* (Princeton, 1998); Liam Kelley, *Beyond the Bronze Pillars: Envoy Poetry and the Sino-Vietnamese Relationship* (Honolulu, 2005); William C. Wohlforth, Richard Little, Stuart J. Kaufman, David C. Kang, Charles A. Jones, Victoria Tin-Bor Hui, Arthur Eckstein, Daniel Deudney, and William J. Brenner, "Testing Balance of Power Theory in World History," *European Journal of International Relations*, 13, no. 2 (2007): 155–85; David C. Kang, *East Asia Before the West: Five Centuries of Trade and Tribute* (New York, 2010).

8 Stephen Krasner, "Organized Hypocrisy in Nineteenth-century East Asia," *International Relations of the Asia-Pacific*, 1 (2001): 173–97, 173; Christian Reus-Smit, "The Constitutional Structure of International Society and the Nature of Fundamental Institutions," *International Organization*, 51, no. 4 (1997): 555–89, 557.

9 Waltz, *Theory of International Politics*, 61.

10 Barry Buzan and Richard Little, *International Systems in World History: Remaking the Study of International Relations* (Oxford, 2000), 5.

11 James Hevia, *Cherishing Men from Afar: Qing Guest Ritual and the Macartney Embassy of 1793* (Durham, 1995), 124.

12 Geun-Ho Yoo, *Chosŏnjo taeoe sasangui hurum* [Flows of Ideologies on Foreign Relations during the Choson Period] (Seoul, 2004).

13 Kenneth R. Robinson, "Organizing Japanese and Jurchens in Tribute Systems in Early Chosŏn Korea," *Journal of East Asian Studies*, 13, no. 2 (2013): 337–60.

14 Joshua Van Lieu, "When is History? The Twenty-first Century Reemergence of the Tributary Model in International Relations Scholarship," *Harvard Journal of Asiatic Studies* (forthcoming).

15 Stephen Krasner, *Sovereignty: Organized Hypocrisy* (Princeton, NJ, 1999), 25.

16 John E. Wills, Jr., "Great Qing and Its Southern Neighbors, 1760–1820: Secular Trends and Recovery from Crisis," http://webdoc.sub.gwdg.de/ebook/p/2005/history_cooperative/www.historycooperative.org/proceedings/interactions/wills.html#_ftn1.

17 Jiyoung Lee, "Hegemonic Authority and Domestic Legitimation: Japan and Korea under Chinese Hegemonic Order in Early Modern East Asia," *Security Studies*, 25, no. 2 (2016): 320–52, 322.

18 Feng Zhang, *Chinese Hegemony: Grand Strategy and International Institutions in East Asian History* (Stanford, 2015), 6.

19 John E. Wills, Jr., "South and Southeast Asia, Near East, Japan, and Korea," in Grandi Opere Einaudi and Maurizio Scapari, eds. *The Chinese Civilization from its Origins to Contemporary Times*, Volume II (forthcoming).

20 Brantly Womack, *China Among Unequals: Asymmetric Foreign Relationships in Asia* (Singapore, 2010), 155.

21 Kang, *East Asia Before the West*, 10.

22 Peter Perdue, "Roundtable on Harmony and War: Confucian Culture and Chinese Power Politics," *ISSF Roundtable*, 4, no. 3 (2012): 1–22, 12.

23 Peter Perdue, "The Tenacious Tributary System," *Journal of Contemporary China* 24, no. 96 (2015): 1002–14, 1004.

24 Victoria Tin-Bor Hui, "Roundtable 4–3 on Harmony and War: Confucian Culture and Chinese Power Politics," ISSF Roundtable, 4, no. 3 (2012); Morris Rossabi, "Review of David Kang's East Asia Before the West," *Political Science Quarterly*, 126, no. 3 (2011): 511–12, 511.

25 Zhongxia Fu (傅仲俠) et al., *Zhongguo lidai zhanzheng nianbiao* (Chronology of Wars in China Through Successive Dynasties), two volumes (Beijing, 2003). And I do mean, "identical": Peter Perdue ("The Tenacious Tributary System," 4) writes, "The Chinese Academy of Military Science estimates that Chinese states fought 3,756 wars from 770 BC to 1912 AD, for an average of 1.4 wars per year," while Callahan (William Callahan, *China Dreams: 20 Visions of the Future* (New York: Oxford University Press, 2013), 48) cites the CWC, writing: "In its long imperial history (770 BC to 1912 AD) China engaged in 3,756 wars, for an average of 1.4 wars per year," and Hui (Victoria Tin-Bor Hui, "How China Was Ruled," *The American Interest*, 2006, www.ou.edu/uschina/texts/Hui.2008.AI.HowChinaWasRuled.pdf) writes: "The Chronology of Wars in China's Successive Dynasties – published by the People's Liberation Army Press in 2006 and compiled from dynastic records – lists 3,756 campaigns from 770 BCE to the end of the Qing dynasty in 1911."

26 David Kang, "War: The Longer Peace," in *East Asia Before the West*.

27 Swope, *A Dragon's Head and a Serpent's Tail*.

28 Kenneth M. Swope, "Manifesting Awe: Grand Strategy and Imperial Leadership in the Ming Dynasty," *Journal of Military History*, 79, no. 3 (2015): 597–634.

29 Alan Shiu Cheung Kwan, "Hierarchy, Status, and International Society: China and the Steppe Nomads," *European Journal of International Relations*, 22, no. 2 (June 2016): 362–83; Joseph MacKay, "The Nomadic Other: Ontological Security and the Inner Asian Steppe in Historical East Asian International Politics," *Review of International Studies*, 42, no. 3 (July, 2016) 471–91.

30 David C. Kang, Meredith Shaw, and Ronan Tse-min Fu, "Measuring War in Early Modern East Asia, 1368–1841: Introducing Chinese and Korean language sources," *International Studies Quarterly*, 60, no. 4 (2016): 766–77.

31 Institute of Military History, (ROK), 한민족 전쟁통사 [Hanminjok jonjaeng t'ongsa] (Wars of the Korean People) (Seoul, 1996).

32 "Measuring War in Early Modern East Asia: Introducing Chinese and Korean Language Sources," (with Ronan Tse-min Fu and Meredith Shaw), *International Studies Quarterly*, 60, no. 4 (December 2016), pp. 766–77.

33 David C. Kang, Dat Nguyen, Ronan Tse-min Fu, and Meredith Shaw, "Vietnamese Wars and the Tributary System in early modern East Asia: Introducing Vietnamese language sources" (unpublished manuscript, 2017), Microsoft Word file.

34 Liam Kelley, "Vietnam as a 'Domain of Manifest Civility' (*Van Hiên chi Bang*)," *Journal of Southeast Asian Studies*, 34, no. 1 (2003): 63–76.

35 Muthiah Alagappa, "Constructing Security Order in Asia: Conceptions and Issues," in *Asian Security Order: Instrumental and Normative Features* (Stanford, CA, 2003), 87.

36 Gi-Wook Shin and Michael Robinson (eds.), *Colonial Modernity in Korea* (Cambridge, MA, 2001); Christopher Hanscom, *The Real Modern: Literary Modernism and the Crisis of Representation in Colonial Korea* (Cambridge, MA, 2013).

37 Seo-hyun Park, "Changing Definitions of Sovereignty in Nineteenth-Century East Asia: Japan and Korea Between China and the West," *Journal of East Asian Studies*, 13, no. 2 (2013): 281–307, 283.

38 Park, "Changing Definitions of Sovereignty in Nineteenth-Century East Asia," 289.

39 Shogo Suzuki, "Japan's Entry into International Society," *European Journal of International Relations*, 11, no. 1 (2005): 137–64, 150.

40 Allen Carlson, "Moving Beyond Sovereignty? A Brief Consideration of Recent Changes in China's Approach to International Order and the Emergence of the Tianxia Concept," *Journal of Contemporary China*, 20, no. 68 (2011): 89–102, 91.

41 Barry Buzan and Ole Wæver, *Regions and Powers: The Structure of International Security* (Cambridge, 2003), 353.

42 Alastair Iain Johnston, "What (If Anything) Does East Asia Tell Us About International Relations Theory?," *Annual Review of Political Science*, 15 (2012) 53–78.

43 Adam P. Liff and G. John Ikenberry, "Racing toward Tragedy? China's Rise, Military Competition in the Asia Pacific, and the Security Dilemma," *International Security*, 39, no. 2 (2014): 52–91, 52; Avery Goldstein, "First Things First: The Pressing Danger of Crisis Instability in U.S.-China Relations," *International Security*, 37, no. 4 (2013): 49–89, 50–55; Ja Ian Chong and Todd H. Hall, "The Lessons of 1914 for East Asia Today: Missing the Trees for the Forest," *International Security*, 39, no. 1 (2014): 7–43, 42; Jonathan Holslag, *China's Coming War with Asia* (Cambridge, 2015).

44 David C. Kang, "Getting Asia Wrong: The Need for New Analytic Frameworks," *International Security*, 27, no. 4 (2003): 57–85; Evelyn Goh, *The Struggle for Order: Hegemony, Hierarchy, and Transition in Post-Cold War East Asia* (Oxford, 2015).

45 Brad Glosserman, "The Regional Implications of 'Peak Japan,'" *The Strategist*, March 31, 2016, www.aspistrategist.org.au/the-regional-implications-of-peak-japan/; Yoshihide Soeya, David A. Welch, and Masayuki Tadokoro (eds.), *Japan as a "Normal Country"?: A Nation in Search of Its Place in the World* (Toronto, 2011); Kent Calder, "Japanese Foreign Economic Policy Formation: Explaining the Reactive State," *World Politics*, 40, no. 4 (1988): 517–41.

46 David C. Kang, *Arms Races, Costly Signals, and American Grand Strategy to East Asia* (Cambridge, forthcoming).

47 McDaniel Wicker, "America's Next Move in Asia: A Japan-Korea Alliance," *National Interest*, February 24, 2016, http://nationalinterest.org/feature/americas-next-move-asia-japan-south-korea-alliance-15301.

48 Evans Revere, "Trilateral Development in Northeast Asia: South Korea, Japan, and China," *National Bureau of Asian Research*, December 15, 2015, http://nbr.org/research/activity.aspx?id=634.

49 Seok-min Oh, "Japan's Greater Military Role Double-Edged Sword for S. Korea," *Yonhap News Agency*, April 28, 2015, http://english.yonhapnews.co.kr/news/2015/04/28/0200000000AEN20150428008400315.html.

50 Sukhee Han, "From Engagement to Hedging: South Korea's New China Policy," *Korean Journal of Defense Analysis*, 20, no. 4 (2008): 335–51; Cheng-Chwee Kuik, "Introduction: Decomposing and Assessing South Korea's Hedging Options," *Asan Forum*, June 11, 2015, www.theasanforum.org/introduction-decomposing-and-assessing-south-koreas-foreign-policy-options/.

51 John E. Wills, Jr. (ed.) *Past and Present in China's Foreign Policy: From "Tribute System" to "Peaceful Rise"* (Honolulu, 2011).

216 David C. Kang

52 Martin Jacques, *When China Rules the World: The End of the Western World and the Birth of a New Global Order* (New York, 2012).
53 Sankaran Krishna, "China is China, not the Non-West: David Kang, Eurocentrism and Global Politics," *Harvard Journal of Asiatic Studies* (forthcoming).
54 Phillips and Sharman, "Explaining Durable Diversity in International Systems."
55 Yuen Foong Khong, "The American Tributary System," *Chinese Journal of International Politics*, 6, no. 1 (2013): 1–47.
56 Brantly Womack, *China and Vietnam: The Politics of Asymmetry* (New York, 2006).

10 Why is China so big? And other big questions

An interview with John E. Wills, Jr., Amsterdam, 2005

By Hendrik E. Niemeijer and Frans Paul van der Putten

Note from the editors: This interview first appeared in the journal *Itinerario: International Journal on the History of European Expansion and Global Interaction*, Vol. 30, No. 1 (2006), pp. 7–15. A postscript, written by John E. Wills, Jr., himself, appears afterwards.

Introduction

John E. Wills, Jr., Jack Wills to all his friends and colleagues, was born in 1936. He completed a B.A. in Philosophy at the University of Illinois in 1956 and went on for an MA in East Asian Regional Studies, 1960, and a PhD in History and Far Eastern Languages in 1967, both at Harvard University. He taught history at the University of Southern California from 1965 to 2004, and now is Professor Emeritus. He lives in the Los Angeles area and has five grown children, seven grandchildren, and two great-grandchildren. This academic year he is a Visiting Scholar at Leiden University. We met him in Amsterdam.

So how did I come out of the Midwest, a thousand miles from salt water, and get involved in maritime history and the history of China? My particular slice of middle America had a number of kinds of latent cosmopolitanism. Our big state universities were and are very open-ended mixes of different kinds of education: business, the arts, the humanities, technology. The one that shaped me, the University of Illinois, was the dominant presence in a small city – 30,000 students in a town of 70,000. My father was a professor of agricultural economics. After World War II the world came to America, especially to the applied faculties of our universities, in search of the secrets of modernization, very much including their agricultural sectors. My father had graduate students from India, Iran, and South Africa. In the general conformism of 1950s America, my high school was remarkably tolerant and hospitable to creativity and intellectual ambition. I was an undergraduate philosophy major at Illinois, and have never stopped reading philosophy, but never had the right temperament for professional philosophy. At Illinois I met my future wife, a history major, whose links to history now are a fascination with vernacular architecture, especially in the old Dutch towns, and real expertise in genealogy, which has led to a lot of volunteer library work.

In 1956–58 I did my military service in San Antonio, Texas. I found in an Army post library Harold Isaacs' The Tragedy of the Chinese Revolution, about the Communists and the Kuomintang in the 1920s. Then I found a not very good translation of the *Analects of Confucius*. Certainly I was moved by Isaacs' passionate account of terrible events obviously important in the shaping of our world, but I think the impact of Confucius was more fundamental. I could not have spent my adult life studying a people whose high culture was obsessed by God or life after death. I had been raised in an environment where organized religion was an option but not central to the way you thought and lived your life.

So how could I go on to learn more about China? The answer came from the American foreign policy establishment. The attacks of McCarthy and his allies on experts on China had the effect that few people wanted to go into the field, and the country was short of specialists on almost every area of Asia. First the Ford Foundation and then the federal government offered fellowships to anyone who would study Chinese, Japanese, Arabic, or a few other weird languages in graduate school. In 1958 we got married and I enrolled in an MA program in East Asian Regional Studies at Harvard.

So China was an attraction because of a more secular mindset?

Confucius has said, "We don't yet know about life, how can we know about death?"[Analects, XI, 12] That doesn't mean that there is no hereafter, but that how to live is more important. In the longer run, I can't think of a better starting point than China for thinking about the transformations of our own times and contributing to this strange new trend we call "world history."

Talking about Confucius, at your age you must have heard and submitted already to the Decree of Heaven. At seventy, Confucius said, you can follow your heart's desire without overstepping the bounds.[Analects, II, 4] Was it your academic heart's desire to compose such an original work as 1688: A Global History?

My dissertation on the Dutch East India Company and China, finished in 1967, ran over 700 pages. In the US we don't publish dissertations as accepted as you do in the Netherlands, but spend years improving and revising the darn things and then finding a press, hopefully a good university press, that will publish the monograph. It was at that point that my doctoral mentor, John King Fairbank, told me that Harvard University Press wasn't looking at 700-page typescripts any more, and asked me to give them no more than 450. So I knocked out the 1680s and the two embassies to Beijing, and the rest became my first book. I published the embassy studies together with two Portuguese embassies in 1984 as *Embassies and Illusions*. This left a third book on the 1680s still to be published. Things I had to know something about for the 1680s book – not just China but the British in India, the Dutch in what is now Indonesia, Jesuits pretty much everywhere – started me accumulating notes on different parts of the world all in one year. I really wanted to do 1687 or 1689 so that I wouldn't have to try to write something sensible about the Glorious Revolution of 1688 in England, but there were a few stories, perhaps most of all the fall of Constantine Phaulkon in Siam, that made 1688 irresistible. My original title was *1688: A World History*. Steve Forman, my excellent editor at W.W. Norton, suggested "global" in place of "world." This nicely raises the flag for all our talk pro and con about globalization. Many of the short pieces in the book are about surprising connections among different parts of the world. There also is an implicit comparative theme, which I'm not terribly surprised that no one has noticed, of the different modes of state-making and political culture within Europe – Golden Age Holland, Restoration England, the France of Louis XIV – and outside, especially in the great empires, Qing, Mughal, and Ottoman, and in Japan. The chapters about the Dutch East India Company even fit in here, as one of the more international, highly-developed examples of mercantilist state-building. And your work [Niemeijer, *Batavia: Een Koloniale Zamenleving in the 17e Eeuw*, 2005] fits in here wonderfully, showing from above and below the transformations of Batavia and its environs by commerce and capitalist agriculture.

Who stimulated you to study seventeenth-century China?

Beats me. The whole ethos of the Fairbank PhD program was that there were so many important things to figure out about China that each of us ought to find something that no one had really worked on before. But both there and in the study of pre-modern foreign relations it got pretty lonely with no one to talk to. Part of what interested me was the theme of center-regional relations and the ways in which the possibilities of the regions to mobilize themselves and pull away from the center were limited. The Ming-Qing transition of course was the last great case of this in pre-modern China. Here I finally found people to talk to, at a wonderful conference that led to the publication of *From Ming to Ch'ing*, which I edited with Jonathan Spence and for which I wrote an article taking maritime Fujian as my case study. I still find people to talk to in the new millennium, have a follow-up essay out in a conference volume edited by Lynn Struve, and am finding ways to link this emphasis on the center and periphery back to my studies of foreign relations; it makes a huge difference to those relations that China is so big.

So what were the forces at work in the Ming-Qing transition?

What I show in both my essays is that in many ways, not all of them obvious, the Manchus made a difference. We can see interactions among different provincial power holders, such as princes of the imperial house, adventurers, and people who rose through the examination system – and that example, by the way, comes right out of the Dutch Company archives and is in my first book! Within the existing Qing structure people found ways to promote themselves, and continued to work within it. I'm still happy to spend a lot of time on the history of political action. I know there are lots of other important things to study, but I think human commitment and contingency come through in such dramatic ways here.

Does that connect to another of your books, Mountain of Fame? *Why did you decide to write a collection of biographies on major Chinese historical figures covering a period of more than 4000 years?*

The book is the result of the worries about political culture we've been discussing and of teaching. The thread of political culture that runs all through the book is the many transformations of the ruler-minister relation, and the moral mystique of the ministerial role. This already is apparent in the traditional life story of Confucius. Then it's enormously helpful for our understanding of the wrenching changes of twentieth-century China to see, about 1898–1911, a lot of very smart people saying "Look, this isn't working any more," and seeking instead some form of the solidarity of the citizens of a nation. The concept of the book is very Chinese, with its focus on stories of ordinary mortals, heroes, sages, villains. Chinese friends jump right into the discussion when you ask them, for example, who they would take as a representative figure from the Northern Song (960–1125).

Is there one person you feel particularly attracted to?

Su Dongpo, from the Northern Song. He had a great deal of interest in Buddhism, especially when he was convicted for opposing the emperor's policies and sent into internal exile. But, more fundamentally, he was interested in human feelings and connections as they're expressed in literature, and also how to be a good and effective person who accomplished something. When he was the magistrate at Hangzhou he supervised the building of dikes along one side of West Lake to control the flood waters; you still can walk on "Mr. Su's Dike."

But here we are interviewing you not for a Chinese studies journal but for Itinerario. *You've also been very much involved in the "overseas history" field.*

Yes, and here early and late there has been a thin but worldwide network of wonderful human connections. I first met Charles Boxer in 1963 or 1964 when he gave some lectures at Harvard, and my wife and I saw him one last time in 1994, when he had just passed ninety, was very frail but still full of ideas and books read. Bailey Diffie taught off and on in the USC Department after his retirement, and I visited him and his wife at the lovely country house at Santiago de Cacem, south of Lisbon. Ts'ao Yung-ho befriended me and advised me in Taipei when he was still a librarian and not yet a famous Academician. But the first memories are of the morning and afternoon coffee gang in the canteen of the old Algemeen Rijksarchief on the Bleijenburg in 1963–64: Om Prakash, Kwame Daaku, John Fynn. Each of us, I think, saw a specialist or two about our eyestrain problems reading the old Dutch manuscripts in the imperfect light of the reading room. But we also shared our sense of amazed discovery; I remember John Fynn looking up in amazement from a map that gave unique clues to the locations of some peoples in the interior of West Africa. And of course upstairs, doing her work and always accessible for our questions, was Prof. M.A.P. Meilink-Roelofsz. I saw Om again in Delhi, at a Vasco da Gama quincentennial conference in Australia, and at the VOC conference in 2003. Kwame, I understand, died young in the service of Clio, promoting oral history in odd and septic corners of Africa. When I finally got a chance to go to Ghana and see Castle Elmina in 1999, I spent a few very pleasant hours with John Fynn.

And then there was the very tall, skinny young Dutchman who turned up on our fourth-floor doorstep in Taipei in 1972, waving an air letter and saying "Boxer said I have to come find you:" Leonard Blussé. I can't count the intersections on several continents or in several fields of common interest. It also was on a Sunday sail on Leonard's extremely slow boat in 1980 that I met Dhiravat na Pombeira, who in 1999 dropped everything and took me to Lopburi, making an important contribution to *1688*, and in 2004 helped me identify a Siamese seal on a photo of a document from the Beijing archives. And this year (2006) I have an office on the corridor in the Leiden Department that is the world vortex of "overseas history": Pieter Emmer, Femme Gaastra, Henk den Heijer, Henk Niemeijer, and Peer Vries perhaps not quite in the field but very important for its interpretative challenges.

The coffee gang of 1963–64 were glad to find each other to talk to, but we didn't have much sense that we were part of something bigger. *Itinerario* was part of the growth of the field, and you can trace a lot of it in its pages. In the late 1980s, I saw a lot happening, and a lot of historians not being aware of it. A first draft of a review article had three books listed at its head. Several years later, after quite a bit of fumbling and development, my "Maritime Asia" review article appeared in *The American Historical Review* with over twenty books listed at the head. Things certainly haven't slowed down since then. It's quite an experience to be around the TANAP students, where everyone is as convinced as I am of the importance of the history of maritime Asia!

You mentioned trips to Ghana, Thailand, and Australia. Is visiting places important for your work as an historian?

Certainly, and a key personal pleasure as well. I didn't travel outside the US as I was growing up, but saw a lot of the American west with my parents, and have always had an itchy foot. Most of my traveling has been more or less "in line of duty," surveying archives and sightseeing on the weekends. A first set of Asian adventures in 1973 took me to the Dominican archives in Manila, the Arsip Nasional in Jakarta, the Tamil Nadu Archives, the Historical Archive in Goa, and others. I have learned a lot from archives and personal connections in Portugal, and my wife and I are very fond of Lisbon. In 1979, after 21 years in Chinese studies, I finally got to mainland China with a delegation of Ming-Qing historians, led by Frederic Wakeman. In 1997, my visit to Australia led to *1688*-related visits to the Dampier Peninsula in the far northwest of the country and to Bali and Ambon in Indonesia. And in 2004, I had a first visit to Vietnam, with some work in the excellent Han Nom Institute and a chance to get a sense of a society very much on the move, despite the authoritarian government; Hanoi reminded me a lot of Taipei in the 1970s.

Did you ever get into disputes with other historians?

Not really. For a long time no one was much interested in pre-modern foreign relations. I've written my share of negative reviews of second- and third-rate books, but I don't think I've ever had a counter-blast from an author.

What do you think of today's academic climate?

It has gotten much too hard to get started as a young historian. Universities are over-producing PhDs without a shred of worry about whether the degree opens up a door to an academic career. Even if you get a "real job," the requirements before tenure are ever more rigid: a book published, and often more signs of continuing "productivity," while the university presses are cutting back on publishing monographs. Do we go to too many conferences? Probably, but Chinese studies have profited a great deal from them. Interaction at article length can get synergies going among scholars a lot faster than waiting for each other's books.

One of the reasons I'm glad to be retired is that I was increasingly uneasy about recruiting young people into a PhD program in the face of the uncertain futures even for the best of them. Another was that I was fed up with the status anxiety that is so prevalent in American academe. About a hundred American universities aspire to be in the inner circle, the top twenty. A few do improve their relative standing, but at the cost of not doing anything different from those who already are in the circle. But the Dutch, British, and German systems now strike me as no better, and as in some ways having deeper systematic problems. A few days ago I saw Peer Vries doing a pile of photocopying. Knowing the range of his interests, imagine how much of this he has to do! In the US, the Department has work-study students who help with such things. The American system doesn't give an almost free ride to the upper-class student whose parents could afford to pay for his or her education. Students who do need financial assistance get a package – a grant, a loan, a job as one of those work-study students. So getting stuff copied becomes a small example of a system that is more equitable than the European. The European low-cost higher education on balance often is a net income transfer to the more affluent.

Do you see any similarities in Sino-Western relations today and in the seventeenth century?

I think there is a tendency among European and American policy-makers, especially American and especially the current batch, to think that there ought to be clear and straightforward basic principles in foreign policy. That is what made some of them so optimistic about the transition from dictatorship in

Iraq. There's no such straightforwardness in relations with China. Human rights and the rights of minority nationalities will remain issues. But, in fact, we all seem to take a many-sided approach. It's right that Human Rights Watch, Amnesty International, and the Free Tibet movement keep the pressure on China, but there also are excellent reasons for maintaining positive relations with the Chinese government. A stable China that sees its interest in stable relations with the rest of the world is in everyone's interest.

The Chinese elite is changing in ways that make such relations possible. Thirty years ago the old guys never really retired, but remained the ultimate decision makers. Now you see ambitious and pragmatic younger people leading many organizations and calling the shots on many issues. But not on Taiwan. No one can get very far from "Taiwan is part of China." There is little realistic sense of how Taiwan has grown away from China. It helps to go there, and see how people, whether of Taiwanese or "mainlander" origin, have become comfortable with being there. Who knows what will happen if and when more mainland officials and opinion-shapers get to visit Taiwan? China is trying to lure Taiwan with opportunities to invest, and is having some success. But the Taiwan political establishment isn't very mature, and politicians tend to seek votes by making strong statements that they know will offend the Chinese leaders. So the whole darn thing remains very dangerous.

I'm still trying to make a contribution to some of this discussion of China's foreign relations by looking at pre-modern Chinese foreign relations and asking if there may be echoes or structural similarities in the way China deals with the world today. For many years I've been trying to argue that the "tribute system" is not a very useful master concept for understanding pre-modern Chinese foreign relations. But one of my best statements on this was in my book about Dutch and Portuguese tribute embassies, and no one seems to have noticed very much. More recently I've been interested in the eighteenth-century relations between the Qing and Annam, which got the name Vietnam in the course of these relations; very interesting stuff, in which the institution of the tribute embassy really was quite useful. But in trying to build a broader framework I turn back to my ideas about Chinese political culture and why China is so big. Maintaining internal unity was the main goal of China's rulers. Foreign adventures or entanglements with foreigners could threaten that unity. So there was a wariness of foreign contacts, a general tendency to defensiveness. Does that persist in any way today? I really don't know, and the specialists on contemporary Chinese foreign relations don't agree. But certainly China's bigness continues to shape its relations with the rest of us, sometimes in confidence in their ability to take a long view, sometimes in frustration at the limits of their power.

You seem pretty busy for someone who's retired. What brought you to the Netherlands this year?

Leonard Blussé had been after me for years to come talk to the TANAP students or get more involved in some way. When he knew that I had retired and that he and his wife Madelon de Keizer were going to Harvard this year, he made me an offer I couldn't refuse: a loose visiting association with the Leiden History Department, helping out where I could with the TANAP PhD students, and a place to live, their house in Amsterdam with Leonard's amazing private library. Then I added a short course for Leiden MA level students on the new big books in "world history." This was a very impressive group of students, and their responses to the books were very instructive. They were particularly taken with John R. McNeill's *Something New Under the Sun*, and environmental history of the twentieth-century world. Clearly they see these big environmental problems as *the* policy challenges of their adult lives. I literally sat there open-mouthed as they all jumped in to argue about all the issues.

And I've been very much impressed with the TANAP students and with the way the program has developed dialogs among young historians whose homes range from Japan to South Africa, who, if they were ordinary members of the historical profession in their home countries, would never have much to do with each other. This became especially clear to me at one of our Wednesday evening seminars when a student from Vietnam talked about the geography of the port area from Hanoi down to the river mouth; pretty soon everyone was jumping in wanting to talk about the rivers of Gujarat, of Siam, and so on.

And you have some research projects for this year? What's all this about opium?

For thousands of years people had taken opium by mouth. Around 1670 they started smoking the stuff, at first mixed with tobacco; you have some of the key citations in your *Batavia*. The greater addictiveness of inhaling makes this a change of world-historical importance. But it's a long way from smoking opium mixed with tobacco to the vaporizing and inhaling of pure opium, and at the moment I'm not getting very far with that project. The one that is getting somewhere is a study of a batch of seventeenth-century Dutch books about distant areas of the world all by one author, Olfert Dapper. I'm interested both in their contribution to a European sense of a wider world and in the information they contain, some of which can be found nowhere else. And working on this in the superb libraries of Amsterdam and Leiden and picking the brains of the experts on book history and Golden Age Amsterdam are great fun.

So you certainly seem to be enjoying your work as an historian. Do you have any advice for young people who might be attracted by the intellectual rewards, despite what you say about the difficulties of getting started?

Actually I think in some crucial personal dimensions young scholars today are making more sensible decisions than most of my generation did. Many of us married young, had children early, and struggled forever after with the competing demands of marriage, parenthood, and "my beautiful career." Now I see, in general, later marriages and very frequently first a book and tenure and then a baby; I just learned of another case last week. I'm less sure about the commitment of a younger generation to contributing to the non-academic cultural life or the "public sphere." My mentor John Fairbank devoted a great deal of time to writing for the general public, as did quite a few of the Harvard faculty of that generation. So did Erik Zuercher at Leiden. Perhaps my generation was more content to seek academic success and to assume that somehow the knowledge we elaborated would "trickle down" to the general public. Now? I don't know. Some younger scholars are deeply involved in some pretty esoteric sub-discourses in Chinese studies and in history in general. But there also is a lot of extra-academic political and cultural involvement in the younger generation. All I can say is we have to worry about this; the public sphere in the US is a big mess, and that in western Europe only marginally better.

2016 postscript to the *Itinerario* interview

John E. Wills, Jr.

Re-reading the interview done ten years ago at the end of a wonderful year at Leiden, I am struck by the ways personal encounters with people and places add enormously to the insights of the student of history. Notice the early cups of coffee with Om Prakash, later to be the doyen of the Delhi school of Asian maritime history, and with Kwame Daaku and John Fynn, my first guides into African views of African history. Some of us think we're pretty good at opening the heritage of a great people to outsiders, but what a difference it makes to be listening to a friend who embodies that heritage! And what a difference it makes to have poked into Elmina Castle in Ghana or the old cemetery in Macao! The concreteness of lived experience of persons and places remains one of the main sources of the humane power of the study of history.

Despite the delights in 2005–06 of renewing old friendships and interacting with a younger generation at Leiden, some of whom now are editing *Itinerario*, I didn't have a very strong sense in 2006 that this work was part of a trend. That came later, starting in 2011, with the excellent conference at Emory that led to the fine book edited by Tonio Andrade and Xing Hang. The range of scholarly perspectives is fully on view in the resulting book, including Adam Clulow's picture of the Tokugawa creating elements of a maritime legal regime without leaving their shores and Robert Batchelor's web of maps, calendars, and diagrams. The editors in their excellent introduction are quite clear about the dominance of the power of the Zheng family in this maritime world. I am the author of one of the ten chapters out of thirteen focused on the Zhengs, but I wonder if we have overdone it a bit. Their dominance of coastal Zhangzhou and Quanzhou is clear. Their power reached at times from the Yangzi to the Pearl River and of course to Taiwan. But there were other good bases and harbors – Hainan, Nanao, Fuzhou, Zhoushan, and even the sources that seem Zheng-centered tell stories of entrepreneurs of trade and violence centered in them.

2015 was the big year for seeing how far our exploratory voyages had come. I will save the festschrift gathering at USC for last. I made two trips to Boston at the beginning and end of May. The first was a gathering of the authors for the Wiley-Blackwell *Companion to Chinese History*. Each of us thought we had an impossible assignment, but I was sure of it: a single short essay giving the main points of the entire history of Chinese foreign relations. I had to limit my sailing and refrain from deflating the tribute system idea again. An excellent summary by Nicola Di Cosmo led me to a focus on a Northern Zone of positive interaction among peoples in early times, and later creativity in that area, ending with Great Qing.

Then I was back in Boston for an excellent conference on "Binding Maritime China: Control, Evasion, and Interloping" organized by Eugenio Menegon and Xing Hang. Here were some old friends from Boston (Menegon, Hang, and more) and Leiden (Blussé, Kwee Hui Kian), some fine connections with cutting edge Qing studies (Peter Perdue, Matthew Mosca), and a welcome reminder, with the participation of Frederic Grant and Lincoln Paine and a viewing of the treasures of the Peabody Essex Museum, that our story also is a piece of American history.

But of course it was the festschrift gathering at USC in March 2015 that made the deepest impression on me, because of the extraordinary honor done me, the great variety of topics and approaches, and the richness of cross-talk and mutual stimulation among the contributors. Not to mention the guns blazing away in about half of the papers. But after all that turmoil, it also was instructive to find Paul Van Dyke's ship full of Chinese passengers coming peacefully down the Pearl River.

In these conferences and in our other articles and books, we are making so many fresh starts in sources used and questions asked that sometimes I wish we would slow down and replicate some of the approaches we already have tried. I don't think I've seen another study of a coastal province and its connections in and out that tells me what I did right and wrong in my study of Fujian in Struve's volume. Am I missing something? Let's all stay in touch.

List of publications by John E. Wills, Jr.

Books

Pepper, Guns, and Parleys: The Dutch East India Company and China, 1662–1681, Harvard East Asian Series, No. 75, Harvard University Press, 1974. Second edition, Los Angeles: Figueroa Press, 2005.

From Ming to Ch'ing: Conquest, Region, and Continuity in Seventeenth-Century China, (co-editor with Jonathan D. Spence). New Haven, CT: Yale University Press, 1979; paperback edition, New Haven, CT: Yale University Press, 1981.

Embassies and Illusions: Dutch and Portuguese Envoys to K'ang-hsi, 1666–1687, Harvard East Asian Monographs, No. 113, Fairbank Center for East Asian Research (distributed by Harvard University Press), 1984. Second edition, Los Angeles, CA: Figueroa Press, 2011.

Mountain of Fame: Portraits in Chinese History. Princeton, NJ: Princeton University Press, 1994; paperback edition 1996, updated reprint with new Afterword, 2012.

1688: A Global History, New York: W.W. Norton and Granta Press, 2001. In Italian, Rizzoli, 2001; in Portuguese, Campus, 2001; in Dutch, Ambo, 2001; in Chinese, Locus Books, Taipei, 2001 and Hainan, Haikou, 2004; in German, Gustav Lübbe Verlag, 2002, paperback 2003; in Spanish, Taurus, 2002; in French, Autrement, 2003; in Japanese, Haru Shobō, 2004. Short-listed for Hessel-Tiltman Prize for History, awarded by British PEN, 2002. Named "number one history book of 2002" by *Damals*, a German popular history magazine.

Eclipsed Entrepots of the Western Pacific: Taiwan and Central Vietnam, 1500–1800 (ed.). Aldershot: Ashgate, 2002.

The World from 1450 to 1700. In series, *The New Oxford World History*. Oxford: Oxford University Press, 2009.

Articles and other publications

"Ch'ing Relations with the Dutch, 1662–1690," in John K. Fairbank (ed.), *The Chinese World Order* (Cambridge, MA: Harvard University Press, 1968), 225–56, 368–80.

"Dutch and Other Archives for Ch'ing History," *Ch'ing-shih wen-t'i*, Vol. 1, No. 10 (February, 1969), 3–7.

"Seventeenth Century Peasant 'Furies': Some Problems of Comparative History," (with Michael O. Gately and A. Lloyd Moote) (review article on R. Mousnier, *Fureurs Paysannes*), *Past and Present*, No. 51 (May, 1971), 63–80.

"This Precious Legacy: Some Notes on Three Studies of History and Traditional Culture in Communist China" (review article on R.C. Croizier (ed.), *China's*

Cultural Legacy and Communism, A. Feuerwerker (ed.), *History in Communist China*, and J.B. Harrison, *The Communists and Chinese Peasant Rebellions*), *Studies in Comparative Communism*, Vol. 5, No. 2–3 (Summer–Autumn, 1972), 319–32.

"Early Sino-European Relations: Problems, Opportunities, and Archives," *Ch'ing-shih wen-t'i*, Vol. 3, No. 2 (December, 1974, [April, 1975]), 50–76.

"De V.O.C. en de Chinezen in China, Taiwan, en Batavia in de 17de en de 18de Eeuw," in M.A.P. Meilink-Roelofsz (ed.), *De V.O.C. in Azië* (Bussum, Netherlands: Unieboek, 1976), 157–92.

"East Asian Historiography," (with Peter Nosco and Michael E. Robinson), *Collier's Encyclopedia*, Vol. 12 (1977), 154.

"History and Its Audiences: A Course and A Concept," *Newsletter of American Historical Association*, Vol. 16, No. 2 (February, 1978), 5–8.

Itinerario (Corresponding Editor), published by the Centre for the History of European Expansion, Leiden University; my notes and reports appeared in *Itinerario*, 1978, No. 2; 1979, No. 2; and 1983, No. 1.

"Maritime China from Wang Chih to Shih Lang: Themes in Peripheral History," in Spence and Wills, *From Ming to Ch'ing* (New Haven, CT: Yale University Press, 1979) 204–38.

"Dutch Ships on Mexico's Pacific Coast, 1747," *Southern California Quarterly*, Vol. 61, No. 4 (Winter, 1979), 337–50.

"State Ceremony in Late Imperial China: Notes for a Framework for Discussion," *Bulletin of the Society for the Study of Chinese Religion*, No. 7 (Fall, 1979), 46–57.

"The Hazardous Missions of a Dominican: Victorio Riccio, O.P. in Amoy, Taiwan and Manila. Les missions aventureuses d'un Dominicain, Victorio Riccio," (both my English and a French translation were published) in *Actes du IIe Colloque International de Sinologie, Chantilly, 1977* (Paris: Les Belles Lettres, 1980), 231–57.

Contributions to Frederic Wakeman, Jr. (ed.), *Ming and Qing Historical Studies in the People's Republic of China* (Berkeley, CA: University of California, Center for Chinese Studies, China Research Monographs, No. 17, 1980): Author of chapters on "Museums and Sites in Northern China" and "Museums and Sites in Central China," 7–33, and section on studies of "Maritime China and Early Sino-Western Relations," 128–30; editor of list of "Nationally Protected Ming-Qing Historical Sites," 158–59. Also in Sun Weiguo, trans., *Zhonghua Renmin Gongheguo de Ming Qing shi yanjiu*, in *Haiwai Zhongguo xue shi yanjiu congshu* (Shangcishu chubanshe, 2008).

"News Notes" for *Ch'ing-shih wen-t'i*, Vol. 4, No. 9 (June, 1983), 103–08.

"Advances and Archives in Early Sino-Western Relations: An Update," *Ch'ing-shih wen-t'i*, Vol. 4, No. 10 (December, 1983), 87–110.

"從外國來看鄭成功 – 西文資料與世界歷史觀法" (Looking at Zheng Chenggong from abroad: Western-language sources and world-historical approaches), in 廈門日報 (Xiamen Daily News) July 29, 1983, 3; also in 鄭成功研究論叢 (Collected studies of Zheng Chenggong), (Fuzhou, 1984), 247–50.

"Taking Historical Novels Seriously," *The Public Historian*, Vol. 6, No. 1 (Winter, 1984), 35–42.

"Some Dutch Sources on the Jesuit China Mission, 1662–1687," *Archivum Historicum Societatis Iesu*, Vol. 54 (1985), 267–93.

"Wu Chia-chi," translations of poems by this early Ch'ing poet, in Irving Y.C. Lo and William Schultz (eds.), *Waiting for the Unicorn: Poems and Lyrics of China's Last Dynasty* (Bloomington, IN: Indiana University Press, 1986), 79–82.

"Tribute, Defensiveness, and Dependency: Uses and Limits of Some Basic Ideas about Mid-Ch'ing Foreign Relations," *Annals of the Southeast Conference of the Association for Asian Studies*, Vol. 8 (1986), 84–90; reprinted in *American Neptune*, Vol. 48, No. 4 (Fall, 1988), 225–29.

"The Dutch East India Company," *The World Book Encyclopedia*, 1989 edition, Vol. 5, 392.

"鄭氏政權的興衰 – 從清鄭談判到清荷攻金廈" (The rise and fall of the Zheng power – From the Qing-Zheng negotiations to the Qing-Dutch attack on Jinmen and Xiamen), in History Research Group, Taiwan Research Institute, Xiamen University, editors, 鄭成功研究國際學術會議論文集 (Collected articles from the international scholarly conference on Zheng Chenggong research), (Nanchang: Jiangxi People's, 1989), 11–16.

"From Wild Coast to Prefecture: The Transformation of Taiwan in the Seventeenth Century," in E.K.Y. Chen, Jack F. Williams, and Joseph Wong (eds.), *Taiwan: Economy, Society and History* (Hong Kong: University of Hong Kong, Centre of Asian Studies, 1991), 374–84.

"China's Farther Shores: Continuities and Changes in the Destination Ports of China's Foreign Trade, 1680–1690," in Roderick Ptak and Dietmar Rothermund (eds.), *Emporia, Commodities and Entrepreneurs in Asian Maritime Trade, c. 1400–1750* (Beiträge zur Südasienforschung, Südasien-Institut, Universität Heidelberg, No. 141, Stuttgart: Franz Steiner, 1992), 53–77.

Fairbank Remembered (Contribution), Paul A. Cohen and Merle Goldman (eds.), (Cambridge, MA: Fairbank Center for East Asian Research, 1992), 109–10.

"Lives and Other Stories: Neglected Aspects of the Teacher's Art," *The History Teacher*, Vol. 26, No. 1 (November, 1992), 33–49.

"Maritime Asia, 1500–1800: The Interactive Emergence of European Domination," *American Historical Review*, Vol. 98, No. 1 (February, 1993), 83–105.

"European Consumption and Asian Production in the Seventeenth and Eighteenth Centuries," in John Brewer and Roy Porter (eds.), *Consumption and the World of Goods* (London and New York: Routledge, 1993), 133–47; reprinted in Peter McNeill (ed.), *Fashion: Critical and Primary Sources*, 4 vols., London: Berg, 2008.

"From Olivença to Peking: Manoel de Saldanha and the Vagaries of Restoration Fortune," in *Mare Liberum* (Lisbon) No. 5 (July, 1993), 113–17.

"A Memo for the Class of 1997: What to Take to College," *Education Week*, Vol. XII, No. 36 (June 2, 1993), 26.

"Brief Intersection: Changing Contexts and Prospects of the Christian-Chinese Encounter from Ricci to Verbiest," in John W. Witek, S.J. (ed.), *Ferdinand Verbiest, S.J. (1623–1688): Jesuit Missionary, Scientist, Engineer and Diplomat*, Monumenta Serica Monographs Series, XXX (Nettetal: Steyler, 1994), 383–94; in Chinese translation of volume, *Nan Huairen (1623–1688)* (Beijing: Shehui kexue wenxian chubanshe, 2001).

"From Manila to Fuan: Asian Contexts of Dominican Mission Policy," in D.E. Mungello (ed.), *The Chinese Rites Controversy: Its History and Meaning*, Monumenta Serica Monographs Series, XXXIII (Nettetal: Steyler, 1994), 111–27.

"What About the Others?," *Education Week*, Vol. XIII, No. 16 (January 12, 1994), 45.

"The Emperor Has No Clothes: Mao's Doctor Reveals the Naked Truth," review essay on Dr. Li Zhisui, *The Private Life of Chairman Mao, Foreign Affairs*, Vol. 73, No. 6 (November/December, 1994), 150–54.

"Maritime Chinese Contexts of the Portuguese Arrival in Japan," in Roberto Carneiro and A. Teodoro de Matos (eds.), *O século Cristão do Japão* (Lisbon: Centro de Estudos dos Povos e Culturas de Expressão Portuguesa da Universidade Católica de Lisboa, 1994), 525–34.

"An Open Door on Early Modern Asia: The Encyclopedic Achievement of Lach and Van Kley," review article on Donald F. Lach and Edwin J. Van Kley, *Asia in the Making of Europe: Volume III, International History Review*, Vol. 17, No. 4 (November, 1995), 759–66.

"The Post-Postmodern University," *Change: The Magazine of Higher Learning*, (March/April, 1995), 59–62.

"After the Fall: Macau's Strategies for Survival, 1640–1690," in Richard Herr (ed.), *Macau and China: The Past As Hope for the Future*, Center for Western European Studies, University of California, Berkeley, Working Paper Series, No. 23 (1997), 12–24.

"Relations with Maritime Europeans, 1514–1662," in Denis Twitchett and Frederick W. Mote (eds.), *Cambridge History of China*, Vol. 8 (Cambridge and New York: Cambridge University Press, 1998), 333–75. Also in Chinese translation in *Jianqiao Zhongguo Mingdai Shi*, Part 2 (2006) 307–53. Also in Wills (ed.), *China and Maritime Europe*.

"'Very Unhandsome Chops': The Canton System Closes In, 1740–1771," in Yen-p'ing Hao and Hsiu-mei Wu (eds.), *Tradition and Metamorphosis in Modern Chinese History: Essays in honor of Professor Kwang-ching Liu's Seventy-fifth Birthday* (Taipei: Institute of Modern History, Academia Sinica, 1998), Vol. II, 873–88.

"The Seventeenth-Century Transformation: Taiwan Under the Dutch and the Cheng Regime," in Murray A. Rubinstein (ed.), *Taiwan: A New History, 1600–1994* (Armonk and London: M.E. Sharpe, 1999), 84–106; expanded edition, same pages and publisher, 2007.

"Asian Participation in An Age of Growth and Global Connection," in *Encarta Encyclopedia*, 1999.

"The Survival of Macau, 1640–1720," in Jorge dos Santos Alves (ed.), *Portugal e a China: Conferências no II Curso Livre de História das Relações Entre Portugal e a China (Seculos XVI-XIX)* (Lisbon: Fundação Oriente, 1999), 105–24.

"Did China have a Tribute System?," *Asian Studies Newsletter*, Vol. 44, No. 2 (Spring, 1999), 12–13.

"Was There A Vasco da Gama Epoch? Recent Historiography," in Anthony Disney and Emily Booth (eds.), *Vasco da Gama and the Linking of Europe and Asia* (New Delhi: Oxford University Press, 2000), 350–60.

"Strange Shores: 442 Years of Anomaly in Macau, and Counting," (co-authored with Paul A. Van Dyke), *Harvard Asia Pacific Review*, Vol. 4, No. 2 (Summer, 2000), 60–64.

"The Knot That Slipped: The Failed Embassy of Tome Pires and the Maritime Silk Route," *Xueshu yanjiu* (Macau) (December, 2000), 19–28.

"The Dutch Re-Occupation of Chi-lung, 1664–1668," in *Maritime History of East Asia and the History of the Island of Taiwan in the Early Modern Period: International Conference in Celebration of the Eightieth Birthday of Professor Yung-ho Ts'ao* (Taipei: Academia Sinica, 2000), also in Leonard Blussé (ed.), *Around and About Formosa: Essays in Honor of Professor Ts'ao Yung-ho* (Taipei: Ts'ao Yung-ho Foundation for Culture and Education, 2003), 272–90.

"Wat Zegt Een Ceremonie? Gezanten van de VOC en het Rijk Groot Qing, 1666–1680," in Gerrit Knaap and Ger Teitler (eds.), *De Verenigde Oost-Indische Compagnie Tussen Oorlog en Diplomatie* (Leiden: KITLV Press, 2002), 239–55.

"Contingent Connections: Fujian, the Empire, and the Early Modern World," Lynn A. Struve (ed.), *The Qing Formation in World-Historical Time* (Cambridge MA and London: Harvard East Asian Monographs, 2004), 167–203. In Chinese translation of volume, *Shijie shijian yu Dongya shijian zhong de Ming Qing bianqian*, 2 vols (Beijing: Sanlian, 2009).

"Canton System," "Empire, Ming," "Empire, Qing," "Entrepot System," "Zheng Family," in John J. McCusker (ed.), *History of World Trade Since 1450* (Detroit, New York, London: Thomson Gale, 2005), 98–100, 234–37, 246–48, 252–54, 827–28.

"Why Is China So Big? And Other Big Questions," interview with JW by Hendrik E. Niemeijer and Frans Paul van der Putten, *Itinerario*, Vol. 30, No. 1 (2006), 7–15.

"The South China Sea Is Not A Mediterranean: Implications for the History of Chinese Foreign Relations," keynote lecture for Conference on Chinese Maritime History, Taipei, August, 2006, published in Tang Xiyong (ed.), *Zhongguo haiyang fazhanshi lunwenji*, Vol. 10 (Taipei: Research Center for Humanities and Social Sciences, Academia Sinica, 2008), 1–24.

"Journeys Mostly to the West: Chinese Perspectives on Travel Writing," *Huntington Library Quarterly*, Vol. 70, No. 1 (2007), 191–201.

"Interactive Early Modern Asia: Scholarship from a New Generation," (review article on eight books from TANAP PhD program at Leiden), *International Journal of Asian Studies* (Japan), Vol. 5, No. 2 (July, 2008), 235–45.

"Taiwan in Three Prisms: Japanese Destination, Southeast Asian Analogue, Chinese Frontier," *Studies in Chinese History/Chūgoku shigaku* (Kyoto), Vol. 17 (2008), 1–10.

"Introduction," in Wills (ed.), *Past and Present in China's Foreign Policy*, 1–9.

"How Many Asymmetries? Continuities, Transformations, and Puzzles in the Study of Chinese Foreign Relations," in Wills (ed.), *Past and Present in China's Foreign Policy*, 23–39.

"Putnam, Dennett, and Others: Philosophical Resources for the World Historian," *Journal of World History*, Vol. 20, No. 4 (2009), 491–522.

"Teapots, Opium Pipes, Guns: From the Canton Trade to the Opium War, 1700–1842," in Beatrice Hohenegger (ed.), *Steeped in History: The Art of Tea* (Los Angeles: Fowler Museum at UCLA, 2009), 190–203.

"Author, Publisher, Patron, World: A Case Study of Old Books and Global Consciousness," *Journal of Early Modern History*, Vol. 13, No. 5 (2009), 375–433.

"Tribute System," "Wokou," and "Zheng Chenggong," *Berkshire Encyclopedia of China* (2009), 2325–29, 2450–53, 2631–32.

"Hansan Island and Bay (1592), Penghu (1683), Ha Tien (1771); Distant Battles and the Transformation of Maritime East Asia," in Evert Groenendijk, Cynthia Viallé, and Leonard Blussé (eds.), *Canton and Nagasaki Compared, 1730–1820: Dutch, Chinese, Japanese Relations*, Intercontinenta No. 26 (Leiden: Institute for the History of European Expansion, History Department, Leiden University, 2009), 255–60.

"Asia occidentale, meridionale, sud-orientale, orientale," in Maurizio Scarpari (ed.), *La Cina, II, L'età imperiale dai Tre Regni ai Qing* (Torino: Giulio Einaudi, 2010), 261–87.

"Making the Social World: The Structure of Human Civilization," (Review article on John R. Searle), in *Journal of World History*, Vol. 22, No. 4 (December, 2011), 811–16.

"Introduction," in Paul A. Van Dyke (ed.), *Americans and Macao: Trade, Smuggling, and Diplomacy on the South China Coast* (with Paul A. Van Dyke) (Hong Kong: Hong Kong University Press, 2012), 1–5.

"Revolutions and Divergences: The Macao Vortex in a Transforming World," in Paul A. Van Dyke (ed.), *Americans and Macao: Trade, Smuggling, and Diplomacy on the South China Coast* (Hong Kong: Hong Kong University Press, 2012), 7–15.

"Functional, Not Fossilized: Qing Tribute Relations with Annam (Vietnam) and Siam (Thailand), 1700–1820," *T'oung Pao*, Vol. 98 (2012), 439–78.

"Armenians and Diasporas: A Breakthrough Book," (review article on Sebouh Aslanian, *From the Indian Ocean to the Mediterranean: The Global Trade Networks of Armenian Merchants from New Julfa*), *Diaspora*, Vol. 16, Number 3 (2007) [published 2013], 416–22.

"On 'Advising Mom and Dad,'" letter to editor, *Perspectives on History: The Newsmagazine of the American Historical Association*, Vol. 51, No. 9 (December, 2013), 34–35.

"A Very Long Early Modern? Asia and Its Oceans, 1000–1850," *Pacific Historical Review*, Vol. 83, No. 2 (2014), 189–203.

"What's New? Studies of Revolutions and Divergences, 1770–1840: A Review Article," *Journal of World History*, Vol. 25, No. 1 (2014), 127–86.

"Back Out to Sea After the End of Empire: Studies of Maritime Asia Since the 1960s," *Education About Asia*, Vol. 19, No. 2 (Fall, 2014), 10–13.

"何謂亞洲: 十八世紀中國變化的邊域," in Lo Kwai-Cheung 羅貴祥, ed., 再見亞洲: 全球化時代的解構與重建 *Resighting Asia: Deconstruction and Reinvention in the Global Era* (Hong Kong: Chinese University of Hong Kong, 2014), 3–25.

"Telling Stories about Lives: The Uses of Biography in Teaching Chinese History," *Education About Asia*, Vol. 20, No. 2 (Fall, 2015), 10–12.

"The First Global Dialogues: Inter-Cultural Relations, 1400–1800," in Jerry H. Bentley, Sanjay Subrahmanyam, and Merry E. Wiesner-Hanks (eds.), *The Cambridge World History*, Vol. VI, Part 2 (Cambridge and New York: Cambridge University Press, 2015), 50–79.

"Yiguan's Origins: Clues from Chinese, Japanese, Dutch, Spanish, Portuguese, Latin Sources," in Tonio Andrade and Xing Hang (eds.), *Sea Rovers, Silver, and Samurai: Maritime East Asia in Global History, 1550–1700* (Honolulu: University of Hawaii Press, 2016), 114–31.

"Ch'ing Trade and Diplomacy with Maritime Europe, 1644–c. 1800," (with J.L. Cranmer-Byng), *Cambridge History of China* (ed. Willard J. Peterson), Vol. 9, Part 2 (Cambridge and New York: Cambridge University Press, 2016), 265–328. Also in Wills (ed.), *China and Maritime Europe*, 183–254.

Inventing Exoticism: Geography, Globalism, and Europe's Early Modern World. *American Historical Review* (Featured review on Benjamin Schmidt), Vol. 121, No. 2 (2016), 527–29.

"The First Inhalers: Clues and Unsolved Puzzles on a World-Historical Question," submitted to *Itinerario*, June 2016.

Index

Taylor & Francis eBooks

Helping you to choose the right eBooks for your Library

Add Routledge titles to your library's digital collection today. Taylor and Francis ebooks contains over 50,000 titles in the Humanities, Social Sciences, Behavioural Sciences, Built Environment and Law.

Choose from a range of subject packages or create your own!

Benefits for you

» Free MARC records
» COUNTER-compliant usage statistics
» Flexible purchase and pricing options
» All titles DRM-free.

Benefits for your user

» Off-site, anytime access via Athens or referring URL
» Print or copy pages or chapters
» Full content search
» Bookmark, highlight and annotate text
» Access to thousands of pages of quality research at the click of a button.

REQUEST YOUR **FREE** INSTITUTIONAL TRIAL TODAY

Free Trials Available
We offer free trials to qualifying academic, corporate and government customers.

eCollections – Choose from over 30 subject eCollections, including:

Archaeology	Language Learning
Architecture	Law
Asian Studies	Literature
Business & Management	Media & Communication
Classical Studies	Middle East Studies
Construction	Music
Creative & Media Arts	Philosophy
Criminology & Criminal Justice	Planning
Economics	Politics
Education	Psychology & Mental Health
Energy	Religion
Engineering	Security
English Language & Linguistics	Social Work
Environment & Sustainability	Sociology
Geography	Sport
Health Studies	Theatre & Performance
History	Tourism, Hospitality & Events

For more information, pricing enquiries or to order a free trial, please contact your local sales team: www.tandfebooks.com/page/sales

 Routledge Taylor & Francis Group | The home of Routledge books

www.tandfebooks.com